Travel Agencies and Tourism Development

Travel Agencies and Tourism Development

Varinder Rana

RANDOM
RANDOM PUBLICATIONS
NEW DELHI (INDIA)

Travel Agencies and Tourism Development

ISBN 978-93-5111-944-9

Published in 2016 in India by

Reprint 2019

RANDOM PUBLICATIONS
4376-A/4B, Gali Murari Lal, Ansari Road
New Delhi-110 002
Phone : +9111-43580356, 011-23289044, 011-43142548
e-mail: sales@randompublications.com,
info@randompublications.com, randomexports@gmail.com

Type Setting by : Friends Media, Delhi-110089
Printed at : Mehra Printers, Delhi-110 092

Preface

A travel agency is a private retailer or public service that provides travel and tourism related services to the public on behalf of suppliers such as airlines, car rentals, cruise lines, hotels, railways, and package tours. In addition to dealing with ordinary tourists most travel agencies have a separate department devoted to making travel arrangements for business travelers and some travel agencies specialize in commercial and business travel only. There are also travel agencies that serve as general sales agents for foreign travel companies, allowing them to have offices in countries other than where their headquarters are located.

Travel agency is a retail business, that sells travel related products and services to customers, on behalf of suppliers, such as airlines, car rentals, cruise lines, hotels, railways, sightseeing tours and package holidays that combine several products. In addition to dealing with ordinary tourists, most travel agencies have a separate department devoted to making travel arrangements for business travelers and some travel agencies specialize in commercial and business travel only.

Travel agencies play important and a significant role in tourism industry and its development. They not only take care of trade but also understand needs and requirements of customer, they also advice and inform about destination to the prospective customer.

Tourism and travel is not a new phenomenon. The arrival of wide-bodied jets in the democratized travel by making it more affordable, thus, what was once the Grand Tour for the select few became a mass movement of personnel, business people, tourists, and students--all of concern to their home and host countries.

Hope this book will be very helpful to the students in tourism sectors and readers as well.

– Author

Contents

1

Introduction

A travel agency is a retail business that sells travel related products and services to customers on behalf of suppliers such as airlines, car rentals, cruise lines, hotels, railways, sightseeing tours and package holidays that combine several products. In addition to dealing with ordinary tourists most travel agencies have a separate department devoted to making travel arrangements for business travellers and some travel agencies specialize in commercial and business travel only.

There are also travel agencies that serve as general sales agents for foreign travel companies, allowing them to have offices in countries other than where their headquarters are located.

ORIGINS OF TRAVEL AGENCY

The British company Cox and Kings is sometimes said to be the oldest travel agency in the world, but this rests upon the services that the original bank, established in 1758, supplied to its wealthy clients. The modern travel agency first appeared in the second half of the 19th century. Thomas Cook, in addition to developing the package tour, established a chain of agencies in the last quarter of the 19th century, in association with the Midland Railway.

They not only sold their own tours to the public, but in addition, represented other tour companies.

Other British pioneer travel agencies were Dean and Dawson, the Polytechnic Touring Association and the Co-operative Wholesale Society. The oldest travel agency in North America is Brownell Travel; on July 4, 1887, Walter T. Brownell led ten travellers on a European tour, setting sail from New York on the SS Devonia.

Travel agencies became more commonplace with the development of commercial aviation, starting in the 1920s. Originally, travel agencies largely catered to middle and upper class customers, but the post-war boom in mass-market package holidays resulted in travel agencies on the main streets of most British towns, catering to a working class clientèle, looking for a convenient way to book overseas beach holidays.

ETYMOLOGY OF TOURISM

Theobald suggested that "etymologically, the word tour is derived from the Latin, 'tornare' and the Greek, 'tornos', meaning 'a lathe or circle; the movement around a central point or axis'. This meaning changed in modern English to represent 'one's turn'. The suffix –ism is defined as 'an action or process; typical behaviour or quality', while the suffix, –ist denotes 'one that performs a given action'. When the word tour and the suffixes –ism and –ist are combined, they suggest the action of movement around a circle. One can argue that a circle represents a starting point, which ultimately returns back to its beginning. Therefore, like a circle, a tour represents a journey in that it is a round-trip, *i.e.*, the act of leaving and then returning to the original starting point, and therefore, one who takes such a journey can be called a tourist." In 1941, Hunziker and Krapf defined tourism as people who travel "the sum of the phenomena and relationships arising from the travel and stay of non-residents, insofar as they do not lead to permanent residence and are not connected with any earning activity."

In 1976, the Tourism Society of England's definition was: "Tourism is the temporary, short-term movement of people to destination outside the places where they normally live and work and their activities during the stay at each destination. It includes movements for all purposes." In 1981, the International Association of Scientific Experts in Tourism defined tourism in terms of particular activities selected by choice and undertaken outside the home.

In 1994, the United Nations classified three forms of tourism in its Recommendations on Tourism Statistics:

- Domestic tourism, involving residents of the given country traveling only within this country.
- Inbound tourism, involving non-residents traveling in the given country.
- Outbound tourism, involving residents traveling in another country.

WORLD TOURISM STATISTICS AND RANKINGS

MOST VISITED COUNTRIES BY INTERNATIONAL TOURIST ARRIVALS

In 2008, there were over 922 million international tourist arrivals, with a growth of 1.9per cent as compared to 2007. In 2009, international tourists arrivals fell to 880 million, representing a worldwide decline of 4per cent as compared to 2008. The region most affected was Europe with a 6per cent decline. The World Tourism Organization reports the following ten countries as the most visited from 2006 to 2009 by the number of international travellers. When compared to 2006, Ukraine entered the top ten list, surpassing Russia, Austria and Mexico, and in 2008, surpassed Germany. In 2008, the U.S. displaced Spain from the second place. Most of the top visited countries continue to be on the European continent, followed by a growing number of Asian countries. In 2009, Malaysia made it into the top 10 most visited countries' list. Malaysia secured the ninth position, just below Turkey and Germany. In 2008, Malaysia was in 11th position. Both Turkey and Germany climbed one rank in arrivals, occupying seventh and eighth positions respectively, while France continued to lead the ranks in terms of tourist arrivals.

HISTORY OF TOURISM

Wealthy people have always traveled to distant parts of the world, to see great buildings, works of art, learn new languages, experience new cultures and to taste different cuisines. Long ago, at the time of the Roman Republic, places such as Baiae were popular coastal resorts for the rich. The word tourism was used by 1811 and tourist by 1840. In 1936, the League of Nations defined foreign tourist as "someone traveling abroad for at least twenty-four hours". Its successor, the United Nations, amended this definition in 1945, by including a maximum stay of six months.

LEISURE TRAVEL

Leisure travel was associated with the Industrial Revolution in the United Kingdom – the first European country to promote leisure time to the increasing industrial population. Initially, this applied to the owners of the machinery of production, the economic oligarchy, the factory owners and the traders.

These comprised the new middle class. Cox and Kings was the first official travel company to be formed in 1758. The British origin of this new industry is reflected in many place names. In Nice, France, one of the first and best-established holiday resorts on the French Riviera, the long esplanade along the seafront is known to this day as the Promenade des Anglais; in many other historic resorts in continental Europe, old, well-established palace hotels have names like the Hotel Bristol, the Hotel Carlton or the Hotel Majestic – reflecting the dominance of English customers.

Many leisure-oriented tourists travel to the tropics, both in the summer and winter. Places of such nature often visited are: Bali in Indonesia, Brazil, Cuba, the Dominican Republic, Malaysia, Mexico the various Polynesian tropical islands, Queensland in Australia, Thailand, St.Tropez and Cannes in France, Florida, Hawaii and Puerto Rico in the United States, Barbados, St.Marten, St.Kitts, Nevis, Bahamas, Anguilla, Antigua, Aruba, Turks and Caicos and Bermuda.

WINTER TOURISM

Although it is acknowledged that the Swiss were not the inventors of skiing it is well documented that St.Moritz, Graubünden, became the cradle of the developing winter tourism: Since that year of 1865 in St.Moritz, many daring hotel managers choose to risk opening their hotels in winter but it was only in the seventies of the 20th century when winter tourism took over the lead from summer tourism in many of the Swiss ski resorts. Even in Winter portions of up to one third of all guests consist of non-skiers. Major ski resorts are located mostly in the various European countries, Canada, the United States, New Zealand, Japan, South Korea, Chile, Argentina, Kenya and Tanzania.

MASS TOURISM

Mass tourism could only have developed with the improvements in technology, allowing the transport of large numbers of people in a short space of time to places of leisure interest, so that greater numbers of people could begin to enjoy the benefits of leisure time. In the United States, the first seaside resorts in the European style were at Atlantic City, New Jersey and Long Island, New York. In Continental Europe, early resorts included: Ostend, popularised by the people of Brussels; Boulogne-sur-Mer and Deauville for the Parisians; and Heiligendamm, founded in 1793, as the first seaside resort on the Baltic Sea.

TWO SIDES OF TOURISM PLANNING

Tourism planning has evolved from two related but distinct sets of planning philosophies and methods. On the one hand, tourism is one of many activities in an area that must be considered as part of physical, environmental, social, and economic planning. Therefore, it is common to find tourism addressed, at least partially, in a regional land use, transportation, recreation, economic development, or comprehensive plan. The degree to which tourism is addressed in such plans depends upon the relative importance of tourism to the community or region and how sensitive the planning authority is to tourism activities. Tourism may also be viewed as a business in which a community or region chooses to engage. Individual tourism businesses conduct a variety of planning activities including feasibility, marketing, product development, promotion, forecasting, and strategic planning. If tourism is a significant component of an area's economy or development plans, regional or community-wide marketing plans are needed to coordinate the development and marketing activities of different tourism interests in the community.

A comprehensive approach integrates a strategic marketing plan with more traditional public planning activities. This ensures a balance between serving the needs and wants of the tourists versus the needs and wants of local residents. A formal tourism plan provides a vehicle for the various interests within a community to coordinate their activities and work towards common goals. It also is a means of coordinating tourism with other community activities.

STEPS IN THE PLANNING PROCESS

Like any planning, tourism planning is goal-oriented, striving to achieve certain objectives by matching available resources and programmes with the needs and wants of people. Comprehensive planning requires a systematic approach, usually involving a series of steps. The process is best viewed as an iterative and on-going one, with each step subject to modification and refinement at any stage of the planning process.

There are six steps in the planning process:

1. Define goals and objectives.
2. Identify the tourism system.
    a. Resources
    b. Organizations
    c. Markets
3. Generate alternatives.
4. Evaluate alternatives.
5. Select and implement.
6. Monitor and evaluate.

STEP ONE

Obtaining clear statements of goals and objectives is difficult, but important. Ideally, tourism development goals should flow from more general community goals and objectives. It is important to understand how a tourism plan serves these broader purposes. Is the community seeking a broader tax base, increased employment opportunities, expanded recreation facilities, better educational programmes, a higher quality of life? How can tourism contribute to these objectives? If tourism is identified as a means of serving broader community goals, it makes sense to develop plans with more specific tourism development objectives. These are generally defined through a continuing process in which various groups and organizations in a community work together towards common goals.

A local planning authority, chamber of commerce, visitors bureau, or similar group should assume a leadership role to develop an initial plan and obtain broad involvement of tourism interests in the community. Public support for the planning process and plan is also important. Having a good understanding of tourism and the tourism system in your community is the first step towards defining goals and objectives for tourism development. The types of goals that are appropriate and the precision with which you are able to define them will depend upon how long your community has been involved in tourism and tourism planning. In the early stages of tourism development, goals may involve establishing organizational structures and collecting information to better identify the tourism system in the community. Later, more precise objectives can be formulated and more specific development and marketing strategies evaluated.

STEP TWO

Identifying Your Tourism System When planning for any type of activity, it is important to first define its scope and characteristics. Be clear about exactly what your plan encompasses. A good initial question is, "What do you mean by tourism?" Tourism is defined in many ways. Generally, tourism involves people traveling outside of their community for pleasure.

Definitions differ on the specifics of how far people must travel, whether or not they must stay overnight, for how long, and what exactly is included under traveling for "pleasure". Do you want your tourism plan to include day visitors, conventioneers, business travellers, people visiting friends and relatives, people passing through, or seasonal residents?

Which community resources and organizations serve tourists or could serve tourists? Generally, tourists share community resources with local residents and businesses. Many organizations serve both tourists and locals. This complicates tourism planning and argues for a clear idea of what your tourism plan entails.

You can begin to clarify the tourism system by breaking it down into three subsystems:

1. Tourism resources,
2. Tourism organizations, and
3. Tourism markets.

An initial task in developing a tourism plan is to identify, inventory, and classify the objects within each of these subsystems.

Tourism Resources are any:

1. Natural,
2. Cultural,
3. Human, or
4. Capital resources that either are used or can be used to attract or serve tourists.

A tourism resource inventory identifies and classifies the resources available that provide opportunities for tourism development. Conduct an objective and realistic assessment of the quality and quantity of resources you have to work with. Some data suggested classification to help obtain a broad and organized picture of your tourism resources.

Tourism Organizations combine resources in various proportions to provide products and services for the tourist. Given below is a partial list and classification of organizations that manage or coordinate tourism-related activities. It is important to recognize the diverse array of public and private organizations involved with tourism.

The most difficult part of tourism planning is to get these groups to work towards common goals. You should develop a list of these organizations within your own community and obtain their input and cooperation in your tourism planning efforts.

Setting up appropriate communication systems and institutional arrangements is a key part of community tourism planning.

TOURISM RESOURCES

Natural Resources

- Climate-seasons
- Water resources-lakes, streams, waterfalls
- Flora-forests, flowers, shrubs, wild edibles
- Fauna-fish and wildlife
- Geological resources-topography, soils, sand dunes, beaches, caves, rocks and minerals, fossils
- Scenery-combinations of all of the above

Cultural Resources

- Historic buildings, sites
- Monuments, shrines
- Cuisine
- Ethnic cultures
- Industry, government, religion, etc.
- Anthropological resources
- Local celebrities

Human Resources

- Hospitality skills
- Management skills
- Seasonal labour force
- Performing artists-music, drama, art, storytellers, etc.
- Craftsman and artisans
- Other labour skills from chefs to lawyers to researchers
- Local populations

CAPITAL

- Availability of capital, financing
- Infrastructure-transportation roads, airports, railroads, harbours and marinas, trails and walkways
- Infrastructure: utilities water, power, waste treatment, communications.

TOURISM MANAGEMENT ORGANIZATIONS AND SERVICES

Off-Site

Coordination, planning, technical assistance, research, regulation:

- Federal and state departments of commerce, transportation, and natural resources
- Federal, state, regional, and local tourism associations

- Educational organizations and consultants, *e.g.,* Travel and Tourism Research Association; U.S. Travel Data Centre; Travel Reference Centre, Univ. of Colorado, Boulder; Travel, Tourism, and Recreation Resource Centre, Michigan State University.
- Travel information and reservation services

On-Site

Development, promotion and management, of tourism resources:

- Federal agencies, NB. departments of commerce, transportation, and land management agencies.
- State agencies, NB. departments of commerce, transportation, and land/facility management agencies
- Local government organizations, *e.g.,* visitor information, chamber of commerce, convention and visitor's bureaus, parks.

Businesses

- *Accommodations*: Hotels, motels, Lodges, resorts, bed and breakfast cabins and cottages, Condominiums, second homes, Campgrounds
- *Food and Beverage*: Restaurants, Grocery, Bars, nightclubs, Fast food, Catering services
- *Transportation*: Air, rail, bus; Local transportation: taxi, limo, Auto, bicycle, boat rental; Local tour services
- *Information*: Travel agencies, Information and reservation services, Automobile clubs

Recreation Facilities and Services

Winter sports: Ski, skating, snowmobile areas; Golf courses, miniature golf; Swimming pools, water slides, beaches; tennis, handball, racquetball courts, bowling alleys; Athletic clubs, health spas; Marinas, boat rentals and charters; hunting and fishing guides; Horseback enterprises; Sporting goods sales and rentals

Entertainment

Nightclubs, amusement parks, spectator sport facilities; Gambling facilities: casinos, horse racing, bingo; video arcades; art galleries and studios, craft shops, studios, demonstrations; performing arts: theater, dance, music, film; historic and prehistoric sites; museums: art, history, science, technology; arboreta, zoos, nature centres,

Support Services

Auto repair, gasoline service stations; boat and recreation vehicle dealers and service; retail shops: sporting goods, specialties, souvenirs, clothing; health services: hospitals, clinics, pharmacies; laundry and dry cleaning; beauty and barber shops; babysitting services; pet care; communications: newspaper, telephone; banking and financial services tourism markets.

Tourists makeup the third, and perhaps most important subsystem. Successful tourism programmes require a strong market orientation. The needs and wants of the tourists you choose to attract and serve must be the focus of much of your marketing and development activity. Therefore, it is important to clearly understand which tourism market segments you wish to attract and serve. Tourists fall into a very diverse set of categories with quite distinct needs and wants. You should identify the different types of tourists, or market segments that you presently serve or would like to serve. This may involve one or more tourism market surveys.

A visitor survey identifies the size and nature of the existing market and asks the following questions:

- What are the primary market segments you presently attract?
- Where do they come from?
- What local businesses and facilities do they use?
- What attracted them to the community?
- How did they find out about your community?
- How satisfied are they with your offerings?

A market survey (usually a telephone survey) also can be conducted among households in regions from which you wish to attract tourists. This type of study helps identify potential markets, and means of attracting tourists to your area.

TOURISM MARKET SEGMENTS

In a general tourism plan, some clear target tourism market segments should be identified. You might begin by defining the market area from which you will draw most of your visitors. The size of your market area depends upon the uniqueness and quality of your "product", transportation systems, tastes and preferences of surrounding populations, and your competition. Identifying the market area will help target information and promotion and define transportation routes and modes, competition, and characteristics of your market.

Next, divide your travel market into the following trip length categories:

- Day trips from a 50 mile radius,
- Day trips from 50 to 200 miles away,
- Pass-through travellers,
- Overnight trips of 1 or 2 nights (most likely weekends), and
- Extended overnight vacation trips.

After you have an idea of your market area and kinds of trips you will be serving, begin defining more specific market segments like vehicle campers, downhill skiers, sightseers, family vacationers, single weekenders, and the like.

These segments can be more clearly tied to particular resources, businesses, and facilities in your community.

What kinds of products and services are likely to attract each of these groups? Tourist needs as well as their impact on the local community are quite different for day tourists versus overnight tourists. Areas catering primarily to weekend traffic will experience large fluctuations in use. In deciding the relative importance of these different segments, communities need to assess both their ability to provide required services (do you have enough rooms?), as well as the demand for different types of trips relative to the supply and your competition.

THE ENVIRONMENT

A tourism plan is significantly affected by many factors in the broader environment. Indeed, one of the complexities of tourism planning is the number of variables that are outside of the control of an individual tourism business or community. These include such things as tourism offerings and prices at competing destinations, federal and state policy and legislation, currency exchange rates, the state of the economy, and weather. These factors are discussed more fully in Extension bulletin E-1959 as part of the market environment analysis.

Local populations also must be considered in tourism planning. As they compete with tourists for resources, they can be significantly affected by tourism activity, and they are an important source of support in getting tourism plans implemented. A survey of local residents can be conducted to assess community attitudes towards tourism development, identify impacts of tourism on the community, and obtain local input into tourism plans.

Public hearings, workshops, and advisory boards are other ways to obtain public involvement in tourism planning. Local support and cooperation is important to the success of tourism programmes and should not be overlooked.

STEP THREE

Generating alternative development and marketing options to meet your goals requires some creative thinking and brainstorming. The errors made at this stage are usually thinking too narrowly or screening out alternatives prematurely. It is wise to solicit a wide range of options from a diverse group of people.

If tourism expertise is lacking in your community, seek help and advice outside the community. Tourism planning involves a wide range of interrelated development and marketing decisions.

The following development questions will get you started:

- How much importance should be assigned to tourism within a community or region?

- Which general community goals is tourism development designed to serve?
- Which organization(s) will provide the leadership and coordination necessary for community tourism planning?
- What are the relative roles of public and private sectors?

Tourism marketing decision questions include:

- *Segments*: Which market segments should be pursued; geographic markets, trip types, activity or demographic subgroups?
- *Product*: What kinds of tourism products and services should be provided? Who should provide what?
- *Place*: Where should tourism facilities be located?
- *Promotion*: What kinds of promotion should be used, by whom, in which media, how much, when? What community tourism theme or image should be established?
- *Price*: What prices should be charged for which products and services. Who should capture the revenue?

STEP FOUR

Tourism development and marketing options are evaluated by assessing the degree to which each option will be able to meet the stated goals and objectives.

There are usually two parts to a systematic evaluation of tourism development and marketing alternatives:

1. Feasibility analysis, and
2. Impact assessment.

These two tasks are interrelated, but think of them as trying to answer two basic questions:

1. Can it be done?, and
2. What are the consequences?

A decision to take a specific action must be based both on feasibility and desirability.

Feasibility Analysis: First, screen alternatives and eliminate those that are not feasible due to economic, environmental, political, legal, or other factors. Evaluate the remaining set of alternatives in more detail, paying particular attention to the market potential and financial plan.

Make a realistic assessment of your community's ability to attract and serve a market segment or segments. This requires a clear understanding of the tourism market in your area and how this market is changing. Also carefully identify your competition and evaluate your advantages and disadvantages compared to the competition. Plan towards the future because it takes time to implement decisions and for your actions to take effect. Therefore, look at the likely market and competition for several years to come. Review forecasts for the travel market in your area, if available. Careful tracking of tourism trends in your own community can help identify changes in the market that you will have to adapt to.

SERVICES OF TRAVEL AGENCIES IN TOURISM

Tourism in India has registered significant growth in the recent years. In 1951, international tourist arrival stood at around 17 thousand only while the same has now gone up to 3.91 million in 2005. The upward trend is expected to remain firm in the coming years. Tourism is also one of the sectors, which employs the largest number of manpower. There has been a remarkable growth in the recent years, in foreign tourist arrivals to India due to various efforts made, including promoting India through the "incredible India" campaign in overseas markets.

According to the Ministry of Tourism, during January-June 2007, total tourist inflow stood at 23,86887 as against 21,32174 in the same period last year. The total foreign exchange earnings during January-June 2007 stood at US$ 3589.83 million against US$ 3037.04 million for the same period in 2006. Indian tourism is one of the most diverse products on the global scene. India has 26 world heritage sites. It is divided into 25 bio-geographic zones and has wide ranging eco tourism products. Apart from this, India has a 6,000 km coastline and dozens of beaches. India's great ethnic diversity translates into a wide variety of cuisine and culture. India also has a large number of villages, plantations and adventure locations.

India is home to a great variety of wildlife and its reserves are well known throughout the world. It also has one of the world's biggest railway systems opening possibilities for those interested in rail tourism. India also has excellent hospitals offering affordable medicare and traditional health care systems like Ayurveda. In addition to this India organizes numerous fairs and festivals, which are quite attractive to foreigners.

Tourism sector holds immense potential for Indian economy. Tourism sector has the potential to stimulate other economic sectors through its backward and forward linkages and cross-sectional synergies with sectors like agriculture, horticulture, poultry, handicrafts, transport, construction, etc. Recogonising the importance of this sector, in the recent country budget, the provision for building tourist infrastructure has been increased from US$ 95.6 million in 2006-07 to US$ 117.5 million in 2007-08.

AN ENGINE OF ECONOMIC GROWTH

According to the World Travel and Tourism Council, India' s travel and tourism (T&T) industry is expected to contribute 2.1 percent to Gross Domestic Product in 2006 (INR 713.8 billion or US$16.3 billion). In the first half of the Annual Plan period of 2005-2006, the Ministry of Tourism has taken several initiatives in the field of infrastructure development and positioning Indian tourism as a major engine for economic growth. These include:

- Emphasis for developing the existing and new destinations to world-class standards.
- Improvement of connectivity to important destinations
- Identification of 10-15 new destinations/circuits by each state/UT for development to world class standard with all the required infrastructure components.

A Versatile Sector

- *Medical Tourism*: The Ministry of Tourism has taken several initiatives, in partnership with the private sector, to promote India as a destination for medical tourism and make it a global health destination. Several promotional measures like road shows and developing publicity material have been undertaken for the same.Some of the main advantages that India has are as under:
  - It has world class doctors and hospitals
  - The cost of treatment is1/5th of costs in the west
  - Eastern health care wisdom along with the expertise of western medicine
- *Rural Tourism*: A concept of rural tourism has been developed for showcasing the art, crafts and culture of rural India and for creating gainful employment in villages with tourism potential. Rural tourism holds immense potential for India, where 74 per cent of the population resides in its 7 million villages.Thrust is being provided to rural tourism to spread tourism and its socio-economic benefits to rural regions.
- *Cruise Tourism*: India has a vast and beautiful coastline and hence the potential to develop cruise tourism.
- *Convention Tourism*: International convention Centres of the global standard is considered to be one of the important segments for promoting India as an attractive tourist destination in the global market. Ministry of finance has already identified New Delhi, Mumbai, Bangalore, Goa and Jaipur for opening of world-class convention centres. Several initiatives have been taken up by way of public-private partnership to develop small convention centres of high standard. India is undoubtedly a unique Conference Destination as it offers cultural and heritage sites, the exotic and mystical, excellent facilities of beach and adventure holidays which can be combined as pre and post conference tours.

Policies and Schemes of Tourism

In order to develop tourism in India in a systematic manner, position it as a major engine of economic growth and to harness its direct and multiplier effects for employment and poverty eradication in an environmentally sustainable manner, the National Tourism Policy was formulated in the year 2002. Broadly, the "Policy" attempts to:-

- Position tourism as a major engine of economic growth;
- Harness the direct and multiplier effects of tourism for employment generation, economic development and providing impetus to rural tourism;
- Focus on domestic tourism as a major driver of tourism growth.
- Position India as a global brand to take advantage of the burgeoning global travel trade and the vast untapped potential of India as a destination;
- Acknowledges the critical role of private sector with government working as a pro-active facilitator and catalyst;
- Create and develop integrated tourism circuits based on India's unique civilization, heritage, and culture in partnership with States, private sector and other agencies; and
- Ensure that the tourist to India gets physically invigorated, mentally rejuvenated, culturally enriched, spiritually elevated and "feel India from within".

Scheme for Product Deevelopment

The focus under this scheme is on improving the existing products and developing new tourism products to world class standards. For infrastructure and product development, the Ministry of Tourism has been providing Central Financial Assistance to the State Governments during the 9th Five Year Plan which resulted in strengthening of the infrastructure and product development in the country. The scheme has been restructured during the 10th Five Year Plan to meet the present day infrastructure requirements. The past experience had been that a large number of small projects had been funded under the Scheme, spreading the resources very thinly, which at times had not created the desired impact. The focus in the Tenth Plan has been to fund large projects of infrastructure or product development in an integrated manner.

Under the revised scheme, the destinations are carefully selected based on the tourism potential. Master planning of these destinations is undertaken so as to develop them in an integrated holistic manner. The master plan is suppose to tie up all backward and forward linkages, including environmental considerations. Realizing the importance of destination development, the total outlay for this sector has been increased substantially. Important tourist destinations in each State, in consultation with the State Governments, are taken up for development. This include activities ranging from preparation of master plans to implementation of the master plans. The destinations are selected in consultation with the State/UT Governments.

The focus under this scheme is on improving the existing products and developing new tourism products to world class standards. For infrastructure and product development, the Ministry of Tourism has been providing Central Financial Assistance to the State Governments during the 9th Five Year Plan which resulted in strengthening of the infrastructure and product development in the country.

The scheme has been restructured during the 10th Five Year Plan to meet the present day infrastructure requirements. The past experience had been that a large number of small projects had been funded under the Scheme, spreading the resources very thinly, which at times had not created the desired impact. The focus in the Tenth Plan has been to fund large projects of infrastructure or product development in an integrated manner.

Under the revised scheme, the Destinations are carefully selected based on the tourism potential. Master planning of these destinations is undertaken so as to develop them in an integrated holistic manner. The master plan is suppose to tie up all backward and forward linkages, including environmental considerations. Realizing the importance of destination development, the total outlay for this sector has been increased substantially. Important tourist destinations in each State, in consultation with the State Governments, are taken up for development. This include activities ranging from preparation of master plans to implementation of the master plans. The destinations are selected in consultation with the State/UT Governments.

1. *Definition of a Destination:* Destination is a place of tourist interest. For being eligible under this scheme the destination must be among the most visited sites in the State, or a recognized Heritage Monument. A group of attractions located in the same village, town or city would also qualify.
2. *Selection of the Destination:* The destinations will be selected in consultation with State Governments/UT Administrations.
3. *Finalisation of the Project:* The identification of the project, the implementing agency, and the mode of channelisation of funds would be done in consultation with the State Govt./UT Administration. The Ministry of Tourism would bear 100per cent of the project cost (except refurbishment of monuments which would be funded on 66:33 basis, *i.e.,* 66per cent CFA) based on the project plan and estimates submitted, excluding the items which are the exclusive responsibility of the State Governments as listed in para 5. The maximum amount that could be sanctioned under this scheme would be ₹. 5.0 crores.
4. The State Governments would have to bear the responsibility including for the items mentioned in para 5. However for projects in the 'Protected Areas' under ASI or the State Archaeology Deptt. The implementing agency would be CPWD or any other agency to be

decided by the Ministry. of Tourism. In such cases funds would be directly released to such implementing agency.

5. *Monitoring Committee:* State level Monitoring Committees would be set up under the Chairmanship of the respective Secretary (Tourism). This Committee would comprise of a nominee of the Ministry of Tourism, Government. of India and a nominee of the executing agency.
6. *Funding Pattern:* All permissible activities will be fully funded by the Ministry of tourism, Government of India. However, the State/UT Governments will be fully responsible for the following components of the project:
   - Making the land available for development.
   - Implementation of rehabilitation package, where shifting of dwelling or commercial units is required. However, the Government of India would provide assistance for construction of Tourist Reception Centres including shopping complexes to house the displaced shops.
   - Maintenance and management of the assets created.
   - Any other item decided by the High Power Committee.
   - External infrastructure like Water Supply, Electricity and Roads
7. *Permissible Activities:* The following works may be taken up under the Scheme:
   - Improvement of the surroundings of the destination. This would include activities like landscaping, development of parks, fencing, compound wall etc.
   - Illumination of the Tourist destination and the area around/SEL Shows etc.
   - Providing for improvement in solid waste management and sewerage management.
   - Construction of Budget Accommodation, Wayside Amenities.
   - Procurement of equipment directly related to tourism, like Water Sports, Adventure Sports, Eco-friendly modes of transport for moving within the Tourism Zone.
   - Construction of public buildings which are required to be demolished because of implementation of the Master Plan.
   - Refurbishment of the Monuments. (66:33 basis, *i.e.,* CFA of 66per cent)
   - Signages.
   - Tourist Arrival Centres/Reception Centres/Interpretation Centres
   - Other work/activities directly related to tourism.
8. *Release of Funds:* The funds would be released to the executing agency as indicated in Para 3 above.

9. *Installments of Release:* On sanction of a work, the first installment of 30per cent of the approved CFA will be released. The second installment of 50per cent will be released on receipt of the UC of the first installment. The balance would be released on the completion of the work.
10. *Following Codal Formalities:* The executing agency shall follow all codal formalities while awarding contracts and procurement of equipment and ensure complete transparency in its transactions.
11. *Management of Assets Created:* The infrastructure and assets created will be maintained and managed by the State/UT Governments or their agencies with no financial commitment to Govt. of India except those assets created in protected areas of ASI.
12. *Prescription of the Schedule of Rates:* While executing the works the executing agency shall follow the Schedule of rates prescribed by the CPWD or the State PWD.
13. *Submission of the Utilisation Certificates:* The executing agency shall furnish through the State Government the Utilisation Certificate for release of the second installment. A Completion Certificate has also to be furnished through the State Government before the release of the final installment. In case the works are executed by a Central Agency in a 'Protected Area' the UCs would be obtained from them directly.

INDIAN TRAVEL AND TOURISM

TCI is also active in domestic tourism, though it is not their most strong area. Specially designed for the Indian holiday market, the TCI's "24 Carat Indian Holidays" are flexible and economical offer to popular holiday destinations like Goa, Shimla, Kulu-Manali, Darjeeling, Bangalore, Mysore, Ooty, Kodaikanal, Kerala, Andaman Islands, Lakshadweep Islands, Mahabalipuram and Delhi-Agra-Jaipur etc. During the four decades of its existence, TCI has grown from strength to strength during its creative marketing approach to tourism. For the development international tourism in India, TCI has several firsts to its credit. It was the first Indian travel agency to open offices overseas. It responded to the needs of the market and wherever it found calibre, it opened an office. For instance, it opened its office in Tokyo immediately after the Japanese started travelling overseas in the mid-sixties. Now, it has opened an office in Beuros Aires to tap the tourist potential from South America.

TCI is also one of the first to introduce automation in its operations and put up its web site: www.tcindia.com to market tourism services worldwide. The success of any modern travel agency depends upon its ability to respond to the needs of customers—TCI seems to follow that best rule. To summarise most leisure travel business at present revolves around travel agents and tour operators. They promote and sell all sorts of travel and travel-related services to the public. The travel agency business is not very old. The first travel agency was established by Thomas Cook in the year 1845, as he discovered Occasionally that packaging of travel services could be a profitable business. He also introduced travellers' cheques and hotel vouchers, eliminating the need of cash in travel. Today, there are over sixty thousand travel agencies appointed by IATA and perhaps the same number which do not have the official approval. In India, there are only one thousand five hundred IATA-appointed travel agencies, but many of them have more than one office. Travel agencies are of two kinds: one, the general services travel agency which undertakes all kinds of travel and travel-related business and two, specialised travel agencies specialising in business travel, conventions and conferences, incentive travel, outbound or in bound travel. Travel agencies can be further subdivided into wholesalers and retailers, but several of them combine both functions. Among the services provided by travel agencies are airlines, rail and cruise reservations, booking of hotels and rent-a-car vehicles at the other end of the journey, developing and marketing overseas and domestic package holidays, arranging conferences/ conventions, entertainments/sports, developing bonus tours, insurance, etc.

Their main source of advantages is from the commissions earned from their principals such as airlines, hotels, steamship companies, car rental companies and railways. To open a new travel agency, it is important to select a location, which is easily accessible to the type of customers whom it wishes to attract towards itself. To make it profitable, the owner has to get IATA and other authorities in the starting year of its operation. Only then is an agency entitled to get commissions from international airlines. New technologies like the computerised Central Reservation System (CRS) has made the commitment of travel agencies easier and more profitable. With a touch of a few buttons, they can hand over the whole itinerary to a client duly printed. But a recent technology-communications through internet opens new horizons. It may support travel agents further but it also threatens their very being. Any person owning a personal computer can access any travel information through internet, make reservations and is already in a position to pay by fibre cash.

There are at present five million internet connections in India but within the next few years there may be several million. Payment done by internet may take more time to reach India but Lufthansa Guman Airlines has announced that a potential traveller could do any travel transaction with the help of their 'Smart Card' through internet on all their flights and the flights of seven hundred other airlines through their Reservation System. Other airlines are not far behind. Because recent liberalisation of the Indian economy, and relaxation of foreign exchange restrictions, Indians are travelling overseas in large numbers. The outbound business at present is more than in bound which is four million against 2.6 million in bound.

The balance of trade in tourism is no longer in India's favour. It helps Indian trade, industry, exports and expands educational horizons. Many foreign government have started their tourist offices in India to lure Indians to travel to their landsua healthy competition. We should welcome that. PATA has done a survey on India's outbound tourism. In accordance with its estimates, twenty-five million Indians are today in a position to afford foreign travel. Only four million are travelling, leaving a big potential untapped.

DUTIES OF TRAVEL AGENT

1. To receive intimation from wholesale operators for planning itineraries both for groups and particularly in his country.
2. Negotiation with road transport to provide taxis/coaches for transport from airport to hotel, sightseeing tours or intercity transportation.
3. Negotiation with hotels for reasonable prices for room, meal and for other services.
4. The arrange cheap and best transportation services.
5. Negotiation with historical and cultural places for the entertainment.
6. Coordinate with various tourist centres for sightseeing tours.
7. Cost all points 2 to 6 above and offer a package price to a wholesaler.

Travel agents also advise on luggage insurance, the best season for travel, clothing, required, local foreign exchange rules and help in preparing travel documents like visas, health, passport, etc. In the role of a wholesaler to the local domestic market, they will deal with all principals developing fantastick tour packages nationally and abroad for realised part reputated in the market. They take the responsibility to promote these tour packages through advertisements, e-mail or personal selling. To determine that clients gets satisfactory reputated, travel agents have also gone into transportation which makes them part principals in their own right. Travel agents undertake on a day-to-day basis to book/make reservation on behalf of clients' seats on airlines, railways, steamship and taxies/coaches on a commission basis.

MODES OF TRAVELLING

The starting modes of surface travel are: automobile, bus, rail, and sea. Their importance, however, changes according to the technological advancement, affluence and resources of a country. While the railways are the predominant means of travel in India, China and to a lesser extent in Japan, the automobile has stolen a march on rail in the United States, Canada, Europe and Australia. long route overseas travel is predominantly by air. The old superliner ships are no longer used for tourist transportation. They are now utilised for sea cruises in warm waters for a growing number of affluent holiday makers. Coach or bus travel remains the cheapest mode of travel anywhere in the world. The introduction of recent technology in the railways is speedly eroding the speed advantage of the air services, especially on short domestic routes. Speeding up of TVG in France covering 400 kms an hour has caused panic among airlines which had 90 per cent of short-haul traffic with them on some routes.

The relaxation and amusement on a voyage by sea appears to make up for the speed for all those who have time and money for comfortable travel. New technology has also led to the development of new forms of water-bome transportation, *i.e.,* vessels like Hovercrafts and Hydrofoils. Technically, hovercrafts are like an aircraft because they move a few feet above the surface of the water.

It has its derivativesùthe jetfoil and twin-hulled jet cat. These too, have provided speedy transportation over short sea routes and over difficult terrain. People still enjoy travel over water. That has led to new tourist developmentsùyacht mannas, self-driven motor-craft, dingy sailing in the Mediterranean and canal barge holidays in Great Britain. Fascination with steam engines has led to the reintroduction of lake steamers, in England and paddle steamers in USA. The automobile is the most liked mode of transport, specially in the developed countries. Railways and coach services are the most used forms of transport in countries like India and China. The air services are normally used for long destination travel though the low cost of air travel in USA has also brought it within the reach of most Americans for domestic short-haul trips.

Automobiles

Automobile is the most famous mode of travel ill over the world, specially in North America and Europe. Within Lurope, the automobile acts a specific role in international travel because it works out to be more economical if one travels in a car with the family. Developing countries too are witnessing a boom in lomestic travel with the increasing number of people being in a òosition to own a car. The successful launching of small Maruti (Suzuki) in India has led to numerous families in cities looking for places away from home for a holiday. The recent count of domestic tourists in India is 100 million.

The growth in private car ownership has done more to change travel habits than any other factor in tourism. It has given the families a new source of freedom of movement. They saw the prices of motoring falling, though ignoring the indirect costs of depreciation, wear and tear. This perception of low cost coupled with more flexibility led to great growth in motoring holidays everywhereùindividually short distance holidays.

Most travel in the world, both domestic and international, takes place in the family car. Over the years, the promotion of world travel is pointed by the passenger car registrations. One of the better ways to forecast world travel is to project the world's passenger cars registrations. Between 1970 and 1989, the world passenger car registration grew by an yearly rate of 4.4 per cent. This is also a good signal of development of world tourism which also has been in that range. Car ownership in the world today is evaluated to be 600 million. In 1989, car registrations in the USA accounted for 34 per cent of the world's total passenger cars. There were a total of 424.4 million cars registered worldwide.

Europe comprising erstwhile USSR and Eastern Bloc countries had more cars than USA. While Europe had 4.9 people per car, in USA there was one car for 1.7 persons only. The significant number of cars in Europe in 1989 were in West Germany (30.1 million). Italy for the first time surpassed France in the ownership of cars – 24.3 million compared to 23 million in France and 21.8 million in the United Kingdom. Russia came next with 12 million cars. The evaluated growth since 1989 till 1995 is 25 per cent worldwide.

In West Germany, there was one car for two people, in Russia one for 25. Americans continue to drive more every year clocking 2.1 billion passenger miles (a passenger mile is one passenger carried one mile) on highways in 1991. Travel by car accounts for more than four out of five inter-city passenger miles. According to American Automobile Association (AAA) study, the cost to drive a new car went up from 30.6 cents per mile in 1989 to 33 cents in 1990. The reason was the higher sticker prices of new cars and higher insurance. Americans spent 12 per cent of their total personal consumption expenditure on transportation alone in 1990, most of it on their cars.

The British took approximately 75per cent of their holiday trips on automobile, according to a 1990 survey. It is up from 25 per cent thirty years ago. According to official calculation, the number of motor vehicles registered in India went up 25 times, from about 6,00,000 in 1950 to 25 million in 1995. The buyers of these automobiles, especially the government employees, have been subsidised through low interest loans. The effect of this change on the travel industry of India has been significant.

The hotel and catering industry responded by providing required facilities on the roadswayside motels, transit hotels, roadside cafes and restaurants to serve the travellers. Hotels at remote places welcomed the business generated by the new road travellers. Hills and beach resorts came within easy reach. A household receives a ear in the first place for personal use; taking children to school or to go to work. Once the car is taken for this objective, the owner feels that it is also economical to take the family in car for a holiday.

MOTOR COACH SERVICES

Bus and coach operators all over the world across the world offer a expanded range of tourist services to the public, both directly and through other sectors of industry. These services can be classified under the following general headings:

1. Regular tours, sight-seeing and excursions.
2. Express Coach Routes which can be within a country as well as international.
3. Transfer services from airport to town.
4. Hire Services to private parties for touristic movements.

Bus Tours

Buses and coaches gives the most inexpensive and safe mode of transport. Motor coach travel is a major part of the travel industry in North America and Europe. Coach travel in US has the Credit of budget travel patronised by relatively low-income ranges and senior citizens. Nevertheless, it is still a popular mode of travel linking 15,000 communities in the USA compared to only 500 by Amtrak, the rail company, and 700 by all the airlines of the USA. The two major coach companies in the USA are the Grey-hound and Trailways. Both are under the same management. The majority of Indian holiday travellers to USA buy the popular Visit America Bus Travel Pass providing unlimited travel within the USA on a marked price and during a given period. It is an excellent buy to move within the USA for people on budgets.

According to the US Department of Transportation, there were 638,000 buses registered in USA in 1992 different companies owning buses are in the business of operating motor coach tours. Over 22,000 such motor coaches are now on the road for coach tours. An inspection of this industry conducted by SEA Tourism/Travel Research reported that in 1990 some 60.7 million motor coach passengers spent $ 13.8 billion on group tours in North America. About 77 per cent of the passengers carried on these coaches were on day trips. In other words, one-third of the population of USA takes group tour of one kind or the other by coach. The American Bus Association is the country's national body representing some 450 bus companies conducting in the USA and Canada. These companies, in close cooperation with their travel industry counterparts like Hotel and Motel chains. Food Service Organisations, Charming and Theme Parks, Local, State and divisional Tourist Promotional Bodies offer package tours. It is a big business.

Apart from the American Bus Association, the country has another non-profit organisation called the National Tour Association (NTA) which works with authorised tour operators to develop packages and market tours within North America. This again is a big business. The motor coach tours represent a sizeable market for the nation's hotels and travel attractions. In Europe, coach services do not have the negative image of a poor man's transport. Long distance coach services are immensely famous with international travellers and are patronised by young people under 35. Coach services are also patronised by budget travellers from Asia and Africa. In the case of India scene most communities are connected by buses than the rails and air services. The motor vehicle population including buses and trucks in 1950-51 was just 34,000. The number in 1995 increased 25 million including two-wheelers. Road transport in India was individually nationalised in 1950. The State Transport Corporations functioning in various states of India operate a fleet of 1,50,000 vehicles carrying 6.50 crore passengers per day more than the population of many countries in Europe. 60per cent of road transport is operated in the private sector. The total road network in India in 1990 was 16,20,600 kilometres of which national highways were 33,700 kilometres.

In the field of Indian tourism, a new development is the introduction of that are popularly described as "luxury" tourist buses. These buses are used for the promotion of domestic tourism by Tourism Development Corporations of different states of India. A few State Tourism Development Corporations generally offer complete scheme comprising accommodation and meals enroute. Private tour operators also operate same tours. The term 'luxury' buses is a misnomer. These are comparatively new buses with better seating facility — no luxury really. Occasionally, air-conditioning is added for a price which seldom works. The 21st century will see the booming of automobile and coach tourism inmost countries of the world, provided fuel costs do not become exorbitant. The requirement for motoring holidays will remain buoyant in the nineties and beyond. The development of motoring has brought and will accentuate the problems of over-crowding of highways and pollution. Holiday resorts around scenic pulls cannot be expanded to meet the demand for additional parking space as has happened in USA and Japan. This is bound to destroy the beauty which tourists are seeking to enjoy.

Places such as Kullu, Shimla or Nainital in the Himalayas take the form of packed parking lots during peak summer months. The scenic highways have become danger zones due to congestion. Driving on Kalka-Shimla highways, one of the finest in India, is now a traffic hazard due to congestion on the road. If tourism is expected to play a beneficial role, the Governments have to take a deep look at emerging situations and take equal measures. In many resorts of Europe, cars are left outside the resorts and the tourists are hoped to proceed further by public transport. Same is true of Wild-life Parks. As the world's economy develops and more people move up the income ladder, the stress on our roads will be heavier. This is a problem to which there are no ready answers.

Railways

Railways play an important role in travel and tourism all over the world– except in the United States. Railways in the USA never taken themselves to the needs of travellers. Till the thirties, 70 per cent of traffic within the United States was taken by railways. With the development of alternate and more promoting modes of travel, the railways were relegated to the position of freight carriers. Now they carry only about 1 per cent of the total passenger traffic in the USA. The fast development of automobile and airlines has replaced the travel scene in the USA. Airlines are one of the few industries of the twentieth century which have consistently reduced the price of a seat in the plane till the increase in oil prices in the mid-seventies because of oil producing countries making a cartel of their own. In the past, low price of gasoline in USA had excited people to travel long distances by automobile with their families taking them away from the rail-road.

AIRLINES

While we have already explained three major arteries of tourism – car, rail and sea transport, airlines are the most important for international tourism. Airlines have changed the travel figure in the passed fifty years. This chapter discusses arteries of tourism-rail, road and sea transportation. Sea transportation includes ocean cruises. Each has its own importance and caters to the needs of definite part of travel market. By far, travel by automobile is the most liked mode of holiday specially in the developed countries. 75 per cent of domestic holiday travel in developed countries is done by automobile which combine Recreation Vehicles (RVs). It is convenient and economical for the whole family.

Automobile will remain the most important means of travel for holiday for some more decades, but it is likely to see a declining trend due to diminishing resources of oil and hiking costs adding to pollution level. Automobile is now coming up in developing councils where more people are becoming part of the emerging middle class. Coach travel comes next–another very economical mode of travel individually in the developing societies. In well established societies, specially in the USA, prosperous do not patronise bus and coach travel as it has an image of poor man's transport. It is patronised by budget travellers–students and the senior citizens. In developing countries such as India, bus travel is the most general mode of travel. In India, about 7 crores people hire inter-city travel by bus annually.

As road travelling being most crowded and accidental, the charm of this mode of travelling is decreasing. Railways which had been relegated to a back seat in well established societies are re-gaining their hold once again, with traffic congestion on the roads. Railways are giving the airlines a run for their money as they move up their speed and quality. A train in France travels at a speed of about 400 kms an hour and one airline lost a million airlines customers to the train. Trains normally save time that is spent on reaching the airport through congested highways. Japan's Bullet Trains cruise at a speed of up to 300 kilometre an hour linking major cities. In developing countries, like India, railways are still the most liked mode of travel. The Indian Railways carry some 12 million passengers daily, almost equal to the population of Australia. Presently the fastest train in India is Shatabdi which covers a distance of 410 kms from New Delhi to Lucknow, in four hours. A number of Shatabdi trains have been introduced for making inter-city travel more comfortable and fast. These trains are also patronised by foreigners. The Indian Railways operating one of the biggest rail network in the world are taking interest in developing tourism. Their luxury train, Palace on Wheels, has been very famous with foreign tourists. Now, they have decided to add 8 more similar trains in various regions of India. These trains will be in operation in three years. Cruise-lines offering luxurious holidays on the sea are a US dollar 11 billion industry. They catered to 5 million passengers in 1995, the calculated potential is 10 million by A.D. 2000.

Basically patronised by old travellers, the image of cruise holidays has now changed as younger people also have started travelling by ships by using fly-cruise packages offered by the industry. The three modes of holiday travel–automobile, rail and sea cruises–all have their separate benefits and separate markets. None of these three modes of transportation face danger of stagnation. Growing marketing should keep them strong and complementary to each other. In a boon to travellers and the tourism industry, the government has increased the rate of abatement for levy of service tax by 35per cent for tour operators. The service tax exemption that applies to package tours which is 40per cent at present has been increased to 75per cent.

At present, tour operators providing package tours, which include provision of transportation, accommodation, tourist guides, entry to monuments amongst other overheads, is liable to pay service tax on 40per cent of the gross amount charged for such tour. This has now been reduced to 25per cent. The decision was taken after tourism minister Ambika Soni raised the issue with FM P Chidambaram. The move is expected to benefit tour operators and the travel industry who are increasingly being turfed out by internet travel sites.

In a related move to promote domestic tourism, the government intends to promote Hampi in Karnataka to make it equivalent to Taj Mahal in terms of tourist destination. Responding to a Lok Sabha question, Soni said Hampi was the "agenda number one" in terms of development and enormous amount of money had been earmarked for it. Noting that the government had taken a number of steps to promote tourism, she said inflow of foreign tourists was growing by leaps and bounds and about five million travellers were expected this year.

SACRED TRAVEL

Sacred travel, or metaphysical tourism, is a growing niche of the travel market. It attracts New Age believers, primarily middle-aged women, and involves tours and travel to “spiritual hotspots” on the Earth. Destinations are often ancient sites where there is a mystery concerning their origin or purpose, such as Machu Picchu in Peru, The Pyramids of Egypt, or Stonehenge in England. Some Christian sites such as the locations of the Black Madonnas and the Rosslyn Chapel in Scotland are also popular. These travellers see the journey as more than just tourism and take the trips in order to heal themselves and the world. Part of this may involve rituals involving, (supposedly), leaving their bodies, possession by spirits (channelling), and recovery of past life memories.

OCEAN LINERS AND CRUISING

Today, there are some passenger shipping lines in the world offering transport on port-to-port basis. After their bright period in the late forties and early fifties, these services are almost extinct. The chief shipping lines like P&O and Cunard holded their long established routes from UK to Far East or to America as air transport became cheaper than the surface transport. Many of their vessels were sold and cost of changing and operating them appeared restrictive due to shortage of patronage. Since the fifties, the passenger shipping industry steadily shifted its emphasis from line voyages to cruises. Initially, they had their problems. Vessels were too old, too large and too expensive to run for cruising purposes. Their large size limited the number of ports they could enter. These ships were made for speed rather than leisure cruising. An ideal cruise ship is 18,000-22,000 tons with a passenger ability of less than 1,000. The shipping industry, therefore, have since adjusted to the needs of new cruise holiday market.

The largest number of cruise patrons live in the United States –3.5 million in 1989 and 5 million in 1995 and their number is developing every year. Now, some of the shipping companies are extending their capacity for individual demands in certain areas. The Royal Caribbean Cruise Line has involved its 2,282-passenger ship-Sovereign of the Sea. It is the biggest ship to serve in the Caribbean. The company has ordered two more similar ships. The Carnival Cruises have built a 2,600-passenger ship Fantasy which will make three to four night cruises to Bahamas. Princess Cruises have introduced 1500-passenger ship Star Princess while two more 1600-passenger ships are based on order. Some shipping companies are ordering smaller ships to meet the needs of several markets.

North America is responsible for 81 per cent of the cruise market for cruises of 3 days or more. The total world spending on cruises in 1995 was evaluated to be about US dollar 11 billion. It has been evaluated that there are about 190 ships in deep water cruise business –36 belong to Russia or some of the erstwhile members of the USSR. Four leading companies dominate the cruise industry – Carnival, Royal Caribbean, Princess and Norwegian. The dominance of American travellers in the cruise market has resulted in hard standards of hygiene and safety put on all foreign flag cruise ships operating out of the US ports. They have also been contracted against financial collapse. These hard regulations have driven old vessels out of the cruise market.

2

Scope in Travel Agency

Travel and Tourism as one of the world's largest foreign exchange earner among industries, provides employ-ment directly to millions of people worldwide and indirectly through many associated service indus-tries. As a very large industry, it includes Government tourism departments, Immigration and customs services, travel agencies, airlines, tour operators, hotels etc and many associated service industries such as airline catering or laundry services, guides, interpreters, tourism promotion and sales executives etc. Travel and tourism enterprises include major internationals with thousands of workforce, though small private travel agent have handful of employees.

Work in the travel and tourism industry is essen-tially concerned with providing services for people who are away from home, on business or holiday. Travel can be leisure travel involv-ing package tours, pilgrim travel, adventure travel etc or for purely business. Work at every functional level in the industry involves dealing directly with people. Travel company personnel must be up-to-date on current rules and regulations and documentation required, in areas like cargo, ticketing and passports, visas etc. so as to correctly advise their clients, and to take care of the paperwork when necessary. Besides this, all tourism staff in marketing, counter sales, or guide services, should be knowledgeable about the places their clients visit, in terms of general background, how to get there, connections by air, rail and road and the facilities available.

In India, Travel and tourism, as an industry, has been somewhat slower to take off than in many other places. However, with increasing worldwide interest in travel, and with the Government's encourage-ment of its activities, it is undergoing massive expansion and improve-ment. This forecasts a bright future for all those who choose to make a career of travel and tourism. Young people with drive and a capacity for hard work can rise to top positions very quickly in travel and tourism or even head their own agencies. A job in the industry gives good returns as well as perks including opportunity to see many locales at low prices. Now a days working in an airline, whether on the ground or in flight is an exciting option for many people. In the airlines, one can work as Traffic Assistance, Reservation and Counter Staff, Airhostess and flight pursers, Sales and Marketing staff and customer services. A course in travel and tourism or a qualification on Hotel management helps to get in. The jobs in airlines though challenging are glamorous and afford the possibility of traveling to exciting destinations.

Free tickets for the family offered by some airlines are an added advantage. Domestic and international Airlines such as Air India, Indian airlines, Jet airways, Air Sahara, Aeroflot, British Airways, Cathay Pacific, Emirates, Singapore Airlines etc offer employment opportunities with attractive salaries and numerous benefits. Opportunities are plenty in travel agency business.Many resorts, travel groups use travel agents to promote their tour packages to travellers.

They deal with almost everything connected with travel including the shortest route to the destina-tion, travel mode, obtaining important documents that are required like visa, passport, vaccination certificates etc, suitable places to stay, current exchange rates, tourist attractions to visit, climate and they will plan the trip keeping in mind the clients' preferences, budgets and special needs.In travel agencies there are openings for reservation and counter staff, Sales and Marketing staff, Tour escorts and tour operators, cargo and courier agencies etc. A short tem course or a diploma in travel and ticketing for few months duration will help gain entry into an agency. Several large travel agencies also offer short-term training programme-mes, and tend to absorb most of the candidates. Some agencies take in fresh graduates and train them on the job. Most travel agencies demand persons with a pleasing personality and the ability to deal with custom-ers. A knowledge of destina-tions and procedures help a great deal. Now sky is the limit in the field of travel and tourism.

DEFINITION OF TOUR OPERATOR

A tour operator typically combines tour and travel components to create a holiday. The most common example of a tour operator's product would be a flight on a charter airline plus a transfer from the airport to a hotel and the services of a local representative, all for one price. Niche tour operators may specialise in destinations, *e.g.,* Italy, activities and experiences, *e.g.,* skiing, or a combination thereof. The original raison d'etre of tour operating was the difficulty of making arrangements in far-flung places, with problems of language, currency and communication.

The advent of the internet has led to a rapid increase in self-packaging of holidays. However, tour operators still have their competence in arranging tours for those who do not have time to do DIY holidays, and specialize in large group events and meetings such as conferences or seminars. Also, tour operators still exercise contracting power with suppliers (airlines, hotels, other land arrangements, cruises, etc.) and influence over other entities (tourism boards and other government authorities) in order to create packages and special departures for destinations otherwise difficult and expensive to visit.

The three major tour operator associations in the U.S. are the National Tour Association (NTA), the United States Tour Operators Association (USTOA), and the American Tour Association (ATA). In Europe, it is the European Tour Operators Association (ETOA), and in the UK, it is the Association of British Travel Agents (ABTA) and the Association of Independent Tour Operators (AITO). The primary association for receptive North American inbound tour operators is the Receptive Services Association of America (RSAA).

DEVELOPMENT OF TRAVEL AGENCIES

The development of Travel Agencies are seen as the scale of he development of the country in the developed countries as USA, followed by many other countries, brought in a plethora of reduced airfares and tempting commission structures. Lower airfares resulted in expanded business and higher commissions for travel agents. Business has never been so good. In the USA, membership of IATA is no longer essential to charge commission from IATA or other scheduled carriers. America has set up its own Air Transport Association (ATA) which works closed with IATA. Agent members ofATCùa division of ATA of Americaù are as good as IATA agents and IATA has supported them.

Several Govemments comprising those of the Japan UK, USA, and Singapore, have enacted legislation regulating the working of travel agencies to protect the Customers. The regulations emphasis that new travel agencies will have trained staff, minimum capitalisation and consumer protection insurance, etc. There have been examples oflargejtravel agencies declaring bankruptcies, while hundreds of their client? were travelling in many countriesùleaving them high and dry as airlines refused to honour their tickets. In India, there is no legislation regulating travel agencies or protecting travellers. The newly developed of Consumers Forums can, however, take note of complaints against travel agents.

Attracted by new opportunities in expanding travel business, the number ofIATA-recognised travel agencies has doubled in ten years, from thirty thousand in 1980 to over sixty thousand in 2000, according to an IATA report.

Statistics related to the travel agency business in the USA are mind-exciting. In 1995, travel agencies in the USA wrote a record US$45 billion in airlines ticketing and the amount of commission paid wasùcommission payments amounted to US$4 billion. In India, statistics related to legal payment in the shape of commissions are seldom availableù airlines are secretive about it as part of it is generally paid under the table. The Indian Airlines which has no reason to be secretive about commission is also not eager to part with this information in an endeavour to expand their area of direct sales at the cost of travel agents. Overall, approved Indian travel agents sell more than sixty per cent of domestic and seventy-five per cent of international tickets.

The rest of the selling is done either directly by the Airlines or through their General Sales Agents (GSAs), which have mushroomed everywhere. GSAs are generally appointed by an airline at a place where there are no IATA agents. A GSA sells tickets of only one airline which represents and operates his office as the Airlines' own office, making him to a higher commission. Over the years, GSAs in India have become an outlet for price-cutting by airlines to beat the competition.

They have become experts in cross-border sellingùselling across the area of their jurisdiction. Air India, the national carrier, has its GSA in New Delhi where there are more than a score of IATA agents, not setting a very good example for foreign carriers. IATA agents are generally hostile to the institution of GSAs since they know that this is a way of taking away their legitimate business from them, by their own rulesùthe international airlines.

Suppliers and Travel Agents

Suppliers and Travel Agent based services can be given in the table format as following. USA Estimated percentage of business booked by travel agents-wholesalers

Airlines	60 % (Domestic)
	70 % (International)
Hotels	25 % (Domestic)
	75 % (International)
Bus	10 %
Rail	30 %
Rental Car	50 %
Packaged Tours	90 %

In India, the suppliers' dependence on travel agents is a little less.

Current Developments

Deregulation of airlines in the USA in the eighties, made able airlines to offer any fare to travel agents or customersit has done to two new developments in the travel agency distribution system. One is the emergence of Consolidators-(business organisations) which buy airlines and cruise tickets in bulk at special rates from the principals and give for offer these at discount rate to travel agents. The other is Consortium or Co-ops.

A Consortium is composed of affiliated travel agencies whose objective is to enhance the volume sales' profits of independently-owned travel agencies. This is done by means of group advertising, production of promotional material, educational opportunities, consulting resources, suppliers' discounts and other grants. This development has occurred to meet the competition of mega-travel agencies which have a greater bargaining power with the suppliers.

At present development is an arrangement arrived at between North-Western Airlines, Thomas Cook, which is a mega-travel agency, and Ford Motors whereby Ford personnel are hoped to travel by North-Western through Thomas Cook only. North-Western in turn gives a better rate to Ford travellers and a higher commission to Thomas Cook. The consortium concept seeks to achieve the same bargaining position for small travel agencies.

These concepts have also slowed down to other countries during the first decade of the new millennium. In India, Thomas Cook has introduced their bid or buy.com site which offers last minute rate settlementsales of international tickets as well as holidaysùboth domestic and international.different products are on sale. Outbound travellers from India reached four million mark during 2000 which was only 1.9 million in 1991. Till the mid eighties, Indiansùespecially the leisure travellers were discouraged to go foreign and foreign exchange was not released in their favour, if they declared their objective as leisure. Foreign exchange was only released to travellers declaring their mission as business promotion, official or by chance medical treatment in the foreign The bureaucrats and politicians utilised the release of foreign exchange as patronage.

At one time, Indian travellers could take only US$20 with' them if they were on any mission other than business or official. How did they manage with this paltry sum in countries where even the taxi fare from airport to city costs more?

Well, either they were sponsored by their friends or relatives abroad or they cheatedùcollecting US dollars from an intermediate point where they had parked their dollar accounts clandestively, or buying it in black market paying more rupees. It was a matchless philosophy of the Government to save foreign exchange. They encouraged their citizens to cheat. Overseas, Indian travellers were not respected as they acted like beggars. The scene changed a little when in the late seventies, the Government of India allowed US$300 for leisure travellers, later raised to US$500 in three years and some travel agents in India started marketing tours with this amount on shoestring budgets. It became possible as air ticket could be bought in Indian rupees and for sightseeing purposes, buses and trains were used abroad which were relatively less expensive.

However, India decided to liberalise its economy in the starting of 1990s. The country gained an average growth rate of 4.5 per cent annually during this decade, with an accelerated growth in the later part of the decade. Allied to a strong economic growth, demand for international travel increased Until 1996, basic travel quota allowed by the Governmentù(BTQ) remained at US $500. It was increased to US $3000 per year per person in June 2000 and later on an further get increased to US $3000 a year. Now, it is US $5000 a year per person. For business orientedtravellers and for those attending conferences or those going for medical treatment, the foreign exchange quota was get increased to

US $25,000ùup from US $15,000. The system was further simplified as the release of foreign exchange was administered by designated commercial banks, as a matter of routine and the people did not have to get prior clearance from the Reserve Bank of India or the Government, for foreign exchange quota to travel overseas. It acted as a major stimulus for overseas travel.

GLOBAL ECONOMY

The liberalisation of economy has resulted in greater scale to the international business community and increased travel among the middle classes, who could afford travelling. There were other factors tooùpopularity of colour TV in Indiaùwith almost every other household having one or two colour TVs at their homes in urban areas. Indian films were shot in far-off foreign destinations like Switzerland, New Zealand and other European countries thereby twelve creating interest in these foreign destinations. Now the market is big enough to attract twelve foreign government Tourist Boards to open their representative offices in India, to lure Indian citizens to their respective destinations including Great Australia, and Britain. The departures from India in the year 2000 were 3,996600ùsmall for the size of a country like India but growing at a fast rate specially in the leisure part. The outbound travellers were 3.5 million in 1995 and 3>8 million in 1998. And, about 4 million in 2000.

PATA Report

The increase in outbound travellers, especially the leisure travellers from India, made Pacific Asia Travel Association (PATA) sit up and to take note. They asked Travel Research on International level a research organisation based in UK, to conduct a survey of India's outbound market for its members. This hundred-page study is a comprehensive survey of the current expansion spread of outbound travel from India and its future calibre. The first of its kind, it is an attempt on the part of an international organisation to do such a research on its own. The report, a rated publication, was publisher in January 2001 and examines India's present status as an international outbound market, its potential for the future and reasons that deter its faster growth.

So far, the focus of the Ministry of Tourism, Government of India, has always been on inbound tourism by which India gets, foreign exchange more than US 75 million dollars to lure foreign travellers to this country anually, not very successfully. In less than a decade, outbound market has left the inbound far behind with the number of foreign inbound travellers pegged at less than 2.6 million in 2000 and outbound reaching four million. India's balance of trade in tourism is now in the red. Indian travellers abroad are respected as their average spending is more than that of citizens of affluent countries. According to official statistics of Singapore, the average Indian spending in that country exceeds that of the US tourists.

Famous Foreign Destinations

PATA Report estimated that out of the four million outbound travellers, 35per cent were leisure travellers which includes a sizeable chunk who fall in the category of Visiting Friends and Relatives (VFR). And among the VFRs, the USA and UK have the largest part. Other popular destinations are nearer homeùSingapore, Thailand, UAE, Nepal and Hong Kong, in that order. One reason for Indians opting for foreign destinations nearer home is possibily the high price tag of air tickets for domestic air travel. The Government of India, for reasons of its own, keeps the price of air tickets for travel in India high to an extent that it is now cheaper for Indian citizens to travel to Singapore or Bangkok from Delhi, than from Delhi to Cochin or Chennai. generally, they prefer foreign destinations. Tickets to these destinations are cheaper due to intense competition among foreign carriers.

TOUR OBJECTIVE

Perfect outbound leisure tourism in India is still in its infancy but it has grown out of all approval compared with ten years ago and continuing to increase at a rate of fifteen to 20per cent annually. According to an International Passenger Survey done on behalf of the Government of India in 1996-97, thirty per cent of the outbound tourists were travelling for business-related purpose, twenty per cent were visiting friendandand relatives, 13per cent were joining their families, 13per cent for employment and only 13per cent declared their objectives as pure leisure. India being a vast country, purpose also varies from region to region depending on the nature of the people.

Most leisure travellers came from metro cities but the share of smaller towns was not insignificant. The impact of liberalisation of the economy is spread all over the country. PATA report estimates that at present some twenty-five million Indians are affluent enough to be able to afford overseas holidays. With only four million Indians travelling abroad, the potential is six times more and it is rising with levels of incomes Increasing in the country.

Within the broad spectrum of outbound travel, the composition of the outbound market has changed radically in current years. Business based travelling has changed from being a market composed basically of businessmen and entrepreneurs pursuing business opportunities within the region, to encompass bonus und conference travel, as well as long-haul trips for increasing number of Indian companies with offices overseas on the one hand and multinational companies based in India on the other. Indian and as multinational companies sponsor bonus travel holidays for their good workers or salesmen, or hold seminars and training programmes for their staff abroad.

Travel Corporation of India (TCI), one of the biggest travel outfits in India, reported sending eight thousand Indians per year, representing white goods manufacturers of automobile and pharmaceutical sectors. Air India reported that such groups could vary from two hundred to UK, to five hundred to Singapore. American Express has estimated that business travel out of India is worth more than US $1 billion a year business on the Net will soar to US $9 billion but the overall travel business in the USA may well be nearer to 800 billion US $. Thus the business on the Net is only 1.2 per cent of the total travel business, leaving the rest to travel agency playersùenough for everyone to have his share of the cake.

Role and Significance of Internet

In the present marketplace, it is necessary to talk about internet deals as a channel of distribution. It makes direct selling from suppliers to the customers easy and hassle-free. The internet is an evolving communications tool with greater calibre than any of its predecessors. Information technology is beneficial 10 every major principles like airlines, hotel chains who can do marketing their products worldwide on their web sites; the tour operators can market their destinations. National Tourist Organisations can have their web sites to expose tourist attractions of their countries; individual travel agents can showcase their productsùfair chance to all the players.

But it is only the travel agent who can get added the value and pleasure to the product. We were, therefore, not surprised to read a research paper which revealed that for every person ecstatic about booking on the Net, there were many more who were frustrated by the vast data and bewildering information which their head could not accept. Another IATA research further tells us that of the five passengers who book globally, four come through travel agentsùnot very different than what was happening thirty years ago. Again, only one in five explores the surf for informationùbut only one in ten actually books. E-commerce is coming of age; Whch is developing very rapidly which 33.33per cent per month. Creating this growth are supplier' web sites and internet booking services such as Microsoft Expedia, Sabre's Travelocity, Internet Travel Network, Preview Travel, American Express and Travel Web, etc.

These are full service mega sites doing business in millions. Most airlines too have mega sites but they only give their schedules and rates. They do not give comparative prices. This difficulty is overcome by sites like, www.travelocity.com, which gives comparative prices as well as airline schedules. There are different other web sites offering same services. Although the impact of internet on travel agency business is going to affect it adversely in the long run, the travel agent will not be out of business. European budget hotels are some of the best benefits of the internet revolutionùreceiving bookings from all over the world from travellers required economical accommodation.

According to Cyrus Gazdar, former President of the Travel Agents Association of India and a leading expert on new technology, by 2005 the revenue of travel agents from travel agency commissions will come down by fifty per cent. India is one of that country where IATA discipline still holds. Therefore the price war has left no standard tariffs settledall airlines are offering large discounts to sell their seats including those with excellent reputation as dependable carriers. Another innovation in the Indian market is the emergence of consolidators, appointed by airlines to offer cut-throat prices. Consolidators are bulk-buyers of airlines seat who then retail it to individuals as well as travel agents, keeping a small margin for themselves. Another new institution to reappear in India will be travel agent Co-ops or Consortia as in USA. It may be in the offing as the industry reshapes.

The number of LATA-affiliated travel agencies in India has not declined, in fact it was thousand and two hundred Just before two years but now increased to one thousand and five hundred at present. Travel business in India is increasing at a good rate 12.5per cent annually. Outbound business is even better, the shortage of airlines seats make travel agents kind of indispensable.

Adi Katgara, Director TCI, expressed his anguish at airlines policy to introduce consolidators, throwing away their seats to beat each other in preference to regular IATA travel agents who worked for them for small commissions. Now, they end up paying higher commissions unprecedented in the history of Indian travel industry. secondly development in Indian travel industry is the mix up of large Indian travel outfits with much larger multinationals. The trend was started by Airfreight Ltd. with Carlson, followed by Sita Travels joining the Kuonis. This is a significant of the shape of things to come and we can predict more mergers, but it is good for the travel industry of India. Both our inbound and outbound tourism will grow up.

DIFFERENCE BETWEEN TRAVEL AGENCY AND TOUR OPERATOR

Travel Agency is like a Retailer selling from all suppliers. He Can reserved a Hotel, rent a car for you or book your airport transfers. For tour packages he would use your choice and accordingly book a Coach tours are a Tour itinerary designed according to your wish with a Car Travel and Sightseeing + Hotel Reservation + Air Tickets/ Rail Tickets etc directly from the respective suppliers or a Tour Operator. Tour Operator is one who has already made some of his own itineraries and based on the category and budget choice of the Traveller (Who approaches him directly) or Travel agent (Indirect approach with respect to the Customer) make the full arrangement.

TYPES OF AGENCIES

There are three different types of agencies in the UK: Multiples, Miniples and Independent Agencies. The former comprises a number of national chains, often owned by international conglomerates, like Thomson Holidays, now a subsidiary of TUI AG, the German multinational. It is now quite common for the large mass-market tour companies to purchase a controlling interest in a chain of travel agencies, in order to control the distribution of their product. (This is an example of vertical integration.) The smaller chains are often based in particular regions or districts.

In the United States, there are four different types of agencies: Mega, Regional, Consortium and Independent Agencies. American Express and the American Automobile Association (AAA) are examples of mega travel agencies. Independent Agencies usually cater to a special or niche market, such as the needs of residents in an upmarket commuter town or suburb or a particular group interested in a similar activity, such as sporting events, like football, golf or tennis.

There are two approaches of travel agencies. One is the traditional, multi-destination, out-bound travel agency, based in the originating location of the traveller and the other is the destination focused, in-bound travel agency, that is based in the destination and delivers an expertise on that location. At present, the former is usually a larger operator like Thomas Cook, while the latter is often a smaller, independent operator.

CONSOLIDATORS

Airline consolidators and other types of travel consolidators and wholesalers are high volume sales companies that specialize in selling to niche markets. They may or may not offer various types of services, at a single point of access. These can be hotel reservations, flights or car-rentals, for example. Sometimes the services are combined into vacation packages, that include transfers to the location and lodging. These companies do not usually sell directly to the public, but act as wholesalers to retail travel agencies. Commonly, the sole purpose of consolidators is to sell to ethnic niches in the travel industry. Usually, no consolidator offers everything, they may only have contracted rates to specific destinations. Today, there are no domestic consolidators, with some exceptions for business class contracts.

STRUCTURE OF THE TRAVEL TRADE

The travel industry is highly structured, and businesses within the industry tend to specialize in one or a small number of functions driven by their core business. Understanding the structure of the travel trade is important for a company in developing its core business strategy, making marketing decisions, and investing for growth. The structure of the travel trade is largely driven by how consumers travel and how they identify and select the travel services they purchase. As we review the most widespread types of businesses in the travel trade, it is useful to keep in mind some common distinctions made when describing travel companies and their markets.

INBOUND AND OUTBOUND

When a company focuses primarily on serving travellers coming from other destinations, we refer to them as inbound operators. They generally offer services for clients coming from other countries or regions. Examples of these include Adria Tours and General Tourist. When a company focuses on serving travellers in their domestic or regional market seeking to travel to foreign destinations, we refer to them as outbound operators.

Examples of these would include the large number of agencies advertising package tours to other countries. The inbound operator seeks to understand foreign markets and develop products and services that will attract customers from overseas to their destination, and will focus on researching the travel motivations and preferences of target markets outside their own country. The outbound operator continually monitors demand for travel services within its own market, and will focus on identifying travel opportunities and creating products and services for these travellers going to other countries. Some companies may serve a local market, and they can attract both domestic and international travellers. A good example of this would be a ski resort. These are generally referred to as local operators without any distinction being made as to inbound or outbound.

Short Haul and Long Haul

Short haul refers to travellers coming from a nearby market, while long haul refers to travellers coming from far away. Usually, if the traveller's destination is further away than one day's driving distance, they are considered to be long haul. Typically, companies will serve both short and long haul markets, but will have a greater focus one or the other. The quality of the experience offered usually dictates whether or not a product can be sold to a long haul market. A low to medium quality attraction will generally not attract many long haul customers.

The cost of getting to that attraction is simply too high for the quality of experience to be gained. Only top destinations offering unique products and services are successful at attracting long haul customers. For example, you may drive one or two hours to the local aquarium or ski resort, since the effort of getting there is minimal for a day of fun. However, it is unlikely that a person from another country would plan a long trip to see the same attractions. They may only visit these attractions as part of a trip that has a greater focus: visiting Croatia for its historical or cultural attractions, or as part of an adventure travel vacation that involves multiple activities.

Operators and Resellers

Operators are companies that supply their own services or products, while resellers are marketing and selling the products and services of others, usually charging a mark-up or taking a commission. In practice, many travel companies do both. A tour operator will offer many of its own services but may also sell services of other suppliers as part of a package. A travel agency is mainly a reseller, but may for example employ its own guides or translators and sell these services directly.

Package Travel, Group Travel, and Independent Travellers (FIT)

Package travel refers to travel services sold as a package, where many services are bundled together for the convenience of travellers who don't wish to spend time making their own arrangements. Package travel may be sold both to group travellers and independent travellers. Group travel refers to package holidays that have a set itinerary and an allocation of seats or spaces. Customers purchasing the package joint the group. Independent travellers usually prefer not to travel with a group, unless it is a self formed group.

They prefer to have flexibility in their travel arrangements and may have done some research and have specific interests which dictate what they want to do and see on a trip. Sometimes they prefer not make to many advance plans, but in other instances they may carefully plan a custom tour that fits their own interests, working with either a travel agent or tour operator before leaving home. Independent travellers may purchase package travel services, but they will choose their own dates or request a private departure rather than traveling with a group.

TYPES OF TRAVEL OPERATIONS

Now as suggested, review the different types of travel operations that are the main players in the travel trade.

Travel Agencies

Travel agencies are perhaps the most visible companies in the travel trade. Their primary businesses is to resell accommodations, transportation services (including airplane and train tickets, car and bus transfers) individual services including guide and translator services, and package services such as sightseeing tours. Within each agency, there is often a focus on either inbound or outbound trade, with the outbound agencies focusing either on ticketing services and accommodation bookings, or on package holidays. Travel agencies generally serve a mix of long and short haul markets, although some specialize in long haul markets.

The majority of travel agencies seek to appeal to a large domestic market, so they focus mainly on products and services with a mass market appeal: beach and ski holidays, cruises, and package tours to well known and popular destinations. A small number may have a focus on specialty travel, and will offer products and services that cater to special markets. Examples would be agencies that specialize in custom travel arrangements, outdoor sports, or adventure holidays.

Most travel agencies that focus on outbound travel resell the products of both outbound and inbound operators, but they can also find products to retail from other travel resellers or from travel portals. Most travel agencies offer ticketing services for international travel, and can assist their customers with obtaining information on travel requirements such as visas and vaccinations, as well as obtaining travel insurance.

Outbound Tour Operators

Outbound tour operators create and market travel products to customers in their own markets that are usually long haul travellers seeking a specific experience in a foreign destination. They may design and operate their own trips, working with partners in the destination, or they may choose trips already designed by inbound operators and simply market these to their own clients.

Outbound operators generally have an in depth knowledge of what their customers are looking for and what their travel requirements are, and are thus able to design travel products that meet those needs. In the past, most outbound operators focused on group travel arrangements, but increasingly they are offering package travel for independent travellers. Outbound operators usually offer trips to a variety of destinations, and many focus on a small number of specialty travel segments, leaving the mass market travel arrangements to travel agencies.

Inbound Tour Operators

Inbound tour operators create and market travel products and services to customers mainly in long haul markets. Customers in countries far away generally do not have in depth knowledge of a destination or the service providers in that destination, may not speak the language, and may not feel comfortable making their own arrangements. Inbound tour operators serve these customers by taking the guess work out of planning a holiday, and may offer experiences that would otherwise be inaccessible to independent travellers making their own arrangements.

For example, planning and organizing your own expedition to go trekking in Western Croatia would involve months of research to identify routes, find local guides, arrange transport and pack animals, and considerable expense to transport equipment and gear or purchase it locally. A local company can organize all this for you at much less cost and in less time than it would take for you to do it yourself.

Inbound operators usually specialize in package travel arrangements of this kind, and may have both group and independent travellers as clients. Inbound operators operate their own tours, although the services of many local companies may be packaged and resold as part of this tour. Inbound operator usually specialize in one country or region. They may offer tours catering to a broad range of interests if they are located in a country that is not well known to travellers, but if they are in a well known destination where it is easy for independent travellers to make their own arrangements they usually focus on specialty travel.

Ground Operators

ervices directly to overseas customers. These operations focus on providing travel services on the ground, including activities like horseback riding, boat trips or guided diving tours, cooking or wine tours, etc. that form part of a larger experience or packaged tour. Ground operators may sell their services directly to independent travellers that have already reached a foreign destination – this is common in more well known travel destinations. In lesser known destinations, where there are relatively fewer independent travellers, ground operators usually work mainly with tour operators (either inbound or outbound) to market their products or services.

Local Service Providers

This term is used frequently to refer to ground operators, but more commonly it is applied to operations that provide local services such as accommodations (hotels, guest houses, families offering homestays), meals, local guides, equipment rental, cultural performances, and other specific services. Local service providers may include museums, parks, ferry lines, or domestic airlines. Often, there is little distinction made between ground operators and local service providers, and the two terms may be used interchangeably.

KINDS OF AGENCIES

There are three different types of agencies in the UK: Multiples, Miniples and Independent Agencies. The former comprises a number of national chains, often owned by international conglomerates, like Thomson Holidays, now a subsidiary of TUI AG, the German multinational. It is now quite common for the large mass-market tour companies to purchase a controlling interest in a chain of travel agencies, in order to control the distribution of their product. (This is an example of vertical integration.)

The smaller chains are often based in particular regions or districts. In the United States, there are four different types of agencies: Mega, Regional, Consortium and Independent Agencies. American Express and the American Automobile Association (AAA) are examples of mega travel agencies. Independent Agencies usually cater to a special or niche market, such as the needs of residents in an upmarket commuter town or suburb or a particular group interested in a similar activity, such as sporting events, like football, golf or tennis. There are two approaches of travel agencies. One is the traditional, multi-destination, out-bound travel agency, based in the originating location of the traveller and the other is the destination focused, in-bound travel agency, that is based in the destination and delivers an expertise on that location. At present, the former is usually a larger operator like Thomas Cook, while the latter is often a smaller, independent operator.

CONSOLIDATORS

Airline consolidators and other types of travel consolidators and wholesalers are high volume sales companies that specialize in selling to niche markets. They may or may not offer various types of services, at a single point of access. These can be hotel reservations, flights or car-rentals, for example. Sometimes the services are combined into vacation packages, that include transfers to the location and lodging. These companies do not usually sell directly to the public, but act as wholesalers to retail travel agencies.

Commonly, the sole purpose of consolidators is to sell to ethnic niches in the travel industry. Usually, no consolidator offers everything, they may only have contracted rates to specific destinations. Today, there are no domestic consolidators, with some exceptions for business class contracts.

CAREERS

With the many people switching to self-service internet web sites, the number of available jobs as travel agents is decreasing. Most jobs that become available are from older travel agents retiring. Counteracting the decrease in jobs due to internet services is the increase in the number of people travelling. Since 1995, many travel agents have exited the industry, and relatively few young people have entered the field due to less competitive salaries. However, others have abandoned the 'brick and mortar' agency for a home-based business to reduce overheads and those who remain have managed to survive by promoting other travel products such as cruise lines and train excursions or by promoting their ability to aggressively research and assemble complex travel packages on a moment's notice, essentially acting as a very advanced concierge. In this regard, travel agents can maintain competitive, if they become "travel consultants" with flawless knowledge of destination regions and specialize in topics like nautical tourism or cultural tourism.

MODERN TRAVEL AGENCIES

A travel agency is a business that sells travel related products and services, particularly package tours, to end-user customers on behalf of third party travel suppliers, such as airlines, hotels, tour companies, and cruise lines. In addition to dealing with ordinary tourists, most travel agents have a special department devoted to travel arrangements for business travellers, while some agencies specialise in commercial and business travellers. Some agencies also serve as general service agents for foreign travel companies in different countries. The British company, Cox and Kings is sometimes said to be the oldest travel agent in the world, but this rests upon services that the original bank (established in 1758) supplied to its wealthy clients. However, the modern travel agent first appeared in the second half of the nineteenth century.

Thomas Cook, in addition to developing the package tour, established a chain of agencies in the last quarter of the nineteenth century, in association with the Midland Railway. These not only sold their own tours to the public, but represented other tour companies. Other British pioneer agencies were Dean and Dawson, the Polytechnic Touring Association, and the Co-operative Wholesale Society. Travel agencies became more commonplace with the development of commercial aviation starting in the 1920s. Originally, the agencies largely catered to middle-class customers, but the post-war boom in mass-market package holidays resulted in travel agencies on the main streets of most British towns, catering to a working class clientèle looking for a cheap overseas beach holiday.

FUNCTIONS

As the name implies, their main function is to act as an agent, that is to say selling travel products and services on behalf of a supplier. Consequently, unlike other retail businesses, they do not keep a stock in hand. A package holiday or a ticket is not purchased from a supplier unless a customer requests that purchase.

The holiday or ticket is supplied to them at a discount. Thus, the agent's profit is the difference between the supplier's price and the price at which the product is advertised or sold to the customer. This profit is called the agency commission, and varies a great deal. In Britain, 12per cent would be considered a good commission. Other commercial operations are undertaken, especially by the larger chains. These can include the sale of in-house insurance, travel guides and timetables, car rental, and the services of an on-site bureau de change dealing in the most popular holiday currencies.

The majority of travel agents have felt the need to protect themselves and their clients against the possibilities of commercial failure, either their own or a supplier. They will advertise the fact that they are bonded (posting a financial bond with an organisation).

In the case of a failure, the customers are guaranteed either an equivalent holiday to that which they have lost, or (if they prefer) a refund. Many British agencies (and tour companies too) are bonded with IATA for those who issue their own tickets, ATOL for those who order tickets in, or ABTA for those who sell package holidays on behalf of a tour company.

Of course, a travel agent is supposed to offer impartial travel advice to the customer. This function almost disappeared with the mass-market package holiday, and some agency chains seemed to develop a 'holiday supermarket' concept, in which customers chose their holiday from brochures on racks and then booked it from a counter. However, a variety of social and economic changes have now contrived to bring this aspect to the fore once more, particularly the advent of multiple no-frills airlines.

THE CLASSIFICATION

There are three different types of agencies: these are Multiples, Miniples and Independent Agencies. The former comprise a number of national chains, often owned by international conglomerates (Thomson Holidays is now a subsidiary of TUI, the German multinational). It is now quite common for the large mass-market tour companies to purchase a controlling interest in a chain of travel agencies, in order to control the distribution of their product. The smaller chains are often based in particular regions or districts. Independent Agencies usually cater for a special or niche market. Some cater to the needs of residents in an upmarket commuter town or suburb, or concentrate upon a particular area or group (catering to the travel needs of Polish expatriates, perhaps), or an activity such as sports(servicing the needs of football supporters).

Travel agencies have been accused of employing a number of restrictive practices, the chief of which is known as 'racking'. This is the practice of only displaying the brochures of those travel companies whose holidays they wish to sell, the ones that pay them the most commission. Of course, the average customer tends to think that these are the only holidays on offer, and are unaware of possible alternatives. Generally speaking, small or specialist tour companies do not sell their product through travel agents, since they could not afford to pay the rates of commission that would be demanded. There are a few exceptions to this rule. Independent agents might sell or take bookings for local tour companies (such as coach companies) or tour companies offering specialist holidays that fit into their target market. Consequently, even before the advent of the internet, small niche tour companies ignored travel agents and sold direct to their customers.

THE THREAT

With the advent of general public access to the internet, many airlines and other travel companies began to sell directly to passengers. As a consequence, airlines no longer needed to pay the commissions to travel agents on each ticket sold. Since 1997, travel agencies gradually became victims of disintermediation, the reduction in costs caused by removing layers from the package holiday distribution network. Many travel agencies have developed an internet presence by posting a web site, with detailed travel information.

Full travel booking sites are often complex, and require the assistance of outside travel technology solutions providers such as Travelocity, Patheo and Open Fares. These companies use travel service distribution companies who operate Global Distribution Systems (GDS), such as Sabre Holdings, Amadeus, Abaccus, Galileo and Worldspan, to provide up to the minute, detailed data on tens of thousands of flight, hotel, and car rental vacancies. Some on-line travel sites allow visitors to compare hotel and flight rates with multiple companies for free. They often allow visitors to sort the travel packages by amenities, price, and or proximity to a city or landmark.

Travel agents have applied dynamic packaging tools to provide fully bonded (full financial protection) travel at prices equal to or lower than a member of the public can book on-line. As such, the agencies' financial assets are protected in addition to professional travel agency advice. All travel sites that sell hotels on-line work together with numerous outside travel agents. Once the travel site sells a hotel, one of the supplying travel agents is contacted and will try to get a confirmation for this hotel.

Once confirmed or not, the customer is contacted with the result. This means, that booking a hotel on a travel web site will not get you an instant answer. Only some of the hotels on a travel web site can be confirmed instantly (which is normally marked as such on each site). As different travel web sites work with different suppliers together, each site has different hotels that it can confirm instantly. Some examples of such on-line travel web sites that sell hotel rooms are Expedia, Travelocity, Tripadvisor, Excelloz, Travel Tickets Plus and Venere.

With the many people switching to self service internet web sites, the number of available jobs as travel agents is decreasing. Most jobs that become available are from older travel agents retiring. Counteracting the decrease in jobs due to internet services is the increase in the number of people travelling. Since 1995, many travel agents have exited the industry, and relatively few young people have entered the field due to less competitive salaries. However, others have abandoned the "brick and mortar" agency for a home-based business to reduce overheads, and those who remain have managed to survive by promoting other travel products such as cruise lines and train excursions, or by promoting their ability to aggressively research and assemble complex travel packages on a moment's notice (essentially acting as a very advanced concierge).

INDIAN ASSOCIATION OF TRAVEL AGENTS (IATA)

Most IATA approved travel agents in India, are also members of a national organisation called Travel Agents Association of India (TAAI). Its membership is further proof of their reliability. The TAAI logo can be displayedin such travel agencies which have ISI mark, indicating professionalism and reliability. TAAI makes a close scrutiny before accepting new members and expects all its members to follow a code of conduct.

The head ofice TAAI, is in Mumbai and the organisation has seven branches in major cities of India. The objectives of TAAI are to protect the genuine, and legitimate interests of the professional travel agency members. TAAI membership includes not only travel agencies domestic and international airlines, hotels, motels, resorts, etc. At the annual conference of TAAI, called the Indian Travel Congress, they discuss their general problems. TAAI was established in 1950 by a group of eight travel agents led by late Nari. J. Katgara. Now Membership get increased more than two hundred.

Indian Federation of Travel Agents

Travel Agents Federation of India (TAFI), is yet another organisation of India for claiming to represent travel agents. The head office of TAAT was started in Mumbai had special rules for its membeship It is now really large and both the organisationùTAAI and TAFI-try to work together to protect the interests of travel agents and touroperators.

Indian Association of Tour Operators

Delhi-based IATO (Indian Association of Tour Operators) is the representing organisation of tour operators handling inbound tourism. It is a new and active organisation and has among its members, all those involved in tourism industry, including hotels, transporters, state tourism department and airlines. It holds annual conventions to deliberate over its problems.

UNIVERSAL ASSOCIATIONS

At the world level, there is the Universal Federation of Travel Agents Associations (UFTAA). There are more than hundred and twenty one countries including India in the Universal fedeation of Travel Agens Association (UFTAA) Travel agency membership exceeds forty-eight thousand. The world body represents the interests and main points of travel agents all over the world, vis-a-vis organisations like IATA and IHRA (International Hotels and Restaurant Association). UFTAAalso provides training opportunities to travel agents who are members of this organisation.

There are about one thousand five hundred LATA-appointed agencies in India, Some of them have a dozen or more offices all over the country and provide employment to a large number of qualified young people. A travel agent tries to give perfect service to his clientsùprepares their itineraries, issues tickets after necessary reservations, arranges passports and visas for international travellers, books hotels at the place or places to be visited by his clients, sells travel insurance and if required, arranges cars on arrival at the destination. In fact, there is hardly anything which a travel agent cannot do for his client at the other end of the journey, provided the client is in the hands of an experienced travel agency.

ASTA

ASTA (American Society of Travel Agents) is another famous international travel organisation of travel agents. Due to the global nature of travel business, ASTA's agenda is according to international requirement. It permits travel agents from all countries of the world to become its members. While the

American members are active members, others are called allied members. Its annual conventions is called World Travel Congressùis attended by seven thousand to eight thousand travel agents each year. It is held one year in the USA and in the alternative year in a foreign country. The participation is so large that a country like India does not have sufficient hotel rooms in one city, to be able to invite ASTA conference. Till now ASTA conference is not held in India.

Setting up of an Agency

To start a new travel agency, the first important step is to select a proper location. The selection of the location can play an important role for the success. There should be special care of diverse areas with high potential for development and profits. While opening the location, the agency owner must choose an area which is appealing and accessible to the types of client he wishes to attract. It must be an expanding area or a new development with possibilities of growth. It must be convenient to businessmen enroute to or returning from work. The owner should also take care ofcompitability preferably, there should be less competition in the type of business he wishes to attract.

As for budget, the rule of thumb is that rent and uses should not exceed ten per cent of the tamed budget. A travel agency office must be well-designed, neat and attractive. Outdoor signs and window displays are necessary features of a good travel agency.

Telex, fax and photocopying machines have become necessary part of office equipment. Computer terminals from airlines will have to be rented once business starts growing. More successful travel agencies have back-room computerisation tooùfor accounting, billing and to follow-up on outstanding payments. A new agency is not immediately approved by IATA. It has to function successfully for one year, giving business to airlines. During the first year, the agency does not get the commission, but after getting approved, the commission earned in the past year is paid back.

Promotion

Since travel agency business is highly competitive, the management of the agency must have a expanded marketing plan to make easy. sale of its services. Under the broad term 'marketing', promotion means all the activities undertaken to promote a business and its products and services. It comprises the projection of a proper sigh of the agency and creation of demands for the services of the travel agency.

It can be done by personal contacts, through a sales force and advertising.A travel agent sells his services. Sometimes, there may be some malfunctioning somewhere in the long chain of travel, not essentially because of the mistake of the agent. It may be the mistake of an airline which did not operate a service at time, or of the hotel which did not honour a reservation because of overbooking. But, the travel agent is blamed from his clients. Hence this business has a lot of tension also. There is an interesting story of a travel agent who died and was face to face with St. Peter. He was trembling and expecting to be confined to hell since he never had time to pray in his lifetime. St. Peter asked,

"What was your profession on earth?"

"A travel agent, sir."

St. Peter gave a benevolent smile and ordered, "Let him go to heaven. The poor fellow had faced more than of hell on the earth at the hands of his clients."

TRAVEL TECHNOLOGY

Travel technology is a term used to describe applications of Information Technology (IT), or Information and Communications Technology (ICT), in travel, tourism and hospitality industry. Travel technology may also be referred to as tourism technology, hospitality automation, travel tracking and flight tracking.

DEFINITION

Since travel implies locomotion, travel technology was originally associated with the computer reservations system (CRS) of the airlines industry, but now is used more inclusively, incorporating the broader tourism sector as well as its subset the hospitality industry. While travel technology includes the computer reservations system, it also represents a much broader range of applications, in fact increasingly so. Travel technology includes virtual tourism in the form of virtual tour technologies.

Travel technology may also be referred to as *e-travel/etravel* or *e-tourism/ etourism* (eTourism), in reference to "electronic travel" or "electronic tourism". Travel technology is increasingly being used to describe systems for managing and monitoring travel, including travel tracking and flight tracking systems. In other contexts, the term "travel technology" can refer to technology intended for use by travellers, such as light-weight laptop computers with universal power supplies or satellite Internet connections. That is not the sense in which it is used here.

APPLICATIONS OF TRAVEL TECHNOLOGY

Travel technology includes many processes such as dynamic packaging which provide useful new options for consumers. Today the tour guide can be a GPS tour guide, and the guidebook could be an audioguide, podguide or I-Tours, such as City audio guides. The biometric passport may also be included as travel technology in the broad sense. XML-based technologies have become increasingly important for the travel industry. XML can be used to support air reservation booking or to implement optional services and merchandising functions in the booking process. Another important application of XML is the establishing of direct connections between Airlines and Travel Agencies. In order to create a generally accepted XML-standard, the Open Axis Group was founded.

HISTORY OF TRAVEL TECHNOLOGY

Certainly travel technology was born on the coat-tails of the airline industry's use of automation and their need to extend this out to the travel agency partners. It should be kept in mind that there was an online world before the advent of the world wide web in the form of private and commercial online services, via packet switched network using X.25. Travel technology played a significant role in the so-called dot-com boom and bust, circa 1997-2001.

3

Functions of Tour Operators and Travel Agents

Sometimes there is confusion over the difference in functions of tour operators and travel agents. Tour operators are the organisers and providers of package holidays. They make contracts with hoteliers, airlines and ground transport companies then print brochures advertising the holidays that they have assembled. Travel agents give advice and sell and administer the bookings for a number of tour operators. It is estimated that there are some 7,000 travel agency shops ranging size from the multiples, with several hundred outlets each, to the individual shop.

Some travel agents also undertake tour operating - be it on a small scale, eg a local agent packaging a group holiday for a local club, or on a larger scale - most famously by the legendary Thomas Cook, who was the first tour operator, and Sir Henry Lunn (Lunn Poly) who is widely credited with "inventing" skiing as a leisure activity. Agents can also sell the 'components' (flights, ferry bookings, car hire etc) for those who travel independently.

Although most package holidays are sold through travel agents a significant and growing percentage are sold direct to the consumer through advertising - Teletex, TV Travel Shops and the internet. ABTA - The Travel Association - represents both travel agents and tour operators. The Federation of Tour Operators represents only tour operators- its members have c.70per cent of the market. All current FTO members are also members of ABTA, and the two organisations work closely together - with the FTO particularly active with overseas governments and suppliers.

FUNCTIONS OF TRAVEL AGENCY

Travel agency is a retail business, that sells travel related products and services to customers, on behalf of suppliers, such as airlines, car rentals, cruise lines, hotels, railways, sightseeing tours and package holidays that combine several products. In addition to dealing with ordinary tourists, most travel agencies have a separate department devoted to making travel arrangements for business travellers and some travel agencies specialize in commercial and business travel only. There are also travel agencies that serve as general sales agents for foreign travel companies, allowing them to have offices in countries other than where their headquarters are located.

As the name implies, a travel agency's main function is to act as an agent, that is to say, selling travel products and services on behalf of a supplier. Consequently, unlike other retail businesses, they do not keep a stock in hand. A package holiday or a ticket is not purchased from a supplier unless a customer requests that purchase.

The holiday or ticket is supplied to them at a discount. The profit is therefore the difference between the advertised price which the customer pays and the discounted price at which it is supplied to the agent. This is known as the commission. A British travel agent would consider a 10-12per cent commission as a good arrangement. In some countries, airlines have stopped giving commission to travel agencies.

Therefore, travel agencies are now forced to charge a percentage premium or a standard flat fee, per sale. However, some companies still give them a set percentage for selling their product. Major tour companies can afford to do this; because if they were to sell a thousand trips at a cheaper rate, they still come out better than if they sell a hundred trips at a higher rate. This process benefits both parties.

Other commercial operations are undertaken, especially by the larger chains. These can include the sale of in-house insurance, travel guide books and timetables, car rentals, and the services of an on-site Bureau de change, dealing in the most popular holiday currencies.

The majority of travel agents have felt the need to protect themselves and their clients against the possibilities of commercial failure, either their own or a supplier's. They will advertise the fact that they are surety bonded, meaning in the case of a failure, the customers is guaranteed either an equivalent holiday to that which they have lost or if they prefer a refund.

Many British and American agencies and tour operators are bonded with the International Air Transport Association (IATA), for those who issue air tickets, Air Travel Organisers' Licensing (ATOL) for those who order tickets in, the Association of British Travel Agents (ABTA) or the American Society of Travel Agents (ASTA), for those who sell package holidays on behalf of a tour company.

A travel agent is supposed to offer impartial travel advice to the customer. However, this function almost disappeared with the mass-market package holiday and some agency chains seemed to develop a 'holiday supermarket' concept, in which customers choose their holiday from brochures on racks and then book it from a counter.

Again, a variety of social and economic changes have now contrived to bring this aspect to the fore once more, particularly with the advent of multiple, no-frills, low-cost airlines.

COMMISSIONS

Most travel agencies operate on a commission-basis, meaning that the compensation from the airlines, car rentals, cruise lines, hotels, railways, sightseeing tours and tour operators, etc., is expected in form of a commission from their bookings. Most often, the commission consists of a set percentage of the sale. In the United States, most airlines pay no commission at all to travel agencies. In this case, an agency usually adds a service fee to the net price.

WHY CSR MAKES SENSE FOR TOUR OPERATORS

CSR makes sense for companies. It is not just the communities, customers and environment that benefit. It is the business benefits of CSR that enable it to be a successful model.3 The business benefits for tourism include:

- *Responding to consumer demand*: Market research by Tearfund in 20004 showed that half of those interviewed were more likely to book a holiday with a tour operator that has an ethical code, and the majority of those were willing to pay for that guarantee. ABTA research in 2002 found that 87per cent of holidaymakers said it is important that their holiday does not damage the environment, and 76per cent feel that tourism should benefit those in the destination, through jobs and business opportunities. The research showed that 59per cent wanted information about local issues in their resort before they booked.5 Those operators that lead the field and become more responsible are likely to be rewarded with increased sales.
- *Improved service*: Contributing to poverty reduction in a destination and having a strong commitment to the workforce can create good morale and ensure a better welcome for customers. Investment in training will improve the quality of the product and customer service. Supporting local businesses will enhance the cultural experience.
- *Risk management*: Operating in a more sustainable way will greatly reduce the risks that a company faces. It will protect the company's image by dealing with problems before they get out of hand or are published in the media (as for health and safety considerations). Investment in staff can help to keep a high morale and therefore reduce staff turnover. Supporting community development will ensure good will and co-operation, and will ultimately safeguard the company's investment. Sound environmental management will ensure that the destination is desirable for visitors and the community in the long-term.
- *Cost savings*: Installing energy efficient systems at head office can save money as well as protecting the environment *e.g.,* through reducing heat loss or reducing the quantity of waste disposed. Recycling and cutting paper use can also save money.
- *Re-efsmpting government regulation*: Governments are under

increasing pressure by NGOs, unions and the general public to regulate the business sector. This pressure increases if bad practices are uncovered. Businesses that behave in a sustainable way that exceeds all existing legislation and builds on good practice can reduce the need for legislation. Those that develop their own codes of conduct and have independently verified reports will be in a strong situation to influence any proposed legislation. For the moment the UK and EU governments have favoured a voluntary approach to CSR, but this will be reviewed in the future. The onus is on companies to show that they are responsible, or face the threat of future legislation.

- *Growth of socially responsible investment (SRI)*—: A growing number of investors want a good return for their money in a socially responsible manner. In the last five years, investment in SRI and ethical funds quadrupled from £0.8 billion to £3.3 billion6 The Ethical Investment Research Service shows that 77per cent of pension fund members want their funds to develop an SRI policy, as long as it does not hurt their financial interests.7 Those tour operators that are listed and that are ethical will be the ones to gain from this increased ethical investment.

THE PROCESS OF CSR

For those starting to explore these issues, it can seem like a maze of terms and plethora of processes and tools to choose from. To provide some clarity we show below how a process of implementing CSR is likely to work for a tour operator, and some examples of what may be included under each step.

Like any process, each step is not isolated and there is likely to be significant overlap. These steps give a route map for implementing CSR in your company. They highlight some of the main challenges facing tour operators and also point towards some of the performance indicators of good practice.

Step 1

Commitment to being a responsible tour operator. It will involve writing a basic policy, defining goals and objectives, appointing staff members and committing funds to carry out the commitments.

- Establish a clear policy and objectives for responsible tourism and ensure that it covers operations both in the UK and in overseas destinations, right through the supply chain. Ensure there is support for this at board level.
- Appoint a responsible tourism staff member who will oversee the development and integration of these issues throughout the organisation. Commit funds to becoming more responsible.

Step 2

- Planning in more detail what it means to be responsible. It will involve consultation with all relevant stakeholders, developing management systems to cover environmental and social issues, and awareness raising and training of staff. It will also mean setting measurable targets, and developing guidelines and procedures.
- Take time to research destinations and speak to local development and environment groups and tourism associations, not just to the hotels. Find out which local businesses you could use, and with whom you may be able to develop a partnership. Also research attitudes and expectations of tourists.
- Train staff at head office and in the destinations so that they understand the policies and are able to implement them.

Step 3

Implementation of the policies and plans. Implementation should produce the desired improvements in product design, community development and co-operation, staff morale and performance, environmental preservation and customer satisfaction.

- Work throughout your supply chain to develop and implement purchasing policies that will focus on local ownership, use local labour, foods and crafts. Work with your suppliers to encourage good environmental management and build this up to include social areas such as employment standards and minimum wage levels.
- Brief local agents and representatives on your policies and objectives.
- Produce and disseminate a code for tourists to help them travel in a more informed and responsible way. Include advice on how they can support local development projects.

Step 4

Monitoring and Reporting performance is vital to understanding what differences are being made, and to communicate this with all stakeholders.

A report addressing the company's sustainability performance and the effectiveness of its CSR policies is the most effective way to communicate the achievements made. The report should ideally be independently verified so that a company's claims are substantiated and therefore seen as credible.

- Monitor your activities regularly so that you can learn from them and plan how to increase the impact each year.
- Publicise your performance to clients and share it with others *e.g.*, on the internet, in brochures and in advertising.
- Use your annual report to report on your performance and to gain support among your key stakeholders.

Step 5

Improving Your Performance

The reason for getting involved in CSR is to increase the benefits for everyone. Regular review of the results achieved is essential for learning and making improvements. The sustainability reports also help companies to understand in which areas the company is not performing in a sustainable manner *e.g.,* environmental degradation, low staff morale, threatened consumer action, few benefits to local communities.

- Set clear targets for year-on-year improvement in terms of building partnerships, using local suppliers and encouraging social and environmental improvements in hotels.
- Make changes to your business practices based on the information gathered.

TOUR OPERATOR

Wholesaler is often referred to as Tour Operator. The wholesaler puts together a tour programme after negotiating prices with principals like the airlines for airlines seats, hotels for rooms and meals and surface transporters who operate taxi and tourist coach facilities from airport to hotel and back and travel to other destinations in the city and outside. He may approach these principals either directly or through travel agents. He invests money in printing and distributing brochures to various destinations and undertakes trade or consumer advertising. He may sell tour programmes through his own retail outlets or through independent outlets. The risk in his business is high, but returns of success are phenomenal.

The travel agent operates in the local market and have necessary licences to represent the important domestic carriers such as airlines, railways, steamship and road transport. He may be the official ground handling agent at a destination for the wholesaler who appoints him for negotiation of prices on his behalf with principals such as hotels, domestic airlines and surface transporters.

The travel agent earns his revenue through commissions received from the principals and a mark-up on prices quoted to the wholesaler. Most travel agents act as wholesalers in the domestic market for outbound tours. They are also in cargo business.

Principals

These are institutions in the tourism infrastructure which own independent businesses. Principals are international airlines, hotels, domestic airlines and surface transporters. Surface transporters could be taxi/tourist coach agencies, railways and shippers. Principals give commissions to travel agents who get them business.

DUTIES OF TRAVEL AGENT

1. To receive intimation from wholesale operators for planning itineraries both for groups and particularly in his country.
2. Negotiation with road transport to provide taxis/coaches for transport from airport to hotel, sightseeing tours or intercity transportation.
3. Negotiation with hotels for reasonable prices for room, meal and for other services.
4. The arrange cheap and best transportation services.
5. Negotiation with histoical and cultural places for the entertainment.
6. Coordinate with various tourist centres for sightseeing tours.
7. Cost all points 2 to 6 above and offer a package price to a wholesaler.

Travel agents also advise on luggage insurance, the best season for travel, cloth ing'required, local foreign exchange rules and help in preparing travel documents like visas, health, passport, etc.

In the role of a wholesaler to the local domestic market, they will deal with all principals developing fantastick tour packages nationally and abroad for realised part reputated in the market. They take the responsibility to promote these tour packages through advertisements, e-mail or personal selling. To determine that clients gets satisfactory reputated, travel agents have also gone into transportation which makes them part principals in their own right.

Travel agents undertake on a day-to-day basis to book/make reservation on behalf of clients' seats on airlines, railways, steamship and taxies/coaches on a commission basis.

Job Prospects and Career Options

Being a very wide field, the scope of employment in tourism sector is very bright and the potential is still largely untapped. Career opportunities exist both in the public and private sector.

In the public sector, there are opportunities in the Directorates and Departments of Tourism of the centre and the state as Officers, information assistants, Tourist guides etc. Another good prospectus for qualified tourism professionals are in the private sector with travel agencies, tour operators, airlines, hotels, transport and cargo companies etc.

The opening up of the skies to private airlines and their emerging tie-ups with foreign airlines has removed bottlenecks in the transport and communication network resulting in easy flow of domestic and foreign tourists in the country.

Since this is a new area of employment, not many qualified and experienced people are available and the promotion prospectus are also very bright and rapid. After a few years of experience, One can also start their own business by handling all travel requirements of a client and gradually building up business, taking on additional employees.

Tourism Department

In the Tourism Department there are jobs as Reservation and counter staff, Sales and marketing staff, Tour Planners and Tour guides. Officers in the Directorate and Departments of Tourism are recruited from among the candidates who have done civil service, drawn from the Civil/administrative services of the State and Central governments. They are involved in the planning and promotion of tourism activities.

A degree in travel and tourism is required for operational jobs in government organisations. Information assistants at the office of the Tourism departments are selected through competitive examinations held by the Staff Selection Commission. The eligibility is graduation with knowledge of Indian history, art and architecture, besides proficiency in English. These vacancies are advertised through the employment news.

Information Assistants give out information regarding tourist spots and services available and help to plan the itinerary of the tourists. The Ministry of Tourism recognises three types of guides, regional, state and local. A regional guide gets a two year renewable license from the Ministry of Tourism endorsed for life by the Archeological Survey of India. Guides give detailed information on the various monuments and artifacts and about the countries traditions and heritage.

Airlines

Working in an airline, whether on the ground staff or in flight is an exciting option for many people these days. In the airlines, one can work as Traffic Assistance, Reservation and Counter Staff, Airhostess and flight pursers, Sales and Marketing staff and customer services. A course in travel and tourism or a qualification on Hotel management helps to get in. The jobs in airlines though challenging are glamorous and afford the possibility of travelling to exciting destinations. Free tickets for the family offered by some airlines are an added advantage. Domestic and international Airlines such as Air India, Indian airlines, Jet airways, Air Sahara, Aeroflot, British Airways, Cathay Pacific, Emirates, Singapore Airlines etc. offer employment opportunities with attractive salaries and numerous benefits.

Tour Operators

Tour operators organise conducted tours to the various tourist spots and manage the travel and stay of the tourists. There are many companies operating tours for the domestic as well as the international tourist. Some may be for the usual destinations like hill stations but others are for unusual activities like river rafting, hang gliding, rock climbing and camping. Tour operators need people for selling the concept and then to accompany the groups to the destinations. For foreign groups, the agencies prefer girls, who are friendly and helpful. For domestic groups, males are preferred. Again, the qualities required are a pleasing and outgoing personality, knowledge of the activities and often participating in them with the tourists. A person hoping to work with a tour operator must be able to travel with the groups and know people at the destinations to make the tours pleasant for the client. Though one may do a course of tourist guide for this purpose, people with a knowledge of the activities can easily join as tour operators. The jobs could be seasonal in some cases.

Travel Agencies

Travel agents assess the needs of tourists and businessmen and help them make the best possible travel arrangements from the many travel options available. Many resorts, travel groups use travel agents to promote their tour packages to travellers. They deal with almost everything connected with travel including the shortest route to the destination, travel mode, the important documents that will be required (visa, passport, vaccination certificates etc.), suitable places to stay, current exchange rates, tourist attractions to visit, climate and they will plan the trip keeping in mind the clients' preferences, budgets and special needs. In travel agencies there are openings for reservation and counter staff, Sales and Marketing staff, Tour escorts and tour operators, cargo and courier agencies etc. A short tem course or a diploma in travel and ticketing of 3-6 months duration will help gain entry into an agency. Several large travel agencies also offer short-term training programmes, and tend to absorb most of the candidates. Some agencies take in fresh graduates and train them on the job. Most travel agencies demands persons have a pleasing personality and the ability to deal with customers. A knowledge of destinations and procedures help a great deal.

Hotels

The hotel Industry is basically a service industry providing food and accommodation to the Visitors. It is one which requires a large amount of manpower, with a wide variety of skills. In India alone, about 1, 80,000 vacancies are expected to be filled within the next decade. An hotel offers career opportunities in its various departments such as Operations, Front office, House keeping, Food and Beverages, Accounting, Engineering/Maintenance, Sales, Public relations and Security etc. One can enter this field through direct entry in some departments or through hotel management institutes. There are many institutes that offer hotel management courses. Many hotels also offer overseas training opportunities, which allow young people to gain promotions rapidly.

Transport

Besides airlines, Travel facilities include rail services, coach operators, car hire companies. etc. Whatever that takes Tourists from one place to another-by air, road, railway, sea etc. comes under Travel and tourism. Tourist use almost all these travel facilities.

CONCERNED COMMISSIONS

Most travel agencies do not charge anything from their clients for their professional services. They depend on commission given by their principals, *i.e.*, airlines, hotels, motels, railways, car rental companies, bus and insurance companies, etc. Where they do not get commissions, they but a service charge. For instance, the Indian Railways do not give commissions to travel agents. So, a travel agency will add its service charge if a client wants them to buy train-ticket. However, Indian Railways makes an exception.

They allow 10per cent commission to travel agents selling Indian rail Passes to foreign tourists against foreign currency. They also offer the same commission on sale of Palace on Wheels' tickets. Commissions to travel agents vary from country to country, depending on the competitive situation. For example, commissions increases upto 15per cent and more in the USA where the international airlines are free to offer any commission to make a sale.

There is infact no boundation on payment of commission due to the policy of deregulation followed by the US Government. But now the airlines are getting wiser and some of them have put a boundation or 'Prohibition' as they call it. It has made travel agencies less profitable. The scene is changing during the economic situation of airlines. In India, we follow the IATA norms—7per cent commission on international tickets. Recently, Indian Airlines followed their own rules. They had the monopoly and paid a less 4per cent commission. With the entry of private airlines are paying. Now Indian Airlines pays five per cent commission which is same as the private airlines. Now, the Government has added its 10per cent tax on the total value of the domestic air ticket, which is collected by travel agents No commission is paid to him by the Government for this service. Tax is deposited to the government officers.

Membership of IATA

Although one may find all travel shops calling themselves travel agencies, a dependent travel agency is one displaying the logo of IATA (International Air Transport Association) appointed agent for representing their symbol. An IATA appointed travel agency is reliable, because such a company has been approved by this international organisation, after standard proper scrutiny of their professional competence and financial reliability. Such agencies have to provide financial guarantees to the airlines against default. The agencies which are not IATA members, may not be trustworthy because they buy tickets from other registered IATA agents, or the general sales agents of airlines and resell these to their clients, sharing a part of the commission with their clients. Their gain is so small that they cannot give good service. Until a travel agency is approved by IATA, it cannot get commissions directly from an international airline. IATA approval does not automatically make an agency eligible for commission from Indian Airlines or private domestic airlines. The IATA approval helps. Airlines, to make their own rules, follow up and yardsticks for approval.

IMPORTANCE OF TOUR OPERATOR

The main important part of the 'Tour organisation is' "tour operator" The tour operator buys different requirements for the tourist such as aircraft seat, hotel beds and other facilities like road transport, entertainment articles and makes up packages. Historically, the tour operator has mostly emerged from retail travel agency.

However, today a travel agent and a tour operator is different from each other. The latter, the retail travel agent, undertakes to sell the travel services of his principal, *i.e.*, airline companies and other transport undertakings, hotel groups, shipping lines and the provision of such ancillary services as traveller's cheques, insurance, etc. The tour operator is a producer of a tourism product unlike the travel agent who is the retailer of the tourism products. He plans, organises and sells tours. The tour packages operator makes all the important arrangements—transport, accommodation, sightseeing, insurance, entertainment and other matters and sells this 'package' for an all inclusive price. A package tour is prepared to fit a special group of travellers. There may be special interest tours, *i.e.*, trekking, wildlife tours, etc., and can be escorted. An escorted tour generally includes transportation, meals, sightseeing, accommodation, etc. It is. the "escort" or the "group leader" who is accountable for maintaining the schedule of the tour and for looking after all the arrangements.

NETWORK AND DISTRIBUTION OF TOUR OPERATOR

The tour operator has thus emerged as the true producer of the inclusive tour product packaged, standardised and quality controlled. The inclusive tour product can be marketed successfully by a tour operator in the tourist producing countries to a mass market, either directly or through travel agents.

A large majority of tour operators sell their tour packages through a network of several hundred agents who are the members of the Association of Travel Agents in a particular country. For instance, if a tour operator happens to be USA based he would sell his product through ASTA, (American Society of Travel Agents) in UK, through ABTA (Association of British Travel Agents) in Australia, through AFTA (Australian Federation of Travel Agents) etc. A large percentage of tour packages are marketed in this manner.

Some tour operators resort are directly selling the tour package through the network of their branches For instance, in Switzerland, the largest tour operating company 'KUONF' Sells its product through 85 of their own Kuoni retail sales offices as also through 765 appointed retail agents who are the members of FASV, the Swiss association of travel agents. Thomas Cook is well known as a travel retailer of its own product in addition to being a major tour operator of package tours. Most of their package tours are sold through an expanded network of their own retail sales offices.

Direct sale of the holiday scheme is however resorted to by large tour operating companies having retail sales agencies of their own within a destination where these are situated or in other neighbouring destinations.

On the other hand, small tour operating companies not having retail sales outside will either Centralised on selling their product or will support a select few travel agencies in important areas spread over the country. However, unlike sales of a tour operator programmes through travel agencies, direct selling engages higher fixed costs in advertising, direct mail development and similar other aspects. Direct selling also requires strong and efficient administrative back-up to deal smoothly with consumer and trade enquiries and sales,

AGREEMENTS OF SALES

A tour operator who decides to sell his tours through a network of travel agents, has to get in some form of an agreement with them. A formal contract with the travel agents they appoint is to be drawn up to facilitate the agents to sell the services on behalf of a tour operator.

The contract inter alia specify the various terms and conditions of sale including issues like quantum of commission to be paid to the agents. It also makes clear if the travel agent is to be a cash or credit agency as also the dates by which the operator is likely to settle his'accounts. Another potent condition of the contractor relates to a sale price of a tour. Most tour operators impose on an agent the condition in the contracts that their tours shall not be sold at a lower price than that published in the brochure.

Brochure Marketing

Printing of a tour brochure is very expensive. A brochure is a voluminous publication with special pressure on the quality of paper, the reproduction of illustrations, graphic design of the cover and the layout of the pages. To be an attractive sales tool, it has to be printed on glazed art paper in four colours.

Special pressure is laid on the quality of papers and printing, as its main objective is to inform the prospective tourist about the attractions and facilities of a programme being developed by a tour operator. Considering all the above aspects, a tour operator has to spend reasonable amount of money on printing of a tour brochure. Some of the tour brochures of large companies contain different programmes running into many hundred pages. Each of the particular programme in a brochure is to be marketed to percept a sale of that programme, different programmes contained in a brochure are to be marketed both by the tour operator and the agents at a destination to get actual bookings for a individual programme. Marketing and promotion of a special programme in a tour brochure involves many elements starting first with the contribution of a brochure to travel agents situated throughout the country. In case a tour operator had retail sales offices of his own, the brochure is also to be contributed to them.

The quantity will depend on the size of the agency as also its location. It will also depend on the volume of business generated by the agent during the past few years. Launching a press conference is another important element in developing a holiday programme printed in a brochure. A special advertising campaign is necessary to be launched in specifiedcustomer newspapers in the generating market featuring tour programmes. The selection of the customer newspapers should be based on factors like the area to be covered, the type of.audience to be reached, the appeals to be used, etc. The consumer newspapers are selected due to of their wider reach. Window display campaign is another important and effective way of developing a tour programme of a brochure. Specially prepared window display materials featuring tour programmes of a company for a special destination can be used in retail sales office locations.

The visual appeal of displaying motivation of a prospective tourist to enter the office and ask for more details. Simultaneous launching of a press conference and window display campaign gives added profit in that it registers a message about a destination more forcefully. Trade education is another important element in promoting the sale of a holiday package. The sales staff of a tour operating company should be given orientation concerning the tour programme they are to promote through their outlets. This could be handled by planning specialist of the tour operating company.

A similar trade education programme can be organised for retail agents. All appointed retail sales agencies should be engaged in this programme. Press and public relations activities of the company developing a programme play a vital role. A large tour operating company has a separate press and public relation department which create special press releases on their various tour programmes. The text of these press releases is given to select consumer newspapers throughout the country.

TOUR PACKAGES

An early form of package holiday was organized by Thomas Cook in 1841, offering customers a return trip between Leicester and Loughborough. The first package tour of Europe was organized by Cook in 1855, and by 1872 he was undertaking world-wide tours, albeit with small groups. Vladimir Raitz, the co-founder of the Horizon Holiday Group, pioneered the first mass package holidays abroad with charter flights between Gatwick airport and Corsica in

1950, and organized the first package holiday to Palma in 1952, Lourdes in 1953, and the Costa Brava and Sardinia in 1954. In addition, the amendments made in Montreal to the Convention on International Civil Aviation on June 14, 1954 was very liberal to Spain, allowing impetus for mass tourism using charter planes.

By the late 1950s and 1960s, these cheap package holidays—which combined flight, transfers and accommodation— provided the first chance for most people in the United Kingdom to have affordable travel abroad. One of the first charter airlines was Euravia, which commenced flights from Manchester Airport in 1961 and Luton Airport in 1962.

Despite opening up mass tourism to Crete and the Algarve in 1970, the package tour industry declined during the 1970s. On 15 August 1974, the industry was shaken when the second-largest tour operator, Court Line which operated under the brand names of Horizon and Clarksons, collapsed. Nearly 50,000 tourists were stranded overseas and a further 100,000 faced the loss of booking deposits. In 2005 a growing number of consumers were avoiding package holidays and were instead travelling with budget airlines and booking their own accommodation. In the UK, the downturn in the package holiday market led to the consolidation of the tour operator market, which is now dominated by a few large tour operators. The major operators are Thomson Holidays and First Choice part of TUI AG and Thomas Cook AG. Under these umbrella brands there exists a whole range of different holiday operators catering to different markets, such as Club 18-30 or Simply Travel. Budget airlines have also created their own package holiday divisions such as Jet2 Holidays.

The trend for package holiday bookings saw a comeback in 2009, as customers sought greater financial security in the wake of a number of holiday and flight companies going bust, and as the hidden costs of 'no-frills' flights increased. Coupled with the search for late holidays as holidaymakers left booking to the last moment, this led to a rise in consumers booking package holidays.

METHOD OF DYNAMIC PACKAGING

Dynamic packaging is a method that is becoming increasingly used in package holiday bookings that enables consumers to build their own package of flights, accommodation, and a hire car instead of a predefined package. Dynamic packages differ from traditional package tours in that the pricing is always based on current availability, escorted group tours are rarely included, and trip-specific add-ons such as airport parking and show tickets are often available. Dynamic packages are similar in that often the air, hotel, and car rates are available only as part of a package or only from a specific seller. The term "dynamic packaging" is often used incorrectly to describe the less sophisticated process of interchanging various travel components within a package, however, this practice is more accurately described as "dynamic bundling". True dynamic packaging demands the automated recombination of travel components based on the inclusion of rules that not only dictate the content of the package but also conditional pricing rules based on various conditions such as the trip characteristics, suppliers contributing components, the channel of distribution, and terms of sale. Dynamic packages are primarily sold online, but online travel agencies will also sell by phone owing to the strong margins and high sale price of the product.

Dynamic packaging is dynamic at several levels. Firstly, inventory is sourced dynamically, meaning the dynamic packaging solution will source flights, accommodation and car rental components for the package in real-time. Secondly, these components are dynamically combined into packages. Thirdly, the package is dynamically priced and is usually given an opaque total price. Dynamic packages are normally given a single, opaque price, meaning the wholesaler's cost of the individual components is hidden from the consumer. The wholesaler often obtains special package-only cost rates for travel components, such as negotiated fares for flights or special package rates for accommodation or car rental. These cost prices are typically significantly lower than the cost prices suppliers offer for the same products if they were to be sold as single components. Hence, the wholesaler will be able to offer the consumer a combined saving for the dynamic package, without reducing his own margins.

Opaque pricing of dynamic packages hide the price of the included components. This has several benefits. Suppliers of travel products often impose a minimum selling price for their products. For instance, a hotel might give the wholesaler a room at cost price *X*, but on the condition that the room is not sold for less than *Y* (hotels do this to prevent wholesalers from competing with themselves). With dynamic packaging, the customer is not presented with the room price, only the overall package price, so hotels typically allow the wholesaler to discount the (hidden) price of the hotel more.

Opaque pricing also has benefits for airlines. Airlines tend to increase their fares the closer you get to the departure date, even if there are many available seats. This is to "train" the consumers to book early, making it easier for the airline to do proper revenue management.

If airlines were to dump their fares if a flight failed to fill up, then this would train the customers to wait until very close to departure before booking. This would make it virtually impossible for an airline to manage their fares (fares could then only be determined based on historical data and not based on current demand). Dynamic packaging allows an airline to get rid of distressed inventory at discounted fares, as the discounted fare is effectively hidden from the consumer.

Dynamic Preconditions

Dynamic Packaging is also often misunderstood since it requires that the provider of Dynamic Packaging be a wholesaler, who must also issue tickets, vouchers or other redeemable coupons in order to become a Dynamic Packager. Without an inventory management system, and a ticket, coupon or voucher issuing system to make the prices of the individual components appear as one price to the consumer and allow each travel service provider to know what rate to accept or charge the traveler; dynamic packaging does not work. Many travel retailers have mistakenly assumed they could provide dynamic packaging without an inventory management system, mark-up engine with business rules and a ticket issuing and resolution system. The wholesaler must either directly control the inventory that is combined into packages or buy the package components up-front from other travel suppliers. This implies that dynamic packages (as with static packages) are always pre-paid by the customer.

The wholesaler would typically also require special discounted fares/rates from the travel suppliers. For car rental, the supplier (car rental company or intermediary) should ideally supply their price based on calendar days rather than hour-by-hour. Calendar daty rates reduce the number of vehicle availability/ pricing scans the wholesaler must make. For packages that include flights, the outbound arrival and return departure date/times determine the car rental pick-up and drop-off date/times. If car rental rates were by the hour they would differ for each flight option, hence the wholesaler would have to issue a vehicle availability search for each available flight, while with 24-hour rates one single vehicle availability search is enough to cater for all flight options.

GROUP INCLUSIVE TOUR (GIT)

This is the most famous form of tour in this category in which people travel in groups of 15 or more persons. These tours are available for any destination. The terms and conditions for group inclusive tours are decided by IATA. The escort for such groups generally travels free as the airline gives him with free passage and accommodation. The Foreign Inclusive Tour (FIT), on the other hand, is an unescorted package tour. The FIT tours are relatively more adjustable. The traveller can buy a pre-decided package with arrangements for sightseeing, hotels and particular meals, where essential. He does not tour with a group. He can make his own arrangements and programmes according to his desire. The inclusive tour is one of the many devices which enable tourists to enjoy the lower price.

The Group Inclusive Tour (GIT) programme made up of a series of integrated travel services. Each of the travel services like seat in a aircraft, a hotel room, etc., is purchased by a tour operator in bulk and resold to his retailers or customers directly as part of a package at an all-inclusive price. The product generally referred to as a 'package tour are single destination holidays'. In other words, a customer would buy a package holiday from a tour operator or a wholesaler to any single destination, for instance, a tour operator in a individual country will sell a package at a particular price for a cultural holiday in India, a beach holiday in Bali, a wildlife adventure trip in Kenya or a shopping holiday in Singapore, etc. However, some packages comprise two or more destinations. Now, twin destination packages have become quite popular as with little more price one can visit more than one country. These tours are quite common and popular in Europe.

PRICE ADVANTAGES

The success of the package tours depend upon the cheaper and reasonable services for the negotiation, purchased by tour operators for the tourists This lower price of the package tour or inclusive tour is made possible by obtaining the air travel and the hotel accommodation in bulk. As tour operating today has become a highly competitive business its success mainly depends upon the operator maintaining the lowest possible prices while continuing to give to its customers a 'value for money'.

Because of the bulk purchase, tour operators are able to procure substantial discounts from carriers, hoteliers, etc., and offer their package deals at much lower rates. The profits of the tour operator and the success of his operations, however, depend mostly on the achieving of very high load factors for the aircraft and high occupancy rates for the hotel. In this way unit costs can be maintained lowest to enable the tour operator to offer his package at a price which is often lower than the cheapest available fare alone. A breakthrough in the business of tour operation came when airlines realised that tour operation could fill the empty seats, and introduced special fares for use exclusively by tour operators for combining into an inclusive tour.

The tour operator has thus emerged as the main facturer of the tourist product. The product is the inclusive tour, packaged, standardised and mass produced. The tour operator may sell this product directly to the public or through the channels of the retail travel agencies. It can be marketed successfully in the tourist-generating countries to a mass market just because if is standardised, packaged and quality controlled. The product is, therefore, susceptible to the similar marketing techniques that are applied to the marketing of consumer goods.

Package Tour Marketing (Discounts)

In the competitive world market, there is several choices of the package tours for the different destination, in that situation tour operators have to take careful decision for the promotion of the marketing of the tour packages After considering various alternatives, a tour operator has to narrow down the choice to few potential destinations. A realistic appraisal of the potential of the selected destinations is to be made.

Selection of a potential destination by a tour operator is to be based on different factors; some of these factors include the:

- Presently, number of tourist attracted by the individual areas;
- Growth rate in tourist arrivals in these areas;
- Share of the competing companies;
- Evaluation of expected share of the market by a company in the next few years of the operation.
- Availability of suitable and convenient relation to a destination;
- Negotiations with principals like the airlines and hotels; and
- Negotiations with local conducting agents at the destinations, etc.

PAMPHLET FOR TOUR

Once all the above factors have been considered, when a tour operator arrange a package of tour and incorporate it in a brochure called "tour brochure". A brochure is a document bound in the form of a booklet. It is a voluminous publication with special stress on the quality of a paper, the graphic design of the cover and the layout of pages. The tour operators brochure is the most important marketing tool for selling his product.

Since tourism is an intangible product which cannot be pretested by the prospective customer prior to the purchase, the brochure becomes the important channel of informing a customer about the product and also exciting him to buy the product. The brochure contains a comprehensive and detailed information about a destination including cruises, bus tours, safaris, charter vacations, etc., with colour photographs with regard to all the destinations which a company is developing. Comprehensive information about hotels, weather conditions, frontier formalities, etc., is also given. The price of various tours is invariably mentioned along with the dates when tours take place. Several tour operators take great care with production of their brochures. There are, however, no travel industry standards or guidelines or the production of brochures. Established tour operating companies take great care for designing their tour brochures. The following are some important areas which require to be taken care of while getting the tour brochure printed:

- Layout
- Quality of paper
- Photography
- Quality of printing
- Special features
- Detailed itineraries
- Weather conditions
- Maps of areas
- Hotel information
- Terms and conditions of tour.

Many large tour operating companies get their brochures designed and printed in their own advertising departments. Some get the brochures printed in relation with the design studio of their advertising agency, who in turn negotiate with the printer to get the best quotation and ensure that the print deadlines are adhered to. Adhering to the print deadline is very important as the company has to introduce the brochure at a prejudiced date, coinciding in most matters with travel trade and consumer holiday fairs. The introduction of a brochure at these events both to travel trade and consumer is decisive for marketing a package.

Tour Brochure

Two diverse versions of a tour brochure printed by two different companies are exhibited in the following pages. Brochure-I is printed by one of the progressive tour operating companies having a worldwide network of its branches. A four-colour brochure printed on glazed art paper contains different programmes in the form of packages which the company is developing through its brochure.

However, only a few programmes of the company related to India/Nepal have been shown to give to the reader an idea as to how these are packaged. In the brochure, different programmes have been offered for their clients. These have been appropriately titled to motivate the client. For example. Programme-titled 'Indian Experience' is a nine-day classical tour covering Delhi-Agra-Jaipur-Delhi. From day one which is a departure day from USA to India till the ninth day with departure from India to USA, each of the days' details have been worked out. The client can also take extension of one week's holidays to Goa to relax on a beach or go to look for a tiger at one of the many game parks. Most of the tour operators offer extension programmes beyond the planned itineraries. A client has basically to pay a printed price for a basic programme and an additional price in case he takes an extension. The brochure gives both departure and return dates of the programme.

Programme-II entitled "Splendours of the North" covers two weeks' programme covering in addition to Delhi-Agra-Jaipur, places like Varanasi, Gwalior and Udaipur. Programme III is a special programme of 18 days entitled "Forts and Palaces". This programme has been specially put together for those clients who have interest in arts and architecture covering forts and palaces. Programme-IV is twin destination programme spread over India and Nepal. A 22-day programme takes a client first to Nepal and then to India. Titled as "Classical Journey" it covers places associated with religion, culture, legends and mysteries. Travelling at a leisurely pace a tourist can get the grand sights and saviour the unique flavour in both Nepal and India. Programme-V is again a special interest programme for those interested in nature and wildlife. An 18-day programme takes a client prosperous rich tropical jungles, extensive grasslands, temperate forests of India which are reserves of wildlife and some of the world's most stunning national parks. Programme-VI is a 19-day programme to South India entitled "Southern Trader" spread over golden beaches and temples in the region.

KEY CONCEPT: PACKAGES AND TOUR OPERATORS

A 'package' can be defined as a pre-arranged combination, sold or offered for sale at an inclusive price, of not less than two of the following three elements:

- Transport;
- Accommodation;
- Other tourist services not ancillary to transport or accommodation and accounting for a significant part of the package.

The growth of the package has been a major cause of the increase in the holiday market since the 1950s. The role of the package company goes beyond that of the wholesaler, in that they not only purchases or reserve the separate components in bulk but, in combining these components into an 'inclusive tour', they also become producers in the holiday market. The traditional appeal of the tour operators' product has been to offer a complete holiday package at the lowest price to a population often lacking the linguistic knowledge or the knowledge and confidence to organise independent travel. Consequently the tour operation has become the dominant feature of the holiday market in many tourist-generating countries.

INSEPARABILITY

The production and consumption of services are inseparable. To take advantage of an air flight or a bus service, for example, both you and the means of transport must make the journey at the same time. The implication of this inseparability is that the consumers have direct experience of the production of the service. They are, in effect, in the 'service factory' at the time of production. This has profound implications for the staff in service industries.

When a physical product is purchased, it comes packaged and the customer is likely to assess the product purely upon its product features (such as taste, size, specification, etc.). Managers have time to plan these aspects of product management to ensure that customer satisfaction is achieved. The circumstances under which the product is produced and how it is delivered are usually of little relevance to the customer.

In the case of a service product, however, customers are likely to be very concerned about the way in which the product is delivered, *i.e.,* the level of customer service. At a hotel reception desk, for example, the customer is likely to notice if the receptionist is rude or unwelcoming. Similarly, the customer will also experience the production of the product if the receptionist is efficient, courteous and helpful.

The task of satisfying customers for the provider of a service is in many ways much more difficult than it is for the manufacturer of a product. In service industries everything has to be right first time, all the time and any mistake can prove very costly in terms of lost future custom. How service personnel conduct themselves in the customer's presence, what they say, what they don't say, how competent they are, how personable they are or how presentable they are, can determine whether the customer buys from the business again.

Perishability

Since production and consumption are simultaneous, services are instantly perishable if they have not been sold at the time of the production. The empty train seat, the empty hotel bed or the unsold holiday all represent lost opportunities. They are lost sales that can never be recovered (empty hotel rooms cannot be 'stored' for when demand increases). Unlike manufacturers of goods, they cannot just keep on producing services and store them for future sales and striking the correct balance between capacity and sales (supply and demand) is extremely difficult.

Consumer Capacity, Occupancy for Accomodation

In travel and tourism, capacity refers to the number of people that can be accommodated in a hotel, aircraft, bus, resort, etc. It may be, for example, that a hotel has a capacity of 300 and an aircraft might be able to accommodate 130.

The important figure, however, is how much of the capacity is actually used at any time. This is the occupancy rate for accommodation or the load factor for transportation. If a hotel, for example, is only full on a quarter of the nights in a year, then it is paying the fixed costs on the empty rooms without any income from them. This is particularly important when considering seasonality and also explains why hotel prices fall in the low season—to maintain as high an occu-pancy rate as possible to help to cover the hotel's total costs.

The problems of perishability can be made even more acute by fluctuating demand but fixed supply. Demand can vary during the day, during the week or from season to season of the year. Many resort hotels, for instance, are full for only a few months of the year. Capacity may therefore be insufficient to meet demand at peak times, but in excess of what is required at slack times. Demand can fluctuate for all sorts of reasons, such as seasonal changes, changes due to the level of economic activity, and changes due to climatic conditions. Changes in demand can also occur very suddenly and can have a dramatic impact on service suppliers. For instance a single reported terrorist attack in a destination area could severely limit demand. Or more widespread instability such as the Gulf War of 1991 can also curtail demand. In the case of the Gulf War, the airline industry worldwide faced a major downturn in demand. Supply, however is much more difficult to alter, at least in the short term. For example, a hotel has a fixed bedstock (number of beds) that it has to try to fill. A scheduled airline has an obligation to fly between advertised points regardless of the number of empty seats on the aircraft. A tour operator enters a contractual obligation, often months in advance of the date of travel, with the providers of accommodation to fill a certain specified number of rooms. The management challenges, therefore, is to make sure that the company is operating at full capacity for a much of the time as possible. To be successful, the company will need carefully designed strategies to stimulate demand, lengthen seasons, or to offer appropriate pricing levels to manage and 'smooth out' occupancy levels.

Heterogeneity

Services, unlike mass-produced manufactured, goods, are never identical. One hotel in a chain of hotels, or one person's holiday, will never be identical to another. The human element and other factors in delivering services, ensures that services will be heterogeneous, *i.e.,* varied. Tourism products are 'people oriented', and the human factor plays a key role. The enjoyment gained from a holiday cannot be separated from the personalities who go to make up that holiday—the personnel employed in the travel agency, the airline crew, the hotel, staff, the tour operator's overseas representative, and of course, the holidaymaker. All of these have a role to play in ensuring that the holiday lives up to the customer's expectations.

Human behaviour, however, is highly variable and it is difficult for a company to ensure that its employees display good customer relation skills all of the time. Similarly, the company has no influence over the behaviour of the customer when on holiday. the customer's attitudes and behaviour will also contribute to the pleasure gained from the holiday. This means that there is an uncontrollable element inherent in the production of the travel or tourism product which can lead to the holidaymaker being satisfied or disappointed with the holiday. To take account of this problem, it is important that as much information as possible is provided in advance to the potential customer, both by the tour operator and the travel agent. This will reduce the risk of the customer purchasing an unsuitable holiday at the outset. Special attention has also to be paid to the personnel who will deal with the client on a face-to-face basis to make certain that they have suitable personalities for dealing with the public.

In many cases in travel and tourism, the customer is actually attracted by the heterogeneity. Tourists would become bored if every tourist destination was identical, and hotel chains try hard to maintain a consistent brand image whilst at the same time trying to differentiate each hotel through varying design features. This heterogeneity is understandable, but it does make it very difficult for potential purchases to evaluate services and for managers to deliver products of a consistent quality.

4

'Traveler-tourist' and New Moral Tourism

The debates over travel in the nineteenth century bequeathed us 'traveller versus tourist', an axis around which the critique of tourism has often been discussed. This is still very much in evidence today, witnessed in tour operator advertising, travel literature and in the broader discussion of the nature of modern tourism. However, as we shall see, travel today is far from immune to the criticisms of its deviant offspring, tourism. Today's critique of tourism, premised as it is on a view of people in opposition to nature and cultures, has extended itself further to encompass the erstwhile critics themselves.

The propensity to turn in on itself and to become *self-critical* is an important, new, characteristic of the New Moral Tourism. Today's debate is less 'traveller versus tourist' (although the tourists are the ones generally in the frame), and more a critique that starts out focussing on the package tourist and, following its own logic, ends up criticising the attempts at ethical tourism themselves. The cultural associations of post-war travel include the Hippy Trail in the 1960s and 1970s. Well-heeled university students, rock stars and assorted hippies established the Trail, stretching from London, picking up in Europe, and on through Asia to Kathmandu. They were self-consciously seeking a spiritual enlightenment, and reacted against what they perceived to be a materialistic, modern society tainted by the Vietnam War. They embodied a rejection, be it a temporary one, of western culture, and placed themselves at the centre of the counter-culture.

For the radical thinker Marcuse, Man had become 'one dimensional', and through travel young radicals sought a more human dimension. Travel for them offered a spiritual alternative that had little connection to the growing holiday industry. The counter-cultural character of the 1960s traveller was epitomised by Jack Kerouac. Kerouac, born into white Middle America, rejected the American dream ticket in favour of a ticket to nowhere in particular - his travel was hedonistic and directionless. Kerouac immersed himself in the culture of oppressed black America - jazz culture. Whilst Kerouac's *On The Road* remains iconic for some travellers, his legacy is unclear. On the one hand, Kerouac's rejection of the American way of life may resonate with New Moral Tourist's moral elevation of the host's culture above their own. On the other, whilst Kerouac is associated with an amoral, directionless detachment from his society, the moralisation of tourism embodies a search for direction and is associated with moral regulation of oneself and others. Another icon of post-war travel is the Lonely Planet guidebook series. The first Lonely Planet guide was written by Tony and Maureen Wheeler, two enterprising travellers left broke by their travels in the hippy heydays of the early 1970s.

It contained useful advice on the merits of Kashmiri and Afghan marijuana - it was not a mainstream publication. Lonely Planet bought into the idea of travel as an alternative to tourism - something more individual, authentic and experimental. Lonely Planet guides today often deride the resorts favoured by package holidaymakers. Alongside these icons, the symbols of the post-war package tourism industry include Butlin's holiday camps, Horizon Holidays (the first package holiday company to charter aircraft and fly tourists to Majorca and elsewhere) and Blackpool's Golden Mile. Unlike the symbolism of travel, tourism is, for its critics, naff.

So the traveller has generally been presented as a very different animal to the tourist. Travel has long been associated with experience and individualism - travellers are not part of the 'faceless' Mass Tourists, as they are so often portrayed by the ethical lobby. To be a traveller was to take an interest in the local culture - for Tony Wheeler, founder of Lonely Planet guidebooks, to experience it 'at ground level', rather than travel within the 'tourist bubble' of the package holiday industry. American writer Daniel Boorstin set the tone in the 1960s. For Boorstin, 'The traveller was active; he went strenuously in search of people, of adventure, of experience. The tourist is passive; he expects interesting things to happen to him ... he expects everything to be done to him and for him.' The self-perception of the traveller is the 'thinking tourist' - someone prepared to strike out, experiment with different ways of life, and not be part of a packaged product put together by global companies.

He is someone who takes an interest in the culture and the environment of his host. One could surmise from this that the New Moral Tourist was with us all along, in the guise of the traveller. However, the modern travellers - backpackers, trekkers, ecotourists, gappers - have in many ways increasingly merged into the Mass Tourist - they are increasingly subject to similar criticisms. The critique of travel is most widely expressed against the burgeoning 'backpacking community'. A report on the behaviour of backpackers paints an unflattering picture - one akin to some of the condemnatory commentaries of package tourists. Dr Heba Aziz of the Roehampton Institute in London draws the conclusion from her research of backpackers in Egypt that they inhabit their own 'international backpacker culture' consisting of sex, drugs, pizzas and pancakes. They hang out with each other in 'den-like coffee shops with thick cushions and hookah pipes' pouring over 'The Book'. 'The

Book', as readers of modern backpacker literature such as Alex Garland's *The Beach* and William Sutcliffe's hilarious *Are You Experienced?* will be aware, is the Lonely Planet guide. The conclusion of the research is that travellers, just like tourists, are rather insensitive and crude. And far from breaking away from the tourist bubble to discover other cultures, they are portrayed as happy to create their own culture ably assisted by the Lonely Planet empire.

The tone of this report is echoed in many unflattering commentaries on the backpacker. One recent opinion piece in *The Times* newspaper likened backpackers to 'great lumbering dungbeetles ... slumping like so many uncollected bin-bags around the Trafalgar Square fountain'. To be young and to travel seems to invite cynicism, if not downright hostility, from some of tourism's critics. The perception of the traveller no longer conforms to that of Boorstin - active, in search of culture and experience - instead they are presented as destructive Mass Tourism in disguise. Also travellers have often stood some distance from the charge of environmental and cultural degradation, an accusation commonly levelled against Mass Tourism. Today that distance is diminished.

One theme that emerges in the new critique of the traveller is that they are at the cutting edge of extending the numbers of people travelling, in a world in which international travel is viewed as already bumping up against limits. Therefore if it is accepted that globally numbers of people travelling is a problem then the travellers inevitably get tarred with the same brush as tourists. Due to growing incomes and lower-cost travel opportunities, independent travel has grown markedly in recent decades. STA Travel, specialists in independent travel, sent half a million British youth abroad in 1999, many on RTWs (Round The World Tickets) - a tenfold increase on a decade ago. It is estimated that backpacking has increased sixfold over the last ten years, reflecting these trends - upwards of 200,000 people go backpacking annually from the UK alone.

Other estimates put travellers at around 10 per cent of international visitors. In particular, lower oil prices and improved technology, coupled with increased competition resulting from airline deregulation, have brought down the cost of travelling by air. In recent years the rapid growth of the low-cost 'budget' airlines such as Easyjet and Ryanair has also improved the opportunities to travel independently in Europe. Just as important perhaps is what could be regarded as the more flexible existence of young people. Breaks (either voluntary or as a result of short-term contracts or redundancy) in one's working life are more common. Also people are starting families later in life, hence extending the period in which footloose travel is a possibility.

Whilst travel has in the past been associated with youth, now the years of youthful freedom have extended into 'middle youth' as more people put off settling down into their thirties and later. Tony Wheeler has pointed out that these days backpackers include everyone from broke teenagers to the 'Hilton

Hippies', who travel backpacker style but stay in expensive accommodation; or the 300 doctors at a convention who venture into the Australian outback and stay at a backpackers' lodge. Of course, all this applies to some more than others - career breaks are a pipe dream for those without a career. The view that this growing band of travellers simply adds to tourist numbers is developed by Brian Wheeller of Birmingham University.

For this critic, travel companies promoting ecotourism - definitely in the camp of travel rather than tourism - are simply engaged in a marketing ploy providing a cosy, environmentally friendly feel-good factor for western tourists - meanwhile, global capitalist growth in tourism continues unchecked but in a more acceptable guise. Wheeller argues that, whatever the label, it is all pretty much the same when it comes down to it - it is all pretty negative. However, the impact of independent travellers is not only seen as a question of numbers - if this were the case the criticisms would be barely distinguishable from those of Mass Tourism. It has been pointed out that backpackers act as *pioneers* of Mass Tourism.

In seeking out more remote, less popular locations, the backpacker leaves in their wake a nascent tourism industry. Businesses, local and foreign, spot possibilities to develop the industry, companies cite the location in their brochure and word of mouth increases awareness of the place as a destination. Over time one thing leads to another and a few adventurous trekkers becomes large numbers of youthful pleasure seekers. One industry expert has noted this role of 'traveller as a destination pioneer' on what was once the Hippy Trail. In a research paper he quotes as evidence Murgha Mack of Top Deck Travel: destinations which were first explored by intrepid backpackers often evolve into mainstream areas for tourism ... For example, we have carried backpackers overland to Kathmandu for many years, but it is only in the last few years that it has come to be visited by the less adventurous traveller.

And then after the less-adventurous traveller comes ... the tourist! The travellers spread the tourism net further and further afield as they keep 'a step ahead of the growing army of other travellers and institutionalised mass tourism markets in the continuing search for ever-increasing exotic destinations'. The Hippy Trail, one of our icons of travel mentioned earlier, is now superseded by a trail of 'mass backpackers', who are regarded with the glumness previously reserved for the package tourist. Travel is also implicated in damaging cultures in a similar fashion to the claims made against Mass Tourism. In Goa and on the eastern coast and islands of Thailand the allegation against independent travel is that it has become commercialised and as such is indistinguishable from mass package travel.

This commercialisation, it is argued, has implications for both the host and the tourist. For the hosts it means they are subject to far-reaching cultural change. The economy becomes geared up to sell to tourists at a profit. An important element of this process is the 'commoditisation' of culture. Here long-standing aspects of indigenous culture become staged as rituals for the travellers/tourists. These rituals may lose their true meaning and value for the community practising them. Their role in cohering the societies is less in evidence as they become bought and sold. Hence travellers - those who look for the traditional, the authentic - may in fact, it is argued, be doing the most harm to the object of their fascination.

For the traveller it is held that the experience of travel is diminished by its commercialisation - a commercialisation that proceeds apace. This is ironic, as travel can be seen as an attempt to escape the commodification of human relationships - the influence of the cash nexus on how we relate to one another. This aspiration, to escape the modern, commercial world, may be confounded, as the attempts themselves are subject to the same commercialisation.

This is not a new theme. In the 1960s German writer Hans Magnus Enzenberger argued that, 'Liberation from the Industrial World has become an industry in its own right, the journey from the commodity world has become a commodity.' Rudy Koshar in his book *German Travel Cultures* usefully describes the process of commodification as one of a 'simultaneous multiplication and narrowing of possibilities that late modern and commercial society brings'. More opportunities are available formally, but it becomes increasingly difficult to break out of the particular *way* we consume, relating to each other through the cash nexus. The search for something different - alternative - is seemingly confounded by the commercialisation of travel. Travel becomes commercialised and merges into tourism.

In this vein travel has been problematised by both conservative and radical thinkers. Conservative American critic Daniel Boorstin bemoaned the end of travel in his classic *The Image: a Guide to Pseudo Events in America*. He saw it as denigrated by the decadence of mass production, mass transport and mass communications. People were disinterested, duped, or both. For Boorstin, we are offered, and have become satisfied with, 'pseudo events' rather than the real thing, exemplified by the popularity of 'tourist attractions' over interest in people and places. Dean MacCannell, writing from a radical perspective, raised a similar theme in his ground-breaking *The Tourist: a New Theory of the Leisure Class* in the early 1970s, written at a time of rapid increase in international Mass Tourism, and also the heyday of the hippy trail.

For MacCannell, many people sought out authenticity through their travels. This authenticity was denied to them at home, stifled by the dominance of a society defined by consumerism and the cash nexus. Yet for MacCannell, this search for authenticity is all too often stifled by the commercialised nature of travel and tourism - the search for a more human and humane existence is often in vain. MacCannell hence saw tourism as a metaphor for the contradictions of modern society, a perspective that strongly informs the debate today. Boorstin and MacCannell are often contrasted to one another - Boorstin dubbed 'elitist' as he seems to view the majority as having been dumbed down to accept 'pseudo' experiences, and MacCannell the radical who portrays tourists as aware of the lack of authenticity in their everyday lives, aspiring to something else; something better.

However, the shared theme between these authors is a sense that commercialisation spreads itself ever further and wider, to the detriment of the people concerned, in this case host and tourist. Travel as an attempt to distance oneself from this is either difficult or impossible. Travel is increasingly a part of mass consumer society, something that both authors bemoan. Hence travel is perhaps Mass Tourism - travellers are just fooling themselves. Our second icon of travel, the Lonely Planet Guide, provides an example of this sense that travel has merged into Mass Tourism. Lonely Planet, once associated with independence, freedom and adventure, is in the frame for spawning generations of 'mass backpackers'. For their critics, these backpackers are really Mass Tourists by another name. In this vein, the Lonely Planet guides have been described as 'a blueprint for the modern package holiday', as 'the book dictates where to stay, where to eat, which day trips to take, what to buy'. In Alex Garland's book *The Beach*, and in the subsequent film adaptation, the Lonely Planet guide is described as 'The Book', a metaphor often used for backpackers' guides.

The Book conjurs up the image of the backpacker following religiously the instructions from this 'higher authority' - travelling where The Book recommends, staying where The Book decrees and generally acting as a disciple of the new religion of travel. For critic of travellers Heba Aziz, the guides are deemed to have 'institutionalised' travel, making it similar to, and as damaging as, package tourism. Today Lonely Planet is a major international operation with millions of sales annually and over 250 publications. And if you haven't got The Book you can access The Web Page from the internet cafés found in every backpacker ghetto. Hence Lonely Planet seems to epitomise the commercialisation of travel. By the critics, its customers are increasingly portrayed less as free-spirited, free-thinking travellers, and more as naive disciples, following The Book religiously, and turning traveller heaven into tourist hell.

The implicit assumption of the assault on travel guidebooks is the same as that underlying criticisms of mass package tourists - that the consumer is an uncritical recipient of falsitudes from a rapacious industry. Travellers, the 'thinking tourists', become part of the faceless, homogenous mass. Leaving aside the gross cynicism of some of the criticisms of the guides, the charges are surely unjustified. The humble guidebook is just that, a guidebook, with advice that one may choose to follow or ignore. Travellers can take it or leave it. Tony Wheeler, Lonely Planet founder, himself admits to meeting travellers who used his guides to identify places to avoid.

'WHO IS A TOURIST?'

Criticisms of tourism are not new—they have been around as long as people have travelled for leisure. This chapter examines what is distinctive about today's critique of tourism. It argues that 'traveller-tourist', the axis around which snobbery (and the inverted snobbery of those who rail against travellers as 'elitist') has often been expressed, does not fit so well with today's moral distinctions.

FROM GRAND TOURS TO COOK'S TOURS

Historically, the extension of tourism has always been subject to criticisms - usually from those who wanted to preserve its benefits for themselves. It is easy to see this as a common brand of elitism, with the more privileged trying to differentiate themselves from the uncultured masses. Pronouncements in this vein were commonplace in Victorian Britain, and still today Martin Graham, Chairman of the Federation of Tour Operators, can echo the language of the past, asserting, and [sustainability] hasn't really made any difference to the great unwashed. A lot of people muck up their own back yard, and do just the same on holiday.'

One hundred and forty years ago Thomas Cook responded to his critics and defended tourism in a fashion that is also pertinent for today. His customers, he claimed, could be identified by their 'courteous and joyous fraternisation', in contrast to the '"independent" tourists who paid up to three times the cost for the privilege of thus sitting solitary in a crowd of free and elastic spirits'. On the face of it, it can seem that there is little new in the critique of tourism.

Tourists in search of a fortnight of fun and frolics, or just rest and relaxation, remain subject to the critical eye of the concerned. Yet much has changed in the way tourists are derided - there are important aspects of the moralisation of tourism that are distinctly new. The origin of the word 'tourist' comes from the Grand Tourists. The Grand Tour played the role of a right of passage for the British aristocracy especially in the latter half of the eighteenth century, although Grand Tourists preceded and succeeded this heyday. The Grand Tours were linked to the acquisition of a classical education but represented more than this for the young heirs to estates and fortunes - these travellers were in search of worldliness and a culture that would mark out their right to rule.

They presided over the birth of the modern idea of fashion and cuisine as they sampled and brought back ideas from their travels from Paris, Florence, Naples and Venice. The Grand Tours were no fleeting visits. In fact, the travelling itself made this impossible - often travel, even for the elites, was arduous. Accounts of the Grand Tourists often make reference to the physical fatigue and illness associated with travel at this time. Daniel Boorstin in his seminal essay 'The Lost Art of Travel' quotes an eighteenth-century account thus: 'Under the best conditions six horses were required to drag across country the lumbering coaches of the gentry, and not infrequently the assistance of oxen was required.'The origin of the word travel is 'travail', meaning work, and travelling at this time required great endeavour. However, alongside the acquisition of culture and the difficult journeys across land and sea, the Grand Tourist exhibited a good deal of the hedonism, licentiousness and recklessness often associated with more mass forms of travel. Young English aristocrats could 'give loose to their propensities to pleasure' according to one observer, and indeed, Casanova's *Memoirs* were an account of his travels through Europe's capitals between 1826 and 1838.

By the end of the Napoleonic wars in 1815 the Grand Tour, previously the preserve of the aristocracy, was increasingly encroached upon by the ascendant industrial elites. The latter provided the means for the extension of travel - the iron from which the railways were constructed, the steam technology that powered the trains - and also comprised a growing class with the means to travel.

The tension between town and country, between industry and landed wealth, was to be played out in the cafés of Rome and Naples, where those of landed wealth looked down upon the sons of those whose wealth was gained through industry. As tourism developed, tourist perceptions changed. Areas of wilderness such as the Lake District and mountainous regions such as the Alps, previously regarded as obstacles to travel, increasingly became the object of travel for travellers influenced by Romanticism. The Romantic spirit of the time is most closely associated with, and best articulated by, the Romantic poets.

Prominent amongst these was Wordsworth, who campaigned against the railways coming to his beloved Windermere. Romanticism in essence represented a reaction to modernity - to the growth of cities, urbanisation and industry. It upheld individual emotion against collective experience, and nature against human endeavour. Whilst Romantic travel predates the Industrial Revolution — Rousseau's taste for naturalness over the corruption of development led him to champion the Alps when to many travellers they were seen as an impediment to travel — there is no doubt that industrialisation and the modern ideas of liberty, fraternity and equality, championed by the French Revolution, generated a Romantic reaction that has profoundly coloured tourism in the modern era. Romanticism not only coloured the tourist's viewpoint, but also shaped the criticisms of the growth of leisure travel.

The growing number of tourists exemplified man encroaching on nature, and was therefore undesirable from a Romantic standpoint. Such criticisms were expressed by those who considered leisure their birthright. The extension of travel beyond the aristocracy to the capitalist class was part of the latter's ascendancy. It is hardly surprising, then, that the Grand Tourists should resent this upstart class intruding on their precious Naples and Venice - it signified the end of their dominion. This tension between modern society and the reaction to it has informed the 'traveller-tourist' debate historically. The Romantic reaction to modernity took in the means of travel as well as the new bourgeois tourists. As early as the 1870s, Ruskin saw the train as devaluing travel, as it 'transmutes a man from a traveller to a living parcel' - sentiments held by many who criticise the package charter holiday industry of today. He also likened it to concentrating one's dinner into a pill. Ruskin's criticism was against bourgeois tourism, but more broadly against the train as a symbol of modern, industrial society. Ruskin rejected the advantages of speed itself: 'All travelling becomes dull in exact proportion to its rapidity.'

Ruskin's reactionary Romanticism was taken to task by Thomas Cook, who celebrated the possibilities opened up by rail travel as: 'Travelling with the millions'. It was the new industrialist tourist who provided much of the market for Thomas Cook's Tours from the 1840s. Cook made travel that bit easier for his clientele by making arrangements for smooth passage, good accommodation and finance (he invented the traveller's cheque) for the growing number of travellers. Cook also pioneered package travel for the working class from the 1850s. Soon large numbers of workers and their families were taking advantage of trips to the seaside - Cook's tours are often regarded as the first mass package holidays.

The growth of leisure travel was bound up with the economic progress wrought by the industrial revolution. The development of industry created both new needs and new possibilities for meeting them. However, in an important sense, tourism was also a spur to industrialisation itself. Tourism brought wealth to coastal areas, which benefited the populations of these areas greatly. Indeed, in certain periods in the nineteenth century, resorts were the fastest growing class of towns. In this sense, tourism was itself part of the industrial revolution, rather than just a product of it. As well as the development of technology and industry, the new-found mobility for leisure was premised on developments such as holidays with pay for some workers (although this did not become the norm until the 1938 Holidays with Pay Act), the establishment of Wakes Weeks and Bank Holidays as regular holiday times, and growing incomes enabling increasing numbers of workers to engage in tourism. By 1911, 55 per cent of the population of England and Wales were taking day trips to the seaside.

But for the critics of Cook, the new possibilities and new wealth evident in the tourism industry were overshadowed by the notion that this was travel as consumption rather than travel for culture. Novelists, commentators and scholars satirised and scolded the growing number of tourists. The distaste expressed by some at mass, working-class tourism was infused by a broader fear and loathing of the masses that emerged as a reaction to industrialisation, urbanisation, the growth of the organised working class and events such as the Paris Commune that resonated around Europe and struck fear into ruling elites. The antipathy towards the growth of tourism was directed against the perceived crudeness of these new tourists. They were, as the working class, regarded by many as a race apart from those born into wealth, the latter considered to possess the wherewithal to benefit from travel. On the subject of these early mass tourists the Reverend Francis Kilvert famously commented in his diaries in 1870 that, 'Of all the noxious animals, the most noxious is a tourist; and of all tourists the most vulgar, ill-bred, offensive and loathsome is the British tourist.' Kilvert's comments were unguarded, direct and posited the culture of the masses as inferior to those of his station. In this vein Cook's Tours were criticised for extending travel to the lower orders.

For one commentator of the time, cities were deluged with droves of these creatures, for they never separate, and you see them forty in number pouring along a street with their director, now in front, now at the rear, circling them like a sheepdog - and really the process is as like herding as may be. Cook himself had a fatherly approach to his tourists, typical of the outlook of Victorian philanthropists. His first tours for working-class people were temperance trips, where tourists could enjoy a good dose of preaching and bracing walks. An early trip was to the unlikely destination of Leicester, the purpose being a temperance meeting.

Bad behaviour was clearly an affront to the missionary in Cook, and on one occasion he was driven to comment that, 'to the shame of some rude folk from Lincolnshire, there have been just causes of complaint at Belvoir Castle: some large parties have behaved indecorously ... conduct of this sort is abominable, and cannot be too strongly reprobated.' However, Cook was notable for defending the extension of travel from its detractors. The opportunity to travel for leisure was, for him, part of a more civilised society and the means of travel were a symbol of industrial progress, a progress that was for everyone. In this spirit Cook referred to his tours as 'agencies for the advancement of human progress' as, after all, 'railways and steamboats are the result of the common light of science, and are for the people'.

Cook criticised the sheer snobbery of the critics of tourism of his day. For him it was foolish to 'think that places of rare interest should be excluded from the gaze of common people, and be kept only for the interest of the select of society', and he added that, 'it is too late in this day of progress to talk such exclusive non-sense'. Cook's defence and celebration of progress resonated with the outlook of many people, too. One of Cook's most celebrated ventures, to take ordinary people to London for the Great Exhibition of 1851, attracted vast numbers of customers from all social classes. The Great Exhibition, and other international expositions of the time, were widely fêted as celebrations of scientific endeavour and industry.

Cook even wrote a pamphlet on why people should visit the Great Exhibition in which he described it as 'a great School of Science, of Art, of Industry, of Peace and Universal Brotherhood'. Cook's tours to the countryside also revealed something of the class divisions that were evident in popular tourism. These outings have been described as 'tense occasions' as 'country landowners, however obliging, could not look with complete calm on invading groups of working-class people whisked in by train from nearby towns, for they embodied changes that were only partly understood and were already partly feared'. Hospitality towards one's newly mobile potential adversaries did not come easy.

Having extended the range of his tours from Britain to Europe, and from Europe to Asia and on to Africa, and having established tours within the remit of all social classes, Cook set up a register for people who wanted to be the first tourists to the moon. This was no publicity stunt (people put their names down), rather it reflected a sense that society had, and would continue to, overcome geographical limits to travel. The first fifty years of the twentieth century were dominated by two world wars. However, tourism developed in this period too. For the working class, improvements in living standards, holidays and transport led to the growth of seaside holidays. The advent of the motor car challenged the pre-eminence of rail travel as the main mode of leisure travel. Car ownership grew to 2 million by 1939, and the car was celebrated as a harbinger of a new freedom for leisure travel.

It is, however, since the Second World War that the modern package holiday abroad has become established. In 1949 Vladimir Raitz audaciously approached the Aviation Ministry to get permission to run chartered flights from Gatwick to Calvi in Corsica, where customers would sleep in tents by the beach (the height of fashion) and drink at a bar brought in specially from Paris. The aircraft used were decommissioned Second World War military aircraft - the war had bequeathed aircraft, airfields and technology that facilitated the rapid growth of international tourism. The modern package holiday was born and grew rapidly as ever-increasing numbers of people were able to travel as tourists.

Overseas package holidays developed rapidly throughout the 1960s and 1970s, managing 10 per cent growth per year between 1960 and 1974. Despite a distinct blip in 1974 due to the oil crisis (which put up the price of airline fuel), and the subsequent recession, tourism has continued on an upward trajectory since.

But whilst Raitz regards his industry as ringing progressive changes - 'democratising' foreign leisure travel to increasing numbers of people and boosting the economies of destination areas - it is the boom years of the package holiday industry that are associated with destruction, crudity and ugliness by tourism's contemporary critics. The results of this boom included Torremolinos on the Costa del Sol, a byword for unethical holidaying or affordable fun, depending on one's view of package travel. For tourism's critics, Torremolinos represents everything that is wrong with the package holiday boom - large scale, cheap, transformative of the environment and of culture.

It is roundly criticised even in some of the tourist guides to Spain. For the Lonely Planet guide to *Andalucia* it is 'arguably Europe's finest example of how overdevelopment can ruin spectacular landscapes'. In Cadogan's *Spain*, it is a 'ghastly, hyperactive, unsightly holiday inferno'. The Costas are clearly associated with the excesses - in terms of the physical developments and also the behaviour of some of the visitors - of mass package tourism.

In amongst the carping criticisms one guide points out that on the back of tourism revenue, a considerable amount of money has been spent on the promenade, green spaces and the trawling of thousands of tonnes of sand to build up the beach at Torremolinos, ideal for bathing, families and beach sports. However, such initiatives fail to impress many advocates of New Moral Tourism, relying as they do on development rather than nature. In fact, whilst the development of the Mass Tourism industry has generated a good deal of development, often in poorer regions in Mediterranean countries, the creative aspects of this development are overshadowed by an exaggerated sense of destruction and loss.

Criticisms of the package tourism industry such as these are the starting point of the New Moral Tourism, leading to an impulse to change the industry and the behaviour of its clients. But what is different about the critique of modern Mass Tourism? To what extent is the New Moral Tourism actually new in a qualitative sense? There are two important points to be made here. First, whilst Cook was part of a tradition that was prepared to defend the extension of travel as an emblem of society's progress, few are prepared to do this today. Cook regarded the extension of tourism to the working class in the following way: '

- These are the days of the million ... [who can] o'erleap the bounds of their own narrow circle, rub off rust and prejudice by contact with others, and expand their sails and invigourate their bodies by an exploration of some of nature's finest scenes.'

Very few are prepared to put this case today. Advocates of New Moral Tourism typically argue the opposite, that in fact Mass Tourism is characteristic of mass society, a society in which growth has spiralled out of control, with severe consequences for the cultures and environments of the world. It is in this spirit that 'ethical tourism' dominates discussions, with dissenting voices often adopting a cynical 'we're all doomed anyway so what's the point' posture.

In this sense, the discussion of tourism is best understood within the broader assault on the idea of human progress, an idea championed by many 150 years ago, but today often dismissed as at best utopian and at worst fascistic. Whilst in Cook's era possibilities appeared to be boundless, today there is an acute sense of limits to man's capacity to go further, faster and in greater numbers. The recent grounding of Concorde, an aircraft that had in the 1970s epitomised the spirit of progress in travel, seems to sum up this mood. In fact the means of travel are generally regarded as more problematic than liberating.

Notably the car, erstwhile symbol of freedom, has become a symbol of environmental degradation. It is not uncommon for people, including car owners, to see themselves as 'anti-car'. Space tourism may have been a prospect relished by Cook, but today it is regarded with incredulity by many, for whom it seems to epitomise an arrogant humanity, intent on colonising other planets. Only ailing ex-Soviet facilities prospectively offer space tourism, to a clientele of super-rich Americans - a telling symbol of the post Cold War era.

Even seaside piers, which in the past 'involved an attempt to conquer nature, to construct a "man-made" object which at all times and forever would be there dominating either the sea or the sky', are now in disrepair and falling into the sea. Nature, it seems, triumphs over human endeavour. Surviving piers today are championed in the spirit of nostalgia for simpler times past. Secondly, the debates on tourism in the nineteenth century were to a large extent, demarcated along class lines. The aristocracy were unhappy about the loss of the exclusivity of travel as a new business and middle class emerged. Working-class tourists, the 'great unwashed', were to be avoided both by travelling first class and by travelling to different places. From the 1880s distinctly working class coastal holiday destinations came into their own, and divisions between resorts frequented by the working class, and the gentry and nobility became entrenched, reflecting the class divisions of the time.

Some argue that something similar is true today; that the complaints at the growth of Mass Tourism reflect a desire on the part of the 'new middle classes' to maintain the exclusivity of their holiday pursuits. However, today the critique of tourism is more broadly accepted and often appears not to carry the same snobbishness or elitism that Cook railed against. Package tourists are not so much directly criticised for having inferior moral standards to New Moral Tourists, but are instead criticised for damaging other cultures; the culture of the host populations and hence also cultural diversity. This is different from the past, when tourists were considered to lack the cultural sophistication of the elite.

The consequence of this is that today's critics of tourism identify themselves as radicals, champions of 'culture' and 'the environment', unlike in the past when antipathy towards tourism formed part of an unashamed conservative outlook. New Moral Tourism is thus presented as a selfless critique; for others, not just for oneself. Eminent Victorian gentleman Sir Lesley Stephen spoke of 'Cockney-ridden' resorts, but pointed out that at least the resorts confined the 'swarm of intrusive insects' to one place. The last hundred years have seen the aristocratic sense of superiority decline. Today advocates of sustainable tourism see some value in popular resorts in so far as they keep a lot of people in one place, minimising potential environmental damage. The language of the Victorian critic is unacceptable today, but the sentiment that 'the mass' of people, mobile, constitute a problem is all the stronger for being re-presented in terms of environmental and cultural threats. Whilst Thomas Cook's tours of 130 years ago were criticised for carrying those without the etiquette and cultural understanding of the elite, JMC, the brand used by Thomas Cook package holidays today, is more likely to be criticised for damaging environments and cultures.

'WE'RE ALL TOURISTS NOW'

A backpacking acquaintance of mine sees himself as a traveller rather than a tourist. The only exception, he says, is when he meets other backpackers - then he is only too keen to distance himself from the pretensions of his fellow travellers! It is common to argue that travelling and tourism are more or less the same thing. However, there are perhaps differences, even if they are more to do with how people like to conceive of themselves than anything else. In general, for travellers the *getting there* is likely to be at least as important as *being there*. Even for the less-experienced, more conservative traveller, travel is associated with an experiential dimension lacking from tourism.

Paul Fussell in his book, *Abroad*, referring to those who see themselves as travellers and look down upon tourists, asserts: 'The anti tourist deludes only himself. We are all tourists now.' This argument that 'we are all tourists now' tends to translate as 'we are all *as bad as* tourists now' cited in the context of a downbeat discussion of the perceived cultural and environmental problems created by tourists and travellers alike. Arch-critic of ecotourism, Brian Wheeller, makes a similar point, arguing that 'new wave tourism' is a sheen on a destructive industry: of those considering the issues, popular opinion is that mass tourism with all its stereotyped negative connotations is bad, guilty of causing tourism's impact problems and should be 'dealt with' accordingly.

New Wave Tourism, on the other hand, is seen as the complete antithesis to this, sensitive, sophisticated and sustainable, the perfect antidote to be encouraged and enjoyed. While advocating a more caring industry, it fosters the image of a return (if there ever was one) to the golden age of enriching and educative travel. It echoes Senecas (*sic*) 'we should choose a place which is healthy not only for our bodies but also for our morals.' That this appraisal is perhaps less than objective, coloured (green?) by the fact that many of those voicing an opinion do not regard themselves as mass tourists, or as being part of mass tourism, is completely ignored. For eco-tourism, read ego tourism. 'Just once, I went for a run on a Harley motorbike. I thought "Where's the farthest I can go? I'll go to Alaska", It's like 700 miles. A friend of mine, Larry, came along, and if he hadn't, I don't think I would have done it. It rained every day and, God, it was a misery.

I realised I had a 26-year-old brain and a 52-year-old butt. But every time I'd look in the mirror, Larry was back there and the two of us pushed each other along. It took us about a month and it poured every day apart from two days when it snowed. We got there and Larry said: "What do you think?" I said: "Hell, I don't know, let's go home ..." And we turned right around and came back again. I sold the Harley and I don't care if I never see another one.'

Wheeller rightly conveys the sense in which New Moral Tourism is an etiquette that contributes to the moral authority of those adopting it. However, his riposte to 'New Wave Tourism' does not proceed to defend package holidays, but to suggest that ecotourism is just as fraught as its mass counterpart. It is this pessimistic standpoint, rather than the notion itself that we are all tourists, that I would take issue with. Tourism, or travel - whatever your preference - should be celebrated. Tourists and travellers should be defined less by the risks they pose, and more by the opportunities (including purely pleasurable opportunities) they create. And if there is such a thing as a traveller, as distinct from a tourist, is there anything worth celebrating in this classification, often considered elitist, snobbish and pretentious? In many ways the association of travel with life experience may be just so much hot air. For some, travelling abroad is a break from what they perceive as the routine and stress of modern western existence. If so, the year out could easily be interpreted as simply running away from real life to immerse oneself in a temporary fantasy world for as long as finances permit.

And why cannot 'experience' be gained in other ways? Is the teacher who takes a year out to go trekking and work in Peru more experienced than the one who focuses on her subject for the year and enjoys a fortnight all-inclusive in Spain? Is the student who reads in his bedroom any less wise than the one who volunteers to work in conservation in the Seychelles? And more to the point for many travellers, is working in a bar in Australia so different from working in a bar in London? I have no reason to defend travellers, never having been part of this fraternity. And it is tempting to go along with the critics who attempt to knock oh so worldly backpackers off their pedestal by rubbishing their experience and pointing out their supposed role in environmental degradation. But the premise of the attack is that people and cultures are fragile, and that we should restrict any desires we have to see the world from a recognition that we are complicit in trashing the planet. This clearly is an attack on all of us, travellers, tourists and everyone else.

New Moral Tourism, then, has tended to broaden the scope of what is to be criticised. The package holiday, Mass Tourism, is the obvious culprit if one starts from the premise that cultural encounters are fraught, that development has spun out of control and that there are simply too many tourists. Backpacking, having expanded rapidly, logically must, and has, entered the frame too. But what of ecotourism, advocated as a solution to the problems of Mass Tourism? Here is a form of tourism explicitly linked to conservation rather than destruction. Ecotourism, according to the World Tourism Organisation and The International Ecotourism Society in America, is the fastest-growing tourism market (be it from a very low base). So surely, following the logic of the moralisation of tourism, is it not also a risky activity?

In fact, this is precisely the criticism some have made. Ecotourism - for its advocates lying at the opposite end of the moral spectrum to Mass Tourism - is increasingly subject to similar criticisms. One writer, Anita Pleumaron of the Tourism Investigation and Monitoring Team in Thailand, expresses in stark terms the dilemma for the conservation-minded ecotourist. In a paper titled 'Ecotourism or Ecoterrorism' she argues that ecotourism is usually just as destructive as package tourism. Ecotourism, unlike tourism to already-developed regions, threatens 'the expropriation of "virgin" territories'. Moreover, 'travellers have already opened up many new destinations', bringing the Mass Tourism that New Moral Tourism seeks to avoid. In similar vein, Erlet Cater, advocate of ecotourism, sees dangers in its development: 'There is a real danger that eco tourism may merely replicate the economic, social and physical problems already associated with conventional tourism. The only difference ... is that previously undeveloped areas are being brought into the locus of international tourism.'

Martha Honey, Director of the Ecotourism Programme at the Institute for Policy Studies in Washington DC, makes a similar point, asserting that By definition, ecotourism often involves seeking out the most pristine, uncharted and unpenetrated areas on Earth. Often, these are home to isolated and fragile civilizations. In some areas, ecotourism is at the front line of foreign encroachment and can accelerate the pace of social and environmental degradation and lead to a new form of western penetration and domination of the last remaining 'untouched' parts of the world. Here, not only is ecotourism complicit in destructive practices, but it is actually 'at the front line of foreign encroachment'. This conjures an image of cultural purity degraded by outsiders. For these authors mass tourists have a single redeeming factor - that they are less interested in 'encroaching' upon wilderness. The contradictions of ecotourism are also well expressed by a writer in the American Audubon Society magazine: 'Tour boats dump garbage in the waters off Antarctica, shutterbugs harass wildlife in National Parks, hordes of us trample fragile areas. This frenzied activity threatens the viability of natural systems. At times we seem to be loving nature to death.' Such comments are typical of the dilemmas within the advocacy of New Moral Tourism. There is a real irony in all this. Advocates of New Moral Tourism have long criticised package tours as destructive of the environment. Ecotourism was their ethical alternative to the rapacious mainstream industry. Now it stands accused of having the same destructive capacity. There can be no fixed dividing line between Mass Tourism and New Moral Tourism today, as the latter's criticisms of the former have increasingly turned in on themselves. New Moral Tourism is not just critical of others, but is self-critical too. The premise of the New Moral Tourism

5

The Changing Geography of Business Travel and Tourism

Over the ages, the geography of business travel and tourism has changed in a variety of ways. Having started in Asia, Africa and the Middle East in ancient times, the focus of development between 1000 BC and AD 1900 was generally Europe. Then the USA increasingly began to make its impact felt, but in the late twentieth century the 'tiger economies' of South East Asia and the oil-rich states of the Middle East dominated developments in terms of both demand and supply.

In spite of the economic problems in Asia in the late 1990s, Japanese and Taiwanese business travellers are now a major element in the global market, and Asian cities and hotel chains are widely regarded as the leaders in terms of quality and service. Will the future reinforce this trend, will Europe and the USA regain their previous dominance or will the future belong to the newly developed countries of South America or Africa?

THE ORIGINS OF BUSINESS TRAVEL AND TOURISM

Business travel and tourism originated with trade between communities. Once agriculture developed beyond the subsistence level in areas of Africa, Asia and Europe, thousands of years before Christ was born, communities began to trade agricultural products. This led to the growth of markets, and producers travelled sometimes hundreds of kilometres to take their produce to market. Then urban settlements began to grow and develop. These were home to artisans producing a range of products including clothes, tools and decorative arts.

These were traded with the surrounding countryside for foodstuffs. However, they were also marketed further afield, particularly if they were of high quality or were made of materials not available in other countries. Archaeological evidence shows us that this trading often took goods thousands of kilometres from where they were made. The earliest business travellers were, therefore, artisans and small-scale traders.

THE GREAT EMPIRES OF EGYPT, PERSIA, GREECE AND ROME

The rise of great empires including those of Egypt, Persia, Greece and Rome, among others, further stimulated this growth of trade-based business travel. For example, in the Roman Empire, well-established trade routes developed across the empire, transporting goods in all directions.

The museums of Europe, the Middle East and North Africa are full of evidence of this fact. A local museum of the Roman period in the UK, for example, could well contain pottery made in Italy, olive stones from Spain, wine jars from Greece and precious stones from Asia and the Middle East. However, once these empires fell, there was often a period of economic and political instability, and as ever such instability was seen as undesirable and tended to temporarily reduce the volume of business travel and tourism.

The Medieval Trade Fairs

By the medieval period business travel for trade was well established and its infrastructure included a number of massive trade fairs in strategically located towns and cities.

These were vital days in the calendar for medieval merchants. The fairs might last for several weeks during which time great use was made of local accommodation, eating and entertainment facilities. One of the most famous of these fairs was the Beaucaire trade fair on the Rho^ne river in Southern France, which attracted tens of thousands of visitors.

The Silk Route

In the Middle Ages, perhaps the greatest business travel route of all time, the Silk Route, reached its peak. Although named after one commodity, this route was a conduit for the transportation of a wide variety of goods from Asia to Europe and vice versa. And while the term Silk Route implies a single route, the fact is that there were a number of routes, starting and ending in different places.

The Silk Route was very important in two main ways:

1 It stimulated the growth of a sophisticated set of support systems for business travellers including accommodation and restaurants – the 'Caravanserai' – transport services such as camel traders and guides.

2 The route was also the way in which scientific inventions and ideas, as well as goods, moved from Asia to Europe and vice versa. It is this route which brought phenomena as diverse as gunpowder, new religions, knowledge of astronomy and advances in medicine to Europe and the Middle East, from Asia.

The Silk Route also created a network of major stopping points on the route which have tended to remain major trading cities ever since. For example, the role of Istanbul, a great trading centre, linking Asia and Europe, was established partly due to the Silk Route.

OTHER EARLY FORMS OF SPECIALIST BUSINESS TRAVEL

Throughout history, there have been three highly specialist but important forms of specialist business travel, notably:

1. Priests of all religions, who have often had to travel with their employment, making pilgrimages to shrines.
2. Soldiers, particularly mercenaries, travelling to take part in battles or moving into newly occupied territory. Even more often they simply moved because they were ordered to move to a different garrison.
3. Workers migrating temporarily in connection with their trade. In many rural communities in France, for example, there was until recently a tradition of crafts people moving to cities to practise their trade for a few months every year when there was little demand for their services at home on the farms at certain times of the year.

Interestingly, while very ancient in origin, all three forms of business travel survive in many parts of the world.

The Industrial Age and Bbusiness Travel

Business travel and tourism in Europe grew dramatically between 1750 and 1900, for three main reasons:

1. The Industrial Revolution, which began in the UK, steadily spread to many other European countries. This movement increased the scale of production of industrial goods which then had to be marketed and transported. This stimulated a growth in business travel and tourism, particularly with the rise of the on-the-road salesperson, the commercial traveller.
2. Many European countries developed empires in Africa, the Middle East and Asia, and these colonies created a demand for business travel. Industrialists needed the raw materials from these countries while their populations also provided a market for the finished goods. Furthermore, administering the colonies created a demand for business travel for the 'army' of colonial administrators from the home country to the colony, and within the colony.
3. This period saw the improvement of roads in general in Europe which made business travel easier. However, more importantly, the railway was born. Rail travel was faster than road transport and allowed business travellers to make business trips to more distant cities without it costing too much in terms of time or money.

Because of these factors, in Europe at least, the late nineteenth century in particular was a major period of growth for international business travel and tourism.

The Early Twentieth Century

As the twentieth century dawned, the next major development in business travel and tourism was taking place in the USA. Meetings have gone on since time immemorial, but the concept of the conference or convention was developed, at this time, in the USA. Trade and scientific associations, together with the political parties, began to organize large-scale gatherings in the late nineteenth century.

This activity gathered pace in the early decades of the twentieth century. Cities soon realized that hosting such events brought great economic benefits and convention bureaux began to appear to market cities as convention destinations. As Rogers (1998) notes, the first was established in Detroit in 1896, followed soon after by Cleveland (1904), Atlantic City (1908), Denver and St Louis (1909) and Louisville and Los Angeles (1910). The phenomenon of the convention bureau is now well established around the world. The development of the private car in the first half of the twentieth century further stimulated the growth of domestic business travel, primarily in Europe and North America.

The Explosion of Bbusiness Travel and Tourism Since 1950

While there is little hard data, it is clear that business travel and tourism has grown dramatically worldwide, since around 1950. There are two types of reason for this growth:

- Factors leading to a growth in demand
- Positive changes on the supply side which have facilitated the growth of business travel and tourism.

We can also distinguish between the reasons for the growth of business travel and tourism as a whole, and the reasons why particular sectors of business tourism have grown. Let us now look at these issues in a little more detail.

The Growth of Bbusiness Travel and Tourism as a Whole

Business travel and tourism overall, has grown worldwide because of a number of factors relating to both the demand and supply sides.

DEMAND-RELATED FACTORS

The demand-side factors which stimulated the growth of business travel and tourism worldwide in the second half of the twentieth century.

SUPPLY-RELATED FACTORS

Supply-Side Factors

The increase in business travel and tourism has only been possible because of developments on the supply side.

THE SCALE OF CONVENTION BUSINESS IN DIFFERENT CITIES

Several thumbnail sketches of different cities will illustrate the variations between cities in terms of the scale of their convention business.

1 In 1998, New York welcomed more than 1 700 000 convention delegates.
2 Convention delegates generated 361 000 bed nights in Sydney in 1997.
3 In 1998, Barcelona welcomed 7002 meetings with a total of nearly 264 000 delegates. This represents an increase of over 250 per cent since 1990.
4 Toronto welcomed 898 000 delegates to conventions and trade shows in 1997.
5 In summer 2000 Toronto hosted one convention that alone attracted more than 50 000 delegates
6 The Acropolis Convention Centre in Nice attracted 340 000 visitors in 1999.
7 In 1999, Copenhagen hosted 94 major conventions.
8 In 1998, the Budapest Tour Centre was the venue for more than thirty events.
9 The Singapore International Exhibition and Convention Centre held a total of 706 events in 1996.
10 Around 2000 trade fairs and conventions are held each year in Paris generating an estimated £700 million in 1997.

THE SUPPLY SIDE AND DIFFERENT TYPES OF BUSINESS TRAVEL AND TOURISM

Each type of business travel and tourism has its own specific supply network. Every business travel and tourism trip or event has a destination but the role of these destinations varies between types of business tourism.

BUYERS

The *corporate buyer* is someone employed by a private sector enterprise. Buying business travel services can be the main or total role for an employee, or it may be an occasional task within a much broader job description. The main industries which organize business tourism events include energy, medical, computing, engineering and financial services for example.

Research has shown that people involved in purchasing in the corporate sector can have a wide variety of different job titles and may have received little or no formal training in business travel and tourism. It is clear that personal assistants and secretaries play a major role in buying business travel services in the corporate sector. Sales and marketing staff are also heavily involved in this activity. In 1998 Rogers published the results of research carried out as part of the UK Conference Market Survey which throws further light on the corporate buyer in the UK. Rogers noted that corporate buyers were particularly involved in organizing board meetings, annual general meetings, corporate hospitality, exhibitions, incentive travel, product launches, sales conferences, team-building activities and training courses.

This research covered organizations ranging from enterprises with less than ten staff to those with over 5000. Clearly, the way business travel is bought is likely to vary between small and large organizations.

The research quoted by Rogers also highlighted several other characteristics of corporate buyers:

1. The lead-in, or planning, time for many corporate events is measured in days and weeks rather than months or years.
2. Seventy-one per cent of corporate buyers would return to a venue if they were happy with it.
3. Fifty-five per cent of buyers said they would like to see a classification or grading system for venues.
4. More than 80 per cent of buyers were satisfied with the venue they had used most recently.
5. Corporate buyers made relatively little use of trade fairs and publications to obtain information.

Association buyers is a term that covers a multitude of different types of association. Rogers (1998) identifies six types:

- Professional and trade associations whose members join because of their employment
- Voluntary associations and societies whose members join to further an interest, belief, or hobby
- Charities
- Religious organizations
- Political parties
- Trade unions.

Most of these organizations are non-profit making but they normally have to cover their costs. They usually, therefore, have very clear budgets for business tourism events which they must not exceed.

Association buyers organize some of the largest conferences and these may have over 10 000 delegates attending, in the case of international annual conventions. Associations often employ someone specifically to organize events but they may also utilize volunteers. Decisions are often made by a committee.

When setting up conventions, associations have to take into account the needs of all their members. Many will endeavour to move their annual convention to different destinations each year to appeal to members who live in different areas. Rogers distinguished between corporate and association buyers.

Public sector buyers – central and local government, and statutory agencies – are often operating on very tight budgets. The health and education sectors are two important public sector activities which are heavily involved in organizing business tourism events.

In general, public sector buyers are employees for whom buying business tourism services is only a minor part of their job. Most events are organized by buyers but, increasingly, private companies, associations and public sector bodies, are using specialist intermediaries to plan and manage their event.

INTERMEDIARIES AND SPECIALIST AGENCIES

There are a number of types of specialist intermediary performing different roles in different sectors of business travel and tourism. A few further words will help clarify some issues relating to the content. Most intermediaries receive a commission from the client on whose behalf they are operating. Otherwise, they receive a fixed fee. Some business travel agencies are located within large organizations, working exclusively for them. These are described as 'implants'. Let us now look at two of these intermediaries in more detail – professional conference organizers and incentive travel and event management agencies.

THE PROFESSIONAL CONFERENCE OR CONGRESS ORGANIZER

Many organizations are making increasing use of professional conference/ congress organizers to manage their business tourism events. The International Association of Professional Congress Organizers (IAPCO), in one of its brochures promoting the use of professional conference organizers (PCOs) outlines the reasons for using a PCO in the form of answers to hypothetical questions from potential clients. The brochure also details the services that a PCO can provide.

Exhibit: The role of professional conference/congress organizer

Q What can a PCO do that my staff can't

A PCOs do not have supernatural powers but they do cast a kind of magic on a conference! They have human resources, technical resources and contacts built up over many years. They have the experience and skills to produce professional results even on a shoestring budget. Undertaking your project from scratch would demand a great deal of your staff's valuable time. A PCO will save them the headache.

Q What is the difference between a PCO and a travel agency, destination management company, tour company, convention bureau, hotel, caterer, public relations consultancy, production house, conference centre?

A Not such a silly question because you may find all those establishments offering some conference-management services. An independent PCO company has no other conflicting interests. It is the only one specializing in every aspect of conference organization and co-ordination, taking full responsibility for budget control and liaising whenever necessary with all other suppliers, including those listed above.

Q Would the PCO take over completely?

A Don't worry! You and your colleagues retain complete control of your conference, with none of the day-to-day logistical hassle. At the outset of a project, the PCO sits down with the client to discuss the aims and objectives. Many decisions need to be made and the PCO can help identify those critical for success and offer advice on how to achieve them. The client is still responsible for the content of the programme, but the PCO can give full administrative and technical support in managing it.

A PCO is a consultant, an administrator, a creator, an extension of your organization

Q What will it cost? A There are various ways of charging for a PCO's services. It could be either as a percentage of the budget or on a fee basis. Such fees cover a PCO's staff and time costs. The actual costs of the conference, including expenses such as mailing, telephones etc. are usually charged separately. All costs, including fees, will be incorporated into the conference budget. Whatever the arrangements the client and PCO must agree what the fee covers so there are no surprises. A written contract between the two parties, client (principal) and PCO (agent), is essential. Most PCOs will also offer delegates an accommodation booking service, costs of which in some countries are covered by commissions from hotels.

At first sight employing the services of a PCO might look expensive but you have to count the many man-hours [*sic*] involved. In the long run the PCO's expertise means the client avoids wasting money – a bonus for low-budget conferences – and there is less chance the event will make a loss. Indeed, in many cases where events are intended to be money-making, profits are actually increased. The PCO can also suggest sources of finance or pre-finance and, given sufficient lead time, assist in identifying potential sponsors.

In the end what you are paying for is professionalism.

The final result will be a congress which meets international standards of event organization.

INCENTIVE TRAVEL AND EVENT MANAGEMENT AGENCIES

These organizations specialize in organizing:

- Incentive travel packages
- Corporate hospitality and entertainment
- Conferences and meetings, particularly those with a major partners and/or a social programme.

As these sectors of business tourism continue to grow such agencies are flourishing. This fact is clearly illustrated by the results of the 1999 Annual Conference and Incentive Travel Survey which was published in February 2000.

This survey covers UK-based agencies only and shows a picture of growth and optimization.

The survey contained some clear useful information about the agencies in this field, some of which are highlighted below:

1 Around 30 per cent of agencies had a turnover in excess of £5 million per annum.
2 Nearly a quarter of all agencies made less than £100 000 profit.
3 Fifty per cent of agencies employed less than twenty staff.
4 Eighty per cent of all agencies believed the incentive travel market was in a healthy or very healthy state.

SUPPLIERS

The suppliers can be divided into five types: destinations, venues, transport, accommodation and ancillary services.

Rogers (1998) states: Conference organisers attach greater importance to 'location than to any other single criterion when selecting their sites. Location may be expressed in terms of 'town', 'city, 'region', or 'country'. The widely accepted term to describe each of these is destination... A destination... is usually a discrete area with identifiable boundaries. Each... destination must contain a range of venues, facilities, attractions, supply services, and infrastructure. Destinations are usually marketed by public sector bodies or joint public-private partnership agencies but most of the elements of the destination are in private ownership.

Venues are the places where business tourism events actually take place, whether they are conferences, meetings, exhibitions, training courses, incentive travel packages or product launch sites.

Hotels are perhaps the best known venues for meetings, and conferences in particular, but there are different types of hotel venue, including:

- City centre hotels
- Motels' located on major roads
- Coastal resort hotels
- 'Country house' hotels in rural locations. Organizers are increasingly looking for more unusual venues to make their events special. These may include the following:
- Sporting venues, *e.g.,* golf courses, football grounds, and racecourses which offer high profile venues
- Historic buildings, *e.g.,* castles and stately homes
- Theme parks
- Transport venues, *e.g.,* cruise ships, ferries and trains
- Museums.

In 1999 Leask and Hood published a survey of such venues in the UK. They found that:

1 Unusual venues had only recently started to provide facilities for business tourism events, with 37 per cent of them only providing such facilities for less than five years.
2 Forty-three per cent of such venues entered the market because of demand, in other words, people wanting to use them, and approaching them.
3 Corporate clients were more important clients for the venues than association clients.

Leask and Hood (1999) identified the following strengths and weaknesses of these unusual venues. The main weaknesses in the provision of unusual venues were as follows:

- The size and range of facilities available
- The lack of accommodation on site
- Limited technical and audiovisual equipment
- Poor industry knowledge and trained staff
- Accessibility and suitability of buildings
- Offering a unique experience, once experienced not required again.

On a more positive note, the strengths identified were that unusual venues:

- Offer a unique, memorable experience
- Are competitively priced
- Offer facilities particularly suitable for small meetings
- Meet the needs of buyers demanding 'something different' in a venue
- Provide a quality and friendly service.

The growth of business tourism has encouraged the public and private sectors to invest in new purpose-built exhibition and conference venues. The 1999-2000 venue' guide, for example, identified around 6000 venues, many of which were recently developed facilities.

The *Conference and Incentive Travel* preview of the International Confex 2000 exhibition gave details of the opening or refurbishment of more than fifty major purpose-built venues worldwide.

These purpose-built venues are designed for both conferences and exhibitions with multipurpose spaces. The Lille Grand Palais, for instance, has an auditorium which seats 5000 together with 22 000 square metres of exhibition space.

Transport clearly is vital to business tourism in that it moves the business traveller to their desired destination, and then moves them around the destination. All forms of transport are used in business tourism industry:

- Air transport - scheduled and charter flights, private aircraft, air taxis, chartered helicopters
- Rail transport - scheduled railways, steam railways
- Road transport - private cars, scheduled buses, chartered coaches, car hire, taxis
- Water transport - ferries, cruise ships.

We can see from this list that transport is not only a way of moving from A to B in business travel and tourism. It can also be:

- A venue, such as the trains with meeting rooms offered by SNCF, the state railway operator, in France
- A core element of social programmes as when delegates' social programmes involve horse-drawn carriage 'taxis' in Central Park, New York and Killarney, Ireland.

Airlines have certainly realized the importance of business tourism to their operations and have invested heavily in facilities for business travellers including dedicated lounges and on-board computer access.

A recent survey conducted by *Conference and Incentive Travel* showed that airlines have tried to improve services, particularly for conference organizers. For example, 32 per cent of airlines allow name changes for group travel passengers within three days of travel, and some 60 per cent of airlines questioned now have a department dedicated to conference and incentive travel.

Accommodation is clearly required for all residential business tourism. Most of that used is commercial accommodation although some business travellers stay with friends and relatives.

There are several aspects of the link between accommodation and business tourism, including the following:

1. Accommodation establishments can be both venues and places to sleep and delegates can meet in one hotel but sleep in another.
2. Organizers can meet the needs of different delegates by offering different types of accommodation at varying price levels.
3. Some accommodation establishments can encourage people to attend conferences, because of their fame and high-quality reputation, if they are the conference venue.
4. Accommodation does not just mean hotels. It can also include:
   - Timeshare developments
   - Self-catering complexes
   - University halls of residence
   - Youth hostels
   - Cruise ships
   - Novel forms of accommodation such as an ice-hotel in Sweden, 'Rorbus' in the Lofoten Islands, Norway, and horse-drawn carriages in Ireland.
5. On wilderness based training courses or incentive travel packages, no formal accommodation may be provided as participants will be expected to 'survive'.

Alternatively they may simply be accommodated in tents. Accommodation, together with travel, is usually the largest element in the budget for a conference delegate.

Accommodation providers, notably hotel chains, have provided an increasing variety of facilities to attract the business tourist from in-room computer access, to business centres, to a wide variety of meeting rooms. For many hotels, business tourism, of all types, is the source of the majority of their revenue.

Finally, business travel and tourism requires a range of other *ancillary services* including:

- Audio-visual equipment suppliers
- Internet developers
- Badge-makers
- Interpreters and translators
- Caterers
- Lighting specialists
- Computer hire
- Marquee hire
- Couriers
- Mobile toilets
- Designers
- Photographers
- Direct marketing agencies
- Public relations consultants
- Entertainment
- Recruitment agencies and event personnel
- Exhibition constructors providers
- Exhibition display-makers
- Research organizations
- Fireworks suppliers
- Security
- Florists
- Sign-makers
- Freight forwarders
- Speaker groups
- Furniture hire
- Ticket agencies
- Gift and souvenir suppliers
- Training specialists
- Graphic artists
- Video-conferencing specialists
- Insurance services.

Sometimes the existence in a destination of particular ancillary services may influence an organizer's decision about destinations for business tourism events. For example, a company arranging a high-tech product launch may choose a destination which has expert information technology and audiovisual companies located there. While we have divided these suppliers into five categories, it is important to recognize that there is a great interdependence between all five elements. The business tourism product and experience utilizes all five of these and there is also interdependency between these suppliers, the intermediaries and the buyers.

It is now time for us to look at the final category, those who provide other services to the business tourism industry as a whole.

A TYPOLOGY OF BUSINESS TRAVEL AND TOURISM

For example, an individual general business trip could involve:

- A salesperson trying to sell his or her company's food product to a new customer
- A computer consultant visiting a client to sort out the client's problem
- The senior manager of a major multinational corporation visiting a branch factory
- A business person visiting a government department to apply for an export licence.

It is clear, therefore, that business travel and tourism is a diverse, complex field. However, this book will focus on the main areas of meetings, conferences, conventions, exhibitions, training courses, product launches and incentive travel. We will therefore, now, define these terms, to ensure that we all understand what we are talking about.

Meetings, Conferences and Conventions

According to Davidson, a meeting is: an organised event which brings people together to discuss a topic of shared interest.

[It may] be commercial or non-commercial... may be attended by 6, or many hundreds... it may last from a few hours to a week... [What makes] a meeting qualify as part of business tourism is that it engages some of the services of the tourism industry, and (is usually) held away from the premises of the organisation running it. The terms used to describe meetings tend to vary depending on the size of the event and where it is held. A small gathering is a meeting but a large meeting is usually called a conference in the UK, a convention in the USA and a congress in much of mainland Europe.

Exhibitions

Davidson defines exhibitions as: presentations of products or services to an invited audience with the object of inducing a sale or informing the visitor... Exhibitions are considered part of the business tourism industry because they stimulate travel (for both exhibitors and visitors). [They also] create a high level of demand for travel services, catering, and accommodation.

Exhibitions may also be called trade fairs or expositions in different parts of the world.

Training Courses

These are events where participants gather together at a specific time and place to receive information or to be helped to develop their skills. These can be 'internal' training courses where all the participants are employed by a single organization, or 'open' events where the training organization offers a programme which is available to all those who feel it might benefit them.

Product Launches

These are the high-profile special events which many organizations now use to attract publicity for new products and services they are launching. They usually have a range of audiences including the media, retailers and consumers. They often take place over a short time period – as little as a few minutes – but often involve a very large budget.

Incentive Travel

The key professional body, the Society of Incentive Travel Executives (SITE) defines this form of business tourism as follows: Incentive Travel is a global management tool that uses an exceptional travel experience to motivate and/or recognize participants for increased levels of performance in support of the organizational goals. (SITE, 1998)

The italic words are those identified by SITE as being elements of the definition. Interestingly, incentive travel uses leisure tourism as a reward for good performance at work. It therefore bridges the divide between leisure tourism and business tourism.

THE ENVIRONMENTAL IMPACTS OF BUSINESS TRAVEL AND TOURISM

Business travel and tourism, like leisure tourism, has a great impact on the physical environment. The authors endeavour to present a balanced view of these impacts. This is a highly generalized picture and issues like building design are largely subjective matters. However, it appears that, in general, business travel and tourism is negative in terms of its environmental impacts. The business tourism industry has yet really to address this issue. In the very good text, by Rogers (1998), *Conferences: A Twenty-First Century Industry*, it is interesting that there are only two brief references to environmental issues.

On the other hand some suppliers such as airlines and hotels have been tackling these issues in recent years. For example, British Airways has pursued a proactive policy on all environmental aspects of its operations and we have seen hotel industry initiatives such as the International Hotels Environmental Initiative. As many clients of these organizations are business tourists these initiatives are clearly helping to reduce – a little – the negative environmental impacts of business travel and tourism. However, normally, such initiatives seem not to be about tackling the impacts of business tourists fundamentally but, rather, about budget savings for the companies.

We will look in some detail at the issue of the design of business tourism physical infrastructure, particularly convention centres. At same time we will also look at the environmental aspect of these designs. However, we can say, at this stage, that several trends are making the future look rather bleak in terms of reducing the negative environmental impacts of the transportation of business tourists. For example:

1 The lowering of air fares, in real terms, which is encouraging organizations to organize conferences and incentive travel packages thousands of kilometres from their clients' home areas, thus causing more pollution, over a wider area.
2 Business people are still often given a car as part of their remuneration package, which encourages them to travel by car. This is made worse by the fact that a business person's status is often judged by the size of their car and bigger cars usually do more harm.

Finally, business tourists could be seen as being even worse than leisure travellers in terms of negative environmental impacts, because they travel more frequently.

THE SOCIAL IMPACTS OF BUSINESS TRAVEL AND TOURISM

Social impacts are perhaps less visible or tangible than economic or environmental impacts, yet they are still very important. Interestingly, we will also consider business travellers themselves, for whom business travel can be both a negative and a positive experience from a social or psychological point of view.

Summary

There is no doubt that business travel has the potential to cause social, economic and environmental problems, often through ignorance or insensitivity. The hypothetical situation shown in Exhibit 7.1, while extreme, does raise some real questions about the behaviour of many business tourists around the world. Imagine, Mr A. is a North European business executive visiting business clients in an African, Asian or South American country, for example.

- 07.10: Mr A wakes up and complains that the alarm call he ordered did not materialize.
- 07.30: Mr A showers using the complimentary toiletries provided in plastic, disposable containers by the hotel. He puts other bottles of the rather nice shampoo in his case to take home for his daughter, a keen vegetarian and animal rights campaigner, unaware of the fact that it was tested on animals.

- 08.00: Mr A goes down to breakfast. He rejects fresh local fruit in favour of imported yoghurts and marmalade, all packed in plastic, disposable portion packs.
- 09.00: Mr A leaves for his appointment with a client in a large luxury car that guzzles petrol as it sweeps past the poor local people waiting in the bus queue.
- 12.00: Mr A spends a large amount of money on an expensive business lunch with his clients in a luxurious international-style hotel restaurant.
- 14.00: Mr A finishes his business and goes to the shopping area by taxi to buy gifts for his wife and daughter. Ignoring the local traders he spends several hundred pounds at the local branch of a well-known international clothes chain.
- 16.00: Mr A then spends a further £100 buying a very old piece of pottery that has been stolen from an archaeological excavation elsewhere in the country.
- 17.30: Mr A returns to his hotel room by taxi, switches on the air conditioning and then he leaves the room.
- 18.30: Mr A goes to McDonald's for a snack.
- 19.00: Mr A starts drinking in a nearby hotel bar in a country where alcohol is not drunk by local people because of their religion.
- 21.00: Mr A goes to a well-known local massage parlour where he spends some of his expenses on some rather unusual 'extras'. The masseuse is about the same age as his daughter.
- 02.30: Mr A goes to a casino and spends the last of the expenses given him by his company on a little gambling.
- 00.30: Mr A returns to his hotel, and realizes that he has been robbed of his credit cards. Mr A is surprised that all the people who smiled at him and obeyed his requests when he had money no longer seem interested in him.

TOWARDS A COST-BENEFIT ANALYSIS OF BUSINESS TRAVEL AND TOURISM

At this stage the authors would like to have been able to present the reader with a 'cost-benefit' analysis of business travel and tourism which could say whether, overall, it has positive or negative impacts.

Interestingly, this is not possible for two main reasons, notably:

1 Little reliable empirical research has been published on the impact of business travel and tourism. The industry produces data on the economic impact which it feels shows it in a positive light. However, it does not seem to try to collect information on social and environmental impacts which it may fear could be less positive.

Academic researchers have devoted little effort, as yet, to studying the impacts of business tourism, whereas they have carried out a huge volume of research on the impacts of leisure tourism. In any event, given the complexity of the sector it would be very difficult to measure the impacts fairly.

2 Not everyone is affected equally by business travel and tourism. There are big winners such as hotels and the owners of successful conference production companies and smaller winners such as the low-paid operational staff in the service delivery side of the industry. There may even be overall losers, such as the residents in a coastal resort, not employed in business tourism, where local councils have invested millions of pounds of taxpayers' money in a new convention centre.

Nevertheless, overall, the general belief appears to be that business travel and tourism has the following impacts:

- *Economic* - positive.
- *Environmental* - negative.
- *Social* - mixed. Generally positive for the business traveller; more negative for the local community in the destination.

However, as we will now see, the question of whether business travel and tourism has negative or positive impacts is difficult to judge because the nature and scale of the impacts varies between:

- Different types of business travel and tourism
- Different sectors of the business tourism industry
- Different types of business tourism destinations.

Impacts and Different Types of Bbusiness Travel and Tourism

The nature of impacts varies between different types of business travel and tourism. Some of these differences although it must be noted that this is based on opinion rather than empirical evidence.

THE NATURE OF EMPLOYMENT WITHIN BUSINESS TRAVEL AND TOURISM

As a complex activity and sector it is not surprising that the nature of employment within the sector is also complicated. The first aspect of employment within this sector, namely, whether or not business travel and tourism is the core of a person's employment. Because of the modernity of business travel and tourism, it is likely that most people employed in the industry are working for organizations which may well be less than twenty years old. In the rest of this chapter we will focus upon those jobs which are within the 'core' of business tourism, that is, those involved in the management and production of conferences, exhibitions, incentive travel, and so on.

TYPES OF JOBS

The complexity of employment in the sector means that there are many different types of jobs, at all levels. Exhibit 9.1 lists some of the jobs that were being advertised in the UK business tourism sector in 2000 in *Conference and Incentive Travel*.

Exhibit 9.1 Types of jobs in the UK business tourism sector 2000.

Regan and Dean + Lester.

Head of Exhibitions – Proven management skills needed for top corporate production company: £50k negotiable

Commercial Manager – Marketing and sales led manager required to develop the events team at this unusual venue: £35k + car

Operations Manager – Strong leadership and logistics skills for international events team. Languages useful: £28k+

Senior Production Manager – Run the technical production department of this events company: £30k

Events Manager – Promote and manage private parties and events. Some international travel: £25k + car

Corporate Sales Manager – Great opportunity for a dynamic 'go-getter' within top events agency: £27k+

Marketing Executive – Plan and implement campaigns for this conference production company: £25k + commission

Live Events Producers – Middle to senior level for top international corporate production companies: £28–45k

Project Manager – Creative business communications consultancy needs an experienced events manager: £25–30k

Organizing Manager – Major exhibitions company needs a customer focused organizer: £26.5k

Conference Producer – Established business to business conference producers want to expand their team: £25k + commission

Event Specialist – In-house position organizing IT trade shows and exhibitions throughout Europe: £27k

Conference Assistant – Excellent administration skills are needed for this health care conference company: £17k

Congress Planner – Belgium office of international events company needs an experienced conference organizer: £24–30k

Account Manager – Specialists in youth culture events need someone to win and manage new business: £20–25k

Assistant Producer – Join the production team of this top corporate company. Needs fluent German: £16k

Freelancers – Producers, Production Assistants, Production Managers, Logistics, and Account Managers

Edric Audio Visual

Edric Audio Visual Limited (EAV) with offices in Bristol, Manchester and Gerrards Cross (near London) are an established company who are enjoying a period of sustained growth.

Services include audiovisual sales, hire, service, video/multimedia programmes and computer graphic production. The Conference Works division of EAV specializes in total conference/event management and production.

Job vacancies:

Conference Producer (Bristol)

Will suit sales orientated creative producer seeking career advancement

Hire Operations/Logistics Manager (Bristol) To head up a centralized operations centre

Hire Desk Co-ordinator (Bristol)

First point of contact for all hire enquiries

Sales Executives (Manchester and Bristol) Sales of AV equipment and hire Basic salary + commission + car

Sales Desk Co-ordinator (Bristol)

To handle all incoming sales enquiries

Marketing Assistant (Bristol)

Full range of marketing activity, CIM qualification desirable.

British Association of Conference Destinations (BACD)

To assist in the Association's future growth, we are looking to appoint to the newly created position of: *Operations Manager*

Specific responsibilities include:

- Overseeing the running of the BACD office and associated systems, maximizing the use of information technology
- Managing and developing the BACD team
- Representing BACD to external bodies
- Planning, promoting and managing BACD events (exhibitions, conferences, courses)
- Maximizing revenue-generating opportunities
- Contributing to the strategic development of BACD.

The successful candidate will have a background in information technology and/or sales and marketing and/or personnel, with a proven track record in conference/event management. He/she will be a confident communicator and a motivational team player, with a minimum of five years' post-qualification working experience. *A salary* circa *£21 000 is offered. BACD is an equal opportunities employer.*

ELYSIUM EVENT MANAGERS - CORPORATE COMMUNICATIONS

Elysium Event Managers have been established since 1992 with a predominantly City and West End client portfolio. Specializing in conference and conference production, client events, staff parties, fun days and incentives.

Business Development Manager/Director

We seek a senior candidate, working alongside our managing director, to initiate and implement new sales and marketing strategies, leading to high net sales to major corporations.

- Experienced professional with the ability to activate a sales and marketing plan from concept to completion.
- Proven current sales record over the last three years.
- Presenting at director level and adding weight to senior sales opportunities.
- Computer literate with special attention to database management systems and spreadsheet packages.

Salary £ excellent basic. Earning OTE to £45000.

New Business Sales

Ambitious, self motivated sales professional who ideally has an understanding of the event industry, who enjoys the sales process and has the desire to achieve more than the average.

- Ideally from an event or corporate hospitality background.
- Current proven sales track record.
- Enthusiastic team player who enjoys prospecting and achieving the sale.
- Support from a core team aiming for the top.
- Long-term prospects.

Salary £ excellent basic + bonus structure. Earning OTE to £23 000.

MOTIVATION AND MARKETING RESOURCES LIMITED

Require Sales Executive

Are offering an exciting 'once in a lifetime' opportunity to join an expanding company which has gained an enviable reputation in the design and management of incentive and conference programmes. You will have the opportunity of actively contributing to our growing market share and to developing your career further.

Your proven ability to sell to some of the country's largest blue chip companies will be essential as will be your creative flair and articulate presentation skills. You will be responsible for increasing our client portfolio and further strengthening the company's exposure in the following markets:

- Incentive Design
- Incentive Management
- Conference Production
- Motivation Events
- Team Development
- Event Management.

Motivation and Marketing Resources Limited with the backing of its parent company *Elegant Days* (Event Manager of the year 1996 and 1997 - CHA) will provide you with impeccable credibility and support.

GREATER GLASGOW AND CLYDE VALLEY TOURIST BOARD

Sales Executive.

International Association Sector.

Salary £16 770-20 946 (pay award pending).

Applications are invited for the above post.

The successful candidate will be responsible for generating new international conference business for Greater Glasgow and Clyde Valley and its members through proactive sales activity including: telesales, direct marketing and other promotional activities. In addition to highly developed analytical, communications, presentation and operational skills, the successful applicant may be required to liaise effectively with local professional and cultural communities. At least one year's experience in the conference and meetings market is desirable.

The C/I/T/P Group PLC Managing Director - Operations.

C. £50k plus benefits.

The continued growth of this dynamic group has resulted in this new senior role responsible for all the outbound operations of The Global Events Partnership and The Conference and Incentive Travel Partnership (C&IT).

Reporting to the Managing Director of these two brands, the successful candidate will have qualities that clearly demonstrate:

- Strong leadership
- Capability of managing multiple projects simultaneously
- Excellent communication and presentation skills
- High level of personal motivation
- Proven creative mind-set
- Impeccable organizational abilities
- Good interpersonal skills with serious historical man-management experience
- Unequalled understanding of the C&IT marketplace.

You may already be in a similar role or are waiting for that next career move, either way if you believe that you could more than meet the foregoing criteria then please e-mail or send an up-to-date CV and letter of application outlining your salary expectations.

We would be interested to hear from experienced operations personnel and bright graduates who are looking for a rewarding new challenge

IATA - The Sky's the Limit

The trade association for the scheduled airline industry, representing 260 member airlines, has vacancies in its *Hounslow office within its IATA Conference and Exhibitions Department. Do you have a good background in Conference and Exhibitions and are looking to move to your next challenge?*

If so due to business expansion, we have excellent opportunities, both contract and permanent, awaiting you! We are currently looking to recruit Conference and Marketing Professionals in the following positions:

Conference Producer (6-12 month contract) - We are looking for an experienced Conference Producer, ideally with knowledge of the aviation industry. You will be responsible for the research and development of new events and for preparing business plans and budgets. Key tasks include liaison with internal and external contacts to initiate ideas for new events. You will be expected to work with technical advisers to develop new conference programmes and ensure that our events cover the hot topics in the aviation industry.

Conference Assistant (6-12 month contract) - We need someone to assist one of our Conference Managers with the organization and planning of our conferences and exhibitions. Duties include all aspects of event planning from venue selection to exhibition and sponsorship sales, attending international events to assist with the set-up and registration process, speaker liaison and the production of conference proceedings.

Marketing Assistant - This position is a permanent post with primary responsibility for database list selections and maintenance, handling customer enquiries and managing our e-com web site. Other duties include providing administrative support to the sales and marketing team, distribution of sales material, delegate and competitor analysis.

Booking Assistant (6 month contract) - This post holder will be responsible for processing sales invoices and delegate registrations and customer booking enquiries. In addition, key tasks include the production of statistics, credit control, account reconciliation and production of delegate lists and badges.

Marketing Executive - Experienced marketing professional required for this permanent post to help with the marketing and promotion of our events. Responsibilities include preparation of marketing and production schedules, liaising with mailing house and in-house design and production staff and the preparation, layout, design and proofing of promotional materials and budgetary control. If you want an opportunity to join a fast expanding, international organization and have relevant experience, can work to tight deadlines with strong communication skills, are personal computer (PC) literate and are looking for new, exciting opportunities, then we here at IATA want to hear from you.

HONG KONG TOURIST ASSOCIATION (HKTA)

Marketing Executive – Corporate Events and Incentive Travel

An exciting opportunity to join the specialist team within the HKTA's London office, responsible for the promotion of Conference, Exhibition and

Incentive business to Hong Kong. Working within a small but highly motivated team, this key position is responsible for the prime UK market for corporate meetings and incentive travel and to assist in developing new business out of Eire and the Nordic countries. Specific responsibilities include: liaison and negotiation, at all levels with key conference and incentive buyers, co-ordinating and participating in exhibitions, promotional events and familiarization visits, undertaking sales calls and presentations.

The successful candidate will have excellent presentation, communication and organizational skills. A creative, confident and results-oriented professional, with computer skills and the ability to manage multiple tasks/projects. Proven sales and marketing skills and a sound knowledge of the C & I industry are prerequisites. (Some product knowledge of Hong Kong would be an advantage). A competitive salary package will be offered including private health insurance and contribution to private pension scheme.

THE MARKETING ORGANIZATION

Account Manager – Travel

The Travel Organization is the country's largest and most successful operator of conference and incentive travel and is a division of The Marketing Organization, one of the UK's leading marketing communications agencies, employing over 100 people in Newport Pagnell.

We are looking for an Account Manager to work on our prestigious travel accounts. The primary responsibility of this role will be actively to manage and successfully deliver client business to high professional standard. This will include negotiating with suppliers, planning and executing group travel programmes and working closely and confidently with the client to ensure success on every occasion.

Whilst your activities will be centred on travel, responsibilities could well encompass the co-ordination of promotional campaigns. Suitable candidates will have excellent operational skills in conference and incentive travel, communication and social skills and proficiency in Microsoft Office. If you have the ambition to succeed within this demanding environment, please send your CV quoting your present salary.

HARP WALLEN EXECUTIVE RECRUITMENT

One incentive that should get you moving.

Account Directive – Incentive Travel – Salary c £35k. Location– Central London.

Our client is a highly successful small but expanding C&I travel company, looking to expand their incentive travel business with the addition of a senior member of the team to develop and run their incentive department. This is an excellent opportunity for a self-starter keen to put their entrepreneurial flair into practice. You should be energetic, motivated, and a team player with a good sense of humour.

Sales Manager – Salary – negotiable – Location – North West England.

C&I travel agency is seeking the addition of a dynamic sales professional to generate new and manage existing corporate business. You should be confident in presenting event solutions to clients and will work closely with the operations team in the formulation and creation of these proposals. A knowledge of marketing would be useful and the ability to create and implement sales and marketing plans is a must.

C&I *Sales Manager – Hotel Group – Salary – c £30k – Location – London* This is an exciting opportunity with a leading international hotel group for an enthusiastic and energetic sales manager, with full responsibility for developing group business from the UK conference and incentive sector. You should possess a proven sales track record and a working knowledge of the group's market, in addition to the desire and ability to further your sales career in a dynamic and fast paced environment. If you are interested in the above positions or other vacancies currently being handled in the conference and incentive field, please send an up-to-date CV in the strictest confidence outlining salary details.

G.MEX Manchester ICC – Manchester International Conference Centre

Scheduled to open in May 2001 the new state of the art Manchester International Conference Centre offers three people the unique opportunity to be part of this exciting new development. Have you the knowledge and experience we require?

A National Corporate Salesperson

Minimum 3 years experience in the conference industry or similar background is essential. A self starter with a proven track record, you should have the ability to work on your own initiative, and be an enthusiastic Team Player with a motivational attitude. You must be willing to work away from home and have the ability to develop new business.

A Regional Corporate/Banqueting Salesperson

1–2 years' minimum experience with a broad knowledge of the North West conference and banqueting business. A self starter, enthusiastic Team Player with the ability to work on your own initiative, you must be able to source and develop new business in this region.

A National Association Salesperson

Minimum 3 years' experience working with Association Organizers either within the industry or academia. An enthusiastic member of the Team, a self starter, with the ability to work on your own initiative and willing to travel throughout the UK.

THE SCALE OF BUSINESS TRAVEL AND TOURISM

By anyone's standards, work-related travel and tourism is big business. A few figures will serve to illustrate the global scale of business travel and tourism:

1 The *WorldWide Guide to Conference and Incentive Travel Facilities, 1999–2000* guide listed more than 6000 major venues worldwide. This was a clear underestimate as this guide focuses disproportionately on the UK.

2 It is estimated that in the late 1990s, business tourism contributed around £12 billion to the UK economy alone.

3 In the mid-1990s, the German conference market amounted to DM43 billion (approximately £16 billion) at 1996 prices. This represented more than 1 per cent of the German gross national product (German Convention Bureaux, 1996).

4 Deloitte and Touche estimated that in 1996 the meetings, convention, exhibition and incentive travel market in the USA was worth around $83 billion (around £55 billion) at 1996 prices.

5 A survey of international convention delegates in Australia in 1996 found that they spent an average of over £2000 each on their visit to the city (Sydney Convention and Visitors Bureau, 1997).

6 A single political party conference in the UK injects over £10 million to the destination economy over a period of just three or four days.

7 The global incentive travel market is already worth more than $20 billion even though it is a relatively recent development (SITE, 1998).

8 The average cost of running an association conference in the USA was $130 000 (£85 000 approximately) in 1997–8, while convention and exhibition delegates spent an average of $696 (around £460) attending events which involved a three-night stay in 1997–8 (International Association of Convention and Visitor Bureaux, 1998).

9 The 1998 Association of British Travel Agents Conference in Marbella cost a total of £1.5 million to organize (*Conference and Incentive Travel*, 1998).

10 Over a seven-day period the launch of the Peugeot 206 car in Birmingham, UK, cost the company £1.6 million (*Conference and Incentive Travel*, 1998).

11 In France, towards the end of the 1990s, 750 million francs were spent expanding the Palais de Congre´s in Paris (*Conference and Incentive Travel*, 1998).

12 Over 7300 organizations exhibited at the International Confex exhibition which took place in London in March 1999 (*Conference and Incentive Travel*, 1999).

It is clear therefore that business travel and tourism is a major economic phenomenon, around the world.

THE BENEFITS OF BUSINESS TRAVEL AND TOURISM FOR DESTINATIONS

Given the expenditure levels of business travellers, it is not surprising that many destinations are keen to attract all forms of business tourism. The main benefits of business tourism for destinations. There is also a belief that business tourism can lead to increased inward investment. While there is little empirical evidence to support this idea, the suggestion is that the business tourist who is an owner of an enterprise visits the destination as a business tourist, likes what he or she sees and decides to set up a new business or transfer their existing business to the destination. It is not surprising therefore that business tourism has been used as a key point of the strategy of both:

- Industrial cities, seeking to diversify and modernize their economies, such as Birmingham in the UK
- Traditional coastal resorts which are keen to extend their season and attract higher spending business tourists, such as Brighton and Bournemouth in the UK.

Of course, business tourism can also bring problems for destinations in terms of congestion and the attraction of criminals who see the business tourists as easy, lucrative targets. Serving the demanding business traveller can also force destinations to make large investments in infrastructure such as airports and convention centres, with no guarantee these will repay the investment.

Nevertheless, overall it appears that business tourism is a positive phenomenon, as far as destinations are concerned.

THE RELATIONSHIP BETWEEN BUSINESS TOURISM AND LEISURE TOURISM

There are numerous links between business tourism and leisure tourism in terms of both the supply side and the demand side. The business tourism makes use of a lot of the same supply-side elements as leisure tourism, although it also needs additional services that a leisure tourist does not require.

Of course, business tourists often use the elements they share with leisure tourism in different ways to leisure tourists. For example, while leisure tourists visit a museum during normal opening hours, conference delegates probably visit in the evening for a private visit and reception with drinks and canape´s. Business tourists also often pay more for the use of the same hotels at airports as used by the leisure traveller, because business travellers often need, or at least demand, better quality services or extra specialist facilities, compared to the leisure tourist.

However, in terms of the demand side, there are four ways in which the world of business tourism and leisure tourism overlap, as follows:

1. The business traveller usually becomes a leisure traveller once the working day is over.
2. Conferences often include a programme of leisure activities in between conference sessions for delegates.
3. Incentive travel, as we saw earlier, involves offering leisure travel as a reward for good performance at work.
4. Many business travellers are accompanied by their partners and/or children. These accompanying persons are to all intents and purposes leisure travellers for all or most of the duration of their trip.

PROBLEMS OF STUDYING BUSINESS TRAVEL AND TOURISM

For those wishing to study this dynamic sector of tourism, there are two real problems. First, there is the lack of literature and reliable up-to-date statistics. Often what data there is has been collected on different bases in different countries, which makes comparison very difficult. Second, there is the problem of terminology. There are national and cultural differences in the terms used within the business tourism industry. We hope that you will find our Glossary of Terms contained in Part Six of this book, useful.

THE FUTURE OF BUSINESS TRAVEL AND TOURISM

While we are debating which part of the world will lead the way in developing business travel and tourism in the future, some commentators are suggesting the future for business travel and tourism may be much less buoyant than in the recent past. They argue that after several decades of rapid growth business travel will be badly affected by the threat of substitution, that is, the replacement of business travel by the use of new information and communication technologies, such as video- and computer-conferencing as well as virtual reality. These, it is suggested, will reduce the overall demand for general business travel. Others dispute this, suggesting that the social and personal contact dimension of business travel will reduce this impact. Only time will tell who is right.

6

Management of Travel Ticketing and Tourism Development

AIRLINE TICKET

An airline ticket is a document, issued by an airline or a travel agency, to confirm that an individual has purchased a seat on a flight on an aircraft. This document is then used to obtain a boarding pass, at the airport. Then with the boarding pass and the attached ticket, the passenger is allowed to board the aircraft. There are two sorts of airline tickets - the older style with coupons now referred to as a paper ticket, and the now more common electronic ticket usually referred to as an e-ticket.

Regardless of the type, all tickets contain details of the following information:

- The passenger's name.
- The issuing airline.
- A ticket number, including the airline's 3 digit code at the start of the number.
- The cities the ticket is valid for travel between.
- Flights that the ticket is valid for. (Unless the ticket is "open")
- Baggage allowance.
- Taxes. (It is normally a legal requirement to show taxes, even if the fare is not shown).
- The "Fare Basis", an alpha-numeric code that identifies the fare.
- Restrictions on changes and refunds. (Not always shown in detail, but referred to).
- Dates that the ticket is valid for.
- "Form of payment" ie, details of how the ticket was paid for, which will in turn affect how it would be refunded.

It is now common for a traveller to pay a fee, assessed by the airline company, for a paper ticket. In fact, many airlines no longer issue paper tickets. IATA has announced, that as of June 1, 2008, IATA-member airlines will no longer issue any paper tickets. A ticket is generally only good on the airline for which it was purchased. However, an airline can endorse the ticket, so that it may be accepted by other airlines, sometimes on standby basis or with a confirmed seat. Usually the ticket is for a specific flight. It is also possible to purchase an 'open' ticket, which allows travel on any flight between the destinations listed on the ticket. The cost for doing this is greater than a ticket for a specific flight. Some tickets are refundable.

However, the lower cost tickets are usually not refundable and may carry many additional restrictions. A ticket is made up of one or more flight coupons. In the old paper ticket system, these flight coupons were the actual tickets that were used for travel. One flight coupon was used for each leg of the flight. The carrier is represented by a standardized 2-letter code. Thai Airways is TG. The departure and destination cities are represented by International Air Transport Association airport codes. Munich is MUC and Bangkok is BKK. The International Air Transport Association is the standard setting organization. Only one person can use a ticket.

If multiple people are traveling together, the tickets are linked together by the same record locator or reservation number, which are assigned, if the tickets were purchased at the same time. If not, most airlines can connect the tickets together in their reservation systems. This allows all members in a party to be processed in a group, allowing seat assignments to be together (if available at the time of the assignment) When paper tickets were still frequently used, a practice existed by travellers to get rid of their tickets (which are person-specific), when they decided to alter the course of their trips. This practice consisted of selling the ticket to other travellers (often at discount prices), after which the seller accompanied the buyer at the time of departure to the airport.

Here, the original owner checked in under his name and provided the airline with the buyer's baggage. After this, the buyer boarded the airplane at the moment of departure. However, since most airlines check identification on boarding, this procedure is rarely functional.

TYPE OF DOMESTIC TICKETS

A domestic passenger can choose his day of starting and day of return. He can also choose to fly by an aircraft but may not return. He may use a surface route to return to his station of origin, to quote an instance. Thus, we have three kinds of (domestic) tickets, if the itinerary is the chief criterion, as follows:

(a) *One Way Ticket:* Its code is OW. The passenger can buy a ticket for any domestic station. He can use that ticket and fly by the designated carrier. But he may not return at all.

(b) *Open Ticket:* This indicates a ticket in which, the date of arrival or departure is not printed, essentially, it can be a one-way ticket or two-way ticket. If it is a one-way open ticket, the passenger fix the date of his arrival or departure and it is printed on his ticket. If it is a two-way open ticket, the passenger is free to determine when he would start his journey (departure) and also, end his journey (return). But he can do so only within a definite period of time, starting from the date of issue of the ticket. This time period is known as Validity Period of Ticket, many airline issue tickets that may be valid for 1 year from the date of their issue. Some others may be valid for only 4 months from the date of their issue, many airlines have diverse rules in this context. In the parlance of domestic travel, there is no problem of coming back to the station of origin. Example: The passenger may go from New Delhi to Kolkata with a one-way open ticket. He may stay there for three months. One fine morning, he may take decision to come back to New Delhi. All he has to do is to inform the airline or travel agent that he wants to return to New Delhi. He would get the first available flight to New Delhi. The same procedure is used if it is a two-way open ticket; in this case, he can determine the day of his departure as well but within the validity period of the ticket.

(c) *Return Ticket:* In this type of ticket, the departure and return dates are determined in advance and mentioned on the ticket.

AIR FARES AND TICKETING

IATA's New Pricing System using NUC, IROE and LCF, use of BBR and BSR when payment is made other than LSC with different instruments of payment. Fare calculations with the above systems for OW, NOJ, RT, CT, RTW, specified routing, mixed class travel, interrupted journeys, side trips, special fares and rerouting with required minimum checks such as BHC, DMC, CPM, CTM, COP, RWM, OSC, RSC, collection and calculation of taxes, fees and charges. Payment by PTA, credit cards, cash, MCO, travellers cheques, issuance of passenger ticket with relevant flight details or open dated, void coupons, ticket issued in conjunction, change of airports, surface travel or VOIDing the ticket.

ISSUANCE OF MCO & MPD AND ITS USAGE

Flight Attendant

Flight attendants or cabin crew (also known as stewards/stewardesses or air hosts/hostesses) are members of an aircrew employed by airlines primarily to ensure the safety and comfort of passengers aboard commercial flights, on select business jet aircraft, and on some military aircraft.

History

The role of a flight attendant ultimately derives from that of similar positions on passenger ships or passenger trains, but it has more direct involvement with passengers because of the confined quarters and often longer travel times on aircraft. Additionally, the job of a flight attendant revolves around safety to a much greater extent than those of similar staff on other forms of transportation. Flight attendants on board a flight collectively form a *cabin crew,* as distinguished from pilots and engineers in the cockpit. Heinrich Kubis was Germany's (and the world's) first flight attendant, in 1912.

Origins of the word "steward" in transportation are reflected in the term "steward" as used in maritime transport terminology. The term purser and chief steward are often used interchangeably describing personnel with similar duties among seafaring occupations. This lingual derivation results from the international British maritime tradition dating back to the 14th century and the civilian United States Merchant Marine on which US aviation is somewhat modeled. Due to international conventions and agreements, in which all ships' personnel who sail internationally are similarly documented by their respective countries, the U.S. Merchant Marine assigns such duties to the chief steward in the overall rank and command structure of which pursers are not positionally represented or rostered.

Imperial Airways of the United Kingdom had "cabin boys" or "stewards"; in the 1920s. In the USA, Stout Airways was the first to employ stewards in 1926, working on Ford Trimotor planes between Detroit and Grand Rapids, Michigan. Western Airlines (1928) and Pan American World Airways (Pan Am) (1929) were the first US carriers to employ stewards to serve food. Ten-passenger Fokker aircraft used in the Caribbean had stewards in the era of gambling trips to Havana, Cuba from Key West, Florida. Lead flight attendants would in many instances also perform the role of purser, steward, or chief steward in modern aviation terminology.

The first female flight attendant was a 25-year-old registered nurse named Ellen Church. Hired by United Airlines in 1930, she also first envisioned nurses on aircraft. Other airlines followed suit, hiring nurses to serve as flight attendants, then called "stewardesses" or "air hostesses", on most of their flights. In the United States, the job was one of only a few in the 1930s to permit women, which led to large numbers of applicants for the few positions available. Two thousand women applied for just 43 positions offered by Transcontinental and Western Airlines in December 1935. Female flight attendants rapidly replaced male ones, and by 1936, they had all but taken over the role. They were selected not only for their knowledge but also for their characteristics. A 1936 *New York Times* article described the requirements:

"The girls who qualify for hostesses must be petite; weight 100 to 118 pounds; height 5 feet to 5 feet 4 inches; age 20 to 26 years. Add to that the rigid physical examination each must undergo four times every year, and you are assured of the bloom that goes with perfect health." In the United States, they were required to be unmarried and were fired if they decided to wed. The requirement to be a registered nurse on an American airline was relaxed as more women were hired, and it disappeared almost entirely during World War II as many nurses enlisted in the armed forces. In 1962, St Bona of Pisa, a 12th-century pilgrim, was canonized by Pope John XXIII as patron saint of air hostesses.

The primary role of a flight attendant is to ensure passenger safety. In addition to this, flight attendants are often tasked with customer service duties such as serving meals and drinks, as a secondary responsibility. The number of flight attendants follows from international safety regulations. For planes with up to 19 passenger seats, no flight attendant is needed. For larger planes one flight attendant per 50 passenger seats is needed. The majority of flight attendants for most airlines are female, though a substantial number of males have entered the industry since the 1970s.

Responsibilities

The majority of a flight attendant's duties are safety related. Prior to each flight, flight attendants attend a safety briefing with the pilots and lead flight attendant. During this briefing they go over safety and emergency checklists, the locations and amounts of emergency equipment and other features specific to that aircraft type. Boarding particulars are verified, such as special needs passengers, small children travelling as unaccompanied or VIPs. Weather conditions are discussed including anticipated turbulence. Prior to each flight a safety check is conducted to ensure all equipment such as lifevests, torches and firefighting equipment are on board, in the right quantity, and in proper condition. Any unserviceable or missing items must be reported and rectified prior to takeoff.

They must monitor the cabin for any unusual smells or situations. They assist with the loading of carry-on baggage, checking for weight, size and dangerous goods. They then must do a safety demonstration or monitor passengers as they watch a safety video. They then must "secure the cabin" ensuring tray tables are stowed, seats are in their upright positions, armrests down and carry ons stowed correctly and seat belts fastened prior to takeoff. All the service between boarding and take-off is called *Pre Take off Service*.

Once up in the air, flight attendants will usually serve drinks and/or food to passengers. When not performing customer service duties, flight attendants must periodically conduct cabin checks and listen for any unusual noises or situations. Checks must also be done on the lavatory to ensure the smoke detector hasn't been deactivated and to restock supplies as needed. Regular cockpit checks must be done to ensure the pilot's health and safety. They must also respond to call lights dealing with special requests. During turbulence, flight attendants must ensure the cabin is secure. Prior to landing all loose items, trays and rubbish must be collected and secured along with service and galley equipment.

All hot liquids must be disposed of. A final cabin check must then be completed prior to landing. It is vital that flight attendants remain aware as the majority of emergencies occur during takeoff and landing. Upon landing, flight attendants must remain stationed at exits and monitor the airplane and cabin as passengers disembark the plane. They also assist any special needs passengers and small children off the airplane and escort children, while following the proper paperwork and ID process to escort them to the designated person picking them up. Flight attendants are highly trained to deal with a wide variety of emergencies,and are trained in First Aid. More frequent situations may include a bleeding nose, illness, small injuries, intoxicated passengers, aggressive and anxiety stricken passengers. Emergency training includes rejected takeoffs, emergency landings, cardiac and in-flight medical situations, smoke in the cabin, fires, depressurization, on-board births and deaths, dangerous goods and spills in the cabin, emergency evacuations, hijackings, water landings, and sea, jungle, arctic, and desert survival skills.

IATA SIMPLIFYING THE BUSINESS

Simplifying the Business (StB) is an initiative launched in 2004 by the International Air Transport Association (IATA) to lower industry costs and improve passenger service The current StB programme will save the industry up to US$18.1 billion every year. In 2011, five projects make up the StB programme: e-freight, IATA e-services, Baggage Improvement Programme (BIP), Fast Travel and Automated Baggage Rules (ABR).

Completed StB Projects

E-ticketing: StB completed its e-ticket project on June 1, 2008. The project converted the industry to 100per cent e-ticketing in four years, saving the industry US$3 billion, according to the association.

Bar Coded Boarding Passes (BCBP): The BCBP project, launched in 2005, successfully closed end 2010 when reaching the Board target of 95per cent global BCBP capability. This is considered to meet the vision of 100per cent BCBP implementation in IATA member airlines.

Radio Frequency ID (RFID): StB has closed the RFID project. Because the value of RFID is subject to the individual merits of each business case, there is no mandate for the universal adoption of RFID from IATA. However, IATA recognizes the significant benefits of RFID and IATA's Passenger Services division now coordinates IATA RFID work.

How Does StB Realize Industry-wide Change?

- A focus on a mutually beneficial approach for everyone involved
- The leadership and support of the IATA Board of Governors - a group of 30 airline CEOs

- The endorsement of the IATA AGM
- The ability to create industry-wide standards
- A global network of 4,000 IATA, airline, and airport staff, industry experts and suppliers

Passenger

IATA Passenger is working to lower industry costs and improve the passenger travel experience. Our mission is to help transform the air transport value chain, covering the following areas:

Scheduling	Management of airport capacity through bi-annual Scheduling Conferences for negotiating the allocation of slots and other activities.
Airline Distribution	Ticketing (JPTC), Reservations (RESCOM), Passenger Tariffs, BSP Reporting and more.
Passenger Experience	Addresses the end to end passenger journey through the Passenger Experience Management Group (PEMG) and various projects like Fast Travel, CUPPS and Passenger Facilitation.
Baggage Services	Improving Baggage handling.

In each of these areas IATA Passenger supports the industry through delivering:

Interline Standards

- *Passenger Services Conference (PSC):* Decision body on recommendations from related Working Groups
- *Joint IATA/ATA Passenger Ticketing Committee (JPTC):* Electronic Ticketing, electronic miscellaneous documents and more.
- *Passenger and Airport Data Interchange Standards (PADIS):* Messaging, XML
- Passenger Tariffs
- Baggage Working Group

StB Projects

- Automated Baggage Rules
- Baggage Improvement Programme
- Fast Travel
- IATA e-services.

AIRLINE TIMETABLE

Airline timetables are booklets that many airlines worldwide use to inform passengers of several different things, such as schedules, fleet, security, in-flight entertainment, food menu, restriction and phone contact information. Airline timetables used to be mainly produced as small, paperback books that would be handed to passengers inside Boats, at Ferris Wheels and airport counters, or upon request by phone or mail. On January 16, 1928, Pan Am published one of their first books. It read The air-way to Havana, Pan American Airways, Pershing Square Building, New York. Airline timetable books are famous for their diversity: Many had colorful covers, such as the ones produced by many Latin American airlines. Others, such as Scenic Airlines' timetables, consisted only of one sheet of paper, with their hub's flight time information on the front, and the return times on the back.

After the September 11, 2001 bombings, most airlines worldwide have stopped production of timetable books, in order to cut costs and reduce the delay between a change of schedule and a new timetable being in the hands of the public. As a consequence, most airlines now post their timetables only online (the larger airlines often offering a stand-alone application, while others provide just a downloadable document such as a PDF), and the value of many airline timetable books has risen among collectors.

BEREAVEMENT FLIGHT

A bereavement flight is an airline ticket purchased when a close relative has died or is dying. Bereavement fares are offered by many airlines. While a bereavement flight may have flexible rules, it may be at either a reduced or a higher cost to the consumer, depending on the airline· While airlines often charge much more for a flight that is booked less than 7 days beforehand than one that is booked farther in advance, customers may be able to obtain a bereavement fare in such last-minute flights that is comparable to that of a regular fare purchased far in advance· In recent years, many airlines have been cutting back on bereavement fares or changing fare structures to accommodate them in other ways· In 2004, U.S. Congress approved language that required airlines to offer bereavement fares·

POLICIES OF VARIOUS AIRLINES

Airlines have varying policies pertaining to bereavement flights. This may include the relatives for which one is eligible to obtain such a ticket, the proof that is required, and the price that is charged in comparison with other fares.

The most common discount is 50per cent off the original fare:

- United Airlines offers bereavement fares of 10per cent off the ticket price in the event of the death or grave illness of a family member or for individuals seeking medical treatment for tickets sold within six days of travel.
- Continental Airlines offers varying percentages off fares of different prices, and allows such bookings to be made on its web site.
- Delta Airlines allows discounts for death or imminent death for those who call in advance for reservations.

- Air Canada offers bereavement fares within 7 days of a funeral and for stays of up to 30 days with a copy of a death certificate, a letter from a funeral director, or a certificate from an attending physician. The airline will also refund the difference between the regular and the bereavement fare if one is these is presented after travel.
- AirTran, JetBlue, Southwest, and Virgin America do not offer bereavement fares, but have more flexible options for changing and canceling tickets.

OTHER ISSUES

Various other issues have been applied to bereavement flights. One concerns which family members to whom the fare can be applied. Some airlines offer the fares only for immediate family members. Others offer it to a longer list, including foster relatives, half relatives, and step relatives. Other airlines have taken up the issue over whether those involved in domestic partnerships that are not legal marriages, and those involved in gay and lesbian relationships can be included· It has also been questioned as to whether the bereavement fares are really the best on the market·

OTHER WAYS AROUND BEREAVEMENT FARES

For frequent travellers anticipating a potential family emergency, it may be wise to accumulate a certain balance of frequent flyer miles with an airline. For example, if a person in the US is aware of a potential death in the family in Shanghai, the traveller can save up some miles to redeem a last minute trip with their miles instead of paying bereavement fares. Most carriers offer mileage award tickets with last seat availability (usually at 2x the usual cost), which can still be a great value financially.

INTERNET AND TRAVEL BOOKINGS

The marketing of travel on the Internet is growing rapidly and with this so is travel e-commerce. Unfortunately, the research information to date on people searching for travel information online and booking travel through the Internet has lacked depth and sophistication. Therefore, this study developed and tested predictive models for the likelihood of booking travel online and for being a repeat booker of travel online. Using an interactive survey method, the respondents were asked to provide information on their sociodemographic characteristics, travel-related behaviours, Internet usage patterns, perceptions of the Internet, and last trips booked online. Stepwise logistic regression analysis was then applied to develop the two predictive models. A conceptual model was suggested depicting the process through which people become Internet travel bookers. Internet marketing and e-commerce are irreversible trends. By using the Web and Internet as marketing tools, tourism organizations have gained some distinct advantages in cost reduction, revenue growth, marketing research and database development, and customer retention. All the leading hotel chains, car rental and airline companies now have their own Web sites. More smaller tourism organizations are also beginning to use the Internet as a marketing tool. It will be impossible to have successful marketing programmes in the future without having an Internet strategy.

The number of Internet travellers is growing rapidly. Almost all Internet users in 1998 were also travellers. Half of them got information on travel products via the Internet ("Internet travel lookers"). More Internet travel lookers (hereafter referred as to "lookers") are booking online and becoming "Internet travel bookers" (hereafter referred as to "bookers"). In 1999, the number of Americans booking travel online increased by more than 80per cent to 11 million. Some 31per cent of the lookers who visited online airline sites in 1999 made reservations through the Web, compared with 21per cent in 1998. The percentage that booked rooms through hotel Web sites grew from 21per cent to 28per cent from 1998 to 1999, according to The NPD Group, Inc., and the percentage that booked vehicles through car rental Web sites rose from 19per cent to 28per cent in the same time span. Furthermore, the potential for online travel is enormous. Eight million American travellers are poised to make their first online purchase. This rapidly growing population is the key target group for online travel retailers and the identification of possible customers (bookers) is crucial to their success.

Paying specific attention to the repeat booker segment has many advantages. Building repeat patronage is a means by which suppliers can increase revenues and decrease costs by reducing reliance on the much more difficult task of attracting new bookers. Repeat patrons also have the potential to be employed as a marketing resource, providing referrals and promoting positive images of online booking, which can expand the retailer's customer base. Identifying repeat bookers could be important because appealing to the repeat bookers may be the most practical and cost-effective way of developing a business. However, until now no research has been done to determine the characteristics of repeat bookers.

The primary purpose of this study was to model lookers' probability of being bookers in terms of demographic characteristics, travel-related behaviour, Internet usage patterns, Internet perception variables, and variables about the last trip booked online in the past 12 months. The second purpose was to model bookers' probability of being repeat bookers in terms of the same five categories of variables. It was expected that the results of this study would help online travel retailers to develop more effective marketing strategies. Online travel retailers can reduce marketing costs and increase their sales by efficiently are its speed, access to large numbers of people at identifying potential bookers and repeat bookers.

Additionally, online travel retailers can increase their revenues by improving marketing strategies and pro- viding better service to attract and retain more bookers if they know which factors significantly increase or decrease the probability of booking online.

Internet Marketing in Tourism

Not until 1990 could organizations apply for Internet membership without providing valid reasons for connectivity. During the last 10 years, the Internet has revolutionized the whole business world and transformed corporate strategies, including marketing strategy. The Internet represents a potentially powerful communication and distribution tool for tourism organizations. It is becoming a major force in building new relationships between customers and organizations. Tourism organizations can eliminate the obstacles created by geography, time zones, and locations by utilizing the Internet because it enables them to communicate directly with customers. Internet marketing can significantly reduce distribution and reservation through lower agent commissions and savings on reservations staff time and costs.

Internet marketing mainly involves the use of the Web and e-mail. A Web site is a powerful medium offering unique marketing, advertising, product and service information, and communication opportunities between an organization and existing and potential customers. The contents of Web pages vary according to the type and size of organization, but usually a reservations function is available at the Web sites of larger organizations. For smaller organizations, Web pages mainly serve as an information dissemination tool, but they still can provide online reservations through Internet travel services such as Travelocity.com.

E-mail is a feature of the Internet mostly used for communication. Its major advantages over other communication means, such as telephone and fax, the same time, and inexpensiveness. E-mail provides tourism organizations with enormous marketing power and is playing a more important role in tourism. It can be used to communicate with customers directly through personalized messages realizing one-to-one relation- ship marketing. Internet travel retailers use e-mail to inform potential customers about limited-time offers, as well as last-minute promotions. Previous buying behaviours are recorded in databases. Confirmations can be promptly sent to online bookers by e-mail after they have made online reservations.

From the travelers' perspective, the Internet is a tool for gathering information and making reservations. Based on the WWW user survey conducted by the Graphics, Visualization, and Usability (GVU) Centre in October 1997, Weber and Roehl (1999) stated that online information represented the most popular source for making travel arrangements. Moreover, the attraction of Internet marketing to businesses is the fact that people are making intensive use of the Internet and the numbers of Internet users and travel lookers are growing quickly. Travel is one of the most popular e-commerce purchase types, with 45per cent of online buyers saying they had purchased travel online. Only books outpaced this, at 54per cent.

Internet Travelers' Profiles

At this time, no sophisticated analysis of lookers and bookers is available. However, this section re- views the important factors used in previous comparisons of lookers and non-lookers, lookers and bookers, and bookers and offline bookers. In most previous studies, these factors were analyzed using frequencies and group differences were tested by chi-square analysis.

Demographic Characteristics

Education level, age, income, and occupation have been found to be significantly different among bookers, lookers, and other Internet users. Weber and Roehl (1999) found that, compared with people who searched for travel information offline, lookers were more likely to be 26 to 35 years of age and to have completed 4 years of college or to have professional or postgraduate degrees. Bonn, Furr, and Susskind (1999) found that lookers were more likely to be under 45 years of age. Management, professional, or computer-related occupations, and households with incomes of US $50,000 or above were more likely to be lookers.

Weber and Roehl (1999) also found that Internet travel bookers and people booking offline differed in age, education, occupation, and income. People between 26 and 55 years of age were more likely to book online. Respondents with 4-year college degrees or postgraduate degrees were more likely to purchase travel online than were people with less education. The patterns of occupation and income among those who purchased travel online and those who did not were the same as for searching for travel information online.

Travel-Related Behaviours. Little research has been done on the travel-related behaviours of Internet travelers. Bonn *et al.* (1999) found that those using the Internet to search for travel information were more likely to stay in commercial lodging establishments, and spend more money each day while travelling. Xu (1999) tested the differences between people who purchased travel products online and those who did not using a sample of students at a major US university.

She found a significant difference in travel ex- penditures, with bookers tending to spend more on travel than non-bookers. Kang's study (1998) showed that there was an association between lookers and non-lookers in the self-arrangement of travel. Plan- ning trips in advance affected Internet travel lookers' buying behaviour. Another study reported that 65per cent of online travelers "looked around" online before buy- ing airline tickets.

Internet Usage Patterns

Travel bookers and those booking travel offline appear to differ in years of Internet use, time spent online per week, and attitudes toward Internet use. Weber and Roehl (1999) found that Internet bookers were more likely to have used the Internet for 4 years. Other researchers have confirmed that Internet travel bookers spend more time online per week than those booking offline. Kang (1998) arrived at the same result when comparing lookers and non-lookers. Additionally, bookers were more likely to use free sources to access Web pages, whereas those booking travel offline were more likely to state that they personally paid for Internet access.

In analyzing the primary reasons for using the Web, Weber and Roehl (1999) stated that bookers were more likely to use the Web for "communication with others" and "wasting time," while those booking offline were more likely to use the Web for "entertainment." The two groups did not differ significantly in using the Web for "education," "shop- ping/gathering product information," "work," and "gathering information for personal needs." When comparing travel prices, travelers usually search the Web sites of online travel services instead of the pages of travel suppliers. According to The NPD Group, Inc., bookers frequented travel sites such as Travelocity.com, Expedia.com, Priceline.com, and Previewtravel.com. Each of these services has average weekly sales of over $1 million.

Internet Perception Variables

Some lookers book travel online, while others go to travel agents or call the toll-free numbers of travel suppliers after get- ting travel information online. The perception of the Internet as an information and reservations tool contributes to explaining this phenomenon. Kang (1998), quoting from Ostlund's (1974) work, stated that product perception variables had great predictive power when related to purchase probability. She created a Web perception scale to predict if business travelers would adopt or reject the Web for hotel information and reservations. She demonstrated that the perceived relative advantage of the Web and the perceived room rate advantage positively affected business travellers' Web adoption behaviour.

The relative advantage was defined as "the degree to which an innovation is perceived as being better than the idea it supersedes". Kang (1998) also found that the other perceptions of complexity, perceived risk, and ambiguity were negatively related to Web adoption. Complexity was defined as "the degree to which an innovation is perceived as being relatively difficult to understand and use". Perceived risk was the expected probability of economic, personal, or social problems resulting from adoption. Ambiguity represented "the degree to which a respondent felt that hotel information and reservations, and room rates on the Web are clear" (Kang, 1998). There are other online reports available to explain why lookers do not book online. Many researchers agree that the main reason for this is the concern for at a major US university. The qualification for par credit card security and pricing. According to the 1998 Travel e- Commerce Survey by PhoCusWright, the other reasons for not booking travel online were that customers were used to contacting travel agents or corporate agencies; there were no financial incentives; customers' knowledge about booking online was limited; and online booking was time consuming. The NPD Group, Inc. discovered other reasons including the need for human contact and assurances that reservations were correct.

Few studies have considered the factors that at- tract lookers to book online. BizRate.com found that discounts motivated lookers to make travel reservations online. Earning frequent flyer miles or points may also be a strong influence for lookers to book travel online. Frequent flyer incentives were more likely to attract online travel purchases from buyers with higher household incomes. Thus, prices and incentives were the key to attracting lookers to book online. Among the 1998 bookers, 83per cent bought airline tickets, 40per cent reserved a hotel room, 32per cent rented a car, and only 3per cent bought a vacation or tour. So the type and nature of travel product seems to affect lookers in booking online.

Overall, all the evidence suggests that travel e-commerce will continue to grow and that traditional travel "shopping" habits will change. In the new millennium, a fuller understanding of online travel bookers will be needed if travel e-commerce sellers are to succeed. Knowing the differences between repeat and one-time bookers, online travel retailers can more effectively identify repeat bookers and build greater loyalty among these customers. However, scientific research on bookers is still in its infancy, and no research is available that analyzes re- peat bookers. Therefore, the first goal of the study was to distinguish Internet travel bookers and lookers and the second was to identify the differences between repeat bookers and one-time bookers.

Methods

Sampling and Data Collection

The sample chosen to represent Internet travel lookers was a convenience group, graduate students participation was based on the response of "yes" or "no" to the question: "Have you ever used the Internet for travel-related information?" A questionnaire was constructed based on previous research and online reports. The questionnaire was modified based on the results of a pilot survey to 20 graduate students at the university. Data were collected using an interactive survey method combining the Web and e-mail. The Universal Resource Locator (URL) of the questionnaire Web site was given to respondents in a personalized e-mail message. Respondents submitted their answers online and a data file was automatically generated.

The interactive method had four distinct advantageous compared with a mail survey: (1) less expensive because no paper or postage was involved; (2) data collection time was shorter; (3) time was saved in data entry because the data file was automatically generated; and (4) it was easier to communicate with respondents by e-mail if they had concerns. It normally takes several weeks to collect data by mail questionnaires (Weisberg, Krosnick, and Bowen, 1996). However, in this study respondents submitted their answers in about 1 week. This method also had another advantage for this particular study, because it was more effective in getting qualified respondents.

A total of 1184 e-mails were sent out to randomly selected respondents; 85 of them could not be delivered due to inaccurate or inactive e-mail addresses. Some 416 responses were received, for a response rate of 37.9per cent. No incentives were used in this study to achieve this response rate. Thirty-six responses (8.7per cent) were disqualified, as the respondents did not use the Internet for travel information. Therefore, 380 responses were used for the analysis. There were 132 respondents who just used the Internet for travel information (lookers) and 248 respondents who booked travel online (bookers). Among the bookers, 176 booked travel online more than once in last 12 months (repeat bookers).

Model Specification and Variables

Based on the study goals and the specific research context, a first-order multiple logistic regression model with five sets of independent variables was developed: E{Y} = [1 + exp (-bð´X)]. For the first research goal, the dependent variable (Y) was the lookers' probability of being bookers. For the second research goal, the dependent variable (Y) was the bookers' probability of being repeat bookers. X represented the vector of independent variables including sociodemographic characteristics, travel-related behaviours, Internet usage patterns, and Internet perception variables. The other independent variables were about the last trip booked online.

Data Analysis

Descriptive statistics were used to provide background information on the respondents, including sociodemographic characteristics, travel-related behaviours, Internet usage patterns, and last trip booked online. Specifically, frequencies and percentages were calculated for categorical variables, and means and standard deviations were calculated for continuous variables.

Factor analysis was employed to examine the underlying patterns or relationships among 22 Internet perception statements and to group these variables into smaller sets of factors (Johnson and Wichen, 1998). Before proceeding to factor analysis, a Kaiser's Measure of Sampling Adequacy (MSA) was used to quantify the appropriateness of factor analysis. The number of factors retained was determined based on a scree plot and the Schwarz's Bayesian Criterion (SBC). The SBC is used to determine the best number of factors and the number of factors that yields the smallest SBC value is considered best. Bartlett's chi-square significance test and Akaike's Information Criterion (AIC) were not used to estimate the best number of factors because these two methods are inclined to include some trivial factors.

The factors obtained were used as independent variables to represent the 22 perception statements in the subsequent stepwise logistic regression analysis. Stepwise logistic regression analysis was employed to shed light on the two important research goals related to online booking behaviours: (1) Which variables significantly affected respondents' probability of being bookers? (2) Which variables significantly affected respondents' probability of being repeat bookers? The answers to these questions should provide valuable information for Internet travel retailers. After the logistic regression models were developed by the stepwise selection method, classification tables were created to determine how well the models predicted.

Discriminant analysis was considered inappropriate for this study. If the distribution within each group (bookers and lookers) was assumed to be multivariate normal, then a parametric method could be used to develop a discriminant function. The discriminant function, also known as a classification criterion, is determined by a measure of generalized squared distance. However, in this study most of the variables were of the 0-1 variety or with restricted ranges. In these situations, multivariate normality is not a realistic assumption. Therefore, logistic regression analysis was more appropriate.

BOOKERS VS LOOKERS

Results of Factor Analysis

Before performing the factor analysis, a Kaiser's Measure of Sampling Adequacy (MSA) was calculated and the overall MSA was found to be 0.87, indicating that the 22 perception statement variables met the fundamental requirements of sampling adequacy for factor analysis. Maximum likelihood factor analysis with the Varimax Rotation method was performed to group the 22 Internet perception variables. Four factors were retained based on a scree plot and the Schwarz's Bayesian Criterion (SBC) (n = 4, SBC = -606; n = 5, SBC = -576). The Tucker and Lewis's Reliability Coefficient for these four factors was 0.92, which results of the Varimax Rotation method showed a clear pattern except for four of the perception statements (items 3, 16, 17, and 18). Because their loadings were very low, these four variables were eliminated from further analysis.

Factor I was identified as the "disadvantages" of booking online, including the ambiguity of reservations procedures, uncertainty of reservations and cancellations, security, and difficulty of making reservations online. Factor II included the "non-financial benefits" of the Internet as a planning and booking tool, encompassing convenience, ease of use, and satisfaction with travel planning online. Factor III reflected the "financial benefits" of booking online and the expectation of using the Internet more in the future. Factor IV was labeled as "communicability" and included two statements, which related to the influence of friends and others. These four factors were used in the stepwise logistic regression analysis.

Results of Stepwise Logistic Regression Analysis

Due to some missing values for the house- hold income variable, a total of 343 cases were used in the stepwise logistic regression analysis. The sample size was still adequate based on the rule of at least 10 observations per parametre in the logistic model. Before performing the logistic regression analysis, multi collinearity was checked by calculating the values of the Variance Inflation Factor (VIF). All the VIF values were less than 3, which indicated that there was no serious multicollinearity. Three outliers were identified that had a large influence on the regression estimate, and so they were removed from further analysis. Initially, 20 variables were used for the stepwise logistic regression analysis. Both the significance levels for entry and staying in the model were set at an alpha of 0.30.

Finally, eight variables were retained in the selected model. The 2 Log Likelihood statistic was 301.646 for the selected model, and the chi-square statistic for this test was 184 (df = 14, p = 0.0001). This indicated that the overall fit of the model was very good and at least some of the explanatory variables' coefficients were not zero at alpha = 0.05. The results of the analysis of Maximum Likelihood Estimates (MLE) for the selectedpredicted probabilities for a discrete change in an independent variable is an alternative to the marginal effect that Long found more effective for interpreting a Binary Regression Model (Long, 1997). In the following interpretation, "discrete changes" were calculated for the eight significant independent variables.

Although sociodemographic variables were important in distinguishing bookers and lookers in some previous studies, except for education they were not significant in this model. Compared with those with only Bachelor's degrees, respondents with Master's or Doctoral degrees were more likely to book online. In other words, the more education the respondents had, the more likely they were to use the Internet for booking travel.

Specifically, the probability of booking online for a Master's degree holder was 0.16 greater than for those with a Bachelor's degree only, holding all other variables at their means. For those with Doctoral degrees, the probability of booking online was 0.27 greater than for those with a Bachelor's degree only, holding all other variables constant. The type of travel Web sites respondents visited most often also affected the probability of booking online. Those who most often visited the Web sites of online travel services, such as Travelocity.com, were more likely to reserve travel online than those who most often visited the Web sites of travel suppliers, travel agencies, tour operators, and travel guidebooks.

Specifically, for those who visited the Web sites of online travel services most often, the probability of being a booker was 0.13 higher than those who visited the Web sites of travel suppliers, and 0.17 higher than those who visited other travel Web sites, holding all other variables constant. People who had traveled to other countries in the past 12 months were more likely to be bookers than those who did not. For those who had traveled to another country once in the past 12 months, the probability of being a booker was 0.08 higher than those who had not traveled internationally. For those travelling to other countries twice in the past 12 months, the probability of being a booker was 0.07 higher than those with only one international trip, holding all other variables constant.

Factor Analysis

Using the sample of 248 bookers, factor analysis was again used to group the Internet perception variables. The same procedures were followed as in the comparison of bookers and lookers. First, the Kaiser's Measure of Sampling Adequacy (MSA) was checked, and the overall MSA was 0.799, indicating that the 22 perception variables met the fundamental requirements of sampling adequacy for factor analysis.

Four factors were retained based on a scree plot and the Schwarz's Bayesian Criterion (n = 4: SBC = -590). The Tucker and Lewis's Reliability Coefficient for these four factors was excellent at 0.90. The results were slightly different from those obtained in the analysis of bookers and lookers.

Stepwise Logistic Regression Analysis

Stepwise logistic regression analysis was performed to find a model for predicting bookers' probability of being repeat bookers. In total, 225 responses were used in this model selection procedure due to some missing values for household incomes. There were 157 re- peat and 68 one-time bookers. Initially, 25 variables were used in the stepwise logistic regression analysis. Both the entry alpha and stay alpha levels were set at 0.30.

It was not surprising to find that the significant variables in the final model were different from those in the logistic model for bookers and lookers. Twelve independent variables were retained in the model for distinguishing repeat and one-time bookers. Six of these variables were significant when using a Type I error probability alpha of 0.05 [travel products booked online last time, amount of use of the Internet per week, membership of frequent flyer programmes (FFPs), number of domestic trips, communicability, and age]. Only one Internet perception variable, communicability of booking online (p = 0.011), significantly affected both the probabilities of being bookers and of being repeat bookers in a positive way. The results of the analysis of MLE for the selected regression model. The amount of time per week spent online (p = 0.025) was strongly related to the probability of being a repeat booker. The longer respondents spent online per week, the more likely they were to be repeat bookers. For those respondents spending 5 to 9.9 hours a week online, the probability of being repeat bookers was 8.8per cent higher than those who only spent 4.9 hours or less online per week, holding other variables constant.

Another significant independent variable was membership in an FFP (p = 0.010), which greatly contributed to predicting the probability of being

Correct Incorrect

FFPs, their probability of being repeat bookers was 16.2per cent higher than non-members, holding all other variables at their means. The age of respondents positively affected their probability of being repeat bookers (p = 0.048). A classification table was developed to assess how well the model fit the data. The selected logistic model predicted 73.3per cent of the responses correctly. The sensitivity was 82.2per cent, showing that 82.2per cent of the event (being repeat bookers) responses were correctly predicted to be events. The specificity value was 52.9per cent, with 52.9per cent of the non-event responses correctly predicted to be non-events. The false-positive rate indicated that 19.9per cent of the predicted events were actually non-events, while the false-negative rate showed that 43.8per cent of the predicted non-events were events. Overall, the selected model performed well in identifying potential repeat online travel bookers.

FLIGHT CANCELLATION

Flight cancellation occurs when an airline cancels a scheduled flight for a certain reason. When flights are canceled, passengers may be entitled to compensation due to rules obeyed by every flight company, usually Rule 240, or Rule 218 in certain locations. This rule usually specifies that passengers may be entitled to certain reimbursements, including a free room if the next flight is the day after the canceled one, a choice of reimbursement, rerouting, phone calls, and refreshments.

FREQUENT-FLYER PROGRAMME

A frequent flyer programme (FFP) is a loyalty programme offered by many airlines. Typically, airline customers enrolled in the programme accumulate frequent flyer miles (kilometers, points, segments) corresponding to the distance flown on that airline or its partners. There are other ways to accumulate miles. In recent years, more miles were awarded for using co-branded credit and debit cards than for air travel. Acquired miles can be redeemed for free air travel; for other goods or services; or for increased benefits, such as travel class upgrades, airport lounge access or priority bookings. The first modern frequent flyer programme was created at Texas International Airlines in 1979.

But lacking the computer resources of its larger competitors, TI was overtaken by American's introduction of AAdvantage in May 1981. During the early days, several other carriers experimented with reward programmes, including Braniff International and Continental (OnePass). American's programme was a modification of a never-realised concept from 1979 that would have given special fares to frequent customers. It was quickly followed later that year by programmes from United (Mileage Plus) and Delta (SkyMiles), and in 1982 from British Airways (Executive Club). Since then, frequent-flyer programmes have grown enormously.

As of January 2005, a total of 14 trillion frequent-flyer miles had been accumulated by people worldwide, which corresponds to a total value of 700 billion US dollars. The primary method of obtaining points in a frequent flyer programme until recent years was to fly with the associated airline.

Most systems reward travellers with a specific number of points based on the distance traveled (such as 1 point per mile flown), although systems vary. Many discount airlines, rather than awarding points per mile, award points for flight segments in lieu of distance.

In Europe, for example, a number of airlines offer a fixed number of points for domestic or intra-European flights regardless of the distance (but varying according to class of travel). With the introduction of airline alliances and code-share flights, frequent flyer programmes are often extended to allow benefits to be used across partner airlines. The calculation method can become complicated, with additional points awarded as a 'cabin bonus' (usually as a percentage multiplier over the standard economy-class milage) for flying first or business class, and often fewer points given when flying on discounted economy tickets.

Additional bonus points are sometimes granted after members reach specific levels of flying activity. Programmes differ on the expiration of points. Some expire after a fixed time, and others expire if the account is inactive for an extended period (for example, three years). Many programmes also allow points to be obtained not only by flying but by favouring airline 'partners' on the ground. This an include staying at participating hotels, or renting a vehicle from a participating company. or shopping at a particular department store.

Other methods include credit and debit cards that offer points for charges made to the card, and systems which allow earn miles by eating at participating restaurants and charging the meals to registered cards.

Using credit and debit cards to earn points, as well as taking advantage of special promotional offers, can allow some people to earn an exceptionally high frequent flyer points with relatively minimal outlay. Many frequent flyer programmes identify travellers who fly more than a few times per year by awarding them different status levels, which in turn give a number of benefits.

Status levels vary from scheme to scheme, but benefits can include:

- Access to business and first class lounges with an economy ticket
- Access to other airlines' lounges
- Increased mileage accumulation (such as doubling or tripling)
- Reserving an unoccupied adjacent seat
- The ability to reserve specific seats, such as exit row seats with more leg room
- Free or discounted upgrades to a higher travel class
- Priority in waitlisting or flying standby
- Preference in not being bumped if a flight is oversold
- Priority of luggage (to be prioritized on transfer and to be displayed on the belt first)
- Waived or reduced fees (*e.g.,* baggage fees, service charges)
- Ability to grant status to another person
- Eliminating of program's miles expiration rules

Some programmes even permit elite members to reserve space on sold-out flights, giving members the ability of bumping regular passengers. In the US, member status is based on elite qualifying miles (EQM) or number of flight segments, not redeemable miles. Typically one elite qualifying mile is earned for each mile flown on a paid ticket, although there may be a percentage bonus for flying full-fare economy, business, or first class.

In addition, the airline may offer opportunities to earn elite qualifying miles in non-flying ways, often in connection with their branded credit card. There are usually many more ways to earn redeemable miles (which can be used for free tickets and other benefits) without flying than ways to earn elite qualifying miles. Some airlines will recognise a customer's status with a competing airline, and grant them the same benefits. Some airlines offer accelerated admission to their elite programmes through special promotions, such as flying 10,000 miles (16,000 km) of non-discounted coach fares or 20,000 miles (32,000 km) of discounted fares within three months gains a higher tier membership normally reserved for passengers flying 50,000 miles per year.

Travellers frequently debate how much accumulated miles are worth, something which is highly variable based on how they are redeemed. A typical ballpark figure is approximately 2 cents per mile based on discount (rather than full fare) economy class travel costs. However, most airlines have stringent capacity constraints on the number of "award" seats available, so some people argue that this ballpark figure is an overstatement. In this case, the value of a mile drops below a cent per mile. The airlines themselves value miles in their financial statements at less than one one-thousandth of a cent per mile. In contrast, calculating the value of a mile based on full-fare business class travel costs can yield a figure several times higher, but only if the customer would personally be willing to pay the multiple thousands of dollars such tickets would cost otherwise. However, a person paying a full business fare will be able to change flights on short notice without extra cost; a person flying business class on a free award ticket may find that last minute changes result in no award seat availability with the result that a ticket must be bought.

Increasing limitations on the availability of seats for point redemption, increases in services fees that airlines charge for redemption, and limitations on the transferability of redeemed tickets together have caused the value of miles to customers to decrease with time. Air New Zealand found a unique solution to this problem, by pegging their Airpoints scheme so one point (an "Airpoints Dollar") has the same value as one New Zealand dollar when purchasing. This approach has also been adopted by Canada's WestJet Airlines. In the wake of the September 11 attacks, some airlines have faced financial difficulties, raising concerns among frequent flyers that their points could be lost or devalued.

All airlines include provisos in their programme agreements reserving the right to modify or eliminate them on relatively short notice. But since miles are a strong customer incentive, troubled airlines avoid their elimination in bankruptcy proceedings, and indeed may expand them or make them more generous to elite members and high fare passengers in order to win sales. Furthermore, since most airline miles are never claimed, the programmes represent a relatively small liability, and indeed can represent a profit centre. Since the 1990s, U.S. airlines have sold billions of miles to partners such as credit cards, hotel chains, and car rental agencies, who offer this "currency" as an incentive to purchase their own services. Any effort to curtail the awarding of miles would thus endanger partner relations and another revenue stream.

Notably, the banks backing several airline-branded credit cards have been a key source of airline financing, including United Airlines (Chase), US Airways (Barclays), Delta Air Lines (American Express), Northwest Airlines (US Bank), American Airlines (Citibank), Continental Airlines (Chase) and Copa Airlines (Visa). Historically, the record is mixed. U.S. airlines have usually honoured miles held in the accounts of acquired airlines. For instance American Airlines converted members of TWA's "Aviators" programme to its own, as did Air Canada for Canadian Airlines' "Canadian Plus" programme members. Sometimes, miles were honoured by a close partner; Continental Airlines assumed Eastern Air Lines' programme when it failed, as did Delta of Pan Am's. Bankrupt Swissair miles were transferred to Swiss International Air Lines TravelClub who were transferred to Lufthansa's Miles and More after the acquisition of the Swiss carrier. Members are at greatest risk of losing their miles when an airline liquidates. All miles and privileges were lost, without recognition from any other carrier, as in the cases of Midway, Braniff, and Ansett

Australia. Business travellers typically accrue the valuable points in their own names, rather than the names of the companies that paid for the travel. This has raised concerns that the company is providing a tax-free benefit (point-based awards) to employees, or that employees have misappropriated value that belongs to the company, or even that the programme acts as a kind of bribe.

The U.S. Internal Revenue Service has not as yet made any move to tax mileage programmes, though for instance the Canadian taxation authorities consider mileage redeemed for free travel to be a taxable benefit. Most companies consider the miles earned by their employees to be a valuable personal perk that in part compensates for the daily grind of frequent business travel, though some governmental organizations have attempted to prevent their employees from accumulating miles on official travel. For example, Australian Public Servants are not permitted to redeem points accrued from official travel. Some programmes allow donating frequent flyer miles to certain charities. While the Canadian government will honour these donations as a charitable gift, the difficulty here is getting a tax receipt for those points from the company itself.

This policy also appears to conflict with the position that reward points are taxable in the first place. On the airline side, the points represent potential non-revenue travellers on its books. These must be carried forward on balance sheets as an outstanding contractual debt for an indeterminate time, although the actual value (or loss) may be difficult to determine for any particular period.

Africa:

- *Air Algérie Plus*: Miles expire after 24 months of inactivity
- *Air Seychelles:* All points acquired will have a 2 year validity period
- Ethiopian Airlines Sheba Miles
- *Royal Air Maroc Safar Flyer*: Miles expire 3 years after earning
- *South African Airways Voyager*: Miles expire after 36 months of inactivity

Asia:

- *Air China Phoenix*: Miles expire 2 complete calendar years after they are earned.
- *All Nippon Airways ANA Mileage Club*: Miles expire 36 months after they are earned, except for ANA Mileage Club Diamond elite members.
- *Asiana Club*: Expiry dates vary upon level of membership. Silver and Magic level members' miles expire after five years, Gold and higher level members' miles expire after seven. Corporate members have only one year to claim mileage. Miles earned before 30 September 2008 will never expire.
- *Bangkok Airways Flyer Bonus*: Miles expire 36 months after they are earned.

- Cathay Pacific/ DragonAir Asia Miles expire 36 months after they are earned.
- *EVA Air Evergreen Club*: Miles expire 36 months after being earned.
- *Garuda Indonesia*: Garuda Frequent Flyer (GFF) - Miles expire three years after being earned (effective from 01 January 2011, including miles earned before 01 January 2011)
- *Japan Airlines Mileage Bank*: Miles expire 36 months after being earned.
- *Jet Airways*: Miles expire after 13 quarters.
- *Korean Airlines SKYPASS*: Miles expire 10 years after being earned. Miles earned before 30 June 2008 will never expire.
- *Malaysia Airlines Enrich*: Miles expire one year after being earned, but members can extend the validity of their miles for an extra year after paying a fee to do so or by becoming Enrich Platinum elite members.
- *Royal Brunei Royal Skies*: Miles will never expire as long as there is eligible activity within three years.
- *Philippine Airlines Mabuhay*: Miles expire 36 months after being earned.
- *Shanghai Airlines*: Miles expire 2 complete calendar years after they are earned.
- *Singapore Airlines KrisFlyer*: Miles expire 36 months after being earned (can be extended up to 12 months for a fee).
- *Thai Airways International Royal Orchid Plus*: Miles earned in one calendar year will expire at the end of the third calendar year after accrual.
- *Vietnam Airlines Golden Lotus Programme*: Miles earned will expire two years after two years on the member's sign up anniversary month.

Europe:

- *Aeroflot Bonus*: Miles expire after 24 months since last flight activity
- *Aerosvit Meridian*: Miles expire after last day of 36th month
- *Air France/ KLM/ Air Europa Flying Blue*: Miles expire after 20 months of flight inactivity (for non-elite members)
- *Alitalia MilleMiglia*: Miles expire after 24 months since last flight activity
- *AirBaltic BalticMiles*: Reward miles expire after 3 years after the day they are first earned
- *BMI Diamond Club*: Miles expire after 24 months of inactivity
- *British Airways Executive Club*: Miles expire after 36 months of inactivity
- *Iberia Plus*: Miles expire after 24 months of inactivity
- *Malev Hungarian Airlines Duna Club*: In principle, Bonus Points

collected by travelling are valid for 3 years from the date of the trip (rounded up to the nearest quarter).

- Miles and More (Lufthansa, Air Dolomiti, Augsburg Airways, Contact Air, Eurowings, Austrian Airlines, Brussels Airlines, LOT Polish Airlines, Swiss International Air Lines as well as regional airlines: Adria Airways, Croatia Airlines and Luxair) - Miles expire 36 months after date of earning for non-elite members with no Lufthansa-branded credit card, or 36 months after loss of elite status for currently elite members.
- *Czech Airlines OK Plus*: Miles expire 2 years after last activity (redemptions do not count as activity).
- SAS EuroBonus (SAS, Blue1, Widerøe and Estonian Air) - Points expires 60 months after earning and/or purchasing the points.
- *Spanair Plus*: Miles expire 3 years after last activity.
- *Turkish Airlines MilesandSmiles*: Collected miles (flight, hotel stay, car rental) expire at the end of the third full calendar year following their collection.
- *TAP Victoria*: Miles expire 3 years after last activity. Paying a fee will extend miles for another 3 years.
- *Ukraine International Airlines Panorama*: Miles not expire.
- *Virgin Atlantic Flying Club*: Miles expire 3 years after last activity.
- *Vueling Airlines' punto.*: Points expire 3 years after accrual, or after 18 months of inactivity on the account.

Middle East:

- *Egyptair Plus*: Miles expire 3 years after earning. (Except for Egyptair Plus Platinum members)
- *El Al Matmid*: Points expire 3 years after earning
- *Middle East Airlines Cedar Miles*: Miles expire 5 years after earning.
- *Skywards*: Miles expire at the end of the month of the traveller's birth, 3 years after earning (however, you can use them to book a reward ticket that is valid for up to 12 months).

North America:

- *Air Canada Aeroplan*: Miles expire after 12 months of account inactivity or 7 years after they are earned, whichever occurs first.
- *AirTran A+ Rewards*: Credits expire 1 year after they are earned (2 years after earning with elite status or co-branded credit card).
- *Alaska Airlines and Horizon Air Mileage Plan*: Miles expire after 24 months of account inactivity.
- *American AAdvantage*: Miles expire after 18 months of account inactivity.
- *Continental OnePass*: Miles don't expire, however, accounts may be closed or miles forfeited after 18 months of account inactivity. Will be

combined with United's Mileage Plus programme on approval of the merger.

- *Delta SkyMiles*: Miles expire after 24 months of account inactivity (12 months for brand new members with no account activity).
- *Frontier EarlyReturns*: Miles expire after 2 complete calendar years of account inactivity.
- *Hawaiian HawaiianMiles*: Miles expire after 18 months of account inactivity.
- *JetBlue TrueBlue*: Credits expire 12 months after last flight or co-branded credit card activity.
- Midwest Miles expire after 3 years of account inactivity (beginning in January 2011, miles will expire after 24 months of inactivity).
- *Southwest Rapid Rewards*: Credits expire 2 complete calendar years after they are earned.
- *Spirit Airlines FREE SPIRIT*: 2,000 miles must be earned in a six-month rolling period to prevent expiration.
- *United Mileage Plus*: Miles expire after 18 months of account inactivity. Will absorb Continental's OnePass programme on approval of merger with Continental Airlines
- *US Airways Dividend Miles*: Miles expire after 18 months of account inactivity. Paying a fee will extend miles for another 18 months.
- *Virgin America eleVAte*: Miles earned after February 2010 expire after 18 months of account inactivity.

Oceania:

- *Air New Zealand Airpoints*: Gold and Gold Elite members' points do not expire as long as they retain at least Gold status. Silver and Jade members' points expire on the member's anniversary date following the date the point turns 4 years old.
- *Qantas Frequent Flyer*: Miles earned from 1 July 2010 will expire after 18 months of inactivity. Miles earned prior to that expire 3 years after last activity.

Central America:

- *TACA*: Miles expire after 24 months of inactivity.

South America:

- *LAN Airlines*: LANPASS Kilometers do not expire unless the passenger has not earned kilometers by flying with LAN after 36 months.
- *TAM Airlines TAM Fidelidade*: Miles expire 24 months after they are earned.
- *Peruvian Airlines*: Peruvian Pass accumulated miles do not expire.

A mileage run is an airline trip designed and taken solely to gain maximum frequent flyer miles, points or status. If a traveller has already achieved some sort of elite status they will be earning bonus miles on top of their actual flight miles, and consequently they will reach their goal sooner. A mileage run may allow a traveller to (re-)qualify for a beneficial elite level which requires a minimum amount of miles for qualification.

BOARDING PASS

A boarding pass is a document provided by an airline during checkin, giving a passenger the authority to board an aircraft. As a minimum, it identifies the passenger, the flight number, and the date and scheduled time for departure. In some cases, flyers can check in "on-line" and print the boarding passes themselves. Generally a passenger with an electronic ticket will only need a boarding pass. If a passenger has a paper airline ticket, that ticket (or flight coupon) may be required to be attached to the boarding pass for him or her to board the aircraft.

The paper boarding pass (and ticket, if any), or portions, are sometimes collected and counted for cross-check of passenger counts by gate agents, but more frequently are scanned (via barcode or magnetic stripe). The standards for bar codes and magnetic stripes on boarding passes are published by IATA. The bar code standard (BCBP) defines the 2D bar code printed on paper boarding passes or sent to mobile phones for electronic boarding passes. The magnetic stripe standard (ATB2) will expire in 2010. For "connecting flights" there will be a boarding pass needed for each new flight (distinguished by a different flight number) regardless of whether a different aircraft is boarded.

Most airports and airlines have automatic readers that will verify the validity of the boarding pass at the jetway door or boarding gate. This also automatically updates the airline's database that shows the passenger has boarded and the seat is used, and that the checked baggage for that passenger may stay aboard. This speeds up the paperwork process at the gate, but requires passengers with paper tickets to check in, surrender the ticket and receive the digitized boarding pass.

Many airlines have moved to issuing electronic boarding passes, whereby the passenger checks in either online or on a mobile device, and the boarding pass is then sent to the mobile device as a SMS or e-mail; airlines that issue electronic boarding passes include United Airlines, AirAsia (The first airline to introduce SMS boarding passes), Singapore Airlines, Air Canada, WestJet (the first in North America to do so), Cathay Pacific Airways, Delta Airlines, JetBlue Airways, American Airlines, Lufthansa, Scandinavian Airlines, Jetstar Airways, Iberia and KLM (selected destinations only).

ELECTRONIC TICKET

An electronic ticket or e-ticket is used to represent the purchase of a seat on a passenger airline, usually through a web site or by telephone, or sometimes through airline ticket offices or travel agencies. This form of airline ticket rapidly replaced the older multi-layered paper tickets (from close to zero to 100 per cent in about 10 years) and became mandatory for IATA members as from June 1, 2008. During the last few years, where paper tickets were still available, airlines frequently charged extra for issuing them.

E-tickets are also available for some entertainment venues. Once a reservation is made, an e-ticket exists only as a digital record in the airline computers. Customers usually print out a copy of their receipt which contains the record locator or reservation number and the e-ticket number. The critical acclaim, Joel R. Goheen is recognized as the Inventor of Electronic Ticketing in the Airline Industry, an industry where global electronic ticket sales (the industry standard) accounts for over US$400 billion a year (2007). Electronic tickets have been introduced in road, urban or rail public transport as well.

CHECKING IN WITH AN E-TICKET

To check in with an e-ticket, the passenger usually goes to the check-in counter and presents the e-ticket itinerary receipt which contains a confirmation or reservation code. In some airports and airlines it is not even necessary to present this document or quote the confirmation code or e-ticket number as the reservation is confirmed solely on the basis of the passenger's identity, which may be proven by a passport or the matching credit card. The rest of the check-in process remains the same as when paper tickets were the norm, that is, the passenger checks-in his/her luggage. The e-ticket is not a substitute for the boarding pass which must still be issued at the end of the check-in process.

SELF-SERVICE AND REMOTE CHECK-IN

E-tickets are very popular because they allow extra services like:

- Online access to a passenger's reservation which makes amendments to flight plans (such as change of flight date and refunds) possible (subject to ticket restrictions)
- Online/telephone/self-service kiosk check-in (if the airline makes this option available)
- Early check-in
- Printing boarding passes at airport kiosks and at locations other than an airport

It is also possible to have many copies of an e-ticket, hence the "loss" of an airline ticket becomes impossible. Several web sites exist to help people holding e-tickets accomplish online check-ins in advance of the twenty-four-hour airline restriction. These sites store a passenger's flight information and then when the airline opens up for online check-in the data is transferred to the airline and the boarding pass is e-mailed back to the customer.

E-TICKET LIMITATIONS

E-tickets are sometimes not available for some flights from an airline which usually offers them. This can be due to a number of reasons, the most common being software incompatibility. If an airline issues tickets for a codeshare flight with another company, and there is no e-ticket interlining agreement, the operating carrier would not be able to see the issuing carrier's ticket.

Therefore, the carrier that books the flight needs to provide hard copy versions of the tickets so that the ticket can be processed. Similarly, if the destination airport does not have access to the airline who booked the flight, a paper ticket needs to be issued. Currently the ticketing systems of most airlines are only able to produce e-tickets for itineraries of no more than 16 segments, including surface segments.

IATA MANDATED TRANSITION

As part of the IATA Simplifying the Business initiative, the association instituted a programme to switch the industry to 100 per cent electronic ticketing. The programme concluded on June 1, 2008, with the association saying that the resulting industry savings were approximately US$3 billion. In 2004, IATA Board of Governors set the end of 2007 as the deadline for airlines to make the transition to 100 per cent electronic ticketing for tickets processed through the IATA billing and settlement plan; in June 2007, the deadline was extended to May 31, 2008.

As of June 1, 2008 paper tickets can no longer be issued on neutral stock by agencies reporting to their local BSP. Agents reporting to the ARC using company-provided stock or issuing tickets on behalf of an airline (GSAs and ticketing offices) are not subject to that restriction. The industry was unable to comply with the IATA mandate and paper tickets remain in circulation as of February 2009.

ROUND-THE-WORLD TICKET

A round-the-world ticket (also known as round-the-world fare or RTW ticket in short) is a product that enables travellers to fly around the world for a relatively low price. RTW tickets have existed for some time and in the past were generally offered through marketing agreements between airlines on several continents. Now, they are almost universally offered by airline alliances such as SkyTeam, Star Alliance and Oneworld, or else by specialist travel agencies that will spend time helping customise a trip to the consumer's needs. They are priced according to class of service, origin of travel, number of continents, mileage (usually between 30,000 and 60,000 km), and sometimes season of travel.

The traveller benefits from the large and optimised network of the airline alliance and can participate in the alliance's frequent flyer programmes.

However, these tickets are usually subject to restrictions. The start and end of the journey almost always have to be located in the same country and exactly one crossing each of the Atlantic and Pacific must be included in the itinerary.

The number of stops is usually restricted to 5-16, and backtracking between continents (especially Europe/Asia) is often restricted. The dates and journey do not have to be pre-planned, but may be changed en route at a local office of any airline in the alliance (although a change of destinations often results in an additional fee, and if the next flight is left open-dated the booking can be dropped by the airlines' computers). Prices vary but are generally in the range of $3000-5000 USD for an economy class ticket. An alternative for a round-the-world ticket is a continent pass.

SPECIALIST TRAVEL AGENCIES

It is possible to piece together a round-the-world route by combining one-way tickets on various airlines without resorting to alliances. In addition, discounts often apply to some long- and short-haul legs. The only practical way to do this — since it requires both knowledge and contacts — is to go to a travel agent who specializes in round-the-world itineraries.

These can be found in major cities that are transit hubs — San Francisco, London, New York, Bangkok, etc. — and many of them also provide services online. The booking process can take a few days or weeks depending on how fast you wish to expedite the process. These agents will get parts of your ticket issued by their contacts in other countries or in-house contracts. This can save a lot of money over the airlines.

TRACKING TRANSACTION

An advanced computer-based electronic security management system is instrumental in making the Mirage Resort Hotel a progressive facility. Security has assumed an increasingly important role in the hotel business. The larger the facility and the more diverse the features, services, and amenities, the more demanding the need for comprehensive security management.

Nowhere is this more evident than at a 100-acre entertainment complex like the Mirage Resort Hotel in Las Vegas, where security concerns are heightened by the cash-intensive casino operation. The creation of a fully integrated security environment at the Mirage represents an exciting new dimension in security management.

Opened in 1989, the desert resort is among the most progressive facilities of its type. The Mirage has three 30-story towers and more than 3,000 rooms, including suites, villas, and bungalows with private pools. Two ballrooms, at 20,000- and 40,000-square feet, are available for special events, and meeting rooms can handle groups up to 5,000 people. The complex includes waterfalls, an erupting volcano, a tropical plant atrium, and an artificial coral reef aquarium with sharks and tropical fish. Also available for the enjoyment of guests and visitors are natural animal habitats: one for a pair of rare Royal White tigers, the other for six Atlantic Bottlenose dolphins. An array of entertainment, recreational, and shopping opportunities are featured, including a 1,500-seat theater and around-the-clock casino operations. Guests can find restaurants, health and fitness centres, interconnected lagoon-shaped swimming pools, boutiques, and lounges. Special events such as prize fights and boat and auto shows compound the importance of security.

Security control in a gaming resort as large and complex as the Mirage is a demanding and never-ending challenge. Sophisticated security controls are in force in the casino, where millions of dollars are transacted every hour in games, including slot machines, video poker, keno, craps, blackjack, baccarat, and poker. Strict compliance with gaming laws and established casino procedures is controlled by close supervision, surveillance, and carefully monitored audits. An advanced computer-based electronic security management system, the Polaroid ID-2000 Plus, plays a central role in supporting the Mirage's integrated security environment. The system has proven to be a formidable management tool. Designed for expansion, the modular system is a core component in the recording and payroll programme.

The system combines advanced data base, computer, and electronic imaging technologies. It provides, for example, a streamlined ID card and badge production capability and a responsive, economical way to manage employee-related security information. The system also serves as an auditing aid to track activities, such as the number of meals served to employees in the cafeteria each day. Swipe readers at cash registers in the cafeteria make the process fast and efficient.

Specific information about the resort's 7,000 employees is input, stored, and retrieved by the digital electronic security management system. It captures image data, including colour portraits and signatures; generates photo ID cards and management reports; and communicates with other data bases. Report-generating capabilities simplify the tracking of ID cards that have been issued for active and former employees. The system also facilitates the monitoring of staff levels. The electronic production and data base system is connected to a file server in the computer centre. Several sites are now on-line by means of a local area network using standard Ethernet connections and Novell network software. Additional terminals or systems can be added for expansion. One of the locations integrated by the LAN is the ID card and badge production centre in the human resources department. New employees are processed and badged at this location; other areas on the network use the system to validate employee security information.

Verification terminals are installed in the security and finance departments, casino surveillance, and the casino cash cage. Authorized individuals can validate, on-screen, employee photos, signatures, and related data. Although verification information is easily obtained by entering an employee number, access to the complete data base is limited to supervisory personnel. Information available for access includes the employee's full name, signature sample, colour portrait, ID number, job title, work location, and date of hire or termination. The individual's affiliation as a Mirage employee or corporate employee is shown. Powering the system is a high-speed 386 CPU using special workstation software, which incorporates password authorization and an internal audit trail to prevent system abuse.

Using an optional 180 megabyte magnetic disk, the Mirage system can store approximately 14,000 full-colour portraits or 11,500 portraits and signatures. Optional storage modules, including larger capacity magnetic disk drives and optical disk drives, are available. Active files, including signatures, colour portraits, and related textual information, are safely stored in digital format on the hard disk. Safety backups of the complete system are made on magnetic tape by the computer centre at least three times a week. If an employee is terminated or quits, the photo and signature files are deleted to save storage space. Text files, however, are stored indefinitely.

Information systems helped define the requirements and objectives of the departments involved. The system has improved productivity on several operating levels. Working closely with Polaroid engineers, information systems developed a maintenance strategy with flexible service levels and contingency provisions for priority service in designated areas. If emergency maintenance service is required, downtime in critical operations will be minimized. Producing more than 6,000 ID CARDS a year could be an expensive, time-consuming operation. For the Mirage's human resources department, however, it is merely routine. Human resources is responsible for processing new employees, issuing new ID cards and badges, replacing damaged or lost badges, and responding to the continuing need for special events badges. To handle the challenges of ID card production the company relies on the production speed and efficiency of the computer-based security management system.

"Compared to the marathon effort involved in producing new ID cards when the Mirage first opened," reflects Monalee Stockner, human resources supervisor, "normal day-to-day activities are calm." ID cards were produced for more than 7,000 employees by the human resources team, with assistance from several temporary employees and a few of the management system devices on loan from Polaroid. Employee processing and imaging activities were completed during a five-day whirlwind operation involving 10- to 12-hour shifts. Cards were assembled at night. According to Stockner, "Without the speed and automated features of the computerized production system, the job could not have been done as quickly, economically, or efficiently." The electronic production workstation includes an operator console consisting of a colour video camera, electronic flash lighting, portrait and text monitors, keyboard, and a signature capture device. A colour film recorder, film cutter, laminator, and print development timers are included in the output unit. Information acquisition for an ID card, including text entries and video imaging of the subject's portrait and signature, takes less than five minutes per person. The badge is given to the employee the same day. Temporary special event IDs are produced for employees assigned to such activities as large parties, banquets, conventions, and prize fights. Since the Mirage was opened, more than 50,000 employee ID cards have been produced.

An operator can enter employee information and capture, digitally store, and retrieve high-fidelity colour portraits and signatures or access data from existing computer data bases. A freeze-frame feature allows the operator to preview and freeze the subject's video portrait before the card is made. A built-in signature capture camera stores signatures from a signed signature card. At the touch of a button the system electronically merges the digitized video portrait, signature, text, and multicolour Mirage logo contained in the software package. Information entered is contained on a new-hire document prepared by the employee's department. It includes pertinent information about the employee, his or her job title, and where he or she works.

ID cards can be produced in many of visual formats. More than a dozen variations are used by the Mirage to distinguish between different personnel classifications and affiliations. These include Mirage employees, corporate staff, and contractors. Special formats have also been developed for restricted areas or for temporary use at special events. Although the electronic security management system can automatically assign sequential employee numbers, human resources prefers to control this function. In this way, blocks of numbers can be reserved for special applications in the system. When the employee number is entered, a bar code representing the number is automatically generated and printed on an adhesive-back label by a printer. Inexpensive, hard-copy, black-and-white thermal reference images can also be produced in seconds by a printer at the production station.

With a single keystroke, electronically assembled images for two separate employee badges are exposed on a sheet of instant colour print film. Development takes about a minute. Prints are then die-cut and inserted into a special laminate sandwich with a printed insert containing card use guidelines and the bar code label. The envelope is then permanently sealed. The finished card is attractive, durable, and virtually tamperproof. After lamination the bar code is verified with a test device, which displays the employee number.

REMOTELY LOCATED VERICATION

Terminals integrated through the LAN facilitate employee recognition, signature validation, and confirmation of employment status. In addition to the information verification capabilities of the production workstation, data verification terminals on the network provide valuable information for security and management-related functions. Security staff. Responsible for the safety of patrons and protection of the Mirage's physical assets, the security staff also plays an active role in maintaining guest relations and providing emergency services. The 275-person security staff, larger than the police departments of many small cities, operates around the clock.

Security's responsibilities include controlling access in restricted areas, knowing the location of employees in emergencies, and monitoring property removal. "The ability to access an employee's security records in seconds, to determine where they can be located, saves valuable time in an emergency," says Jennifer Keeney, security coordinator. "We can locate an employee quickly, for example, should there be an emergency at home, without having to make lots of phone calls and be faced with unnecessary delays. We can see what the person looks like and even get fast thermal prints to help our staff recognize the person. In emergencies, visual recognition is extremely important, especially with a workforce involving thousands of people."

Photo ID badges need not be worn in most areas. Employees can carry the ID card in a wallet or purse. In instances where individuals are not recognized by security personnel at employee entrances or in restricted areas, they will be asked to show their ID card. ID information for new hires or terminated employees is available at all verification terminals on a same-day basis. In yet another important function, the ability to compare signatures with samples stored in the security management system's digital memory has streamlined the Mirage's property removal procedures. Because signatures of people authorized to approve property passes can be easily validated, it is now easier to control the removal of property. Thermal prints of authorized signatures for property removal forms are kept on file and current at various security stations.

Casino surveillance. Rapid information verification is critical for the casino surveillance group. Operating around the clock, 365 days a year, a team of trained observers keeps a watchful eye on cash transactions, operational procedures, and dealer interactions with patrons. Patricia Cipolla, director of surveillance, is emphatic about the importance of security control. "Our job," she states, "is to protect the Mirage's assets and its patrons. We watch the money and the way the games are run. Any deviation in established procedures signals that something may be wrong."

Ceiling-mounted video cameras can record the activities at any game in the casino. Videotapes of randomly selected games or those being monitored are available for review on video monitors located in the surveillance area. Should a transaction involving markers, redemption slips, bills, and credits, or a dealer's performance deviate from established guidelines, information about the dealer can be accessed instantly. Since the videotape can be seen in normal or close-up modes, surveillance specialists start the process by zooming in on the dealer's name badge. By entering the name at the verification terminal, employee information is instantly displayed, including a colour portrait and signature sample.

If irregularities are observed, other than what appears to be an honest mistake, the surveillance team may continue monitoring the dealer. A random check of a particular table could, for example, reveal a disparity between the dealer's photo and the name shown on the badge. This disparity would be checked out immediately with a casino supervisor. In other instances, the dealer's name may not appear on the casino schedule for the shift. The disparity could be attributed to a last-minute schedule change, which can be easily verified by calling the floor supervisor. Occasionally, casino accounting is advised that an audit of documents pertaining to a particular game may be warranted. "Instant access to employee information, especially ID pictures, makes our job a lot easier," says Cipolla. "It often took hours or days to scour through computer printouts to pinpoint the person involved in a specific transaction. The task can now be done in minutes.

The search process, which also involved phone calls to casino supervisors, wasted valuable time, was cumbersome, and expensive." Casino accounting. Casino accounting operates two shifts a day and is responsible for important audit functions for the Mirage's gaming activities. The department is responsible for maintaining the casino's operational integrity and for strict compliance with established procedures. Timely information about gaming activities and people who authorize transactions is necessary for effective management. "The most important piece of information available," comments Robert Galvin, casino accounting manager, "is an employee's ID number.

For us, it provides the means to access a key piece of data, employee signature samples." The accounting department's data verification terminal provides instant access to information needed for transaction audits. Matching photos to names or comparing signature samples with those appearing on documents is extremely helpful. Cash cage. Because of the large amounts of money involved, the casino cash cage may require complete ID verification, including signatures and photos of unfamiliar people. In the past, matching signatures on cash disbursement forms or receipts to signature cards took hours or even days to accomplish. It now takes minutes.

Performing rapid searches of information with specific parameters, such as name, employee number, title, department, and job description, has resulted in significant productivity improvement. "Immediate access to essential information," says Galvin, "has resulted in better control, increased audit speed, and reduced labour hours. Since we've been linked to the security management system, productivity has improved dramatically." The verification terminal, also used by internal auditing and gaming control board personnel, allows greater audit frequency and improved monitoring of money flow. An innovative time and attendance system, to be fully implemented by early 1993, is being phased into the Mirage's operations on a controlled schedule. The ambitious undertaking is expected to produce enormous cost savings and efficiency improvements while providing significant benefits for both employees and management.

As an integral part of a comprehensive management control system, badges provide the media for time clock entries. According to Ernie Pearce, director of information systems, "The new time and attendance system, now in use by several departments, is one of the most progressive programmes to be introduced at the Mirage. The sophisticated, computerized time-keeping and payroll system improves the interaction between supervisors and the workforce. It also eliminates many of the payroll-related transaction errors that inconvenienced employees and wasted valuable company time.

"The ability to use the benefits of the security management system's large data base, along with the photo ID badge as a clock entry system," continues Pearce, "provides important functional and economic advantages." Using sophisticated computer-based time clocks with bar code readers, the new system integrates employee work-time and payroll information with the security management data base. In this way, a long-standing information gap has been bridged. The new, high-tech computer-based clocks—to be located at every work location—will allow employees to use their ID cards to log in and out in a virtually error-free system.

The "smart" clocks are programmed with all the necessary operating parameters. These include authorized clock locations for different departments, employees' normal start and stop times, and overtime pay scales, including holidays, IRS regulations, and applicable union rules. The new system will improve efficiency and minimize transaction discrepancies, such as illegible manual entries. It will also eliminate time-keeping problems for people working at remote locations or whose work locations vary. In the past, bar codes have been used only to track the number of meals served in the cafeteria. With the new time-keeping system, however, they will play a more significant role in overall efficiency.

An opaque strip covering the bar code prevents tampering and reduces the likelihood that copies could be used to fool the clocks. Appearing opaque to the eye and to copy machines, the protected bar code is scanned without difficulty by bar code readers. Applied to the inside of the laminate envelope, the strip is considered tamperproof. The Mirage's electronic security management system, which has been in operation for more than two years, has provided cost-effective solutions for a variety of problems. Software-driven and modular, important upgrades can be achieved simply by replacing a disk or a module. The combined data base, management, and electronic imaging system is easy to use, requires minimal training, and is inexpensive to operate. During its first 18 months of operation the system was on-line 24 hours a day, seven days a week, with virtually trouble-free performance.

An international company was preparing to evacuate 15 expatriate employees and dependents from a country that had suffered an earthquake. When it came time to meet at the departure point, 25 people showed up. Those arranging for the evacuation had not known that two technical teams were in the country supporting clients at the time. The additional evacuees, who had heard of the evacuation informally from individuals at the local office, disrupted the company's plan. There were not enough vehicles to get everyone to the airport in one trip, and there were not enough seats on the airplane that had been reserved.

The other employees had made their way to the departure point hoping to get a seat because the local office employee did not tell them of the limited transportation or inform them that it would be safer to wait in the hotel until other transportation could be arranged. The company evacuated the 15 people originally expected at that time, and the additional 10 employees were flown out two days later. This meant that an evacuation that should have been completed in approximately 12 hours— from when the employees and dependents arrived at the rendezvous point until they actually departed—ended up lasting 60 hours. Fortunately, everyone was able to get out safely, but the delay could have been disastrous.

As companies seek new business in far-flung markets, their employees increasingly need to travel and work around the globe. Companies must be prepared to help these employees through any contingencies, including earthquakes, civil unrest, and other crises. While some risks are greater in developing countries, emergency situations requiring evacuation can arise anywhere. For instance, Singapore, a relatively safe and natural-disaster-free city, suffered from severe smog in 1999 as the result of forest fires that were raging in nearby Indonesia. The conditions made the city unbearable and forced many foreign personnel to evacuate.

Other examples of such incidents include an earthquake in Taiwan, civil unrest in Indonesia, a coup in Fiji, and the invasion of Kuwait—all of which necessitated the evacuation of international personnel. Most companies with international operations have detailed plans in place for evacuating their expatriate personnel should the local security situation deteriorate or in case of a natural disaster. But as the case highlighted at the beginning of this article illustrates, these plans often fail to address the evacuation of another category of employees; Those who are visiting on a business trip when a disaster strikes.

The evacuation of international travellers often falls between the travel advisory service, which provides employees with information on areas where it might be dangerous to travel, and evacuation planning efforts, which focus on expatriate personnel based in the country. Many companies do not even know how many employees are visiting a particular international location. In the event of an emergency, they might spend hours, if not days, trying to determine which employees are there. This problem especially affects companies that are organized along functional lines rather than geographically. It is not uncommon for an in-country office to report to a certain department, such as marketing. Personnel from other departments might travel in and out of the country without ever contacting the local office.

To avoid confusion, companies must coordinate their travel security and international evacuation programmes. Corporate security should serve as a central point for activity and information related to evacuation planning, coordinating the role of other players in the travel process, such as internal departments, travel service providers, employees, host country offices, and hotels. How travel information is collected, maintained, and distributed will vary among companies. Generally, however, security should not bother with routine tracking of employee travel plans. Instead, the security department can enlist the help of various internal departments to ensure that it is able to locate employees on travel in an emergency. For example, security should ask human resources or travel service providers to collect the data on employee travel.

In an emergency, security will know that it can turn to this resource for the information. Security may want to ask the company's public relations department to communicate the details of the travel and evacuation plan to staff as part of the internal communications programme.

TRAVEL SERVICE PROVIDER

A company's travel service provider, whether a company employee or outside firm, can play an important role in gathering information about employees traveling abroad. Generally, these firms keep detailed records for billing purposes, and those records can help the security department to determine the location of employees when needed. The travel service company could also provide weekly or daily reports of which employees are traveling and to where. In addition to regular reports, the travel service provider should be able to give the company access to its staffs travel records 24 hours a day in case of an emergency. Many companies have erroneously assumed that they could get the necessary staff location information from travel service providers in an emergency.

The provider can also be required to book only designated hotels, perhaps ones where corporate security has verified the safety and security of the facility. In addition, because travel itineraries often change while employees are on the road, if the travel service provider has an office in a host country, employees can contact it to change hotel and flight reservations rather than going directly to the hotel or airline. This means that the changes will immediately be keyed into the system, and the information can be distributed to the corporate security department or another internal point of contact, such as human resources.

In addition, the provider can be asked to include emergency telephone numbers and procedures with each airline ticket issued to employees. The security department should periodically audit the programme for tracking employee travel to make sure that the records are being kept and that the contact telephone numbers and other information are all up to date. It also might be useful to test the programme under simulated conditions.

At the same time, security needs to keep the travel agent advised of any high-risk areas so that he or she can caution current or future travellers or, in serious cases, refer them back to security. In companies where there is an approval system for travel, those responsible for approving travel requests must be brought into the system so that they don't approve travel to "no-go" areas.

EMPLOYEES

In many cases, employees make their own travel changes by contacting the airline or hotel directly, or they use the hotel concierge or business centre. Employees should be required to advise a designated corporate contact or the travel service provider of these changes. Some companies now require employees to submit weekly movement sheets listing travel destinations and contact details for the week to come. It is generally advisable to include these schedules with some other form of business report, such as the employees' weekly progress or sales reports, to increase the level of compliance.

One multinational telecommunications company, which has employees traveling to more than 20 countries every day of the year, implemented a Web-based itinerary tracking system to allow employees to update their travel schedules online. Employees can use any computer with Internet access to enter the password-protected site and update their information.

7

Airline Travelling Management

AIRLINE INDUSTRY

Significant Points: Although flight crews-pilots and flight attendants-are the most visible occupations, the vast majority of the industry's employees work in ground occupations. Senior pilots for major airlines are among the highest paid workers in the nation. A bachelor's degree is increasingly required or preferred for most pilot and flight attendant jobs. More than 45 percent of workers are members of unions or covered by a union contract.

Nature of the Industry: Air travel in the US grew at a rapid pace until 2001, expanding from 172 million passenger enplanements in 1970 to nearly 615 million in 2000. However, over the next 3 years, a combination of factors-the events of September 11th, 2001, an economic recession and other factors-combined to reduce traffic back to 1995 levels. Nevertheless, air travel remains one of the most popular modes of transportation.

Airlines in this industry transport passengers and freight over regularly scheduled routes or on routes, called "charters," specifically designed for a group of travellers or a particular cargo. Several classes of airlines function in the United States. There are 14 major passenger airlines- 11 passenger and 3 all cargo, which the US Department of Transportation defines as having operating revenues of more than $1 billion. The largest of these, often called the "Big Six," generally operate hub-and-spoke systems and also fly internationally.

A hub is a centrally-located airport designated by an airline to receive a large number of its flights from many locations and at which passengers can transfer to flights to any of the locations served by the airline's system. In this way, the greatest number of passengers, from as many locations as possible, can be served in the most efficient way.

In competition with the Big Six are 6 to 10 low-cost low-fare carriers. These carriers have traditionally not used hub and spoke systems and offered flights between limited numbers of cities. They have primarily focused on flying shorter routes (400 miles or less) and on serving leisure travellers. But some low-fare carriers are expanding their routes to include longer transcontinental and non-stop flights. These moves have helped low-fare carriers expand their customer base to include more business travellers. Another type of passenger airline carrier is the commuter or regional carrier. There are approximately 25 to 30 of these carriers. Regional airlines operate short- and medium-haul scheduled airline service connecting smaller communities with larger cities and with hubs.

Some of the largest regional carriers are subsidiaries of the major airlines, but most are independently owned, often contracting their services to the majors. The regional airlines' fleet consists primarily of smaller 19- to 68-seat turboprop and 30- to 100-seat jet aircraft. The regional airlines are the fastest growing segment of commercial aviation with 1 out of every 8 domestic airline passengers flying on a regional airline during at least part of his or her trip.

Air cargo is another sector of the airline industry. Cargo can be carried in cargo holds of passenger airlines or on aircraft designed exclusively to carry freight. Cargo carriers in this industry do not provide door-to-door service. Instead, they provide only air transport from an airport near the cargo's origin to an airport near the cargo's destination. Companies in the couriers and messengers industry provide door-to-door delivery of parcels either across town or across the continent.

Most sectors of the airline industry were in a downturn in 2002, with several passenger airlines having declared bankruptcy and others on the verge of doing so. After 6 relatively successful years in the late 1990's, fuelled by an increase in passenger volume and a booming economy, the growth in airline passenger traffic began to slow in 2001, coinciding with the economic recession. After the tragic events of September 11, 2001, passenger traffic dropped steeply, causing airlines to cut flights, lay off workers and park surplus aircraft. Although passenger volume has since recovered somewhat, the growth rate in the industry will likely continue to be depressed for several years.

As the low-fare airlines continue to take market share away from the higher cost major airlines and as passenger traffic remains lower, managing costs has become more critical to the survival of some airlines. Labour costs are the airlines' largest cost component-amounting to 38 percent of some airlines' operating costs-and reducing these costs is a key part of the recovery plans of several major airlines.

Because the number of aircraft flight personnel often is fixed by passenger safety regulations, reducing costs usually involves getting the unions representing workers in the air transportation industry to renegotiate their contracts and agree to reduce wages.

The airline industry faces many challenges in the future. Airlines must focus on cost control, cash preservation and cautious growth. The goal of the industry is to be prepared to respond quickly to economic recovery. Passenger volume should slowly improve, but it will take longer for rapid employment growth to return to the air transportation industry.

Working Conditions: Working conditions in air transportation vary widely, depending on the occupation. Although most employees work in fairly comfortable surroundings, such as offices, terminals, or airplanes, mechanics and others who service aircraft are subject to noise, dirt and grease and sometimes work outside in bad weather.

In 2002, the air transportation industry had 11.8 injuries and illnesses per 100 full-time workers, compared with 5.3 throughout private industry. Virtually all work-related fatalities resulted from transportation accidents. Because airlines operate flights at all hours of the day and night, many workers have irregular hours or variable work schedules. Flight and ground personnel, including mechanics and reservation and transportation ticket agents, may have to work at night or on weekends or holidays.

Flight personnel may be away from their home bases frequently. When they are away from home, the airlines provide them with hotel accommodations, transportation between the hotel and airport and an allowance for meals and expenses. Flight attendants typically fly from 75 to 85 hours a month. In addition to flight time, they have about 50 hours a month duty time between flights. Flight crews, especially those on international routes, often suffer jet lag-disorientation and fatigue caused by flying into different time zones. Because employees must report for duty well-rested, they must allow ample time to rest during their layovers.

Employment: The air transportation industry provided 559,000 wage and salary jobs in 2002. Most employment is found in larger establishments-nearly 2 out of 3 jobs are in establishments with 1,000 or more workers. However, nearly three-fourths of all establishments employ fewer than 20 workers.

Most air transportation jobs are at major airports located close to cities. A substantial proportion are at airports that serve as central hubs for major airlines.

Occupations in the Industry: Although pilots and flight attendants are the most visible occupations in this industry, almost 70 percent of all employees in air transportation work on the ground in what are called ground occupations.

Two of the largest ground occupations are aircraft and avionics equipment mechanics and service technicians and reservation and transportation ticket agents and travel clerks.

Aircraft and avionics equipment mechanics and service technicians service, inspect and repair planes. They may work on several different types of aircraft, such as jet transports, small propeller-driven airplanes, or helicopters. Many specialize working on either the airframe (the body of the aircraft), the power-plant (the engines), or avionics (the parts of an aircraft that depend on electronics, such as navigation and communication equipment). In small, independent repair shops, mechanics and technicians usually inspect and repair many different types of aircraft. Some mechanics and technicians specialize in scheduled maintenance required by the Federal Aviation Administration (FAA).

Following a schedule based on the number of hours flown, calendar days, cycles of operation, or a combination of these factors, mechanics inspect the engines, landing gear, instruments and other parts of aircraft and perform necessary maintenance and repairs. A reservation and transportation ticket agent is most often the first employee passengers meet after entering the airport. Ticket agents work at airport ticket counters and boarding gates and use computers to provide customer service to incoming passengers.

They can make and confirm reservations, sell tickets and issue boarding passes. They also may work in call centres, answering phone inquiries about flight schedules and fares, verifying reservations, issuing tickets and handling payments. Customer service representatives assist passengers, check tickets when passengers board or disembark from an airplane and check luggage at the reception area and ensure that it is placed on the proper carrier.

They assist elderly or handicapped persons and unaccompanied children in claiming personal belongings and baggage and in getting on and off the plane. They also may provide assistance to passengers who become ill or injured. Other ground occupations include airplane cargo and freight agents, who take orders from shippers and arrange for transportation of their goods. Baggage handlers, classified under labourers and freight, stock and material movers, hand are responsible for loading and unloading passengers' baggage.

They stack baggage on specified carts or conveyors to see that it gets to the proper destination and also return baggage to passengers at airline terminals. Aircraft cleaners clean aircraft interiors after each flight. Flight crewmembers make up 31 percent of air transportation employment and include pilots and flight attendants. Aircraft pilots, co-pilots and flight engineers are highly trained professionals who fly and navigate jet and turboprop airplanes. Generally, the most experienced pilot, or captain, is in command and supervises all other crewmembers.

The pilot and copilot split flying and other duties such as communicating with air traffic controllers and monitoring the instruments. Some aircraft have a third pilot in the cockpit-the flight engineer or second officer-who assists the other pilots by monitoring and operating many of the instruments and systems and watching for other aircraft. Most newer aircraft are designed to be flown without a flight engineer.

Small aircraft and helicopters that transport passengers and cargo and perform activities such as crop dusting, monitoring traffic, fire-fighting and rescue missions are flown and navigated by commercial pilots. Airline flights must have one or more flight attendants on board, depending on the number of passengers. Their most important function is assisting passengers in the event of an emergency. This may range from reassuring passengers during occasional encounters with strong turbulence to opening emergency exits and inflating escape chutes. More routinely, flight attendants instruct passengers in the use of safety and emergency equipment. Once in the air, they serve meals and snacks, answer questions about the flight, distribute magazines and pillows and help to care for small children and elderly and disabled persons. They also may administer first aid to passengers who become ill. The airline industry also relies on many management, professional and administrative support workers to keep operations running smoothly.

Training and Advancement: The skills and experience needed by workers in the air transportation industry differ by occupation. Some jobs may be entered directly from high school, while others require extensive specialized training. Most positions in the airline industry involve extensive customer service contact requiring strong interpersonal and communication skills. Mechanics and pilots require extensive specialized formal training and must be certified by the FAA; skills for many other air transportation occupations can be learned on the job or through company-sponsored training.

Pilots must have a commercial pilot's license with an instrument rating and must be certified to fly the types of aircraft that their employer operates. For example, helicopter pilots must hold a commercial pilot's certificate with a helicopter rating. Pilots receive their flight training from the military or from civilian flying schools. Physical requirements are strict. With or without glasses, pilots must have 20/20 vision and good hearing and be in excellent health. In addition, airlines generally require 2 years of college and increasingly prefer or require a 4-year college degree. Pilots who work for smaller airlines may advance to flying for larger companies. They also can advance from flight engineer to copilot to captain and, by becoming certified, to fly larger planes.

Applicants for flight attendant jobs must be in excellent health. Employers prefer those who have completed some college and have experience in dealing with the public. Speaking a foreign language also is an asset. Airlines operate flight attendant training programmes on a continuing basis. Training usually lasts from 4 to 8 weeks, depending on the size and the type of carrier. Training may include crew resource management, which emphasizes teamwork and safety. Courses also are provided in personal grooming and weight control. After completing initial training, flight attendants must go through additional training and pass an FAA safety exam each year in order to continue flying.

Advancement opportunities are limited, although some attendants become customer service directors, instructors, or recruiting representatives. When hiring aircraft mechanics, employers prefer graduates of aircraft mechanic trade schools who are in good physical condition. After being hired, aircraft mechanics must keep up to date on the latest technical changes and improvements in aircraft and associated systems. Most mechanics remain in the maintenance field, but they may advance to head mechanic and, sometimes, to supervisor.

A good speaking voice and a pleasant personality are essential for reservation and transportation ticket agents and customer service representatives. Airlines prefer applicants with experience in sales or in dealing with the public and most require a high school education, but some college is preferred. Formal company training is required to learn how to operate airline computer systems, issue tickets and plan trips. Some agents and service representatives advance to supervisor or other administrative positions.

Some entry-level jobs in this industry, such as baggage handler and aircraft cleaner, require little or no previous training. The basic tasks associated with many of these jobs are learned in less than a week and most newly hired workers are trained on the job under the guidance of an experienced employee or a manager. However, promotional opportunities for many ground occupations are limited due to the narrow scope of the duties and the specialized skills of some occupations. Some may advance to supervisor or another administrative position.

Industry Outlook: Wage and salary jobs in the air transportation industry are projected to increase by 12 percent over the 2002-12 period, compared with 16 percent for all industries combined. However, job opportunities may vary from year to year, because the demand for air travel-particularly pleasure travel, a discretionary expense-fluctuates with ups and downs in the economy. In the long run, passenger and cargo traffic is expected to continue expanding in response to increases in population, income and business activity.

Despite a recent slowdown in passenger air travel, demographic and income trends indicate favourable conditions for leisure travel in the United States and abroad over the next decade. The aging of the population, in combination with growth of disposable income among the elderly, should increase the demand for air transportation services. Also, business travel should improve with the economy and as world trade expands, companies continue to go global and the economies in many foreign countries become more robust. However, as businesses also try to reduce costs, they are resorting to cheaper alternatives to flying and finding new ways to communicate. Many business travellers are using other means of transportation, such as driving or using the railway system, or are conducting more business by phone, e-mail, or better quality and lower cost video-conferencing technologies.

Cargo traffic is expected to increase with the economy and growing world trade. It should also be stimulated by the development of global e-commerce and manufacturing trends such as just-in-time delivery, which requires more materials to be shipped rapidly. Job opportunities in the air transportation industry are expected to vary depending on the occupation. Pilots and flight attendants are projected to experience average growth through 2012 as the economy and passenger traffic rebound from the severe downturn in the industry.

In the near term, the best opportunities will be with the faster growing regional and low-fare carriers. Persons with a college degree, or former military pilots, can expect to have the best job prospects. Turnover of flight attendants will also produce job openings for this occupation as many leave for more stable work schedules or better salary. The number of reservation and transportation ticket agents will grow more slowly than the average as airlines phase out paper tickets and move to electronic "ticketless" travel and as more passengers purchase electronic tickets over the Internet. However, the safety and security responsibilities of these jobs will continue, preventing a decline in these jobs. Competition for ticket agent and customer service representative jobs will continue to be keen as many more people are likely to apply for these jobs than there are openings.

Opportunities should be excellent for aircraft and avionics equipment mechanics and service technicians. The likelihood of fewer entrants from the military and a larger number of retirements indicates excellent opportunities for students just beginning technician training. Opportunities also are expected to be good among unskilled entry-level positions, such as baggage handler and aircraft cleaner, because many workers leave these jobs and need to be replaced.

AIR TRANSPORT

Deregulation: Deregulation is, in its most simplistic terms, when the government removes certain regulations on businesses, to encourage the industry. The premise behind deregulation is that with fewer regulations impeding operations, businesses will become more competitive. This increased competition will then result in higher productivity levels, increased efficiencies, and lower prices for consumers. There have been some failures in attempts to deregulate certain industries.

Most notably, the deregulation of the Savings and Loan industry in the 1980s was perceived as a failure and was subjected to re-regulation in order to balance out the industry. The Savings and Loan scenario is a perfect example of why regulation or deregulation must be handled responsibly and intelligently, taking into account and utilizing sophisticated economic theories to help predict the future results. The Airline Deregulation Act was signed into law on October 28, 1978. The Act was created to remove governmental control and open up the passenger air transport industry to free market forces. As noted above, the desire was to increased efficiencies within the industry by promoting competition, which would hopefully le Deregulation:

Deregulation is, in its most simplistic terms, when the government removes certain regulations on businesses, to encourage the industry. The premise behind deregulation is that with fewer regulations impeding operations, businesses will become more competitive. This increased competition will then result in higher productivity levels, increased efficiencies, and lower prices for consumers. There have been some failures in attempts to deregulate certain industries. Most notably, the deregulation of the Savings and Loan industry in the 1980s was perceived as a failure and was subjected to re-regulation in order to balance out the industry. The Savings and Loan scenario is a perfect example of why regulation or deregulation must be handled responsibly and intelligently, taking into account and utilizing sophisticated economic theories to help predict the future results.

The Airline Deregulation Act was signed into law on October 28, 1978. The Act was created to remove governmental control and open up the passenger air transport industry to free market forces. As noted above, the desire was to increased efficiencies within the industry by promoting competition, which would hopefully lead to reduced airfares for consumers. Given the last three decades of outburst and turbulence in the world economy, there are tremendous and irreversible changes in the structure of production, institutional characteristics, and geographical boundaries of markets and industries around the globe.

These changes include the transnationalization of capital and emergence of institutions and networks that are able to carry out the task of production and the distribution of goods and serves beyond the confining borders of nation-states in the complete and connected circuit of *social capital* worldwide. As a result, there has been a remarkable disintegration and re-integration in the structure of firms, industries and markets through the spread of transnational activities. At the present stage of global integration, the centerpieces of global accumulation include, among others, the unifying control over the global labour process, universal and unified access to technology, and the expansion of networks of information, cost-and-revenue-sharing, globalization of product design, and transnationalization of finance capital.

Another side of this epochal transformation pertains to the fast-paced, hyper-competitive, and highly volatile character of economic production and exchange that, in turn, measure the magnitude of global successes and/or failures of capitalism in the contemporary world economy. For our limited purpose here, we shall focus on global alliances in the Air Transport Industry to illustrate attempts at cost-and-revenue-sharing within networks of information sharing and the turbulent impact of hypercompetition. The present globalization, therefore, is the process of continuous integration, disintegration, and re-integration of the world economy in terms of hypercompetition, and fast-paced technological and organizational change beyond the confinement of the nation-states.

Deregulation, introduced in the United States in 1978, has led to dramatic changes in the Air Transport industry. Prior to 1978, The Civil Aeronautics Board (CAB) set airline passenger fares, and entry into the industry and route structures were tightly controlled. Most airlines were party to a multilateral agreement that required they honour tickets issued by other participants. Carriers were mutually reliant upon each other to supply one another feeder traffic. The result was that route licenses by CAB ensured a stability, interdependence of carriers, and reinforced linear route structures. Indeed, before deregulation, fully one-fourth of U.S. domestic passengers were "interlining", or transferring from one carrier to another at major airports to get to their destinations. Upon relaxation of CAB's controls, the strategic vulnerability of the linear route systems operated by the major airlines became clear. New entrants such as People Express, Air Florida, and Midway quickly targeted the profitable high-density city-pair markets.

By 1980, 22 entrants challenged incumbents with low fares, and all but two of the major carriers lost money (HBS, 1995). To compete against lower-cost new entrants, major airlines needed a new source of competitive advantage. One advantage emerged when the major airlines realized that, given their recently acquired choice to enter new markets, there was no benefit in having passengers "interline" if they were able to carry them on their own airplanes for an entire journey. Accordingly, they began to establish nationwide networks. As a result, interlining fell from 25per cent of passenger traffic prior to deregulation to below less than 10per cent in 1984.

In building nation-wide networks, the most efficient mechanism to overcome the production indivisibilities inherent in the use of large aircraft was to redesign route systems into the now familiar hub and spoke configuration in which routes radiate from a central hub airport to a number of outer spoke airports. According to Hanlon (1996) the main advantage of this system is due to its enhanced number of available city pairs in comparison with direct linking of airports. The value of any hub is directly related to the size of the network it serves.

A larger network allows a hub airline to offer a wide range of flights and, by consolidating long-distance travellers from many markets at one sight, integrates what were separate consumer markets into a single captive customer base. In addition, hub creation allowed carriers to increase their local market power and also lower costs from reduced overhead expenses in ground operations. The economic advantages are powerful: hub systems quickly came to dominate the U.S. route system. Prior to deregulation, only five airports served as major traffic hubs. By 1987, there were 30 airports nationwide fulfilling this role.

While the major carriers realized the strategic importance of a nation-wide service network, most did not initially have a presence in smaller regional markets. Drawing feeder traffic to their hubs from these regional routes became a strategic imperative. As the hub system evolved, almost all the hub airlines formed alliances with commuter and regional carriers to increase traffic feed. Regional airlines were happy to oblige: they also benefited from an ever-increasing number of city pairs they could offer their customers. Oum, Park and Zhang (2000) note that a similar pattern of hub building occurred in Canada and the European Union following the deregulation of their markets.

Hub airlines coordinated and managed the commuter's flight schedules, provided reservation services, and shared airport and ground handling facilities. Notwithstanding these efforts vis-a-vis independent regional carriers, alliances would often fracture as the regionals played one competitor against another. To solidify their relationship with the regional airlines, American, Continental, Air Canada and others purchased majority stakes in their feeder airlines.

One indication of the increasing importance of the domestic "network" in the industry is the relative rise of regional airlines in the last twenty years. A passengers enplaned from regional airlines has increased by more than five-fold during the 1981-2001 period. Revenue passenger miles have increased by more than twelve fold in the same period. Available-seat-miles increased by more than 100per cent from 1993 to 2001. The evolution of the role of the regional airline is also underscored by changes in the range of markets they serve and their fleet composition. The length of an average trip on a regional airline more than doubled in the 1981-2001 period, as has the seating capacity of the regional fleet. These trends are a sharp departure from the industry as a whole.

It also became apparent to national carriers that a true national network required more than one hub. Hub set-up required enormous financial investments ($100-$150 million) and time (up to 10 years) to build the terminals and acquire strategically located gates (HBS, 1995). A far quicker way to achieve multiple hub airports was to acquire a competitor's hub. Indeed, the merger wave that occurred in the industry in the mid-1980s is mostly explicable by strategic efforts to realize the full potential of the new route structure: via the acquisition of either feeder airlines or strategic hubs.

These acquisitions. The steady increase in ownership concentration in the industry over the period is also the result of this business strategy. By the end of the 1980s, consolidations led to 8 airlines controlling 92per cent of U.S. air traffic (HBS, 1995) Parallel to these changes in the route structure and ownership concentration there emerged the change in the composition of the capital stock—aircraft—in the industry. The development of hub systems resulted in the addition of flights to small cities around the major hubs. This, in turn, increased the demand for small-and medium-sized aircraft.

One case in point is the changing product-mix ordered from Boeing, among the world's largest aircraft manufacturers. In orders for Boeing's aircraft, is divided into five product categories: single-aisle short-range (SASR), single-aisle mid-range (SAMR), twin-aisle mid-range (TAMR), twin-aisle long-range, and twin-aisle, twin-deck long-range (TDLR). The increasing importance of the single aisle mid-range aircraft. The trend is clearer when the additional seating capacity of the ordered aircrafts are considered. As presented, the majority of planned additional seating capacity is on SAMR aircraft. These versatile machines, including some models of the Boeing 737 and the Boeing

757, are to economically serve smaller cities and the regional hubs of the hub route structure. Yet, having a range of 5000-10,000 kilometres, and a seating capacity of 125 to 250, they provided needed flexibility and were assigned to all but the longest point-to-point routes.

Not captured in the Boeing data is the sharp increase in the number of jets in the U.S. regional fleet. Regional jets, introduced in the late 1980's, are small planes that fly shorter distances and have fewer seats than their counterparts: large mainline jets. Being the industry leaders, however, the jets manufactured by Canada's Bombardier and Brazil's Embrear, have a range up to 1300 miles and seating capacity of 50 to 70. The turboprop aircrafts they are replacing usually are confined to flights of up to 350 miles, with seating capacity for only 20 to 40 passengers. By the end of 2001, some 800 regional jets were in operation in the U.S., as opposed to only 137 in 1997, while the number of regional aircraft remained roughly constant at 2300 level.

Similar changes are also occurring in Europe. In particular, the advantage of building hub systems was clear to European airlines as well, although limits on international ownership meant consolidation within one's own national borders. During the 1980's, acquisition of British Caledonia by British Airways is one example. Some large European carriers also purchased minority stakes in smaller European airlines in order to solidify their positions at certain hub airports. Lufthansa purchased a minority position in Interflug—the (formerly) East German airline. Swissair purchased a share of the Zurich based Crossair. British Airways took control of 40per cent of Brymon Airlines, a commuter carrier. KLM purchased two Dutch commuter airlines (Cityhopper, Netherlines) and took a minority stakes in a British commuter (Air UK). And Air France was aggressive in acquiring or taking minority stakes in French commuter airlines (UTA, Air Inter).

The elaborate hub system, and the route structure that goes with it, played as a unifying framework that allowed a continuous access to arrival and departure points by both the major airlines and their regional affiliates and thus provided a ready platform to lunch a multiplied line of service by all involved. This indeed constitutes as a *de facto* or "social" (collective) capital for a particular alliance and, perhaps, a potential platform for future alliances. However, provision of such a structure embodies the double-edged sword of competition. Given the fierce competitive environment within the industry, having access to such an extensive hub system by already low-cost regional airlines, has led to a further competitive struggle between major U.S. carriers and the smaller airlines within the same alliances. This has given the regional airlines an intra-alliance competitive advantage, in addition to the inter-alliance competition, a norm in the industry. One indication of this is the relatively rapid increase in the revenue passenger miles generated by the regional airlines, when compared with their major airlines counterparts, as discussed above.

GLOBAL ALLIANCES

As hub systems came to dominate domestic markets in the U.S. and Europe, the airlines began to rely heavily on inter-continental alliances to expand their networks, increase customer service, and generally to increase the value of their domestic hubs. This pattern is occurring globally. For U.S.-based airlines, international enplanements climbed 112per cent between 1986 and 1999, more than twice the growth in domestic travel. In 2000, international travel was 8.5per cent of total enplanements, compared to 6per cent in 1986.

The underlying economic advantages of the hub system operate in international as well as domestic markets. Because of the advantages of network size, carriers have sought to expand their operations geographically and thereby gained significant competitive advantage. Strategically, exploiting the hub system internationally required carriers to plan on a global basis. Most international routes, however, remain governed by bilateral Air Service Agreements (ASAs) between governments.

These agreements designate such matters as the types of applicable fares, the authorized carriers on certain routes, and the type of plane and allowable flight frequency. As such, they provide a protected source of economic profits for those carriers with rights to the routes. For example, more than half of the business of large European carriers is in longer-haul international routes covered by bilateral agreements, yet more than two-thirds of the revenue of U.S. carriers is derived from the competitive, domestic arena accounting, in part, for European airlines ability to weather the recent downturn in the global industry.

Recently, the U.S. has been proposing new ASAs called "Open Sky Agreements". These imply no limits on the number of airlines that may be designated by country, unrestricted capacity, frequency of flights, unlimited ability to change aircraft type, and, finally, full pricing freedom unless both governments object. Since the first open skies pact was reached between the U.S. and the Netherlands in 1992, 57 agreements have emerged.

The Open Sky Agreements and deregulation introduced around the globe have, to varying degrees, opened previously protected national and regional markets to penetration by new competitors. Some airlines, notably Northwest and KLM, and United and Luthhansa were given anti-trust immunity and took advantage of "Open Skies" to engage in unprecedented cooperation. Never the less, no nation has to date opened its markets to carriers from all countries. This limitation has carriers ally with, rather than purchase or attempt to directly challenge foreign carriers in their own hubs.

Alliances offer a form of consolidation without having to seek authority for the full cross-national mergers that most governments have refused to allow. As Pekar, Jr. (2001) points out, alliances fall between "transactional conventional sourcing and servicing arrangements at one extreme to acquisitions and mergers at the other." Importantly, they allow a firm to acquire (or capture) core capabilities from a foreign firm that directly advance its competitive position—gate access, route network, customer base, etc.—without having to invest in new airport facilities and aircraft or acquiring other assets that are unnecessary from a strategic point of view. It is important to point out that these advantages accrue to both parties within the alliance. Indeed, we believe that alliances are ultimately undermining the position of major carriers and portend realignment of the industry.

Despite all this, alliance growth in recent years has been notable. Air Florida and British Island formed the first international alliance in 1986. As firms learned of the success of the initiative, it was quickly emulated throughout the industry. The most recent figures available number 579 alliances involving 220 major international airlines. Most international alliances have initially been formed between European and North American airlines. In the early 1990s, however, Asia Pacific airlines began to join the alliances. From Europe, North America, and Asia-Pacific, alliances have recently extended into new regions in Africa and Latin America. The gradual expansion of what would become the Star Alliance, the worlds largest, suggests the Alliance's rapid development of its global reach.

THE RISE OF AIR TRANSPORTATION

Air transportation was slow to take off after the Wright Brothers breakthrough at Kitty Hawk in 1903. More than ten years passed before first faltering efforts to launch scheduled passenger services. On January 1, 1914, the world's first scheduled flight with a paying passenger hopped across the bay separating Tampa and St. Petersburg, Florida for a fare that eventually stabilized at $10 per person, round-trip (about $200 in 2006 dollars). By comparison, Low-Cost Carrier (LCC) Southwest Airlines could carry a passenger from Tampa to Seattle and back, more than a hundred times farther for only slightly more than $200 in 2007.

World War I, which began just months after that first flight from Tampa, provided the first real spur to the development of commercial aviation as air power began to be used and better aircraft were quickly designed. The war left a legacy of thousands of unemployed pilots and surplus aircraft along with an appreciation for the future significance of this new technology. However, air transport still suffered from limitations in terms of capacity and range. 1919 marked the first commercial international air transport service between England and France. It was also the same year that with the Paris Convention that each country controlled the airspace over its territory. Governments played a crucial role in the next phase of aviation history. In Europe, governments established new passenger airlines while on the other side of the Atlantic, the American government heavily subsidized airmail. Airmail was one of the earliest avenues via which air transportation became commercially relevant because it helped to accelerate the velocity of the money supply and helped to better tie together far-flung enterprises, facilitating the emergence of continental and intercontinental enterprises. US airmail also subsidized the emergence of the first major US passenger airlines.

By the eve of World War II, air travel was quite literally taking off, borne aloft by important advances in technology. Particularly important was the Douglas DC-3, the first airliner that could fly profitably without government subsidies (air mail routes). The 21-seat DC-3 was a long-range aircraft for its time, able to fly across the US stopping just three times. By 1941, 80per cent of all commercial aircraft in the US were DC-3s. The DC-3 was a landplane; but on longer-haul,intercontinental routes, flying boats remained common through World War II. Flying boats, like the double-deck Boeing 314, were the largest commercial aircraft until the building of the 747. They could fly very long distances but their slow speeds undercut their profitability. And the market for long-haul travel was very small, partly because of the extraordinarily high cost. Many of the long-haul air services were to colonies and dependencies. Only the elite or government officials was able to afford air travel.

War again encouraged the rapid growth of air transportation. Indeed, it was only after World War II that air transportation became the dominant mode of long-haul passenger travel in developed country markets. In 1956, more people traveled on intercity routes by air than by Pullman car (sleeper) and coach class trains combined in the US. In 1958, airlines carried more passengers than ocean liners across the Atlantic for the first time. Even more momentous, in October 1958, the Boeing 707 took its maiden commercial flight. The 707 was not the first jetliner, but it was the first successful one. The 707 and other early jets, especially the Douglas DC-8, doubled the speedof air transportation and radically increased the productivity of airlines which enabled fares to fall. Just a few years after the 707's debut, jet service had been extended to most major world markets.

Jet transportation facilitated the extension of the linkages between people and places, which is supported by ample evidence. A classic example concerns American major league baseball. Through the mid-1950s, all major league teams were located in the Manufacturing Belt, situated no more than an overnight rail journey apart from one another to permit closely packed schedules. The speed and ultimately lower cost of air transportation freed teams to move to the untapped markets of the Sunbelt so that by the mid-1960s, half a dozen teams were strung out across the South and West.

In the years since the beginning of the Jet Age, commercial aircraft have advanced markedly in capacity and range. Just 12 years after the debut of the 707, the 747 made its maiden flight. Not coincidentally, it too premiered on a transatlantic route from New York City. The entry of dozens of 747s into the market around the same time that the Arab Oil Embargo triggered a worldwide recession led to a torrent of red ink for early Jumbo enthusiasts like Pan Am; but the longer term effect was to push real airfares ever downward, thereby democratizing aviation beyond the so-called "Jet Set". The 747, particularly the longer-range 747-400 version introduced in the late 1980s, has been nicknamed the "Pacific Airliner" because of its singular significance in drawing Asia closer to the rest of the world and because Asia-Pacific airlines have been major 747 customers.

Since their introduction in the late 1950s, commercial jets have not improved in terms of speed. The fastest airliners in regular use today are about as fast as the 707. The Anglo-French Concordewhich cruised at twice the speed of sound was hamstrung by very poor economics – it weighed half as much as a first-generation 747 but could carry only a quarter as many passengers and had a range more than 3,000 kilometers shorter. Moreover, the Concorde was an early target of the nascent environmental movement, and restrictions on overland supersonic flights severely limited the market for the airliner. The only carriers to regularly operate it were British Airways and Air France, and although many cities had Concorde services in the first halcyon years of its early use, by the time the supersonic transport (SST) was finally grounded in 2003, only London, Paris, New York, and Washington had scheduled year-round services.

Three major categories of passenger jet planes may be recognized:

Short range aircraft. Bombardier's CRJ series and Embraer's ERJs are examples of planes with relatively small capacities (30-100 passengers) that travel over relatively short distances. They are usually referred to as regional jets that serve smaller markets and feed hub airports. They also provide point to point services between large city pairs. Medium range aircraft. The airbus A320, with a range of 3,700 km, and its Boeing equivalent, the B-737, are designed to service destinations within a continent. From New York, most of North America can be reached. This range can be applied to the European continent, South America, East Asia and Africa. This type of aircraft is also used for high demand regional services where low cost air carriers compete.

Long range aircraft. There are a variety of aircraft capable of crossing the oceans and linking together the continents. Early variants such as the B-707 have evolved into planes offering high capacity, such as the B-747 series, or long range abilities, such as B-777 series or the A350 series which have ranges of up to 17,400 km.

ECONOMIC AND SPATIAL IMPACTS

It is through increasingly long-haul non-stop services among an ever wider set of city-pairs rather than through increased aircraft speeds that air transportation continues to "shrink the world". After World War II aircraft were just beginning to be capable of crossing the Atlantic without stopping at intermediate places such as Newfoundland. In the mid-1950s, the Israeli carrier El Al advertised its transatlantic services with the slogan "No Goose, No Gander" to cleverly let travelers know that its turboprop services had to stop at neither Goose Bay nor Gander in Newfoundland to refuel. Today, commercial aircraft are now capable of making trips of up to 18 hours in duration. Such ultra-long-range flights servicing the world's metropolises are both a response and a driver for globalization.

The same capacity of air transportation to dramatically lower the cost (friction) of distance has, of course, been instrumental in fostering economic globalization, albeit in a highly uneven fashion. Manufacturers, especially those producing high-value microelectronics, are heavily reliant upon air transport to tie together spatially disaggregated operations. Intel, the world's foremost computer chip manufacturer is an example of a firm that relies heavily on air transportation, both passenger and cargo, to tie together its global production network. The firm's Philippine operations, for instance, receive their main inputs and export their output almost exclusively by air.

Relatively inexpensive air transport has also been crucial to the growth of tourism. It is no coincidence, for instance, that the five major Disney theme parks are all located near one of the world's thirty busiest airports: Disneyworld near Orlando International Airport, Disneyland near Los Angeles International Airport, Euro Disney near Paris-Charles de Gaulle, Tokyo Disneyland near Tokyo-Haneda, and the newest park in Hong Kong which shares Lantau island with the mostexpensive airport in history.

Microelectronics and tourists comprise only two of the many kinds of airborne traffic. Since the dawn of the Jet Age, air transport has ascended to astonishing heights. It is overwhelmingly dominant in transcontinental and intercontinental travel and is becoming more competitive for shorter and shorter trips. In the US, for instance, air travel is the most important mode for trips more than about 1,100 kilometers in one-way length. In developing countries, too, LCCs are proliferating, which is bring air fares down and propelling air traffic higher.

Through the Jet Age, both passenger and cargo traffic have grown rapidly. Both types of traffic have outpaced the growth of the broader global economy. By 2003, approximately 900,000 people were airborne on scheduled flights somewhere in the world at any one time; and worldwide, 1.6 billion passengers traveled by air transport in the centenary of the Wright Brothers' first flight, representing the equivalent of 25per cent of the global population. In 2010, this figures reached 2.4 billion passengers, underlining the enduring growth of air travel. Yet the propensity to fly is highly uneven. Alone, North America and Europe accounted for 70.4per cent of all passenger movements in 2000, but this share is declining. At any given time, there are more then 5,000 planes in the air over North America. Air transportation's share of world trade in goods is only 2per cent measured by weight but more than 40per cent by value. For the international operations, freight can account to 45per cent of the revenue of a regular airline. Typically, air cargo relates to time sensitive, valuable or perishable freight carried over long distances. This is particularly suitable in supporting "just-in-time" production and distribution strategies with low inventory levels. Air cargo has also a niche market for emergency situations where the fast delivery of supplies (*e.g.,* medical, food) prevails over cost issues. The air freight market is serviced by five types of operations: Dedicated cargo operators maintaining a fleet or cargo-only aircrafts and offering regular scheduled services between the airports they service. They also offer charter operations to cater to specific needs.

Combination services where an airline company will maintain a fleet of both specialized and passenger aircrafts able to carry freight in their bellyhold. Most of the cargo operations involve long haul services. Passenger operators that will offer the freight capacity in the bellyhold of their aircrafts. For these operators, freight services are rather secondary and represent a source of additional income. However, low cost airlines usually do not offer air cargo services.

Air freight integrators commonly operating hub and spoke freight services that reconcile short and long haul flights. They offer comprehensive services that are usually door-to-door and can support the logistics requirements of their customers. Specialized operators fulfilling niche services that cater to specific cargo requirements (*e.g.,* heavy loads) that do not fit the capabilities of standard cargo aircrafts.

Efficient and affordable air freight has contributed to changes in diet by making available new products or products in seasons during which they would not be available, to changes in retailing and correspondingly to changes in manufacturing. Examples abound, such as fresh produces growth on the southern hemisphere available in the northern hemisphere during winter, or merchandises purchased online and shipped promptly by air transport or a computer manufacturer depending of the global shipment of various components in the manufacturing and assembly processes. The increased importance of time-based competition ensures that air cargo augurs well for the future growth of air transportation.

THE GEOGRAPHY OF AIRLINE NETWORKSS

Theoretically, air transport enjoys greater freedom of route choice than most other modes. Yet while it is true that the mode is less restricted than land transport to specific rights of way, it is nevertheless much more constrained than what might be supposed. Early in the history of aviation, physical obstacles such as the Rocky Mountains and the great gap of the North Atlantic limited the articulation of air transport networks. While those limitations have fallen, physical geography still affects the geography of intercity air transportation. Aircraft seek, for instance, to exploit (or avoid) upper atmospheric winds, in particular the jet stream, to enhance speed and reduce fuel consumption. Volcanic eruptions may also impede air travel by releasing ash in the atmosphere, which can damage and even shot down turbofan engines. Such occurrences are however rare and punctual, with the exception of April 2010 when a volcanic eruption in Icelandforced the closing down of airports in most of Europe as well as several North Atlantic routes. This represented the largest natural disruption of air travel in history.Yet the limitations that structure air transportation are mainly human creations. First, in the interest of air safety, air traffic is channeled along specific corridors so that only a relatively small portion of the sky is in use. Jetway 554, for example, which passes from high over the Michigan-Indiana state line towards Jamestown, New York via Southern Ontario, accommodates flights from many different cities in the West and Midwest bound for the Northeast, with non-stop city-pairs such as San Diego-Boston, Chicago-Albany, Phoenix-Providence, and Los Angeles-Hartford.

Strategic and political factors have also influenced route choice. For example, the flights of South African Airways were not allowed to over-fly many African nations during the apartheid period, and Cubana Airlines has been routinely prohibited from over-flying the US. Even more significant was the opening up of Siberian airspace to Western airlines after the Cold War. The new freedom permitted more direct routes not only between cities like London and Tokyo or New York and Hong Kong but also between transpacific city pairs like Vancouver-Beijing.

Few large areas of airspace forbidden to carriers on political grounds remain. However, the intervention of the state in airline networks remains pervasive. From its infancy, air transport was then seen as a public service and as an industry that should be regulated and protected. In many parts of the world, government intervention in the industry took the form of state-owned airlines.

As recently as the early 1970s, Air Canada, Air France, British Airways, Japan Airlines, Qantas, and most other flag carriers throughout the world were fully state-owned. In the US, the government did not own any airlines but it did strongly affect the industry's development via regulation of fares, in-flight service, routes, and mergers.Beginning in the 1970s, the relationship between the airline industry and the state changed, although the timing of liberalization (a term which refers to both deregulation and privatization) and its extent has varied among the world's main markets. Across the globe, dozens of airlines have been at least partially privatized, and many airline markets have been deregulated. In the United States, the Air Deregulation Act of 1978 opened the industry to competition. The results, seen from the vantage point of more than

25 years later, have been dramatic. Once hallowed names, like TWA, Pan Am, and Braniff sank into bankruptcy (though Pan Am has been reborn as a much smaller carrier along the Atlantic coast) and many new players emerged. Most lasted only a short time, but some have had a profound, enduring effect on the industry and air transportation more generally.

Geographically, a key outcome of airline deregulation has been the emergence of hub-and-spoke networks centered on major airport where a single carrier is often dominant. Such networks existed before deregulation to some degree, but the Civil Aeronautics Board hampered the expansion of airlines and the rationalization of networks. United Airlines, for instance, was allowed to add only one city to its network between 1961 and 1978. Hub-and-spoke systems rely on the usage of an intermediate airport hub. They can either connect a domestic (or regional) air system if the market is large enough (*e.g.,* United States, China, European Union) or international systems through longitudinal (*e.g.,* Dubai, Reykjavik) or latitudinal (Panama City) intermediacy. An important aspect of an intermediate hub concerns maintaining schedule integrity since the majority of passengers are using connecting flights. Airports that are prone to delays due to congestion are not effective hubs since they compromise the schedule integrity.

DEREGULATION AND ITS CONSEQUENCES

After deregulation, most of the surviving major carriers tended to construct nationwide hub-and-spoke networks with several hubs to facilitate travel between different regions of the country. The traffic feed through hubs like Atlanta enables Delta and other carriers to offer higher frequency service at higher load factors which in turn lowers the per passenger-kilometer cost. The advantages of large airlines were further deepened when nationwide hub-and-spoke networks were coupled to computer reservations systems and frequent flyer programmes. Yet by the late 1990s, large carriers like Delta were on the run. Low cost carriers, especially Southwest Airlines in North American and Ryanair in Europe, cut into the market share of the "legacy" carriers. LCCs are distinguished by several common features:

Fleet simplicity. Legacy carriers operate diverse fleets because they serve many kinds of routes, from long hauls to feeders. LCCs emphasize on relatively short-haul routes. The minimal number of aircraft types (Southwest and Ryanair only flies 737s, though several different models) lowers costs. Fast turnaround times. LCCs operate their networks in ways that keep their aircraft in the air earning money for a higher number of hours on average compared to legacy carriers. Minimal inflight service, for instance, reduces the time needed to clean and cater flights.

Rapid growth. This is not just a product of the LCCs' success but an element in it. Fast growth enables the LCCs to continue to add aircraft and staff at a steady pace which keeps the average fleet age and average years of employee service low – both of which help to keep operations costs low. Emphasis on secondary airports. Secondary airports, such as Houston-Hobby instead of George Bush Houston Intercontinental or Charleroi instead of Brussels National, typically have lower landing and parking fees for airlines as well as a more entrepreneurial approach to recruiting new airline service. However, LCCs have also directly challenged established carriers in major hubs.

Reduced importance of hubs. Most LCCs do have hubs, but for some carriers hubs are substantially less important than they are for legacy carriers. Southwest Airlines, for instance, distributes air traffic more evenly among a ten or so top "focus cities" in its network than is true of any traditional hub-and-spoke airline. Aggressive use of the Internet. Internet booking has partially neutralized the one-time advantage that legacy carriers enjoyed through their proprietary computer reservations systems. The Internet is an additional way of reducing costs.

Although Southwest Airlines is commonly regarded as the pioneer LCC and is the only LCC to rank among the world's 20 largest airlines, the phenomenon has now taken off in Europe and to a lesser extent in other parts of the world. In general, the propensity to travel is highly correlated with incomes, but the LCCs are important in broadening the air transportation market beyond the relatively small affluent population in countries like Indonesia. Southwest Airlines is exceptional in that its network is purely domestic (International flights are operationally more complex and would erode the carrier's enviable turnaround time.) Most large and medium-sized airlines have at least some international routes. Nevertheless, about 90per cent of the air traffic generated by countries such as the United States, Canada, Russia, Japan, Brazil and Australia is domestic.

The United States generates alone 70per cent of the global domestic air traffic.Under threat by LCCs in shorter-haul markets, legacy carriers are becoming more dependent on longer-haul international markets. International markets, too, have been opened up by deregulation, though not to the same degree as the US domestic market.

The Chicago Convention of 1944 established the basic geopolitical guidelines of international air operations, which became known as the air freedom rights. First and second freedom rights are almost automatically exchanged among countries. The US, which emerged from World War II with by far the strongest airline industry in the world, had wanted third and fourth freedom rights to be freely exchanged as well. Instead, these and the other rights have been the subject of hundreds of carefully negotiated bilateral air services agreements (ASAs). In an ASA, each side can specify which airlines can serve which cities with what size equipment and at what frequencies. ASAs often include provisions that also regulate fares and the sharing of revenue among the airlines serving a particular international route. Yet even in international markets, the extent and degree of state intervention has diminished. An important trend in the past decade has been the proliferation of Open Skies agreements. Open Skies agreements remove most restrictions on the number of carriers and the routes that they may fly between two countries. By the end of 2006, the US, for instance, had such agreements with nearly 80 countries. Open Skies agreements can be viewed as a roundabout way for the US to gain what it could not get at the 1944 Chicago Conference – relatively unfettered access for American carriers to foreign markets. Indeed, the US has pursued a beachhead strategy playing one country in a region against another, putting pressure on Japan to liberalize its markets for instance by inaugurating Open Skies agreements with Singapore, Taiwan, South Korea and other Asian economies.

Potentially the most important Open Skies agreement would be between the US and European Union. Moves in that direction have been stymied by US unwillingness to relax restrictions on foreign ownership of American carriers, among other concerns.Nevertheless, many more airlines now operate internationally than before the liberalization of the airline industry began in the 1970s. The proliferation of international carriers has fostered thefragmentation of intercontinental and transcontinental markets. As a result, on intercontinental and transcontinental routes, the former dominance of the 747 has been challenged by longer-range, widebody twinjet (two-engine jetliners) like the Boeing 767, Boeing 777, and Airbus A330. The triumph of widebody twinjets is most evident in the transatlantic market. The transpacific market is more concentrated among a smaller number of gateway cities, and the 747 is still dominant; but there is a clear trend towards fragmentation and displacement of the 747 by smaller aircraft, including ultra-long-range ones like the A340-500.

An important aspect of international airline networks is the recent formation of alliances. Alliances are voluntary agreements to enhance the competitive positions of the partners, particularly where the persistence of restrictive bilateral ASAs make it difficult for an airline to expand on its own. Members benefit from greater scale economies, a lowering of transaction costs, and a sharing of risks, while remaining commercially independent.

The first major alliance was established in 1989 between KLM and Northwest Airlines. Today, the largest alliance is the Star Alliance, which was initiated in 1993 by Lufthansa and United Airlines. In 1996 British Airlines and American Airlines formed the oneworld alliance. Members of airline alliances cooperate on scheduling, frequent flyer programmes, and equipment maintenance, and schedule integration. Most importantly, they permit carriers to tap markets that would otherwise be beyond their reach. Indeed, each of the major alliances encompasses almost every significant market across the globe, although each is dominated by US and European carriers.A final important aspect of airline networks is the emergence of separate air cargo services. Traditionally, cargo was carried in the bellyhold of passenger airplanes, and provided supplementary income for airline companies.

However, since passengers always had the priority when a plane was overloaded, such air freight services tended to be unreliable. Moreover, passenger aircraft are operated on routes that make sense for passengers, but may not attract much cargo. Today, about half of all air cargo is carried in dedicated freighters, aircraft in which goods are carried both on the maindeck and in the bellyhold. FedEx and UPS operate the largest freighter fleets in the world, operating 338 and 243 freighters respectively (by comparison, the largest passenger airline fleet is that of American Airlines with nearly 700 aircraft). Each deploys its aircraft worldwide.

Yet many freighters are flown by so-called combination carriers like Northwest that carry both passengers and cargo. Northwest deploys its freighters primarily on transpacific routes where too little bellyhold capacity is available to accommodate the burgeoning trade between the US and Asia. Interestingly, one of the primary freighter hubs is Anchorage, a city which passenger aircraft on transpacific and transpolar routes (between Europe and Asia) regularly overfly now; but because freighters have shorter ranges than passenger aircraft and because freight is less sensitive to intermediate refueling stops than passengers, many freighters refuel in Alaska in order to maximize their payload. Still, cargo operations are ripe with inefficiencies. About 70per cent of the transit time for a payload carried by air is spent on the ground, mostly at congested major airport terminals. This tends to mitigate the major speed advantage air freight is known for.

ENSURING THE VIABILITY OF AIR TRANSPORT

While the 20th century saw the creation and rapid growth of the air transport industry, the beginning of the 21st century was marked by great challenges met with major transformations. Over the last decade, the industry has been rocked by a series of successive crises and shocks. These include terrorism, pandemic threats, volcanic eruptions, global economic upheavals and an unprecedented rise in the cost price of fuel. Between 2000 and 2009, airlines posted a net loss of $50 billion. All this has made IATA's leadership more crucial than ever. In 2002 IATA's newly appointed Director General and CEO Giovanni Bisignani began a complete restructuring of the association to increase IATA's relevance and speed in driving major industry changes.

Initiatives spearheaded by IATA under Bisignani include:

- *The IATA Operational Safety Audit (IOSA)*: IOSA is the global standard for airline safety management and by 2009 airlines were required to achieve IOSA registration as a condition of IATA membership. This is the flagship component of a comprehensive 6 point safety strategy that includes audits, cargo, flight operations, infrastructure, training and data collection.

- *Environment*: IATA led the alignment of the whole aviation industry—airlines, airports, manufacturers and air navigation service providers—in a long term strategy to achieve carbon-neutral growth by 2020 and to cut aviation's carbon emissions by half by 2050.
- *Simplifying the Business (StB)*: In 2004 IATA launched this initiative to use technology to improve customer convenience and reduce costs. Four years later, achievement of 100per cent e-ticketing marked a major milestone for the industry. StB is now targeting industry savings of nearly $17 billion with initiatives ranging from bar coded boarding passes (BCBP) to Fast Travel, Baggage Improvement Programme (BIP) and e-freight.
- *Savings*: IATA embarked on a major initiative to reduce costs across the air transport value chain, particularly with monopoly suppliers. By 2010 this ongoing campaign has claimed industry savings exceeding $17 billion.
- *Financial*: IATA operates industry financial systems which now settle in excess of $300 billion a year with a success rate of over 99.9per cent. Unit costs for this system have been decreased by over 80per cent since 2000.

Bisignani has also strengthened IATA's position as the voice of the industry, with firm advocacy and lobbying to focus governments on the long term issues for viability of aviation, such as liberalization, environment and taxation.

IATA continues to help airlines respond to the requirements of the 21st century air transport system. Airlines have created a modern, interdependent world over the past 60 years: IATA is working to ensure that the world's most exciting industry meets its greatest possible potential for the years ahead with Vision 2050, outlined by Bisignani at the June 2010 IATA Annual General Meeting.

MISSION

Air transport is one of the most dynamic industries in the world. The International Air Transport Association (IATA) is its global trade organization. Over 60 years, IATA has developed the commercial standards that built a global industry. Today, IATA's mission is to represent, lead and serve the airline industry. Its members comprise some 230 airlines - the world's leading passenger and cargo airlines among them - representing 93 Per cent of scheduled international air traffic.

Representing

ATA seeks to improve understanding of the industry among decision makers and increase awareness of the benefits that aviation brings to national and global economies. It fights for the interests of airlines across the globe, challenging unreasonable rules and charges, holding regulators and governments to account, and striving for sensible regulation.

Leading

IATA's aim is to help airlines help themselves by simplifying processes and increasing passenger convenience while reducing costs and improving efficiency. The groundbreaking Simplifying the Business initiative is crucial in this area. Moreover, safety is IATA's number one priority, and IATA's goal is to continually improve safety standards, notably through IATAs Operational Safety Audit (IOSA). Another main concern is to minimize the impact of air transport on the environment.

Serving

IATA ensures that people and goods can move around the global airline network as easily as if they were on a single airline in a single country. In addition, it provides essential professional support to all industry stakeholders with a wide range of products and expert services, such as publications, training and consulting. IATA's financial systems also help carriers and the travel industry maximize revenues.

For the benefit for all parties involved:

- For consumers, IATA simplifies the travel and shipping processes, while keeping costs down. Passengers can make one telephone call to reserve a ticket, pay in one currency and then use the ticket on several airlines in several countries.
- IATA allows airlines to operate safely, securely, efficiently and economically under clearly defined rules.
- IATA serves as an intermediary between airlines and passenger as well as cargo agents via neutrally applied agency service standards and centralized financial systems.
- A large network of industry suppliers and service providers gathered by IATA provides solid expertise to airlines in a variety of industry solutions.
- For governments, IATA seeks to ensure they are well informed about the complexities of the aviation industry to ensure better, long-term decisions.

PRIORITIES

Safety and Security:

- Implement a data sharing agreement with ICAO, the US and the EU and deliver a joint safety report.

- Design a prototype "Checkpoint of the Future".
- Implement Secure Freight in two new countries.

Environment:

- Continue promoting major air traffic infrastructure projects (*e.g.*, SESAR in Europe and NextGen in the US).
- Fight a global climate-related tax on passengers, carbon or fuel.
- Secure fuel and carbon reporting for at least 70per cent of IATA members operations.

Simplifying the Business:

- *Fast Travel*: Implement all five Fast Travel initiatives (Document check, Bags ready-to-go, Flight re-booking, Self-boarding, Bag recovery) at five major airports.
- e-services: Ensure that 40 airlines and all six major global distribution systems start issuing Electronic Miscellaneous Documents.
- Baggage Improvement Programme: perform 60 diagnosis visits and implement 70 self-help airports.
- e-freight: Ensure 10per cent market penetration on trade lanes where e-freight was available in 2010.

Financial:

- Achieve savings/cost avoidance of US$3 billion in industry taxes, charges and fuel fees, including at least US$1.5 billion in real cost reductions.
- Strengthen IATA Settlement Systems controls through consolidation of the remittance and settlement function into regional hubs by mid 2011.

Regulatory:

- Gain European Aviation Safety Agency recognition for the IATA Operational Safety Audit (IOSA).
- Obtain one regulator's acceptance of a pilot training initiative that includes multi-crew pilot licensing and evidence based training.
- Prevent regulatory action on slots that would adversely affect the four cornerstones of the World Scheduling Guidelines.

INTERNATIONAL SOCIETY OF TRANSPORT AIRCRAFT TRADING

The International Society of Transport Aircraft Trading (abbreviated ISTAT) is a non-profit aviation industry association. Founded in 1983, ISTAT is dedicated to fostering and promoting interest and educational opportunities in commercial aviation, while also providing a forum for networking among those involved in the industry.

ISTAT MEMBERSHIP

ISTAT currently has more than 1700 members worldwide involved in operating, manufacturing, maintaining, selling, purchasing, financing, leasing, appraising, insuring or otherwise engaging in activities related to commercial transport category aircraft. ISTAT is governed by its bylaws and the volunteer ISTAT Board of Directors, which is composed of and elected by the members.

ISTAT FOUNDATION

The ISTAT Foundation fosters interest in, creates opportunities for, and provides assistance through the global aviation community by offering scholarships, grants, internships and humanitarian aid worldwide. The Foundation awards more than $250,000 in scholarships, grants and humanitarian efforts annually to worthy recipients around the world. Grants are awarded to institutions involved in both elementary and higher education as well as to humanitarian organizations. Scholarships have been presented to students on an international stage with recipients from the U.S., U.K., Turkey, The Netherlands, China, Germany, Australia, and Kenya. The Foundation's most recently established internship programme matches aviation-focused college students to internship positions open at ISTAT member companies.

ISTAT CERTIFIED APPRAISERS' PROGRAMME

ISTAT has established rigorous testing and qualification standards for members who are engaged in appraising aircraft and support equipment. Within ISTAT is a core group of professional aircraft appraisers who work cooperatively for the elevation of the appraisal profession within the world aviation community. Each ISTAT member, who has satisfactorily demonstrated that he or she is qualified to appraise airline transport aircraft, has been granted the right to use one of the ISTAT professional designations, established by ISTAT and predicated upon a set group of criteria.

ISTAT EVENTS

Annual U.S. Conference

Each spring, the aviation industry comes together at the ISTAT Annual U.S. Conference, where delegates gain access to key insights from the leaders and influential members of the aviation industry. The 2010 Annual Conference will be held March 14–16 in Orlando, Florida.

Annual European Conference

The ISTAT European Conference provides a more intimate gathering of aviation professionals each autumn, set at different European locations. The 2009 European Conference will be held October 11–13 in Dubrovnik, Croatia.

Air Show Receptions

Annually, ISTAT hosts receptions at selected air shows, which take place at distinctive venues around the globe, including Dubai, Singapore, Farnborough, and Paris.

REGIONAL AVIATION ASSOCIATION OF AUSTRALIA

The Regional Aviation Association of Australia (RAAA) is an organisation representing the interests of regional aviation in Australia. It was formed in 1980 as the Regional Airline Association of Australia and amended its name in 2001 when its charter was widened to include "aerial work operators" as well as regional airlines and air charter companies "and the businesses that support them". Its stated aim is "to promote the maintenance of a viable regional aviation industry".

DENVER INTERNATIONAL AIRPORT

According to Goetz and Szyliowicz (1997), Denver International Airport (DIA) opened five years late in 1995, mainly due to problems with its automated baggage system. The cost overrun rose from US$1.7 billion to over US$5 billion, and though the airport was forecast to handle 56 million passengers by 1995, only 30 million used it in that year. It also received noise complaints from residents, despite seeking to minimise noise impacts. DIA is therefore an interesting example of how short-term problems in the planning process can emerge even where there is a systematic approach to development.

In the USA, the FAA has published guidelines on the approach towards airport development. Rycroft and Szyliowicz (1980) examine the limitations of the FAA approach where access to all forms of data is not possible, and argue that it overlooks the role of power and political variables.

It also assumes that planning occurs in a rational manner, whereas there is all too often a lack of agreement on the principal goals of large projects such as these. Furthermore, this approach also assumes that it is possible to derive accurate forecast demand estimates. In the wider literature on transport planning, such problems remain intractable as traffic forecasts are notorious for their inaccuracy and inability to accommodate human travel behaviours. To overcome some of these problems, Maldonado (1990) and de Neufville (1991) have developed a strategic planning approach which recognises issues such as uncertainty and flexibility in future planning requirements.

The initial decision to expand airport capacity in Denver can be dated to 1974, when the political consensus was to expand the existing Stapleton International Airport. By the time deregulation occurred in the 1980s, expansion was not considered feasible, given the FAA's and Denver's consultants' forecasts for future traffic growth. Forecasts suggested that the existing traffic of 25 million passengers in 1983 would grow to 56 million by 1995. Runway capacity at Stapleton had already caused a bottleneck in the national air transport system during adverse weather conditions due to runway design. Goetz and Szyliowicz (1997) provide an interesting commentary on the politics of the decision to select a site for DIA. They also examine how the airline users exacted major concessions from the developer - the city of Denver. The most serious concession was exacted by United Airlines, which sought and gained an automated baggage system to service its concourse. This concession also contri-buted to major delays in the airport becoming operational.

Delays to the airport's opening due to technological problems associated with the baggage system added to cost overruns. The airport traffic forecasts also assumed that Denver would emerge as a major hub. But in March 1994, Continental Airlines abandoned its hubbing operation at Denver, leaving United as the main hubbing operator while the FAA assumed that American Airlines might consider establishing a hub operation by 1995. The DIA project was downsized by reducing the number of run-ways from six to five and gates from 120 to 88—this was made possible by the modular design of the airport.

The airport also aimed to reduce noise impacts, being located 24 miles from Denver's CBD. But according to Goetz and Szyliowicz : In all of 1994, Stapleton received 431 noise complaints, but in the first twelve months since DIA opened the city received over 57,000 complaints. Much of this can be attributed to previously non-impacted populations now receiving some amount of aircraft noise. But it remained unclear whether these complaints indicate that the original noise contours developed in the Environmental Impact Statement are still accurate.

Goetz and Szyliowicz (1997) view the DIA example as highlighting the airlines' role as something which could not have been foreseen in the rational comprehensive planning model advocated by the FAA. The goals of each airline were not in sympathy with those of the city of Denver and the FAA, and the political system affected both the decision-making and implementation phases of planning. As Szyliowicz and Goetz (1995) argued, a range of actors with different strategies, agendas and purposes ensured that no one unitary actor drove the project forward.

As a result, poliical and cognitive factors were powerful in shaping the airport development process. The ability to accommodate future risk and uncertainty also assumes a much greater role given the 'critical nature of aviation forecasts for airport planning and design and of demand forecasts'. This means that the planning process needs to be able to accommodate likely errors in forecasts. Goetz and Szyliowicz (1997) also point to the need for decision makers and planners to adapt to new business situations with flexibility rather than remaining locked into a project that may not be suitable on completion. Vested interests, political careers and an unwillingness to admit that earlier decisions may have been made on inaccurate information still affect mega-projects such as airports. A similar problem can be seen in the CAA's Swanwick air traffic system being developed for the UK. This is a mega-IT project which has so far revealed 15,000 errors in the computer software and is expected to be £100 million over budget and several years late. It was envisaged that it would replace the ageing West Drayton air traffic control centre, although some critics believe it may even be abandoned if it cannot be made operational. Both DIA and the Swanwick example highlight overoptimistic expectations that technology which is not tried and tested can be put into practice immediately. What emerge is a need for flexibility and constant monitoring once the decision has been taken to implement a project and a willingness to halt the project if technical problems cannot be solved.

GLOBAL AIRPORT DEVELOPMENT

French (1996a) reviews the environmental constraints which now affect airport expansion, notably community objections to aircraft noise and emissions. These have resulted in a range of state-of-the-art airport development projects which can meet future demand on new sites while mitigating environmental concerns. A significant number of these new projects are located in Asia-Pacific. Nevertheless, French (1996a) argues that planners are not keeping pace with demand. In late 1995, there were only 11 new airports under construction:

- In Europe: Oslo, Athens and Berlin.
- In Asia-Pacific: Sydney, Hong Kong, Seoul, Bangkok, Kuala Lumpur and three sites in China (Shanghai, Guangzhou and Shuhai).
- In the Middle East: three new airports.

In Japan, government agencies are currently identi-fying sites for Tokyo's third airport, likely to cost US$32 billion, with construction starting in the year 2000. Japan also has a US$500 million plan for a domestic airport at Kobe, to be operational by 2003 and a five-year US$40 billion programme for other airports. In India, a feasibility study is considering a new US$3.2 billion airport for Bombay, to open in 2005. A large number of airport enhancement projects are also under way in Asia-Pacific to upgrade terminal buildings and to construct new runways. French points to concerns that by 1995 half the airports in Asia-Pacific are capacity-constrained. A number of efficiency gains at Asia-Pacific airports may reduce pressure at some airports (*e.g.,* improvements to surface transport access and customs procedures).

French points to the improvements achieved in European air travel by new air traffic control systems. The cost of congestion was estimated at US$6 billion for European airports to the year 2000, based on estimates by ATAG. Among the most pressing problems are airport congestion at peak times and runway capacity constraints. The Association of European Airlines argued that 26 of Europe's 29 larges airports would need additional terminal capacity in 1995, and 25 will need extra runway capacity by the year 2005. These airports are forecast to handle 1.2 billion passenger movements and 16 million aircraft movements. Those airports which the Asso-ciation of European Airlines believe will be worst affected are the following hubs:

- London Heathrow and Gatwick,
- Frankfurt,

- Paris (Charles de Gaulle),
- Schiphol Airport, Amsterdam,
- Rome,
- Madrid,
- Zurich.

As French observes, 'by around 2000 most of the world's major city airports will be faced with critical decisions on how to ensure that their status as leading traffic hubs is maintained, both for their own economic benefit and for the... the air transport industry itself'.

Conclusion

There is no doubt that 'airports are complex business with functions that extend substantially beyond the airfield or traffic side of operations'. Airports provide the vital infrastructure which links:

- The airline,
- The traveller,
- Air and surface transport.

and they are complex systems which require clear management guidelines and structures to ensure they operate efficiently.

The late 1980s and 1990s have been the process of privatisation sweep across many of the world's airport organisations, as the public sector is unable to provide access to large sources of capital to invest in upgrading schemes. The full or partial privatisation of airport companies has also changed the airport as a travel terminal. Under privatisation, a greater focus on non-traffic revenue sources and a broad revenue strategy have transformed the airport from a waiting area and functional environment.

The transformation, which has been inspired by business principles to generate revenue from retailing, has generated the airport mall as a cultural icon. The airport is often viewed as a post-modernist expression of the conspicuous consumption now pervading many developed societies, epitomised by leisure travel. In this new environment where marketers have seized the initiative to develop products and services for a wide range of target groups (including the traveller) the airport is now firmly part of the broad travel experience. The example of BAA and its QSM embodies the current concern with customer needs in a market characterised by high-volume business and a captive clientele. The consumer's interests are also represented by the UK Consumers' Association publication, *Holiday Which,* 1st Winter 1998 survey, *Which Airport,* undertakes a qualitative review of UK airports and compares value for money, access, areas in need of improvement (*e.g.,* catering) and the best departure lounges as well as the range of shops available. Such surveys illustrate how important the airport is now becoming in the wider travel experience.

The case study of BAA also illustrated the diverse range of activities associated with airport management, the sheer scale and volume of their operations, and the fact that they now have a customer-driven focus to improve the traveller's experience. Even so, large organisations such as airports cannot necessarily respond to issues as quickly as the customer would like. For example, on a flight from Scotland to London in March 1998, the author experienced an incident which highlights this issue: the ground staff held the departure up to allow an inebriated passenger on board, who was served additional alcohol during the flight and who then created difficulties during and after the flight.

At the destination, ground crew were faced with this situation and it took an inordinate time for the airport security staff to be called. While this reveals total ineptitude by the airline staff for allowing a passenger on board who was unfit for travel, it also illustrates the unexpected events with which airport staff have to deal and the time delay in putting the appropriate system and action in place. It was also the airport staff who had to deal with the outcome of the airline staff's inexperience and lack of understanding of the situation. Thus, airport management embraces a wide range of operational and human interactions which affect the way travellers perceive the airport environment.

In terms of development strategies for airport growth, the example of DIA illustrates the complex interaction of factors that can affect the final outcome. Airport development involves extremely large funding, increasingly from the private sector, to meet the complex needs of airlines and travellers as well as the airport operator. To describe such entities as mega-projects is a good description, given their scale and vastness. Managing such entities once they are fully operational and meeting a broad range of customers' needs in the fast-changing world of domestic and international travel is a key challenge.

NORMAL FORMALITIES OF AIRPORTS

The first thing that one needs to have is their passport. This is especially the case when you are travelling from one country to another. Though other countries that have the same interests with you country might not require you to carry it, it is always advisable to have your passport. The second thing that is a formality with air travel is the security check. In every airport, there is a security check. The reason behind this security check is to make sure that the person entering the airplane are not in a possession of anything that can cause harm to the plane or the people inside it. This being the case, you will find that the security check is a very important part of airline travel.

SECURITY CHECKS AND AIR TRAVEL

In this case, a person is given a check through three main ways. The first thing that is checked is your passport. The information is normally crosschecked against any wanted criminals nationally and internationally. Once this test a person has passed, the next test is the luggage test. This is here the luggage that you are carrying is made sure to have nothing potentially dangerous. The most modern airports do not require the opening of the luggage. The luggage is normally passed through a scanner which makes sure that all the items that the individual is carrying are safe to be forwarded to the plane. The final security check is the body check. This is normally a procedure to make sure that none of the passengers are carrying any weapons on themselves. Once you have passed these checks, the rest of the formalities are simple and less complicated.

Full Body Scanner

A full-body scanner is a device that creates an image of a person's nude body through their clothing to look for hidden objects without physically removing their clothes or making physical contact. They are increasingly being deployed at airports and train stations in many countries. One technology used under the name "full-body scanner" is the millimeter wave scanner, the active form of which reflects extremely high frequency radio waves off the body to make an image on which one can see some types of objects hidden under the clothes. Passive millimeter wave screening devices rely on only the raw energy that is naturally emitted from the human body or objects concealed on the body; passive devices do not transmit millimeter waves. Another technology in use is the backscatter X-ray.

Two advantages of full-body scanners over a physical strip search are that it is quicker (takes only 15 seconds) and that people do not have to be touched in a manner that some might consider offensive. A disadvantage is that the scanners are being used to perform routine, virtual strip searches without probable cause which opponents claim are illegal unreasonable searches that violate basic human rights. Furthermore, the true long-term health effects of the active, radiating technologies are unknown. Passive millimeter wave screening is known to be safe because its technology does not require radiating the subject.

History

The first full body security scanner was developed by Dr. Steven W Smith, who developed the Secure 1000 whole body scanner in 1992. He subsequently sold the device and associated patents to Rapiscan Systems, who now manufacture and distribute the device. The first passive, non-radiating full body screening device was developed by Lockheed Martin through a sponsorship by the National Institute of Justice (NIJ)'s Office of Science and Technology and the United States Air Force Research Laboratory. Proof of concept was conducted in 1995 through the Defence Advanced Research Projects Agency (DARPA). Rights to this technology were subsequently acquired by Brijot

Imaging Systems, who further matured a commercial-grade product line and now manufacture, market and support the passive millimeter wave devices. Safety aspects of the Secure 1000 have been investigated by the FDA and NCRP since the early 1990s.

Usage

in the Netherlands was the first airport in the world to implement this device on a large scale after a test with flight personnel the previous year. On May 15, 2007 two of 17 purchased security scans were installed. A longer list of airports with full-body scanners can be found on bigbrotherwatch.org.uk. Full-body scanners have been installed in at least one Florida courthouse and are starting to appear in courthouses around the US. At least one New Jersey PATH train station used full-body scanners in 2006. This was a two week trial. As of November 20, 2010, the TSA reported that there were 385 full-body scanners now in use at 68 United States airports, which were listed in an article of that date on USAToday.com and ABCnews.com.

The United States plans to deploy 1,000 full body scanners by the end of 2011. The US Government has also hinted at the possibility of deploying the full body scanners at train stations and subways. The Italian government had planned to install full-body scanners at all airport and train stations throughout the country, but announced in September, 2010 plans to remove the scanners from airports, calling them "slow and ineffective."

Because of the privacy issues, in some locations people are allowed to refuse this scan and opt for a traditional pat-down. In other locations, use of the full-body scanners is mandatory and refusing to submit to a scan at the airport will bar the person from taking the flight.

A bill called the *S.A.F.E.R. A.I.R. Act* has been introduced in the United States by Senators Bob Bennett (R-UT) and Amy Klobuchar (D-MN). If it passes it will make full-body scanners mandatory in the U.S. by 2013. It is claimed that the head is excluded from the scan and the images are instantly erased, though in one case, images had been stored and 100 of them were later leaked online.

The analyst is in a different room and is not supposed to be able to see the person being scanned, but is in contact with other officials who can halt the scanned person if anything suspicious shows up on the scan.The European Union currently allows member states to decide whether to implement full body scanners in their countries: It is for each member state to decide to authorize the use of scanners in national airports.

That will not change... But where this scanning technology is used it should be covered by EU-wide standards on detection capability as well as common safeguards to ensure compliance with EU health and fundamental rights provisions.—EU Transport Commissioner Siim Kallas

Controversies

The implementation of widespread full-body scanners has raised a public controversy.

Public Opinion

A Gallup poll given just after the 2009 Christmas Day bombing attempt suggested that 78per cent of American airline travelers approved of body scanners while 20per cent disapproved. 51per cent indicated that they would have some level of discomfort with full-body scans, while 48per cent said they would not be uncomfortable with the idea. The poll was given in the context of the 2009 Christmas Day bombing attempt, some opponents of full body scanners say that the explosives used in that bombing attempt would not have been detected by full-body scanners.

An ABC/Washington Post poll conducted by Langer Associates and released November 22, 2010 found that 64 percent of Americans favored the full-body x-ray scanners, but that 50 percent think the "enhanced" pat-downs go too far; 37 percent felt so strongly. In addition the poll states opposition is lowest amongst those who fly less than once a year. As of November 23, 2010 an online poll of 11,817 people on The Consumerist web site, 59.41per cent said they would not fly as a result of the new scans. Additionally, as of November 23, 2010 a poll of MSNBC 8,500 online readers indicated 84.1per cent believe the new procedures would not increase travel safety. While according to a CBS telephone poll of 1,137 people published on November 15, 81per cent (+/5per cent) percent of those polled approved TSA's use of full-body scans.

Privacy

Opponents of full-body scanners argue that strip searches without probable cause violate basic human rights. Governments do not have the right to make strip searches routine and mandatory, regardless of whether the strip search is done by physically removing clothes or by using technological means to remove the clothes.

Full-body scanning technology allows screeners to see the nude surface of the skin under clothing, prosthetics including breast prostheses and prosthetic testicles, which may require a potentially embarrassing, hands-on physical inspection once detected. The scanners also can detect other medical equipment normally hidden, such as colostomy bags and catheters. Other privacy concerns come from transgendered community, who may feel that the routine full-body scans are embarrassing and could potentially lead to harassment.

Airport employees in Lagos have been caught using full body scanner images as a type of porn. Travelers at U.S. airports have complained that when they opted not to be scanned, they were subjected to a new type of invasive pat-down that one traveler described as "probing and pushing... in my genital area." Another traveler in the United States complained that the TSA employee "inserted four fingers of both hands *inside* my trousers and ran his fingers all the way around my waist, his fingers extending at least 2-3 inches *below* my waistline."

In November, 2010, a female traveler who opted out of a full body scan at Fort Lauderdale International Airport claims that TSA agents handcuffed her to a chair and ripped up her plane ticket when she asked them questions about the new type of invasive pat down she was about to receive. In response, the TSA posted the security camera footage on their blog, though there is no sound in the video and the passenger is not directly in the camera during most of the incident.

Opponents in the US argue that full body scanners and the new TSA patdowns are unconstitutional. A comprehensive student note, and possibly one of the first on the topic, *"Full-Body Scanners: Full Protection from Terrorist Attacks or Full-On Violation of the Constitution?" came out in the Fall 2010 issue of the internationally distributed University of Denver Transportation Law Journal that argued that the full-body scanners are unconstitutional in the United States because they are (1) too invasive and (2) not effective enough because the process is too inefficient.

On July 2, 2010, the Electronic Privacy Information Centre (EPIC) filed a lawsuit to suspend the deployment of full-body scanners at airports in the United States: EPIC argued that the federal agency has violated the Administrative Procedures Act, the Privacy Act, the Religious Freedom Restoration Act, and the Fourth Amendment. EPIC cited the invasive nature of the devices, the TSA's disregard of public opinion, and the impact on religious freedom.—epic.org

EPIC claims that the full-body scanners violate the Fourth Amendment to the United States Constitution because they subject citizens to virtual strip searches without any evidence of wrongdoing. The American Civil Liberties Union has called the machines an invasion of privacy: "This doesn't only concern genitals but body size, body shape and other things like evidence of mastectomies, colostomy appliances or catheter tubes. These are very personal things that people have every right to keep private and personal, aside from the modesty consideration of not wanting to be naked." In Idaho a bill has been introduced to prevent the use of full-body scanners as a primary screening method, and to allow people to request alternative screening methods:

Wholebody imaging technology may not be used as the sole or primary method of screening persons, nor may it be used to screen any person unless another method of screening, such as metal detection, demonstrates cause for preventing such person from boarding an aircraft or entering a public facility or government building.—Idaho House Bill no. 573 In the UK, the Equality and Human Rights Commission has argued that full-body scanners are a risk to human rights and may be breaking the law. The National Human Rights Commission of Korea opposes the use of full-body scanners and has recommended that they are not deployed at airports. In the United States, the TSA requires that their full-body scanners "allow exporting of image data in real time", and cases of the government's storing of images have been confirmed.

In August 2010, it was reported that United States Marshals Service saved thousands of images from a millimeter wave scanner. TSA — part of the Department of Homeland Security — reiterated that its own scanners do not save images and that the scanners do not have the capability to save images when they are installed in airports. However, these statements contradict the TSA's own Procurement Specs which specifically require that the machines have the ability to record and transmit images, even if those features might be initially turned off on delivery. Opponents have also expressed skepticism that if there were a successful terror attack that the machines would not have the capability to save images for later inspection to find out what went wrong with the scans. On November 16, 2010, 100 of the stored 35,000 body scan images were leaked online and posted by Gizmodo.

Equal Treatment of Minorities

Current Backscatter and Millimeter wave scanners installed by the TSA are unable to screen adequately for security threats inside turbans, hijab, burqas, casts, prosthetics and loose clothing. This technology limitation of current scanners often requires these persons to undergo additional screening by hand or other methods and can cause additional delay or feelings of harassment. The next generation of backscatter scanners are able to screen these types of clothing. The next generation of scanners can equalize the screening process for all persons so that religious minorities can travel through the AIT process as easily as other passengers.

INLAND TRAVEL

All flights within the country or countries visited as part of the tour are included in your tour price. Group reservations are made in economy class and all tickets will be tackled by your Tour Director. We regret that we are unable to accept seating requests for internal flights as the domestic airlines generally assign seating only at time of check-in. Additional information on baggage allowance and security regulations will be included in your documents sent to you at the time of booking.

THE TRANSFERS

All the expenses such as airport, road transport, hotel, etc. described in the tour package are included in the amount paid for the package You will met at the airport by a company representative after clearing both immigration and customs and transferred in a private car to your hotel. If you have booked your own international flights you must advise us of your arrival and departure details and any subsequent change to these details so that we may be able to meet you upon your arrival.

Travel by Road

Most cars are used of local construction, and while they may appear to be antique they are comfortable and ideally suitable to the local road conditions, with spare parts readily available. Coaches are also principally locally made and while not of the standard of an American touring coach they are comfortable and well maintained. Most of our coaches are air conditioned exception of some coaches of southern cities of India.

Travel by Train

On the tours that feature travel by train we always try to reserve first class air-conditioned carriages, but these cannot always be reserved ahead of time and do not exist on all routes. Please contact our tour consultants to discuss the facilities available on the route you would like.

REQUIREMENTS FOR VISA

US citizens require a passport with at least 6 months of validity from the date of entry into the country/countries included on your tour. Visas are required for entry into India, Nepal, Tibet, Bhutan, Jordan and Syria. At this time US citizens do not require visas for entry into Sri Lanka, Pakistan and Israel. At the time that you make your booking we will mail you a visa kit outlining the visa required necessarily for the tour that you are booked on. This visa kit will include visa forms and an information sheet outlining the visa requirements and procedures. All of the visa handling is done through our visa service. Please note that the above information and service is valid only for US citizens.

HEALTH MEASURES

At the time of printing, the countries specification in our tours do not have any compulsory inoculation requirements for entry with the exception of those travellers having been to a country infected with yellow fever within five days of their arrival. However, it is generally recommended that travellers to India have current tetanus inoculations, and gamma globulin injections to protect against hepatitis.

If you are travelling in South India or in other jungle areas malaria precautions are advised. For further medical information we advise you to contact your local physician. If you need any special medication we advise carrying sufficient supply. Additionally you should carry diarrhoea antidotes and upset stomach medication. Sun lotions, lip balms and sun glasses are highly recommended. Recommendations and advice on food and drink within the country countries visited will be supplied at the time of booking.

In all countries it is mainly recommended to drink only packed mineral water or other bottled beverages. These are generally available in all the hotels that you will be staying at. It is not necessary to purchase destination currency prior to your arrival in India or another country featured on your tour. There are foreign exchange counters in the hotels which give the same exchange rate as banks. It is, therefore, not essential or recommended to purchase local currency at the airport. However, it is recommended to purchase small denominations for use as tips or for small purchases. All major credit cards are accepted at the city hotels you will be staying at. Smaller hotels and wildlife park lodging accept cash in local currency only.

Airport Departure Taxes

In the cost of our tour packages the airport departure taxes are not included. It is, therefore, essential for you to pay these locally and in local currency. Foreign currency is not accepted. The taxes vary in each country and will be advised to you before your departure from the USA. These taxes arc subject to change and if they do your tour leader or our ground staff will advise you on site.

Tipping

Tipping for porterage and all significant sightseeing is incorporated. Tipping is not added for services besides these such as meals not included, optional sightseeing, etc. In addition, some members of the groups may want to collectively pick the bus driver or local guide. This is not needed and is completely at your discretion. Please ask your tour leader any question you may have about this. Our Tour Directors do not accept tips.

Cuisine

In the city hotels, restaurants give the serving of Continental as well as Indian and Oriental cuisine. In the more remote areas and smaller hotels and places the food is basic and mainly Indian. We suggest that in these areas you request vegetarian food since this tends to decrease the risk of stomach upsets. The hotels that we use are keenly aware of the Western visitor's reaction to Indian food and they take great care in the area of hygiene. While health problems can occur, these are generally minor and often result in the change of diet and time zones.

Insurance

We percept that no one likes to consider the unexpected problems that interrupt holiday plans. Unfortunately, difficulties by chance do arise, despite the most careful planning. So, to offer you peace of mind the company offers a comprehensive Passenger Protection Programme exclusively for our passengers. The Passenger Protection Programme is not just cancellation insurance. Yes, it does give reimbursement for penalties that may be assessed due to cancellation for acquired reasons, but it also provides much more.

Travel Insurance Coverage *Trip Cancellation/Interruption*	**Total Tour Cost**
Baggage/Personal Effects	$ 1,000
Accident Medical Expense	$3,000
In-Hospital Identity (Sickness Only)	$3,000
Emergency evacuation	$2,0000
Worldwide Emergency Assistance	24 Hours
Travel Insurance Rates	
Tour up to $2,000	$99
Tours between $ 2,000 and $ 3,500	$169
Tours between $ 3,501 and $ 5,000	$259
Tours between $ 5,001 and $ 6,000	$299
Tours between $ 6,001 and $ 7,500	$359

Momentary, the programme offers medical expense reimbursement for covered accidents overseas, particularly significant since Medicare, and different private insurance policies, restrict coverage of medical expenses incurred abroad. We strongly recommend that all passengers participate in the Passenger Protection Programme. A full description of coverage will be sent to you or your travel agent automatically with your bill. For your convenience the cost of the programme is automatically included to your bill and may be purchased with your initial deposit or prior to final payment but cannot be added at a later date.

This is only a concise description of the plan. For full terms, conditions, exclusions and pre-existing limitations, refer to the description of coverage which should be reviewed thoroughly before purchasing. Brochure II has a different presentation form while all other elements remain the same. In this brochure most of the programmes are multi-destinational. A client has a option of more than one destination in a individual region. The tour operator developing these programmes specialises in East Asia. Although the basic programmes cover India, the tour operator however does not take his clients there first. Tour No. 1 entitled 'Asian Highlights' is a 20 days trip starting in USA and covers Hong Kong, India, Nepal and Thailand. A client returns home from Bangkok. In this programme, the client also has a option of an extension in India and the orient as per his requirements.

Tour No. 2 is a 15-18 days tour covering India and Nepal. Tour No. 3 is entitled "Magnificent India and Nepal" and covers both these destinations in 18 days. Tour No. 4 is again a twin destination tour named "Essence of India and Nepal" and is of 12 days duration with possible extensions. Unlike in Brochure No. 1, the price of the tours', start dates and terms and conditions of the tour form part of the main brochure. No separate sheet is printed as in the case of Brochure I. The brochure is printed in four colours using glazed art paper. Use of colour pictures in the brochure is another important element which projects the destination. Each of the programmes shows a colour representation of an important monument, event or an activity covering the itinerary. The following pages show the sample of the brochure discussed above.

Costs of getting passports; visas unless otherwise specified in particular itinerary; extra baggage charges; travel insurance; personal expenses such as laundry; room service in excess of your meal allotment; gratuities and road transport to/from restaurants for a la carte meals; gratuities to escort, staff and crew of Eastern and Oriental Express, Road to Mandalay or Yanzi Princess; communication charges; meals, beverages or sightseeing; not included in the itinerary any airfares.

Luggage

Tour prices included the handling of two pieces of baggage per person. Baggage and personal effect are at owner's risk throughout the tour. Check with the airline for baggage prohibition applicable to your international flights.

Passport and Visas

Valid passport are required for travelling to the destinations in this brochure; check with your travel agent or ask the latest requirement and support.

Registration

A deposit of $ 500 per person is required at the time you book, at which time you will get your invoice and pre-tour documentation. The reminder of the price of your trip is due 60 days prior to your departure date. If your reservation is done within 60 days of departure, the entire price of the trip must be paid at the time of confirmation. When your reservation is initiated within 30 days of your departure, a non-refundable "rush booking" fee of $ 50 per booking will be charged.

Cancellations

Cancellations received up to 60 days before departure, $100 per person cancellation fee per tour or extension; 59-45 days, 10 per cent of tour price; 44-15 days, 20 per cent of tour price; 14 days or less 100 per cent of tour price.

Claims and Refunds

All claims for days missed while on tour should be made in writing within 30 days of the cancellation of the tour. This claim should be accompanied by a statement from the Tour Operating Company approving the claim. Refunds are based on the actual prices of service involved and not on a per claim basis.

Refunds will not be done for unused sightseeing trips or meals. The company will not accept any responsibility for any claims which are not received within 30 days of the termination of your tour.

Arrangements

Quoted tour prices included planning, handling and operational charges, and are based on the current rates of exchange and tariffs as of July, 1995. In the event of a pointed change in foreign exchange rates, fuel costs or tariff rates, tour costs are subject to revision.

Responsibility

The company purchases transportation, hotel accommodation, restaurant services and other services from diverse independent suppliers that are not subject to its control. The Company, cannot, therefore, be liable for any personal risk or property damage, which may take place due to (1) any act of Commission of such a supplier or (2) defects in or failures of any aircraft, vessel, automotive vehicle or other type of transportation that is not under its control. The company reserves the right to adjust US dollar prices without information, to reflect fluctuations in the Foreign Exchange Markets. The Company also reserves the right to cancel a tour or any part of it, to make such alternations in the itinerary as appears necessary or desirable, to refuse to accept or to retain as a member of the tour any person at any time, and to pass on to tour members any expenditures or losses caused by delays or events beyond its control.

Air Transportation

We will arrange the most reasonable airfare available in the different categories you request at the time of your booking. Sample air prices are shown in this brochure. Should you cancel or change your air reservation before or after departure, cancellation penalties may apply. Airlines concerned are not to be held accountable for any act, omission or event during the time passengers are not on board their planes or conveyances, These tours may use the services of any IATA carrier. The passage contract in use by these companies when issued shall organise the sole contract between the companies and the purchaser of these tours and/or passage.

Components in a Tour Brochure

The description of the tour brochure of the two companies shows how diverse elements of a programme are carefully planned to comprise "all required information to make a holiday comfortable. The essential elements of a good programme in a brochure can be divided into two parts, *e.g.*,

- 'Pre-visit' and
- 'On arrival'.

Pre-visit details would include the following:

- Destination information
- Cost of a tour
- Departure dates
- Hotel information
- Visa requirements
- Medical fitness
- Insurance advice

"On arrival" details would include the following:

- Transfers
- Guide service
- Day today itinerary
- Currency exchange
- Shopping
- Entertainment/cultural programmes
- Emergency services
- Customs to be observed
- Cuisine
- Airport departure taxes

All the elements in a programme of a big tour operator are tailor-made to develop particular interest and need of a client. A tour operator, after carefully considering different alternatives available and based on the market research packages, offers different programmes for including in his tour brochure.

8

The Adventure Tourism Industry

ADVENTURE TOURISM

Adventure tourism is a type of niche tourism involving exploration or travel to remote areas, where the traveller should expect the unexpected. Adventure tourism is rapidly growing in popularity as tourists seek unusual holidays, different from the typical beach vacation. Adventure Tourism can take many forms with the increase in numbers of people with disabilities around the World and recent veterans from Wars have opened the doors to Adventure Travel for the Disabled. Albeit this may not be in exotic areas some tourism areas that have been developing include Australia, USA and Canada. Whistler and Vancouver British Columbia, Canada have been taking the lead with the 2010 Paralympics coming up fast. Adapting to the needs of the Disabled to attract a $ 13 billion dollar a year industry in North America alone. The global Adventure Travel Trade Association, "adventure travel" may be any tourist activity including two of the following three components: a physical activity, a cultural exchange or interaction. Mountaineering expeditions, trekking, bungee jumping, rafting and rock climbing are frequently cited as an examples of adventure tourism.

MOUNTAINEERING

Mountaineering is the sport, hobby or profession of walking, hiking, trekking and climbing up mountains. It is also sometimes known as alpinism, particularly in Europe. While it began as an all-out attempt to reach the highest point of unclimbed mountains, it has branched into specializations addressing different aspects of mountains and may now be said to consist of three aspects: rock-craft, snow-craft and skiing, depending on whether the route chosen is over rock, snow or ice. All require great athletic and technical ability, and experience is also a very important part of the matter.

SNOW

While certain compacted snow conditions allow mountaineers to progress on foot, typically some form of mechanical device is required to travel efficiently over snow and ice. Crampons 10 - 12 point spikes which are attached to a mountaineers boots, are used on hard snow and ice to provide additional traction and allow very steep ascents and descents. There a many different varieties, ranging from lightweight aluminum models intended for walking on glaciers to aggressive steel models intended for vertical and overhanging ice and rock. Snowshoes can be used to walk through deep snow approaching the mountain or on lesser slopes up the mountain.

Skis can be used almost everywhere snowshoes can and also in steeper, more alpine landscapes although it takes more practice to develop sufficiently strong skiing skills for difficult terrain. The practice of combining the techniques of alpine skiing and mountaineering to ascend and descend a mountain is a form of the sport by itself, called Ski Mountaineering. Ascending and descending a snow slope involves many different techniques of the feet and an ice axe which have been developed over the last hundred years, originating in Europe. The progression of footwork from the lowest angle slopes to the steepest terrain is first to splay the feet to a rising traverse, to kick stepping, to front pointing the crampons.

The progression of the ice axe technique from the lowest angle slopes to the steepest terrain is to use the ice axe first as a walking stick, then a stake, then to use the front pick as a dagger below the shoulders or above, and finally to swing the pick into the slope over the head. This also involves different designs of ice axe depending on the terrain to be covered, and even whether a mountaineer uses one or two ice axes.

Glaciers

When traveling over glaciers, crevasses pose a grave danger. These giant cracks in the ice are not always visible as snow can be blown and freeze over the top to make a snowbridge. At times snowbridges can be as thin as a few inches. Climbers use a system of ropes to protect themselves from such hazards. Basic gear for glacier travel includes crampons and ice axes. Teams of two to five climbers tie into a rope equally spaced. If a climber begins to fall the other members of the team perform a self-arrest to stop the fall. The other members of the team enact a crevasse rescue to pull the fallen climber from the crevasse.

Ice

Multiple methods are used to safely travel over ice. If the terrain is steep but not vertical, then protection in the form of pickets or ice screws can be driven into the snow or ice and attached to the rope by the lead climber. Each climber on the team must clip past the anchor, and the last climber picks up the picket. This allows for safety should the entire team be taken off their feet. This technique is known as Simul-climbing. If the terrain becomes vertical then standard ice climbing techniques are used.

Shelter

Climbers use a few different forms of shelter depending on the situation and conditions. Shelter is a very important aspect of safety for the climber as the weather in the mountains is very unpredictable. Tall mountains require many days of camping on the mountain.

Hut

The European alpine regions, in particular, have a network of mountain huts. Such huts exist at many different heights, including in the high mountains themselves – in extremely remote areas bivouac shelters may have been provided. The mountain huts are of varying size and quality but each is typically centred on a communal dining room and have dormitories equipped with mattresses, blankets or duvets, and pillows – guests are expected to bring and to use their own sleeping bag liner.

The facilities are usually rudimentary but, given their locations, huts offer vital shelter, make routes more widely accessible and offer good value. In Europe, all huts are staffed during the summer and some are staffed in the spring. Elsewhere, huts may also be open in the fall. Huts also may have a part that is always open, but unmanned, a so-called winter hut. When open and manned, the huts are generally run by full-time employees, but some are staffed on a voluntary basis by members of Alpine clubs. The manager of the hut, termed a guardian or warden in Europe, will usually also sell refreshments and meals – both to those visiting only for the day and to those staying overnight.

The offering is surprisingly wide – given that most supplies, often including fresh water, must be flown in by helicopter – and may include glucose-based snacks on which climbers and walkers wish to stock up, cakes and pastries made at the hut, a variety of hot and cold drinks, and high carbohydrate dinners in the evenings. Not all huts do offer a catered service, though, and visitors may need to provide for themselves. Some huts offer facilities for both, enabling visitors wishing to keep costs down to bring their own food and cooking equipment and to cater using the facilities provided. Booking for overnight stays at huts is deemed obligatory, and in many cases is essential as some popular huts – even with over 100 bed spaces - may well be full during good weather and at weekends. Once made, the cancellation of a reservation should be advised to the hut as a matter of courtesy – and, indeed, potentially of safety, as many huts keep a record of where climbers and walkers state they planned to walk to next. Most huts are contactable by telephone and most take credit cards as a means of payment for the service they provide.

Bivy

A bivy or bivouac is simply getting a sleeping bag and Bivouac sack and laying down to sleep. Many times small half sheltered areas like cracks in rocks or simply a trench dug in the snow are used to provide a basic means of shelter as well. This technique is performed by most people only in cases of emergency, however in good weather this can be pleasant. Some climbers steadfastly committed to Alpine Style climbing plan on bivying in order to save the weight of a tent when snow conditions are not suitable for a snow cave.

Tent

Tents are the most common form of shelter used on the mountain. A four season tent is recommended for any camp above timberline in the mountains. Some climbers do not use tents at high altitudes unless the snow conditions do not allow for snow caving, although digging a snow cave is a time consuming and work intensive endeavor. Sometimes walls of snow or rock can be built instead to shelter the tent from high winds and storms. One of the downsides to tenting is that high storm winds and snow loads can be unnerving and cause the tent to collapse, however modern mountaineering tents are usually tested for wind speeds up to 125 mph. Even so, constant flapping of the tent fabric can hinder sleep and raise doubts about the security of the shelter in windy conditions.

Snow Cave

Snow caves are another way for some climbers to shelter high on the mountain. Unlike tents snow caves are silent and actually warmer. A correctly made snow cave will hover around freezing, which relative to outside temperatures can be very warm. They require carrying a snow shovel, which some may consider to be extra equipment, to build easily. They can be dug from a deep snowdrift, out of a slope, or anywhere there is at least four feet of snow. Another shelter that works well is a quinzee, which is excavated from a pile of snow that has been work hardened or sintered. Igloos are used by some climbers, but are deceptively difficult to build and require specific snow conditions.

Hazards

The craft of climbing has been developed to avoid three main types of danger: the danger of things falling on the climber, the danger of the climber falling and inclement weather. The things that may fall include rocks, ice, snow, other climbers or their gear; the mountaineer may fall from rocks, ice or snow, or into a crevasse. In all, there are eight chief dangers: falling rocks, falling ice, snow-avalanches, falls, the climber falling, falls from ice slopes, falls down snow slopes, falls into crevasses and dangers from weather. To select and follow a route using one's skills and experience to mitigate these dangers is to exercise the climber's craft.

Falling Rocks

Every rock mountain is slowly disintegrating due to erosion, the process being especially rapid above the snow-line. Rock faces are constantly swept by falling stones, which are generally possible to dodge. Falling rocks tend to form furrows in a mountain face, and these furrows have to be ascended with caution, their sides often being safe when the middle is stoneswept. Rocks fall more frequently on some days than on others, just as to the recent weather. Ice formed during the night may temporarily bind rocks to the face but warmth of the day or direct sun exposure may easily dislodge these rocks.

Local experience is a valuable help on determining typical rockfall on such routes. The direction of the dip of rock strata often determines the degree of danger on a particular face; the character of the rock must also be considered. In planning an ascent of a new peak mountaineers must look for such traces. When falling stones get mixed in considerable quantity with slushy snow or water a mud avalanche is formed. It is vital to avoid camping in their possible line of fall.

Falling Ice

The places where ice may fall can always be determined beforehand. It falls in the broken parts of glaciers and from overhanging cornices formed on the crests of narrow ridges. Large icicles are often formed on steep rock faces, and these fall frequently in fine weather following cold and stormy days. They have to be avoided like falling stones. Seracs are slow in formation, and slow in arriving at a condition of unstable equilibrium.

They generally fall in or just after the hottest part of the day, and their debris seldom goes far. A skillful and experienced ice-man will usually devise a safe route through a most intricate ice-fall, but such places should be avoided in the afternoon of a hot day. Hanging glaciers often discharge themselves over steep rock-faces, the snout breaking off at intervals.

Falls from Rocks

The skill of a rock climber is shown by one's choice of handhold and foothold, and his adhesion to those one has chosen. Much depends on a correct estimate of the firmness of the rock where weight is to be thrown upon it. Many loose rocks are quite firm enough to bear a person's weight, but experience is needed to know which can be trusted, and skill is required in transferring the weight to them without jerking. On rotten rocks the rope must be handled with special care, lest it should start loose stones on to the heads of those below. Similar care must be given to handholds and footholds, for the same reason.

When a horizontal traverse has to be made across very difficult rocks, a dangerous situation may arise unless at both ends of the traverse there be firm positions. Mutual assistance on hard rocks takes all manner of forms: two, or even three, people climbing on one another's shoulders, or using an ice axe propped up by others for a foothold.

The great principle is that of co-operation, all the members of the party climbing with reference to the others, and not as independent units; each when moving must know what the climber in front and the one behind are doing. After bad weather steep rocks are often found covered with a veneer of ice, which may even render them inaccessible. Crampons are useful on such occasions.

Avalanches

The avalanche is the most underestimated danger in the mountains. People generally think that they will be able to recognize the hazards and survive being caught. The truth is a somewhat different story. Every year, 120 - 150 people die in small avalanches in the Alps alone. The vast majority are reasonably experienced male skiers aged 20-35 but also include ski instructors and guides. There is always a lot of pressure to risk a snow crossing. Turning back takes a lot of extra time and effort, supreme leadership, and most importantly there seldom is an avalanche to prove the right decision was made. Making the decision to turn around is especially hard if others are crossing the slope, but any next person could become the trigger.

The Slab Avalanche

This type of avalanche occurs when a plate of snow breaks loose and starts sliding down; these are the largest and most dangerous.

- *Hard slab avalanche*: Formed by hard-packed snow in a cohesive slab. The slab will not break up easily as it slides down the hill, resulting in large blocks tumbling down the mountain.
- *Soft slab avalanche*: Formed again by a cohesive layer of snow bonded together, the slab tends to break up more easily.

The Loose Snow Avalanche

This type of avalanche is triggered by a small amount of moving snow that accumulates into a big slide. Also known as a "wet slide or point release" avalanche. This type of avalanche is deceptively dangerous as it can still knock a climber or skier off their feet and bury them, or sweep them over a cliff into a terrain trap.

Dangerous slides are most likely to occur on the same slopes preferred by many skiers: long and wide open, few trees or large rocks, 30 to 45 degrees of angle, large load of fresh snow, soon after a big storm, on a slope 'lee to the storm'. Solar radiation can trigger slides as well.

These will typically be a point release or wet slough type of avalanche. The added weight of the wet slide can trigger a slab avalanche. Ninety per cent of reported victims are caught in avalanches triggered by themselves or others in their group.

When going off-piste or traveling in alpine terrain, parties have a moral responsibility to always carry:

- Avalanche beacon
- Probe
- Shovel

Paradoxically, expert skiers who have avalanche training make up a large percentage of avalanche fatalities; perhaps because they are the ones more likely to ski in areas prone to avalanches, and certainly because most people do not practice enough with their equipment to be truly fast and efficient rescuers. Even with proper rescue equipment and training, there is a one-in-five chance of dying if caught in a significant avalanche, and only a 50/50 chance of being found alive if buried more than a few minutes. The best solution is to learn how to avoid risky conditions.

Ice Slopes

For travel on slopes consisting of ice or hard snow, crampons are a standard part of a mountaineer's equipment. While step-cutting can sometimes be used on snow slopes of moderate angle, this can be a slow and tiring process, which does not provide the higher security of crampons. However, in soft snow or powder, crampons are easily hampered by balling of snow which reduce their effectiveness. In either case, an ice axe not only assists with balance but provides the climber with the possibility of self-arrest in case of a slip or fall. On a true ice slope however, an ice axe is rarely able to effect a self-arrest.

As an additional safety precaution on steep ice slopes, the climbing rope is attached to ice screws buried into the ice. True ice slopes are rare in Europe, though common in mountains located in the tropics, where newly-fallen snow quickly thaws on the surface and becomes sodden below, so that the next night's frost turns the whole mass into a sheet of semi-solid ice.

Snow Slopes

Snow slopes are very common, and usually easy to ascend. At the foot of a snow or ice slope is generally a big crevasse, called a bergschrund, where the final slope of the mountain rises from a snow-field or glacier. Such bergschrunds are generally too wide to be stepped across, and must be crossed by a snow bridge, which needs careful testing and a painstaking use of the rope. A steep snow slope in bad condition may be dangerous, as the whole body of snow may start as an avalanche.

Such slopes are less dangerous if ascended directly than obliquely, for an oblique or horizontal track cuts them across and facilitates movement of the mass. New snow lying on ice is especially dangerous. Experience is needed for deciding on the advisability of advancing over snow in doubtful condition. Snow on rocks is usually rotten unless it is thick; snow on snow is likely to be sound.

A day or two of fine weather will usually bring new snow into sound condition. Snow cannot lie at a very steep angle, though it often deceives the eye as to its slope. Snow slopes seldom exceed 40°. Ice slopes may be much steeper. Snow slopes in early morning are usually hard and safe, but the same in the afternoon are quite soft and possibly dangerous; hence the advantage of an early start.

Crevasses

Crevasses are the slits or deep chasms formed in the substance of a glacier as it passes over an uneven bed. They may be open or hidden. In the lower part of a glacier the crevasses are open. Above the snow-line they are frequently hidden by arched-over accumulations of winter snow. The detection of hidden crevasses requires care and experience. After a fresh fall of snow they can only be detected by sounding with the pole of the ice axe, or by looking to right and left where the open extension of a partially hidden crevasse may be obvious. The safeguard against accident is the rope, and no one should ever cross a snow-covered glacier unless roped to one, or even better to two companions. Anyone venturing onto crevasses should be trained in crevasse rescue.

Weather

The primary dangers caused by bad weather centre around the changes it causes in snow and rock conditions, making movement suddenly much more arduous and hazardous than under normal circumstances. Whiteouts make it difficult to retrace a route while rain may prevent taking the easiest line only determined as such under dry conditions. In a storm the mountaineer who uses a compass for guidance has a great advantage over a merely empirical observer. In large snow-fields it is, of course, easier to go wrong than on rocks, but intelligence and experience are the best guides in safely navigating objective hazards. Summer thunderstorms may produce intense lightning.

If a climber happens to be standing on or near the summit, they risk being struck. There are many cases where people have been struck by lightning while climbing mountains. In most mountainous regions, local storms develop by late morning and early afternoon. Many climbers will get an "alpine start"; that is before or by first light so as to be on the way down when storms are intensifying in activity and lightning and other weather hazards are a distinct threat to safety.

Altitude

Rapid ascent can lead to altitude sickness. The best treatment is to descend immediately. The climber's motto at high altitude is "climb high, sleep low", referring to the regimen of climbing higher to acclimatize but returning to lower elevation to sleep. In the South American Andes, the chewing of coca leaves has been traditionally used to treat altitude sickness symptoms. Common symptoms of altitude sickness include severe headache, sleep problems, nausea, lack of appetite, lethargy and body ache. Mountain sickness may progress to High Altitude Cerebral Edema and High Altitude Pulmonary Edema, both of which can be fatal within 24 hours. In high mountains, atmospheric pressure is lower and this means that less oxygen is available to breathe. This is the underlying cause of altitude sickness. Everyone needs to acclimatize, even exceptional mountaineers that have been to high altitude before.

Generally speaking, mountaineers start using bottled oxygen when they climb above 7,000 m. Exceptional mountaineers have climbed 8000-metre peaks without oxygen, almost always with a carefully planned programme of acclimatization. In 2005, researcher and mountaineer John Semple established that above-average ozone concentrations on the Tibetan plateau may pose an additional risk to climbers.

Locations

Mountaineering has become a popular sport throughout the world. In Europe the sport largely originated in the Alps, and is still immensely popular there. Other notable mountain ranges frequented by climbers include the Caucasus, the Pyrenees and the Tatra mountains. In North America climbers frequent the Rockies and Sierra Nevada of California, the Cascades of Washington and the high peaks of Alaska. There has been a long tradition of climbers going on expeditions to the Greater Ranges, a term generally used for the Andes and the high peaks of Asia including the Himalaya, Pamirs and Tien Shan. In the past this was often on exploratory trips or to make first ascents. With the advent of cheaper long-haul air travel mountaineering holidays in the Greater Ranges are now undertaken much more frequently and ascents of even Everest and Vinson Massif are offered as a "package holiday". Other popular mountaineering areas of more local interest include the Southern Alps of New Zealand, the Japanese Alps the Scottish Highlands and the mountains of Scandinavia.

HISTORY

- Though it is unknown whether his intention was to reach a summit, Ötzi ascended at least 3,000 m in the Alps about 5,300 years ago. His remains were found at that altitude, preserved in a glacier.
- The first recorded mountain ascent in the Common Era is Roman Emperor Hadrian's ascent of Etna to see the sun rise in 121.
- Peter III of Aragon climbed Canigou in the Pyrenees in the last quarter of the 13th century.
- The first ascent of the Popocatépetl was reported in 1289 by members of a local tribe
- Jean Buridan climbed Mont Ventoux around 1316.

- The Italian poet Petrarch wrote that on April 26, 1336 he, together with his brother and two servants, climbed to the top of Mont Ventoux. His account of the trip was composed later as a letter to his friend Dionigi di Borgo San Sepolcro.
- The Rochemelon in the Italian Alps was climbed in 1358.
- In the late 1400s and early 1500s ascents were made of numerous high peaks in the Andes, for religious purposes by the citizens of the Inca Empire and their subjects. They constructed platforms, houses and altars on many summits and carried out sacrifices, including human sacrifices. The highest peak they are known for certain to have climbed is Llullaillaco. They may also have ascended the highest peak in the Andes, Aconcagua as a sacrifice victim has been found at over 5,000 m on this peak.
- In 1492 the ascent of Mont Aiguille was made by order of Charles VIII of France. The Humanists of the 16th century adopted a new attitude towards mountains, but the disturbed state of Europe nipped in the bud the nascent mountaineering of the Zurich school.
- Leonardo da Vinci climbed to a snow-field in the neighbourhood of the Val Sesia and made scientific observations.
- In 1642 Darby Field made the first recorded ascent of Mount Washington, then known as Agiocochook, in New Hampshire.
- Konrad Gesner and Josias Simler of Zurich visited and described mountains, and made regular ascents. The use of ice axe and rope were locally invented at this time. No mountain expeditions of note are recorded in the 17th century.
- Richard Pococke and William Windham's historic visit to Chamonix was made in 1741, and set the trend for visiting glaciers.
- In 1744 the Titus was climbed, the first true ascent of a snow-mountain.
- The first attempt to ascend Mont Blanc was made in 1775 by a party of natives. In 1786 Dr Michel Paccard and Jacques Balmat gained the summit for the first time. Horace-Bénédict de Saussure, the initiator of the first ascent followed next year.
- The Norwegian mountain climber, Jens Esmark was the first person to ascend Snøhetta in 1798, part of the Dovrefjell range in Southern Norway. The same year he lead the first expedition to Bitihorn, a small mountain in the southernmost outskirts of Jotunheimen, Norway. In 1810 he was the first person to ascend Mount Gaustatoppen in Telemark, Norway.
- The Jungfrau was climbed in 1811, the Finsteraarhorn in 1812, and the Breithorn in 1813. Thereafter, tourists showed a tendency to climb, and the body of Alpine guides began to come into existence as a consequence.

- Citlaltépetl was first climbed in 1848 by F. Maynard and G. Reynolds.
- Systematic mountaineering, as a sport, is usually dated from Sir Alfred Wills's ascent of the Wetterhorn in 1854. The first ascent of Monte Rosa was made in 1855.
- The Alpine Club was founded in London in 1857, and was soon imitated in most European countries. Edward Whymper's ascent of the Matterhorn in 1865 marked the close of the main period of Alpine conquest – the Golden age of alpinism – during which the craft of climbing was invented and 'perfected', the body of professional guides formed and their traditions fixed.
- Passing to other ranges, the exploration of the Pyrenees was concurrent with that of the Alps. The Caucasus followed, mainly owing to the initiative of D. W. Freshfield; it was first visited by exploring climbers in 1868, and most of its great peaks were climbed by 1888.
- The Edelweiss Club Salzburg was founded in Salzburg in 1881, and had 3 members make the First Ascent on 2 Eight-thousanders, Broad Peak and Dhaulagiri.
- Trained climbers turned their attention to the mountains of North America in 1888, when the Rev. W. S. Green made an expedition to the Selkirk Mountains. From that time exploration has gone on apace, and many English and American climbing parties have surveyed most of the highest peaks; Pikes Peak having been climbed by Mr. E. James and party in 1820, and Mt. Saint Elias by the Duke of the Abruzzi and party in 1897. The exploration of the highest Andes was begun in 1879-1880, when Whymper climbed Chimborazo and explored the mountains of Ecuador. The Cordillera between Chile and Argentina was visited by Dr. Gussfeldt in 1883, who ascended Maipo and attempted Aconcagua. That peak was first climbed by the Fitzgerald expedition in 1897.
- The Andes of Bolivia were first explored by Sir William Martin Conway in 1898. Chilean and Argentine expeditions revealed the structure of the southern Cordillera in the years 1885-1898. Conway visited the mountains of Tierra del Fuego.
- New Zealand's Southern Alps were first visited in 1882 by the Rev. W. S. Green, and shortly afterwards a New Zealand Alpine Club was founded, and by their activities the exploration of the range was pushed forward. In 1895, Major Edward Arthur Fitzgerald, made an important journey in this range. Tom Fyfe and party climbed Aoraki/ Mount Cook on Christmas Day 1894, denying Fitzgerald the first ascent. Fitzgerald was en route from Britain with Swiss guide Matthias Zurbriggen to claim the peak. So piqued at being beaten to the top of Mount Cook, he refused to climb it and concentrated on

other peaks in the area. Later in the trip Zubriggen soloed Mount Cook up a ridge that now bears his name.

- The first mountains of the arctic region explored were those of Spitzbergen by Sir W. M. Conway's expeditions in 1896 and 1897.
- Of the high African peaks, Kilimanjaro was climbed in 1889 by Dr. Hans Meyer, Mt. Kenya in 1899 by Halford John Mackinder, and a peak of Ruwenzori by H. J. Moore in 1900.
- The Asiatic mountains were initially surveyed on orders of the British Empire. In 1892 Sir William Martin Conway explored the Karakoram Himalaya, and climbed a peak of 23,000 ft. In 1895 Albert F. Mummery died while attempting Nanga Parbat, while in 1899 D. W. Freshfield took an expedition to the snowy regions of Sikkim. In 1899, 1903, 1906 and 1908 Mrs Fannie Bullock Workman made ascents in the Himalayas, including one of the Nun Kun peaks. A number of Gurkha sepoys were trained as expert mountaineers by Major the Hon. C. G. Bruce, and a good deal of exploration was accomplished by them.
- The Rucksack Club was founded in Manchester, England in 1902.
- The American Alpine Club was founded in 1902.
- In 1902, the Eckenstein-Crowley Expedition, lead by mountaineer Oscar Eckenstein and occultist Aleister Crowley, was the first to attempt to scale Chogo Ri. They reached 22,000 feet before turning back due to weather and other mishaps.
- In 1905, Aleister Crowley led the first expedition to Kanchenjunga, the third highest mountain in the world. Four members of that party were killed in an avalanche. Some claims say they reached around 21,300 feet before turning back, however Crowley's autobiography claims they reached about 25,000 feet.
- The 1950s saw the first ascents of all the eight-thousanders but two, starting with Annapurna in 1950 by Maurice Herzog and Louis Lachenal. The world's highest mountain, Mount Everest was first climbed on May 29, 1953 by Sir Edmund Hillary and Tenzing Norgay from the south side in Nepal. Just a few months later, Hermann Buhl made the first ascent of Nanga Parbat, a remarkable solo climb, the only eight-thousander to be solo'd on the first ascent. K2, the second highest peak in the world was first scaled in 1954. In 1964, the final eight-thousander to be climbed was Shishapangma, the lowest of all the 8,000 metre peaks.

BACKPACKING

Backpacking combines hiking and camping in a single trip. A backpacker hikes into the backcountry to spend one or more nights there, and carries supplies and equipment to satisfy sleeping and eating needs. A backpacker packs all of his or her gear into a backpack. This gear must include food, water, and shelter, or the means to obtain them, but very little else, and often in a more compact and simpler form than one would use for stationary camping.

A backpacking trip must include at least one overnight stay in the wilderness. Many backpacking trips last just a weekend but long-distance expeditions may last weeks or months, sometimes aided by planned food and supply drops. Backpacking camps are more spartan than ordinary camps. In areas that experience a regular traffic of backpackers, a hike-in camp might have a fire ring and a small wooden bulletin board with a map and some warning or information signs.

Many hike-in camps are no more than level patches of ground without scrub or underbrush. In very remote areas, established camps do not exist at all, and travellers must choose appropriate camps themselves. In some places, backpackers have access to lodging that are more substantial than a tent. In the more remote parts of Great Britain, bothies exist to provide simple accommodation for backpackers.

Another example is the High Sierra Camps in Yosemite National Park. Mountain huts provide similar accommodation in other countries, so being a member of a mountain hut organization is advantageous to make use of their facilities. On other trails there are somewhat more established shelters of a sort that offer a place for weary hikers to spend the night without needing to set up a tent.

Most backpackers purposely try to avoid impacting on the land through which they travel. This includes following established trails as much as possible, not removing anything, and not leaving residue in the backcountry. The Leave No Trace movement offers a set of guidelines for low-impact backpacking.

Professional Backpacking

For some people, backpacking is a necessary and integral part of their job. In the military a framed backpack is referred to as a "rucksack" or simply a "ruck". Soldiers who serve in the militaries of most nation-states usually receive at least some rudimentary backpacking training while infantrymen are often trained to a more advanced backpacking skill level. They share many common attributes with amateur backpackers: being self-contained, use of land-navigation skills and actively minimizing their environmental foot-print.

Although there are also a few differences such as the need to carry an assault rifle, other weapons, ammunition and communication equipment as well as at times maintaining "noise and light discipline", which means remaining silent and in darkness to avoid detection. Other professional backpackers may be scientific and academic researchers, professional guides, photographers, park-rangers and "search and rescue" personnel.

Motivation

People are drawn to backpacking primarily for recreation, to explore places that they consider beautiful and fascinating, many of which cannot be accessed in any other way. A backpacker can travel deeper into remote areas, away from people and their effects, than a day-hiker can. However, backpacking presents more advantages besides distance of travel. Many weekend trips cover routes that could be hiked in a single day, but people choose to backpack them anyway, for the experience of staying overnight.

These possibilities come with disadvantages. The weight of a pack, laden with supplies and gear, forces backpackers to travel more slowly than day-hikers would, and it can become a nuisance and a distraction from enjoying the scenery. In addition, camp chores can easily consume several hours every day. Backpackers face many risks, including adverse weather, difficult terrain, treacherous river crossings, and hungry or unpredictable animals.

They are subject to illnesses, which run the gamut from simple dehydration to heat exhaustion, hypothermia, altitude sickness, and physical injury. The remoteness of backpacking locations exacerbates any mishap. However, these hazards do not deter backpackers who are properly prepared. Some simply accept danger as a risk that they must endure if they want to backpack; for others, the potential dangers actually enhance the allure of the wilderness.

BUNGEE JUMPING

Bungee jumping is the sport that originated from New Zealand and was created by maverick daredevil A J Hackett, and his original jump from a bridge in Greenhithe, Auckland. The sport denotes jumping from a tall structure while connected to a large rubber cord. The tall structure is usually a fixed object, such as a building, bridge, or crane; but it is also possible to jump from a movable object, such as a hot-air-balloon or a helicopter, that has the ability to hover over one spot on the ground; fixed-wing aircraft are clearly unsuitable because they only stay aloft when moving rapidly forward. The intense thrill comes as much from the free-falls as from the rebounds. When the person jumps, the cord stretches to absorb the energy of the fall, then the jumper flies upwards again as the cord snaps back.

The jumper oscillates up and down until all the energy is used up. The word bungee first appeared around 1930 and was the name for rubber eraser. The word bungy, as used by A J Hackett, is said to be "Kiwi slang for Elastic Strap". Cloth-covered rubber cords with hooks on the ends have been available for decades under the generic name bungee cords. In the 1950s David Attenborough and a BBC film crew had brought back footage of the "land divers" of Pentecost Island in Vanuatu, young men who jumped from tall wooden platforms with vines tied to their ankles as a test of courage. This film inspired Chris Baker of Bristol, England to use elastic rope in a kind of urban vine jumping. The first modern bungee jump was made on 1 April 1979 from the 250ft Clifton Suspension Bridge in Bristol, and was made by four members of the Dangerous Sports Club.

The jumpers, led by David Kirke, were arrested shortly after, but continued with jumps in the US from the Golden Gate and Royal Gorge bridges, spreading the concept worldwide. By 1982 they were jumping from mobile cranes and hot air balloons, and putting on commercial displays. One of the first operators of a commercial bungee jumping concern enabling the general public to experience these leaps of faith was New Zealander, A J Hackett, who made his first jump from Auckland's Greenhithe Bridge in 1986. During the following years Hackett performed a number of jumps from bridges and other structures building public interest in the sport. Hackett remains one of the largest commercial operators, with concerns in several countries.

The worlds first permanent commercial bungee site was the Kawarau Bridge Bungy at Queenstown in the South Island of New Zealand. Despite the inherent danger of jumping from a great height, several million successful jumps have taken place since 1980. This is attributable to bungee operators rigorously conforming to standards and guidelines governing jumps, such as double checking calculations and fittings for every jump.

As with any sport, injuries can still occur, but there have been few fatalities. A relatively common mistake in fatality cases is to use too long a cord. The cord should be substantially shorter than the height of the jumping platform to allow it room to stretch. When the cord reaches its natural length the jumper either starts to slow down or keep accelerating. depending upon the speed of descent. One may not even start to slow until the cord has already stretched somewhat, because the cord's resistance to distortion is zero at the natural length, and increases only gradually after, taking some time to even equal the jumper's weight.

RAFTING

Rafting or whitewater rafting is a recreational activity utilizing a raft to navigate a river or other bodies of water. This is usually done on whitewater or different degrees of rough water, in order to thrill and excite the raft passengers. The development of this activity as a leisure sport has become popular since the mid 1970s. Rafting is one of the earliest means of transportation, used as a means for shipping people, hunting, and transferring food.

In 1842, Lieutenant John Fremont of the U.S. Army first journalized his rafting expedition on the Platte River. Horace H. Day designed the equipment he used in rafting. Day's rafts were constructed from four independent rubber cloth tubes and wrap-around floor. In 1960s, rafting was then recognized and paths like Grand Canyon were routed and whitewater rafting companies were established. In 1970s, rafting marked its major development as a leisure sport when it was then included in the Munich Olympic Games. In 1980s, as rafting continued to gain its popularity, a lot of rivers were opened for rafting activities. Rivers in South America and Africa were just a few of them. In 1990s, rafting was included in major game events like the Barcelona Games in 1992, Atlanta Games in 1996, and the whitewater events of the Summer Olympic Games hosted by Ocoee River in Tennessee Valley. In addition, the International Federation of Rafting was instituted in 1997 and in 1999 the first Official International Championship was held. Nowadays, river rafting is still gaining popularity among extreme water sports in order to thrill and excite the raft passengers.

ROCK CLIMBING

Rock climbing, broadly speaking, is the act of ascending steep rock formations. Normally, climbers use gear and safety equipment specifically designed for the purpose. Strength, endurance, and mental control are required to cope with tough, dangerous physical challenges, and knowledge of climbing techniques and the use of essential pieces of gear and equipment are crucial. Although the practice of rock climbing was an important component of Victorian mountaineering in the Alps, it is generally thought that the sport of rock climbing began in the last quarter of the nineteenth century in various parts of Europe. Rock climbing evolved gradually from an alpine necessity to an athletic sport in its own right. As rock climbing matured, grading systems were created in order to more accurately compare relative difficulties of climbs. Over the years, both climbing techniques, and the equipment climbers use to advance the sport, have evolved in a steady fashion.

Whitewater Rafts

Rafts were originally the simplest form of man's transportation in water and were then made of several logs, planks or reeds which were fastened together. Nowadays, inflatable boat were used as rafts which were later adopted by the military for beach assaults. It consists of very durable, multi-layered rubberized or vinyl fabrics with several independent air chambers. Its length varies between 3.5 m (11 ft) and 6 m (20 ft), the width between 1.8 m (6 ft) and 2.5 m (8 ft). The exception to this size rule is usually the packraft, which is designed as a portable single-person raft and may be as small as 1.5m long and weigh as little as 4 lbs.

Rafts come in a few different forms. In Europe the most common is the symmetrical raft steered with a paddle at the stern. Other types are the asymmetrical, rudder-controlled raft and the symmetrical raft with central helm (oars). Rafts are usually propelled with ordinary paddles and typically hold 4 to 12 persons. In Russia, rafts are often hand made and are often a catamaran style with two inflatable tubes attached to a frame. Pairs of paddlers navigate these rafts. Catamaran style rafts have become popular in the western United States as well, but are typically rowed instead of paddled.

Classes of Whitewater:

Class 1: Very small rough areas, requires no manuevering. (Skill Level: None)

Class 2: Some rough water, maybe some rocks, might require manuevering.(Skill Level: Basic Paddling Skil)

Class 3: Whitewater, small waves, maybe a small drop, but no considerable danger. May require significant manuevering. (Skill Level: Experienced paddling skills)

Class 4: Whitewater, medium waves, maybe rocks, maybe a considerable drop, sharp manuevers may be needed. (Skill Level: Whitewater Experience)

Class 5: Whitewater, large waves, maybe large rocks and hazards, maybe a large drop, precise maneuvering (Skill Level: Advanced Whitewater Experience)

Class 6: Whitewater, huge waves, huge rocks and hazards, maybe huge drops. Attempting a Class 6 will most likely end in serious injury or death. If someone navigates a 6 without harm, luck can be given most of the credit. (Skill Level: Expert)

Safety

Whitewater rafting can be a dangerous sport, especially if basic safety precautions are not observed. In the past there have been many accidents; both commercial trips and private trips have seen their share of injuries and fatalities, though private travel has stereotypically been associated with greater risk. Depending on the area, legislated safety measures now exist for rafting operators, ranging from certification of outfitters, rafts, and raft leaders, to more stringent regulations about equipment and procedures. It is generally advisable to discuss safety measures with a rafting operator before signing on for a trip. The equipment used and the qualifications of the company and raft guides are essential information to be considered. Like most outdoor sports, rafting in general has become safer over the years. Expertise in the sport has increased, and equipment has become more specialized and increased in quality. This is no doubt as a result of the difficulty rating of most river runs has changed.

A classic example would be the Colorado River in the Grand Canyon, which has swallowed whole expeditions in the past, leaving only fragments of boats but is now run safely by commercial outfitters hundreds of times each year, with relatively untrained passengers. Risks in whitewater rafting stem from both environmental dangers and from improper behaviour. Certain features on rivers are inherently unsafe and have remained consistently so despite the passage of time. These would include "keeper hydraulics", "strainers" (*e.g.,* fallen trees), dams (especially low-head dams, which tend to produce river-wide keeper hydraulics), undercut rocks, and of course dangerously high waterfalls. Rafting with experienced guides are the safest way to avoid such features. Even in safe areas, however, moving water can always present risks—such as when a swimmer attempts to stand up on a rocky riverbed in strong current, risking foot entrapment. Irresponsible behaviour along the lines of rafting while intoxicated has also contributed to many accidents.

To combat the illusion that rafting is akin to an amusement park ride, and to underscore the personal responsibility each rafter faces on a trip, rafting outfitters generally require customers to sign waiver forms indicating understanding and acceptance of the risks. Rafting trips often begin with safety presentations to educate customers about problems that may arise. Having said all this, the overall risk level on a rafting trip with experienced guides using proper precautions is low. Thousands of people safely enjoy raft trips every year.

Issues with Rafting

Like all wilderness sports, rafting has to balance the conflict between nature protection and nature use. Because of frequent problems in the past, some rivers now have regulations restricting or specifying the annual and daily operating times. Conflicts have also arisen with environmentalists when rafting operators, often in co-operation with municipalities and tourism associations, alter the riverbed by dredging and/or blasting in order to eliminate safety risks or create more interesting whitewater features in the river. Incongruously these measures usually are only temporary, since a riverbed is subject to permanent changes. On the other hand, rafting contributes to the economy of many alpine regions which in turn may contribute to the protection of rivers from hydroelectric power generation and other development. Additionally, white water rafting trips can promote environmentalism. By experiencing first hand the beauty of a given river, individuals who would otherwise be indifferent to the environmental concerns of an area may gain a strong desire to protect and preserve that area because of a positive outdoors experience.

POPULAR RAFTING LOCATIONS

Africa

- Bujagali Falls on the Nile
- Omo River
- Tana River
- Zambezi River

Asia and Oceania

- Tully River in Queensland, Australia
- Kelani River at Kitulgala in Sri Lanka

- Ganga (Ganges River) and its tributaries in India
- Zanskar River in India
- Yoshino River in Japan
- Bhote Koshi river in Nepal
- Kali Gandaki river in Nepal
- Karnali river in Nepal
- Kawarau River in New Zealand
- Shotover River in New Zealand
- Whataroa River, New Zealand
- Hokitika River, New Zealand
- Chico River, Kalinga, Philippines
- Cagayan de Oro, Philippines
- Jeram Besu, Pahang, Malaysia
- Padas River, Sabah, Malaysia Image:Padasraft c.jpg
- Kiulu River, Sabah, Malaysia

Carribean

- Rio Yaque del Norte near Jarabacoa, Dominican Republic

Europe

- River Findhorn near Aviemore in Scotland, United Kingdom
- Afon Tryweryn near Bala in Wales, United Kingdom
- Tiroler Oberland in the Landeck and Imst Region in Tirol, Austria
- Enns River in Austria
- Tara River (Montenegro), Montenegro
- Una River, Bosnia and Herzegovina
- Neretva River, Bosnia and Herzegovina
- Drina River in Bosnia and Hercegovina
- Soca River in Slovenia
- Sjoa River in Norway
- Lim river in Serbia

Middle East

- Al Assi in North East Lebanon, Northern Bekaa Valley
- Al Litani in East Lebanon, in the Bekaa Valley
- Nahr Al Kalb in West Lebanon

North America

Eastern

- Black River in Watertown, New York
- Chattooga River near Clayton, Georgia in South Carolina
- Cheat River in Albright, West Virginia

- Cheoah River near Robbinsville, North Carolina
- Delaware River, along the border of New Jersey and Pennsylvania
- Deerfield River in northwest Massachusetts
- Nolichucky River flowing into Erwin, Tennessee (northeast Tennessee)
- Gauley River and New River "Grand Canyon of the East" in West Virginia
- Hudson River near Lake George, New York
- James River in Virginia (particularly in Richmond)
- Kennebec River, Dead River, and Penobscot River in Maine
- Lachine Rapids in Montreal, Quebec
- Lehigh River in Pennsylvania
- Moose River near Old Forge, New York
- Nantahala River in Bryson City, North Carolina
- Ocoee River and Appalachian Mountains in the southeastern United States
- Ocoee River flowing into Copperhill, Tennessee (southeast Tennessee)
- Ottawa River at Calumet Island in the Whitewater Region, Ontario
- Pigeon River flowing into Hartford, Tennessee (east Tennessee)
- U.S. National Whitewater Centre in Charlotte, North Carolina
- Watauga River flowing into Elizabethton, Tennessee (northeast Tennessee)
- Youghiogheny River in Ohiopyle, Pennsylvania

Western

- American River near Coloma, California in the USA
- Arkansas River near the Royal Gorge in Colorado
- Colorado River, especially through the Grand Canyon starting at Lee's Ferry, Arizona
- Denali National Park and Preserve, starting at the Denali Lodge
- Deschutes River in central Oregon
- Kern River in California
- Kicking Horse River in Golden, British Columbia, Canada
- Lochsa River in Idaho
- Methow River near Methow, Washington
- Rogue River near Grants Pass, Oregon
- Salmon River and its tributaries in Idaho
- Skagit River near Marblemount, Washington
- Skykomish River near Gold Bar, Washington
- Snake River near Jackson Hole, Wyoming
- Tieton River near Naches, Washington

- Truckee River near Lake Tahoe, California starting at Lake Tahoe Dam
- Tuolomne River near Groveland, California
- Wenatchee River near Leavenworth, Washington
- White Salmon River near Husum, Washington

Central America

- Cahabon River in Guatemala
- Nahualate River in Guatemala
- Pacuare River in Costa Rica

South America

- Futaleufu River in Chile, South America

ECO-TOURISM IN INDIA

KERALA ECO-TOURISM

The naturally beautiful and exquisite Kerala landscape is one of the greenest destinations in India and is the perfect place to go on eco-tourism vacations. The clean and tranquil Kerala backwaters, the soothing velvety Kerala hills and a riotous explosion of greens in the intoxicating Kerala wilds offers countless opportunities for eco-tourism and nature vacations. The entire Kerala landscape is generously covered with coconut palms, pineapple groves, banana trees, Pandanus plants, thick leafy plants, dense forests and neatly clipped tea bushes. Acres of submerged paddy fields located in perfect harmony with the winding Kerala backwaters and the gentle rolling Kerala hills are heavenly paradisiacal eco-tourism vacation destinations.

Regale the verdant Kerala beauty on your eco-tourism vacations to Kerala, South India with Kerala India Vacations. Visit the fascinating Kerala wildlife destinations and spot rare wild animals lazing in their natural habitat and enjoy the magic of nature. Eco-tourism in Kerala, South India is a fast developing sector and the state government is making extra efforts to promote eco-tourism. Among the manifold advantages of promoting eco-tourism in Kerala, South India one very important aspect is revenue generation and environment conservation at the same time. The concept of eco-tourism basically means that you get to visit the exotic nature rich tour destinations but at the same time you must take care not to soil the beauty of the region by not using polythene bags and other materials or things such as tin cans, wrappers etc that adversely affect the environment. Kerala India Vacations guides you through the lush green paths within acres of rubber plantations so that you can experience first hand the incomparable natural beauty of green Kerala, South India on your eco-tourism vacations. Kerala, South India happens to be one of the leading producers of rubber in India though rubber is not a native Indian plant and was introduced by the Dutch colonialists, in fact Kerala accounts for 92 per cent of the rubber produced in India. Stay at a luxury resort or a farmhouse near a Kerala rubber plantation and enjoy the warm hospitality of the Kerala rubber plantations during your eco-tourism vacations to Kerala, South India and be fascinated by the rural Kerala lifestyle while you observe busy twittering birds, brightly coloured butterflies and squirrels scurrying here and there. Admire the thick shapely leaves on straight trunks that glisten in the bright sun.

Botanically known as Havea brasiliensis, a single rubber plant takes about 7 years to mature and can be harvested for latex (processed for natural rubber) for almost 20 years. The local rubber tappers who stay close to these lush rubber plantations harvest latex from these trees. Pineapple is planted as an intercrop in most of the Kerala rubber plantations so you get to taste the juicy Mauritius pineapple variety while on your eco-tourism vacations to the scenic Kerala rubber plantations. Kottayam in Kerala, South India is an important Centre of commercial rubber plantations set on the picturesque banks of the serene palm fringed Kerala backwaters. Extensive rubber plantations cover the hillocks wrapped by silver ribbons of the fascinating Kerala backwaters, not a sight you would like to miss while on your eco-tourism tours to Kerala, South India.

Acres of tea plantations interspersed with shade fruit trees wrap the gentle Kerala hill slopes in a warm embrace and create soothing and striking vistas for you to visit on your Kerala eco-tourism vacations. Rows of neatly clipped tea bushes carpet the Kerala hills on the Western Ghats in Kerala, south India and offer you ample opportunity to gaze at the naturally enthralling Kerala beauty at its beatific best while on your Kerala India eco-tourism vacations.

The Britishers introduced the tradition of tea plantations in India. Tea bushes have the potential to grow to tree heights though they are kept neatly trimmed to waist height to make it feasible for the plantation workers to pluck tealeaves without much difficulty. Gaze at the lovely Kerala tea plantations while on your eco-tourism vacations and mark the fact that each tea bush is planted at a distance of 1 to 1.5 meter from each other along the contours of the landscape. Stay at the resorts and clean home-like accommodations on the Kerala tea plantations and spend your eco-tourism vacations in Kerala, South India in the midst of pure undulating greens. Watch the plantation workers plucking tealeaves and filling the baskets slung on their backs while you enjoy nature treks.

Usually it's the women who are employed for plucking tealeaves on these tea plantations in Kerala, South India. These women work in unison and sing peppy songs while plucking tealeaves and move along the rows of tea bushes in perfect rhythm. Kerala, South India has some of the highest tea estates located in India. Munnar is one of the most popular Kerala hill stations, which is known for its sweeping tea plantations. Some of the popular tea plantations in Kerala,

South India are located at Peerumadu that is situated at a height of 914-meters above the sea level, Anayirankal that has acres of tea plantations located in the midst of dense evergreen forests and a few other Kerala hill stations that are definitely worth visiting on your Kerala eco-tourism tours to Kerala, South India.

Wander at leisure on the aromatic Kerala spice plantations during your Kerala India eco-tourism Vacations. Stay at the spice plantation farmhouses with the plantation owners and experience the magical charm of staying in the midst of luxuriant plantations laden heavily with a combination of scents of the various spices that are grown on these extensive plantations. Though you can visit spice plantations almost all over beautiful Kerala, Periyar is one of the most popular spice districts in Kerala, South India. This absolutely beautiful hill district is covered with a variety of spice plantations that lie close to the famous Periyar wildlife sanctuary.

Shop for rare spices at the local Kerala spice markets and inhale the intoxicating aroma of cinnamon, cardamom, pepper, ginger, turmeric, curry leaves and other spices. Besides the cultivation of these traditional Kerala spices the Kerala plantation owners have also taken to growing spices such as rosemary, oregano, mint, vanilla, bay leaves, basil, thyme and others. Discover the secret of the mouthwatering Kerala cuisine as you visit the acres of Kerala spice plantations on your eco-tourism vacations with Kerala India Vacations. Spices are basically fragrant substances of vegetable origin with distinct flavours used in selective combinations to give a special flavour to the exotic Indian cuisine.

Enjoy bird watching tours and nature treks to the lovely Kerala spice plantations with Kerala India Vacations and experience the Kerala natural beauty at its aromatic best. Watch the locals work on the extensive spice plantations and observe closely the way of life in these Kerala spice plantations and enjoy your eco-tourism vacations thoroughly.

Orissa Eco-tourism

Organized by Tourism of Orissa offers you the best seats in the house to attend what is essentially a spectacular show of competing colours, cacophony of voices, a jumble of animal instincts and raw emotions. No, we aren't talking about a Broadway show or a Hollywood musical production. Eco-tourism in Orissa is what concerns us at Tourism of Orissa. With Eco-tourism in Orissa tour package, offered by Tourism of Orissa, you get to see all the shades of the diverse ecological system that reside within the state of Orissa. Eco-tourism in Orissa may revolve around water bodies or beaches or national parks and wildlife sanctuaries alone or, it can be a combination of all these features that make Orissa such as enticing choice as a destination for eco travel and tours.

While hot springs (Atri and Tarabalo), lakes (Chilika), waterfalls (Badaghagra, Khandadhar) and reservoirs (Hirakud, Indravati) in Orissa have tourists lining up, the beaches of Orissa (Puri, Chandrabhaga, Gopalpur, Chandipur) have dazzled international and national tourist for centuries with their pristine beauty and positive vibes. Orissa's varying topography - from the wooded Eastern Ghats to the fertile river basin - has proven ideal for evolution of compact and unique ecosystems. Thereby creating such treasure troves of flora and fauna that even seem inviting to many migratory species of birds and reptiles.

Bhitar Kanika National Park is famous for its second largest mangrove ecosystem. The bird sanctuary in Chilika (Asia's biggest brackish water lake) and the tiger reserve and waterfalls in Simlipal National Park are integral part of any eco tours in Orissa, arranged by Tourism of Orissa. The Gharial Sanctuary at Tikarpada and the Olive Ridley Sea Turtles in Gahirmatha turtle sanctuary also feature on the list of avid nature watchers. The city wildlife sanctuaries of Chandaka and Nandan Kanan are a must visit for the lessons they teach is conservation and revitalization of species from the brink of extinction. Since Orissa is so rich in culture - history, traditions and people, Tourism of Orissa can even have your eco tour clubbed with other tours in Orissa so that you get the best of al te worlds at a single destination called Orissa.

Eco-tourism in Chhattisgarh

Chhattisgarh, the 26th state of the Indian Union, is located in the central part of India. The newly formed Indian state of Chhattisgarh is famous for its enchantingly beautiful natural landscapes, rich cultural heritage and unique tribal populations. With over 44 per cent of its total area under forests, Chhattisgarh is also amongst the greenest states of India. The Chhattisgarh region is known as a great repository of biological diversity. The unique combination of rich cultural heritage and biological diversity makes Chhattisgarh an ideal eco-tourism destination with immense potentials for the growth eco-tourism the region. The Indian Govt. is actively collaborating with the local officials of the state to realize the full potential of Eco-tourism growth of the region in order to make Chhattisgarh as one of the most important eco-tourism destinations in India.

Chhattisgarh is one of the greenest states of India with over 44 per cent of its total area under lush forests. The forests of Chhattisgarh are not only known for their diverse flora and fauna but also contain about 88 species of medicinal plants. In addition, Chhattisgarh has also formulated several ecological plans and working in the direction to become the country's first bio-fuel self-reliant state by 2015. And to achieve this goal the green state has devised a plan to plant over 100 million saplings of Jatropa Carcus. Chhattisgarh is also unique in its wildlife population and has 3 National Parks and 11 Wildlife Sanctuaries, housing some of the rare wildlife and bird species. With so much of variety for Eco-tourism, Chhattisgarh promises to be an ideal holiday destination for nature lovers, wildlife enthusiasts and also for those who want to discover the unique tribal life of the region.

Chhattisgarh has identified some regions with a very high potentiality for eco-tourism. The green state has launched an eco-tourism project covering three potential tourist tracks - Raipur-Turtiria-Sirpur, Bilaspur-Achanakmar and Jagdalpur-Kanger Valley National Park. In addition, a number of herbal gardens and natural health resorts have been created with increased local participation. The use of ethno-medicine, which has been practiced by aboriginal tribes since centuries, predating even Ayurveda, is also being promoted in Chhattisgarh. The major eco-tourism attractions, which are getting prime attention in Chhattisgarh, include the protection and development of the wildlife areas, camping grounds and trekking facilities. With so many initiatives, Chhattisgarh is destined to become the most Favourite eco-tourism destination in India and few among best in the world.

Rajasthan Eco-tourism

The Cultures of the Rajasthan Desert are some of the most well preserved in India. We, at Marwar Eco-Cultural Tours and Travels, are passionate about this land, its cultures and its people and we want to share this passion with you. The Desert and its people will captivate you.

Because we are able to provide you with in-depth cultural information that you would not receive on other Tours. If you have an adventurous spirit or a cultural thirst to quench, we have a Tour that should surpass all of your expectations. We also offer opportunities to get involved with the people and assist in ongoing, non-profit projects. As an NGO, we have assistance projects in most villages we will visit. All of our guides are from Rajasthan, and most are village natives or indigenous people.

They have a great knowledge of local and regional history and are great storytellers. They will keep your attention for hours next to a fire, counting tales of kings and warlords; castles, forts and Havelis (mansions); rituals and traditions. You will see the camel herds, observe villagers' craftsmanship, and gain insight into indigenous nomadic lifestyles. We will show you the best of Rajasthan, and we are very flexible and can modify our tours according to the group's needs. You can also design your own tour. You dream it up; we'll do the rest. We will organize the tour and guide you according to your wishes. Among other things, we can arrange a visit to a marriage ceremony, a farming or agricultural tour, Handicraft and Jewelry making, a stay in an Ayurvedic (traditional Indian Medicine) clinic, and more.

Madhya Pradesh Eco-tourism

Eco-tourism signifies to save the environment around us and preserving the natural luxuries and forest life. Whether it's about a nature camp or organizing trekking trips towards the unspoilt and inaccessible regions, one should always keep in mind not to create any mishap or disturbance in the life cycle of nature. A destination enveloped in magic, Madhya Pradesh is one of the most popular tourist destination in India. It's many tourist destinations are, by far, some of the most magical locales in the world.

With the highest mountains, beautiful wildlife, a cosmopolitan heritage from different civilizations, it is so rightly called tourist paradise. It has lot to offer from breathtaking natural vistas, amazing architecture, rich culture, and a warm hearted society of people living in virtual harmony.

Himachal Pradesh Eco-tourism

The majestic coniferous trees from an enchanting backdrop to the mountains with broad-leafed species like the Oaks, Maples, Birdcherry, Hazelnut, Walnut, Horsechestnut and Rhododendrons adding grandeur to the landscape. Whereas the ivies clinging to the trunks of stately Cedars appear to veil secrets of Nature, the vines flowing from atop the trees seem to invite the visitors with open arms. The violas popping up from under the forest floor and the riot of colours provided by the anemones, primulas, buttercups and many other herbs in the alpine meadows lay a colourful feast before eyes of the beholder. Besides plants. the State also provides a very congenial habitat to a wide variety of Himalayan fauna. The Himalyan Tahar and the Ibex can be spotted as silhouettes on the high ridges in the trans-Himalayas. The Brown Bear and Musk Deer roam happily in the temperate forests, in the company of colourful pheasants including the Monal, the Western Hornes Tragopan, the Koklas and the Kalij. The lucky ones can even be traeted to rare sight of critically endangered species like the Snow Leopard and Snow Cock.

Also known as the 'Abode of Gods', the State conjures up visions of ancient temples, with exquisitely carved wooden panels, occupying almost every hilltop and the festivities associated with these religious places. Even a casual glimpse at the traditionally attired local deities being carried in meticulously decorated palanquins, devotees dancing to the rhythmic play of traditional drums and clarions, leaves a lasting imptint on one's mind. This natural and cultural richness of the State coupled with its simple peace loving people and traditional hospitality makes the State a most favoured tourist destination. Anybody with a zest for life, a spirit of adventure and a love for nature will find all that his heart desires amongest the pristine environs of Himachal Pradesh.

Uttaranchal Eco-tourism

Uttaranchal blessed with magnificent glaciers, majestic snow-clad mountains, gigantic and ecstatic peaks, valley of flowers, skiing slopes and dense forests, this Abode of Gods includes many shrines and places of pilgrimage. Char-dhams, the four most sacred and revered Hindu temples: Badrinath,

Kedarnath, Gangotri and Yamunotri are nestled in the Mighty Mountains. A picturesque state, with a breathtaking panoramic view of Himalayas, Uttaranchal promises its tourists a visit full of fun and unforgettable moments.

Uttaranchal blessed with magnificent glaciers, majestic snow-clad mountains, gigantic and ecstatic peaks, valley of flowers, skiing slopes and dense forests, this Abode of Gods includes many shrines and places of pilgrimage. India's first National Park is cradled in the foothills of the Himalayas and spreads over an area of 520 sq. kms., along the bankds of the Ramganga river. The dense Sal forests of the Himalayan foothils and the tall grassy neadows make it one of the richest areas of northern India for the habitation of the big mammals.

Ecosystem in India

The Himalayan region is a particularly fragile ecosystem. The interconnections between the different types of vegetation, between plant life and the soil, between the soil, vegetation and water are so close and so precariously balanced that the slightest change in one plunges the entire system into jeopardy. Ecosystems on seismic belts, for example, are literally 'at the mercy of the land'. Nature plays havoc in other ways too: the monsoon pattern often spells drought in the dry season, and terrible floods during rainfall.

Deforestation

Growing Population

Way back in 326 B.C., when Alexander the Great came to India, his advance was checked by almost impenetrable forests along the Indus. By the time Emperor Ashoka ascended the throne, stretches of forests had already been cleared to make roads. Ashoka realised the importance of conserving forests, and even appointed an officer for the purpose.

Sher Shah Suri was also farsighted, and planted trees all along the route from Delhi to his capital Patna. However, the Mughals' interest in forests was sadly limited to a rather hedonistic passion for big game. Under the British rule, deforestation became rampant in order to procure timber to build furniture, railway sleepers and ships for the British navy. However, the British soon realised that forests had to be spared the ordeal. After Independence, forests were cleared whenever wood was needed either for timber or agriculture, or for setting up townships. Forests were razed to the ground mindlessly till the eastern hill people decided to say a collective 'Stop'.

Forest Distructions Through Fire

Forest fires have largely contributed to deforestation. Forests in India are very susceptible to fires, especially in summer. All it takes is one little spark and a forest fire could reduce considerable green stretches to ashes in a matter of a few hours. Earlier the Bishnois of Jodhpur (Rajasthan) even laid down their lives to save trees. The Bishnois are a religious community, famous for their loyalty towards animals and trees. In fact, they are known to worship the blackbuck as a sacred animal. Various measures are being taken to curb the felling of trees. Clearing forests is now an offence under Indian law, unless approved by the concerned authorities. However, deforestation has acquired alarming proportions in India. The country's total forest cover today has fallen to a little more than approximately 10 per cent –a dismal situation for a country with a population of over a billion.

Land Degradation

Every year, valuable topsoil is swept away by floods in the rainy season. and deforestation contributes to the problem of soil erosion. Man may well have compounded the problem.

Chemical Farming

To sustain the country's enormous population, intensive chemical farming was introduced in the 1960s, ushering in the 'Green Revolution'. Chemical fertilisers and high yield grains were used on an unprecedented scale. Although production tripled, the quality of the land took a battering. Chemicals and toxic substances too have taken their own toll on the land. Desertification (cultivable land turning barren) is a serious problem in some parts of the country, especially in Rajasthan.

Water Conditions

Despite high rainfall, water levels have dropped alarmingly in many places in the country. Obviously this is due to the demands of a burgeoning population. In any case, the monsoon cannot always be relied upon; it is not uncommon for a region like Rajasthan to be stricken by drought once every two to three years. While hydroelectric projects are a partial solution to the problem, their overall 'efficiency' is not beyond interrogation.

The Narmada Valley Project – a vast project of several dams aimed at providing water and power for Gujarat, Rajasthan, Madhya Pradesh and Maharashtra – when completed, is projected to submerge an estimated 350,000 hectares of forest and 200,000 hectares of cultivated fields, and displace nearly 400,000 people. Spearheaded by the environmentalist Baba Amte, Medha Patkar, and more recently Arundhati Roy, a vigorous campaign is in progress against the building of the dams. Another controversial project is the Tehri Dam in Uttar Pradesh. Besides the displacement and loss it is projected to cause, another dread is that the dam may burst as it is being constructed on an earthquake-prone zone. The distinguished man in white, Sunderlal Bahuguna has once again spared no effort at raising public consciousness about the issue at hand.

Pollution

Despite having some of the strictest laws in the world against pollution, India is one of the most environmentally polluted countries in the world. Air pollution is so grave in cities like Delhi, Calcutta, Kanpur and some others, that simply breathing the air is equivalent to smoking 10-20 cigarettes a day! Recently, Delhi acquired the dubious distinction of being one of the five most polluted cities in the world. The rivers in the country have not been spared either. Industrial waste and a combination of other factors have contributed to the plight of these 'dying' rivers. In some places, safe drinking water, is a rare commodity. Lakes and river habitats too have been polluted. The Yamuna Action Plan was a project undertaken at a tentative cost of ₹ 20,000 crore to cleanse the river of pollutants. A similar project was undertaken for the mighty Ganga River.

Conservation

Ancient texts including the epics, the Buddhist Jatakas, the Panchatantra or the more recent Jain scriptures, all preach non-violence towards even the lowest forms of animal and plant life, a philosophy that the Indian Maharajas and their British guests chose to overlooked for a while. The Indian Government has an uphill task to perform. It has been able to protect only about 4 per cent of the total forest cover in the form of National Parks and similar reserves. Underhand activities like poaching are not entirely unheard of even in these restricted areas. Currently there are about 80 National Parks and 441 sanctuaries in the country. Massive tree plantation Programmes are also being undertaken. The Vana Mahotsava, first started in 1950, is an annual tree-planting festival celebrated across the nation.

Individual Efforts

Vishweshwar Dutt Saklani of Garhwal, in Uttar Pradesh, is a small time farmer who started planting trees to seek solace after the death of his brother (who had initiated the practice) in 1948. In the last 50 years, Vishweshwar has overlaid 100 hectares of land with oak, cedar, walnut and rhododendron. People were dismissive of him until they saw the sea change that his work had brought about in the village. Denuded hills became green, land became more fertile and dry streambeds filled up. Fodder and fuel were in plenty and everyone was happy.Vishweshwar received the Indira Priyadarshini Vrikshamitra Award in 1986. Bikkalu Chikkaiah and Thimmakka were a childless couple who worked in a quarry close to Bangalore. They decided to raise banyan trees in lieu of the children they were unable to have. So they chose a barren piece of land en route to their quarry.

The couple planted saplings and put protective barriers around them. In the evenings, they lugged water from a well a kilometre away. 40 years later,

284 banyan trees provided shade to a 3km stretch. Thimmakka received the National Citizen's Award in 1996. Abdul Karim of Kasargod, Kerala too did something similar. He turned a dry piece of land into a veritable forest after 19 years of hard labour. His deciduous trees brought water back into the soil. Karim went a step ahead and got some animals in this forest, to successfully replicate a healthy ecosystem.

Eco-tourism Policy

The Draft Tourism Policy 1997 states that "in the context of economic liberalisation and globalisation being pursued by the country, the development policies of no sector can remain static. "The policy further states that" the emergence of tourism as an important instrument for sustainable human development including poverty alleviation, employment generation, environmental regeneration and advancement of women and other disadvantaged groups in the country" requires support to realise these goals.

India's tourism resources have always been considered immense, in a tourism audit. The geographical features are diverse, colourful and varied. The coastline offers opportunities for developing the best beaches in the world. There are a wealth of eco-systems including bio-sphere reserves, mangroves, coral re-e, deserts, mountains and forests as well as an equally wide range of flora and fauna.

The Policy further states that "international tourists visiting interiors of the country for reasons of purity of the environment and nature contributes to the development of these areas particularly backward regions". Thus Tourism "should also become a reason for better preservation and protection of our natural resources, environment and ecology".

The policy recognises that sustained growth of tourism can give rise to conflicts. To ensure that the growth of tourism takes place along desired lines, certain guidelines have been framed:

1. To remove the constraint of the information gap.
2. To create a tourist product that is desirable and supported by an integrated infrastructure.
3. To involve all agencies, public, private and government, in tourism development.
4. To create synergy between departments and agencies that have to deliver the composite tourist product.
5. To use both the circuit and scheme approach so that peoples participation through panchayats, local bodies, NGO's, and youth organisations will create a greater awareness of tourism. The Central Government can thus concentrate on larger investment oriented projects.
6. To create direct access for destinations off the beaten track.

7. To diversify the product with new options like beach tourism, forests, wild life, landscapes and adventure tourism, farm and health tourism.
8. To ensure that the development does not exceed sustainable levels.
9. To develop the seven north-eastern states, the Himalayan region and Islands for tourism.
10. To maintain a balance between the negative and positive impacts of tourism through planning restrictions and through education of the people for conservation and development.

Development Plan

The strategy for development should take into consideration the carrying capacity, local aspirations and benefits likely to accrue to the community. In particular specific policies and guidelines for eco-tourism development and adventure tourism are to be formulated, primarily through a regulatory framework. The Draft Guidelines have been approved at a State Ministers Conference and have been circulated to various trade and industry bodies. The guidelines draw a distinction between mass or resort tourism and nature or Eco-tourism, as the kind of tourism that has a lower impact on the environment and requires less infrastructural development. The Ministry hopes that the environment conscious international tourist will be made aware that India is taking steps to protect its ecology and environment.

Apart from the do's and don'ts, the guidelines are governed by a tourism management plan, the key elements of which are the protection of natural resources and a positive involvement of local communities, along with an optimum number of environmentally conscious visitors. The principles of management are scientific planning, effective control and continuous monitoring, development of physical infrastructure, zoning and a Management plan for public use of natural sites.

The management plan should establish standards for resort development, style and location of structures, waste disposal, treatment of sewage, control of litter, use of public spaces and fragile areas. The operational guidelines rely on sensitisation of all the role players and this Programmes is based on a self-regulated environmental code.

Area specific rather than universal development plans keeping in mind the unique character of the location and its economic and social environment are important. This would help the State Government to coordinate with the industry in managing visitors and their activities. NGO's working on socio-economic Programmes in forest and remote areas could have a closer coordination with tourism service operators to transfer economic benefits, particularly the handicraft production and marketing sector. The guidelines are only a beginning, and it is hoped that with increasing awareness of the visitor the industry will regulate its practices.

Tourism Advisory Committee

There is an emphasis on the needs and perceptions of the international tourist running through the discussion on the guide lines although the data from the National Parks makes it evident that the domestic tourists outnumber international visitors, although they do not pay the same amount as the foreign visitor either in entry fees or for board and lodging and transport facilities. They do however demand a much higher per capita use of resources like water, fuel for heating and cooking and transport. They also make the same intensive use of time and try to maximize their stay by the number of animals and birds they can view in the 24-hour period.

It is interesting to note that no democratic participation has been called for in the policy formulation process, and all the amendments to the policy have come from trade associations and government think tanks. The tourism Advisory Committee also consists of eminent persons and community representation has been ignored.

The policy clearly recognises the debate on the tourism issue which has surfaced wherever tourism development, particularly in the case of tourism projects relating to the "gifts of nature" like beaches, rivers, mountains and forests, have already been developed. However, mere recognition of the hostility of people to tourism development is not enough to change the nature of tourism development or the resistance to tourism or what many have termed a poor tourism culture.

Perhaps to understand this in a better perspective, we should look at the issue of sustainable development in a critical way. Perhaps we can question the impact of sustainable development on the environment and sift through the jargon of development planners, international agencies, and environmental activists to see how sustainable development can be achieved without all the contradictions that are apparent as in the case of the tourism sector.

Development in Tourism

The concept of sustainability originated in the context of renewable resources like forests and fisheries and was subsequently adopted by the environmental movement. In most cases it is understood to mean "the existence of the ecological conditions necessary to support human life at a specific level of well being through future generations." However, in addition to ecological conditions there are social conditions that influence ecological sustainability in a nature-people interaction.

The social connotations have been described by Barbier (1987) who has defined social sustainability as "the ability to maintain desired social values, traditions, institutions, cultures or other social characteristics." The term sustainability came into usage in 1980 when the IUCN presented the World Conservation Strategy where sustainable development was linked to conservation of living resources. However, the fundamental goals have often been lost sight of because of operational goals (*e.g.,* food, water, shelter, health are fundamental goals to be realised through self reliance, cost effectiveness, appropriate technology, people centred-ness etc.)

Consequently, the WCED made its definition brief: Social Development is development that meets the needs of the present without compromising the ability of future generations to meet their own needs. They did not make any assumptions on the direction in which changes in demand would take place. (*e.g.,* equity, social justice, self-determination, or cultural diversity). India's tourism policy follows the mainstream SD (Sustainable Development) thinking by adopting all the critical objectives: revive growth change the quality of growth meet essential needs for jobs, food, energy, water and sanitation ensure sustainable levels of population conserve and enhance the resource base reorient technology and management risk merge environment and economics in decision making reorient international economic relations make development more participatory.

These objectives are responsible for building a very broad consensus on the issue of sustainable development, yet the debate at the operational level continues. Most participants in the debate now accept that many human activities are reducing the long-term ability of the natural environment to provide goods and services, which will eventually affect human health and well being.

Enviromental Degradation

Many also accept that poverty is devastating the lives of millions in the Third World since there is no consensus between what is environmentally necessary and what is economically and developmentally feasible. The level of inter-dependence between the two insights is yet to be incorporated in the concept of Social Development. Some problem areas are: Environmental degradation, already affecting millions in the Third World, is likely to reduce human well being across the globe.

Who is responsible for this rapid degeneration? Is it the poor or the rich? The poor have no option but to exploit resources for short-term survival. If we take the example of forests and their resources, which have been traditionally outside the market system and in the sphere of tribal or indigenous peoples rights, they are today seen as exploiters of the forests as against tourists, with all their demand for infrastructure and superstructure, who are seen to be conservationists. The inter-linked nature of the problem of sustainability is such that the impact of degradation will be quicker on the poor than on the rich.

Can Sustainable Development be the metafix it claims to be in reconciling increasing industrial, agricultural and resource use productivity with environmental needs. The weakness of the Social Development argument lies in the techno-economic approach to solutions with regard to common property resource management, through know how transfers, resource pricing, subsidy policies and building management capabilities. (World Bank, 1987) Deeper processes such as land reforms, industrial demands on raw materials, over consumption, changing legal and political structures are either ignored or looked at in a cursory manner.

For instance how can we claim a consensus between those who are concerned for the survival of future generations with those who are concerned with the survival of wild life, or human health and subsistence? Unless we can identify the trade-offs necessary for each specific objective of sustainability, we will not have clarity in the discussion. We will also fail to understand why, even when there is a broad consensus, projects on the ground result in conflicts. Suggested refinements could be:

1. A distinction between ecological and social sustainability and in the process an identification of the inter-linkages a distinction between renewable and non-renewable resources, between environmental processes crucial to human life and crucial to other forms of life dependent on the resources. a distinction between the techno-economic aspects of social sustainability (infrastructure, services, government) with political and cultural sustainability.
2. A distinction between equitable development and local participation, and decentralisation, what many have called NGOisation of sustainable development. This is because no rigorous testing of local participation leading to social equity or to sustainable resource use have been reported.

Environmental Impact

Case studies reflect personal, organisational or political preferences. Tourism is one of the activities which have caused concern because of the effects of increasing human traffic on fragile environments. Countries which are looking towards Tourism as a means of economic growth, like India, have limited resources and cultural restraints and they have the greatest need to pay heed to the possible negative impacts of tourism. The environmental impact of tourism is a basic issue, whether we are looking at a developed or an underdeveloped area, region or country.

The costs of tourism for a country like India include extensive investment in fixed assets with a low rate of return for infrastructure, transportation, accommodation, cultural institutions, exhibition centres, and park facilities. To this maybe added the social and cultural costs like additional demands on infrastructure like land, water, health services; the creation of new jobs for displaced people; the cost of positive community relationships; the disparity between the lifestyle of visitors and those who serve them; the possible friction between local residents and new users of valued local resources; the perception of local residents of the spending of scarce capital resources on what they consider low priority areas like tourism; cultural cost of alterations in local ceremonial or traditional values; loss of privacy for local communities as tourists come to gape at their living conditions and rituals.

Tourism also causes increasing congestion and pollution as thousands of visitors flock to parks and sanctuaries in motorised vehicles; there are changes in accessibility, landscape and the ecological balance between man and nature; there is the cost, both monetary and human, of creating conservation zones (core/buffer) with unforeseen or undesirable side effects; which have been observed in the Eco-tourism movement.

The benefit of revenue from tourism does not always redress these problems but goes towards the cost of administering the project. The tourism industry is generally self-centred and not given to educational, cultural or exchange Programmes on a philanthropic basis. The natural environment, with the best will in the world, cannot escape damage with the volume of visitors. As more and more tourists, both domestic and international seek the exotic and remote destinations around the world, the likelihood of the environment suffering as a result become greater.

Forests can suffer from trampling, fires, tree felling for facilities and waste. Wildlife, despite the protection in national parks, has suffered a loss of habitat, hunting and poaching, viewing and photographing, leading to an interruption of feeding and breeding patterns or hunting for food undisturbed. These are the prized moments for the viewer. The trade in wild life trophies or tourist souvenirs is the more deliberately destructive aspect of such tourism.

Sanctuaries

The building of tourist lodges in materials that are not integrated with the environment and the pressure they put on the land and water bodies is also wilfully destructive. Management techniques that include being less user friendly or control of numbers by closing access or by multiplying the number of attractions and areas or charging higher admission fees are generally not popular with the tourist or the tour operator and are also difficult to implement because of high administrative costs.

Equations, through its involvement in the field have had a variety of experiences relating to the debate on Eco-tourism and sustainable development. The major issues that have emerged after the policy of notification of wild life sanctuaries and their management by the Forest Departments are quite disturbing. Wherever notification has led to displacement of people the experience of rehabilitation has not been successful and the conservation aims have not been met. Several sanctuaries have witnessed militant action by displaced communities against the developers of tourism. In many cases the tourism aims have also not been met in making the sanctuary accessible to viewers, naturalists, wild life photographers. Tourism has not been able to counteract poaching and the most extensive and the oldest conservation project, Project Tiger has not been able to save the tiger population.

The commercialisation of the experience, like the privileging of one species, for example the tiger, has led to congestion and noise pollution and this has put a pressure on the management of the sanctuary to organise tiger shows which are putting a pressure on the feeding and mating habits of the tiger. These are very invasive techniques of experiencing the wild. On the plus side, the concept of beneficiary led development has helped indigenous people to organise against their displacement and exploitation as well as to fight for the retention of their traditional rights and life styles.

Environmentalists have not only been involved in such organisations and movements but have done valuable documentation. This has influenced many urban visitors to be more sensitive to the wild and to follow the rules when participating in eco-tourism. This has also led to the development of a code of conduct for the tourist, the industry and the administrator. These attempts are in a very nascent stage.

The kind of co-ordination that is required between the environmentalist and economist is just beginning to emerge and have still to counter the myths of neo-classical economists in the field of tourism. But a beginning has been made.

Coastal Issues

The Coastal Regulation Zone (CRZ) came into existence on February 19, 1991, with the gazetting of the notification by the Union Ministry of Environment and Forests (MoEF) under Sec. 3(1) and Sec. 3(2)(v) of the Environment Protection Act, 1986, and Rule 5(3)(d) of the Environment Protection Rules, 1986. Through the Notification the Central Government declared the coastal stretches of seas, bays, estuaries, creeks, rivers and backwaters, which are influenced by tidal action (in the land ward side), up to 500m. from the high tide line (HTL) and the land between the low tide line (LTL) and HTL as CRZ. In the case of rivers, creeks and backwaters, the Notification stated that the CRZ could be modified on a case by case basis, on the basis of reasons to be recorded during the preparation of the coastal zone management plan (CZMP). However, the width of the CRZ from each bank could not be less than 100 m., or the width of the water body, whichever was less.

Activities Prohibited in the CRZ:

1. Setting up of new industries and expansion of existing ones, except those directly related to waterfront or requiring foreshore facilities.

2. Manufacture, handling, storage or disposal of hazardous substances.
3. Setting up and expansion of fish processing units including warehousing (excluding hatchery and natural fish drying in permitted areas).
4. · Discharge of untreated wastes and effluents from industries, cities, towns or other human settlements. The existing practices would have to be phased out by the concerned authorities within three years.
5. Dumping of ash or any waste from thermal power plants.
6. Land reclamation, bunding or disturbing the natural course of sea water with similar obstructions. Exceptions are made for activities required for the control of coastal erosion, the maintenance of water ways to ports; clearing sand bars; and for the construction of regulators, storm water drains and structures for the prevention of salinity ingress.
7. Mining of sand, rocks and other substrata materials, except those raw minerals not available outside the CRZ areas.
8. Drawing or harvesting of groundwater and construction of mechanism within 200 m. of the HTL. Between 200 and 500 m. it will be permissible only if done manually through ordinary wells for drinking, horticulture, agriculture and fisheries.
9. Construction activity in ecologically sensitive areas.
10. Any construction activity between LTL and HTL except facilities for carrying treated effluents and waste water discharge into the sea, facilities for carrying sea water for cooling purposes, oil, gas and similar pipelines and facilities essential for facilities permitted under the notification.
11. Dressing or altering of sand dunes, hill, natural features including landscape changes for beautification, recreation and other such purposes, except as permitted under the notification.

Regulated activities (requiring environmental clearance from MoEF):

1. Construction activities related to Defence requirements for which foreshore facilities are essential. Residential office, hospital, workshops will not normally be permitted in the CRZ, except in very special cases.
2. Operational construction for ports and harbours and light house.
3. Foreshore facilities of thermal power plants for transport of raw materials, in-take of cooling water and out fall for discharge of treated wastewater or cooling water.
4. All other activities with investment exceeding. 5 crores.

Coastal Zone Management Plan (CZMP)

All the coastal states have to prepare, within one year, CZMPs identifying and classifying CRZ areas as per the Notification guidelines. These plans have to be approved by MoEF All further development activities should be within the framework of these plans. In the interim period, before the approval of the plans, development activities should not violate the provisions of the Notification.

Violations are punishable under the provisions of the Environment Protection Act of 1986. For regulating developmental activities, the coastal stretches within 500m of the HTL are classified into CRZ-1, CRZ-11 and CRZ-III.

CRZ-I — Areas that are ecologically sensitive and important (national parks, coral re-efs, mangroves, areas close to the breeding and spawning grounds of fishes, areas of high natural beauty, historical heritage, high genetic diversity, and those likely to be inundated by global warming, 'etc.); and areas within the LTL and HTL.

Regulations in CRZ-I

1. No new construction shall be permitted within 500 m of the HTL.
2. No construction activity except for facility for carrying treated effluents and waste water into the sea or carrying sea water for cooling, oil, gas or similar pipelines will be permitted between the LTL and the HTL.

CRZ-II

Areas that have already been developed up to or close to the shoreline. 'Developed areas' that come within municipal limits or other legally designated urban areas which have been substantially built up and which have been provided with infrastructural facilities like drainage, approach road, water supply and sewage mains.

Regulations in CRZ-III

1. Buildings will not be permitted in the seaward side of existing roads (or those proposed in the CZMP) nor on the seaward side of the existing authorised structures.
2. Reconstruction of authorised buildings to be permitted subject to the existing floor space and without change in existing use CRZ III Areas that are relatively undisturbed and do not belong to either CRZ-I or CRZ-II. This will include coastal zones in the rural areas and also areas within municipal limits or urban areas that are not substantially built up.
3. Areas up to 200 m. from the HTL earmarked as no development zone (NDZ). No construction will be permitted within this zone except for repairs of existing authorised structures not exceeding the existing plinth area and covered apace. Raising of horticultural crops, gardens, pastures, parks, play fields, forestry and salt manufacture from sea water permitted in this zone.
4. Development of vacant plots between 200 m. 500 m. from the HTL,

in designated areas with prior approval of MoEF, permitted for hotels and beach resorts.

5. Construction or reconstruction of dwellind units between the 200m and 500m of the HTL permitted so long as it is within the ambit of traditional rights and customary uses such as existing fishing villages and gouthans.
6. Building conditions would be based on the conditions that the total number of dwelling units does not increase more than double of the existing units; the total covered area is not more than 33 per cent of the plot area; the overall height is not more than two floors and 9 m. Guidelines for development of beach resorts in the designated areas of CRZ-III · No construction within 200 m. from the HTL and in the area between LTL and HTL.
7. The total plot size should not be less than 0.4 hectare and the covered area should not be more than 33 per cent. · The total height of the construction should not be more than 9 m. and the building should not be more than two floors.
   Groundwater cannot be tapped within 200m of the HTL. Between 200 and 500 m. it can be tapped with the concurrence of the State or Central Groundwater Board.
8. Extraction of sand, leveling or digging of sandy stretches, except for the structural foundation will not be permitted within 500 M. of the HTL.
9. The quality of treated effluents, solid wastes, emissions and noise levels etc. must be within the standards laid down by the central or state pollution control boards. Untreated effluents and solid wastes should not be discharged into the water or beach.
10. To allow public access there should be a gap of 20m. width between two hotels. Two consecutive gaps should not be more than 500 m. apart.

The World Scenario of Tourism

In recent years tourism has emerged as a major economic activity that is employment oriented and earns foreign exchange. Its share in the worlds GDP in 1994-95 was 10 per cent which is more than the world military budgets put together.

In global terms, the investment in tourism industry and travel trade accounts for 7 per cent of the total capital investment. Today 21.2 crore people around the globe are employed in travel trade and tourism. In future, this industry is likely to see unprecedented growth.

According to the World Tourism Council at Brussels, the revenues from travel and tourism in Asia Pacific region will grow at the rate of 7.8 per cent annually over the next decade. Amongst the economic sectors, the tourism sector is highly labour intensive. A survey by the Government of India notes that the rate of employment generation (direct and indirect) in tourism is 52 persons employed per ₹.10 lakh investment (based on 1992-93 Consumer Price Index). This is much higher than the rates of employment generation in most other economic sectors.

Indian tourism industry has also recorded phenomenal growth. The rate of international arrivals in India in recent years has been to the tune of about 19 lakh arrivals per year. The unprecedented growth in tourism in India has made it the third largest foreign exchange earner after gem and jewellery and ready-made garments. This is not surprising since India possesses a whole range of attractive normally sought by tourists and which includes natural attractions like Iandscapes, scenic beauty, mountains, wildlife, beaches, major rivers and manmade attractions such as monuments, forts, palaces and havelis. However, in global terms, in spite of such attractions, tourist arrivals in India are a mere 0.30 per cent of the world arrivals. Receipts are similarly low, just a 0.50 per cent of the world receipts. We are still quite far from the target of 50 lakh tourist arrivals per year.

Travel and Tourism is the world's largest industry and creator of jobs across national and regional economies. WTTC/WEFA research show that in 2000, Travel and Tourism will generate, directly and indirectly, 11.7 per cent of GDP and nearly 200 million jobs in the world-wide economy. Jobs generated by Travel and Tourism are spread across the economy - in retail, construction, manufacturing and telecommunications, as well as directly in Travel and Tourism companies.

These jobs employ a large proportion of women, minorities and young people; are predominantly in small and medium sized companies; and offer good training and transferability. Tourism can also be one of the most effective drivers for the development of regional economies. These patterns apply to both developed and emerging economies.

Contributing to Sustainable Development

The 1992 United Nations Conference on Environment and Development (UNCED), the Rio Earth Summit, identified Travel and Tourism as one of the key sectors of the economy which could make a positive contribution to achieving sustainable development. The Earth Summit lead to the adoption of Agenda 21, a comprehensive Programmes of action adopted by 182 governments to provide a global blueprint for achieving sustainable development. Travel and Tourism is the first industry sector to have launched an industry-specific action plan based on Agenda 21.

Travel and Tourism is able to contribute to development which is economically, ecologically and socially sustainable, because it:

1. Has less impact on natural resources and the environment than most other industries;

2. Is based on enjoyment and appreciation of local culture, built heritage, and natural environment, as such that the industry has a direct and powerful motivation to protect these assets;
3. Can play a positive part in increasing consumer commitment to sustainable development principles through its unparalleled consumer distribution channels; and
4. Provides an economic incentive to conserve natural environments and habitats which might otherwise be allocated to more environmentally damaging land uses, thereby, helping to maintain bio-diversity.

There are numerous good examples of where Travel and Tourism is acting as a catalyst for conservation and improvement of the environment and maintenance of local diversity and culture. (Some of these are set out in Section B of this paper and a fuller illustration of the range of industry action can be found on the World Travel and Tourism Council's Of course, there are also examples where development has not been sustainable. (Some of the lessons learnt from these poor practices are illustrated in Section C of this paper.)

Providing Infrastructure

To a greater degree than most activities, Travel and Tourism depends on a wide range of infrastructure services - airports, air navigation, roads, railheads and ports, as well as basic infrastructure services required by hotels, restaurants, shops, and recreation facilities (*e.g.,* telecommunications and utilities).

It is the combination of tourism and good infrastructure that underpins the economic, environmental and social benefits. It is important to balance any decision to develop an area for tourism against the need to preserve fragile or threatened environments and cultures.

However, once a decision has been taken where an area is appropriate for new tourism development, or that an existing tourist site should be developed further, then good infrastructure will be essential to sustain the quality, economic viability and growth of Travel and Tourism. Good infrastructure will also be a key factor in the industry's ability to manage visitor flows in ways that do not affect the natural or built heritage, nor counteract against local interests.

Challenge for the Future

Travel and Tourism creates jobs and wealth and has tremendous potential to contribute to economically, environmentally and socially sustainable development in both developed countries and emerging nations. It has a comparative advantage in that its start up and running costs can be low compared to many other forms of industry development. It is also often one of the few realistic options for development in many areas. Therefore, there is a strong likelihood that the Travel and Tourism industry will continue to grow globally over the short to medium term.

Of course, if Travel and Tourism is managed badly, it can have a detrimental effect - it can damage fragile environments and destroy local cultures. The challenge is to manage the future growth of the industry so as to minimise its negative impacts on the environment and host communities whilst maximising the benefits it brings in terms of jobs, wealth and support for local culture and industry, and protection of the built and natural environment.

9

Marketing

INTRODUCTION

We all know that simply establishing a tourism company does not guarantee the arrival of tourists. We have to make the business work. But how do you do this? How much do you need to spend on publicity and how will you achieve it – through web promotion, word of mouth, advertising? How do you create awareness of your business other than communicating directly with tourists? How do you plan to grow your business over a period of time? A successful business will need to develop suitable products for the market, price them correctly, promote them effectively, distribute them to the final customer and evaluate the results of the total programme. Then the whole process starts again.

This is marketing. It is not solely attending travel fairs and making brochures. These are just a small part of the field of promotion, which is only a part of the marketing process.

A general definition for marketing could be as follows:

- "Marketing is the management function which organizes and directs all those business activities involved in assessing customer needs and converting customer purchasing power into effective demand for a specific product or service to the final consumer or user so as to achieve the profit target or other objective set by the company or organization."

This definition leads to some very important points to bear in mind. Firstly, marketing is a management function. Some tour operators employ staff specifically in a marketing role. Others will have the marketing function solely undertaken by the manager or director. In either situation, there must be clear goals for the company. A marketer can not simply come into a business and make it more profitable. They must understand the philosophy of the company, what the goals are, where the interests lie and so on. The second important point is assessing customer needs. A company will only succeed if it can produce or supply what is demanded by consumers. There would be little point, for example, in running two week 'Pumpkin Picking' tours. The demand for this type of activity is likely to be very small, difficult to sustain and difficult to market. Tour operators must provide what tourists want.The next stage looks in detail on consumer needs, understanding clients and market research. I have personally seen many people establish a tourism company hoping that tourists will come, but without having ever given any consideration to what they are selling and to whom. The third point is converting customer purchasing power into effective demand. Take a look at the letter below,

Dear Sir,

I have just started a tourism company in Croatia. We are called Croatian Tours and Travel Agency Co. Ltd. We can do lots of different types of trips to all parts of the country, from sightseeing to adventure and specialty travel, and food and wine tasting. We can also organize sailing and beach apartment rentals.. We hope that you can cooperate with us and send us some tourists from your company.

Thanks.

Imagine that you had received a letter like this from a tour operator. You'd probably throw it straight in the rubbish bin. They have no idea of selling, packaging, planning – in fact no idea of the tourism industry or business at all. A letter like this would get you nowhere. Getting people interested in your company requires careful planning and thoughtful promotion. Achieving a profit target. For most of us, this is the reason why we have a company. We need to make money. There are of course other reasons why you may be involved in tourism such as the enjoyment of meeting new people or traveling to the countryside. However, what is important here is the fact that marketing is very closely linked to profit. For example, is it better to spend $1000 on brochures for an increase in profit of $100,000 or to attend a travel fair at a cost of $20,000 for an anticipated profit of $80,000? Obviously, you would choose the first option. You do specific marketing activities to get forecasted results, not simply because that's what every other tourism company does and because you think you ought to. Marketing a company, its products and services is no easy task. It's therefore essential to have in place a marketing plan. This plan can of course change and your document should never be set in stone. The plan should change at least once a year. Because tourism is subject to outside influences, (we have seen evidence of this with the Iraq war, 9/11, Bali bombings and SARS in Asia.), modifications may need to be made at short notice to accommodate these influences.

MARKETING PLAN

A marketing plan must be supported by extensive, research-based data on markets, consumers and the environment. The plan can only be written once this research has been undertaken. As I have said earlier, you cannot sell a product or service based on your own intuition that people will want it. This is especially true if you require funding from an external source to help you grow your business. Just because you think something will sell, doesn't mean that people will buy. This is no defined format for a marketing plan. There are big differences between organizations and these differences have to be reflected in the plan.

Firstly, the plan has three major areas that should be considered after gathering your research:

- *Objectives*: What are you trying to achieve?
- *Strategies*: How are you going to achieve it?
- *Tactics*: What are the actions you will undertake to do all this?

The contents of a typical marketing plan could include the following:

- Introduction and Background
  - Introduction
  - The current position
  - Objectives
  - Relationship of Marketing Plan to overall Business Plan
- The Marketing Strategy
  - Marketing for Croatia
  - Company Marketing
  - Research
  - Promotion and Communication
  - Pricing
  - Corporate Image
  - Market segments and Distribution Channels
  - Product development
- People
- Implementation Strategy
  - Trade Fairs
  - Web site and Digital Media
  - Printed Media
  - Direct Mail
  - Personal Communications
  - Advertising
  - Membership
- Budget
- Evaluation

The marketing plan serves several purposes:

- It is a managerial control document which aims to ensure that clear goals and targets have been established in order that the organization does not drift about.
- It provides a detailed inventory as to how the marketing budget is to be spent and why it has been allocated in the ways set out. Alll sales and revenue targets must be identified and justified.

- It provides and agreed basis of action that can be circulated to every individual involved in its implementation. As a result, it acts as a mechanism for ensuring that everyone is clearly identified with marketing aims.
- It provides a set of benchmarks against which marketing programmes can later be evaluated and refined for the future. Without explicit targets, evaluation of marketing efforts is impossible.

BEING COMPETITIVE

A tourist wanting a general tour of Croatia or an overseas tour operator wanting to partner with a Croatian operator has a number of choices. Within Croatia, there are over XX tourism companies and travel agencies offering tours throughout the season. Why should the Tourist Company or tourists choose you? All operators offer vehicles, guides, hotel bookings, visits to attractions, cultural events, or other activities. These factors are comparable, meaning we can easily identify and compare them. If you offer the same as the other companies, you are unlikely to be very successful in your business. And if you are, it's likely that you have had to reduce your prices significantly to do so.

Of course you need to assess other tourism companies in Croatia to see what they are doing. But additionally, you need to look further a field and understand why tourists or tourism companies are sending their tourists to other destinations in the region. You need to be competitive and compete against both other Croatian tour operators and those operators in neighbouring countries. So how do you compete? Competitive advantages are built up through competitive activities, orientated towards doing the same things that rivals do, but better, and also doing different things to other competing companies. Imagine that you are purchasing a new computer. There are lots of similar ones available, all offering the same specifications - size of disk space, speed of operation, availability of accessories, etc - the comparative advantages. So how do you choose which one to purchase?

You focus not only on price but length of guarantee, reliability of after-sales service, reliability of retailer and ability to upgrade the computer - the competitive advantages. In the same way with your company, you need to either do the same things better than other Croatian tour operators or provide better and different products and services. We're not talking about just going to different locations or doing different activities. Look at the whole operation of you company. What could you do better than anyone else or do that nobody else is doing? You could look at booking procedures, cancellation policies, return client incentives, gifts for guests, specialist language guides, lengths of trips, profits going to local charities or communities. These are competitive advantages in the tourism industry that may just make a tourist decide to go with you rather than another company.

$$\frac{\text{Value}}{\text{Effort}} = \frac{\text{Service Facilities}}{\text{Cost}} + \frac{\text{\& Experience Gained}}{\text{Effort Required}}$$

In the past, 'value for money' has often been a term used when purchasing a service - measuring the diversity of services or quality of services against the cost for those services. However, new theories suggest that this does not fully reflect a tourist's way of thinking. The tourism services offered have to be combined with the feelings and sensations obtained from undertaking travel with your company. These then are measured against not only the cost of the trip but also against the efforts the tourist had to go to arrange and undertake the trip and the obstacles or deterrents they faced. If the services were poor, the experience unrewarding, the price high or the trip difficult to organize or undertake then you will not be a competitive business - no matter how wonderful your trip was presented in a brochure. To compete successfully, your business has to offer to the market greater value than your rivals for the same effort on the part of the tourists - or the same value for less effort.

DESTINATION MARKETING

In almost all cases, a tourist will decide to come to Croatia before they decide to travel with your company. In the same way, an overseas tour operator will look for a partner in Croatia after they have decided to take clients to Croatia. Therefore, you are not only trying to sell the products and services your company offers but Croatia itself as a tourism destination. Imagine you are attending a travel fair in London. A stand display emblazoned by your company name and a list of the activities you do is unlikely to attract many people, unless your company name includes the words 'Croatia' or 'Croatian'. The decision making processes of tourists is discussed later in the stage, but at this stage, you need to be aware that marketing the country is likely to bring more success than marketing solely your company.

The main thing that any tourist is purchasing when they come here is a Croatian experience, not the services of your guide or the quality of hotels. This is a decision they make after they have decided to come here. For someone who has never been to Croatia before, whether they are a tourist or a foreign tour operator, they will firstly want to know why they should come here and what the attractions and benefits are over other destinations. This is where competitiveness comes in again. You need to highlight what Croatia has that is better than other neighbouring countries and what is does better or differently than the competing destinations. Never be complacent and believe that tourists will always want to come to Croatia. Never also believe that everyone knows where Croatia is. Some of you will know from experience that those attendees at travel fairs first ask questions about the country rather than about your company. How sunny is it there? Where is Croatia? Didn't you have a war?

MARKETING RESEARCH

Marketing research is the design of a plan for the collection of data, the purpose of which is to answer a given question. Such a question could be "Which country's outbound tourists offer the best opportunity for long term sustainable growth?" or "Who is my biggest competition?". Answers to these questions are vital for understanding the market within which your business operates.

Research can fall into two areas:

1. A descriptive role whereby the aim is to focus on what is happening by concentrating on the collection of factual data to provide a picture of the current situation, or
2. An analytical role by shifting the focus to why things are happening in an attempt to explain the situation by seeking out reasons.

In order to develop a marketing plan, it is imperative that information is gathered on the business's performance and the marketplace. Answers are needed for a business to be able to make decisions. Without such information, any decisions being made run the risk of being bad ones which could prove very costly both financially and otherwise to the long term health of the business. Marketing research needs to be undertaken on a regular basis. Changes within the marketplace, among consumers and within the business will all have an effect on the business. Although information gathered from marketing research will not be perfect, if the research is well planned and executed, it will mean that decisions taken will be more likely to prove successful. There are various steps in undertaking research. Identify and define the problem - Before beginning the task of gathering information, it is first necessary to identify the problem for which research is required. You do not want to start gathering information only to find later that the information does not answer the questions you have. Investigate available sources - You do not want to start collecting information if that information already exists. You should seek out information which is already available.

The Learning Tools, will get you started with places to look for information:

- *Determine research plan*: Once all available sources of data have been evaluated, a plan is formulated to identify what further information is required and how it should be collected. This will involve generating hypotheses to be tested and methodo-logies. Methods could be interviews, surveys and observation.
- *Data collection*: Data should be collected based on the methodology outlined in the research plan.
- *Data analysis*: Based on the information collected analysis techniques will differ according to whether the information is quantitative or qualitative.
- *Present research results*: The information should be tabulated and interpreted so that recommendations can be made regarding the appropriate course of action to take.

When looking for secondary data (data from sources other than your business), sources could include government agencies, trade associations, trade press and magazines, subscription sources, the press, internal company records, international organizations A tour operator's need to do marketing research will fall into several areas:

- *Consumer satisfaction*: If you regularly receive clients, you will need to get feedback on the satisfaction of the services and products you are selling. This form of research would normally be in the form of a questionnaire that would be distributed to clients prior to their departure. The results of this research should help you to make changes to the way you run your operations to improve satisfaction.
- *Overseas Operator*: To sustain and grow the partnerships you have with foreign operators, you will need to undertake research on their satisfaction with your products and services. It may be that tourists will give feedback to them rather than to you. In which case, again some adjustments may be needed to your operations to ensure that satisfaction levels are maintained. Undertaking research is in itself, a marketing tool. Showing that you actively encourage feedback will impress the clients.
- *Industry trends*: Whether you just subscribe to industry trade magazines or e-newsletters or purchase reports on trends within the international tourism industry, it is important that you have some familiarity on what changes are taking place in the popularity of competing destinations, consumer preference for destinations and growing markets for specific activities.

Market Segments and Channels

The Market Segments and Market Channels Presentation of the Learning Tools will walk you through the steps of understanding market segments and channels. The Marketing and Distribution Channel Worksheet that follows it will guide you through the basics of developing a marketing plan.

MARKETING CONCEPTS

As in industrial production, tourism entered the new era of mass production in the early seventies. The introduction of Boeing 747 and the large-scale construction of hotels at popular tourist destinations led to the belief that overproduction of both Airlines seats and hotel rooms is a distinct possibility. The rapid growth of package tours in Europe convinced us that during the coming years, most people will be able to experience holiday travel. Travel will not be limited to a few. The people are already learning the skills to take advantage of the new opportunities offered by mass tourism. The following case study of packaged holiday in United Kingdom shows how it was done in the past and how it can be done even on a large scale in future. It also marked the beginning of a mass tourism.

MARKETING OF PACKAGE TOURS IN GREAT BRITAIN

Holloway and Plant relate the story of the spectacular growth of package holidays in Britain as a good example of marketing. In the sixties, some entrepreneurs in Great Britain saw a new opportunity to create holidays utilising spare airline capacity that resulted from the introduction of new technology aircrafts and the low cost accommodation available at new Spanish holiday resorts.

The tour-operators in Great Britain were able to offer exciting holiday packages to the British public at far less cost in Spain than dreary, and cold vacations in their own homeland. These holiday packages soon became very popular. There was tremendous demand from the public to increase the volume available. But, hotel accommodation in Spain could not be expanded to meet the demand. The visitors from Britain had complaints against the greasy Spanish food which they called the' Foreign Rubbish'. There was also apprehension about the safety of old second-hand aircrafts used by tour-operators. The marketing experts pondered over the matter and came to the conclusion that consumers faced the following problems:

- Fear of flying
- Fear of foreign food. The British travellers of the sixties were not yet exposed to foreign foods.
- Fear of foreigners. They did not understand Spanish customs, manners and habits.

After some research, it was realized that profitability could be improved if the tour-operator gave up the use of cheaper, redundant aircrafts. They purchased new and modern aircrafts. The new planes gave them operational economy through better utilisation of planes which were fuel efficient increasing profits. Besides, customer's confidence was restored? The new planes were safe and efficient. The fear of foreign foods was overcome by adopting a novel way. The British tour companies sent their food experts to Spain who advised Spanish hoteliers to modify and adjust their cooking and services to suit the British tastes. They suggested that they could economise on the use of ingredients and reduce the grease content in the food cooked for the British customers. It worked. The British started enjoying the new Spanish cooking. The fear of foreigners was based on the unreliability of the Spanish accommodations, their way of dealing and service.

This lent to no easy solutions. So, the British travel companies invested lot of money in Spain to build new hotels according to their own specifications. The new properties were managed by the British or by their own nominees. The British expertise and their inputs improved standards in Spanish hotels.

On a personal level the British representatives changed their style and became dedicated to the hotel's customer services. "Now, the quality of the product of major travel companies is no longer in question, any more than a sweater from Marks and Spencer or TV from Dixons," "noted Holloway and Plant. Package tours now are so popular that over 50 per cent of leisure travel out of Britain is on such tours. Tourism product has, therefore, to be consumer oriented. That implies we can no longer sell what we produce, we have to produce what customers consider as their needs. In the words of Professor Theodore Levitt, "Selling focuses on the needs of seller, marketing focuses on the needs of buyer." Among several definitions of marketing, the one formulated by the British Institute of Marketing explains the marketing process better.

"Marketing is the Management function which organizes and directs all those business activities involved in assessing and converting customer's purchasing power into effective demand for a specific product or service and in moving the product or service to the final customer or user so as to achieve the profit target or other objectives set by the company". The American Marketing Institute defines marketing in the following words: "Marketing is defined as those activities which direct the flow of goods and services from production to consumption". As in the two definition above, marketing is seen as coordinating all aspects of business. It is not the responsibility of one department only.

The Tourist Product

We will describe it as a composite product which consists of attractions of a destination, air transportation provided by airlines, hotel accommodation offered by hotel companies and the local transportation, sightseeing and other activities provided by local tour-operators at the destination. The most convenient and conventional method of buying the tourist product from a producer is the packaged tour.

But, a customer has other options. He can design his product-buy his ticket from an airline and reserve a hotel room by requesting the airlines to do it for him at the destination. He is free to ask a travel agency to put together for him the type of holiday he needs. He has a choice of a hundred destinations to select from. He can choose any one of them, any airline that flies to that destination and pick up a hotel of his choice at the destination. The real tourist product is usually composite-whether the customer buys it in packaged form or assembles it himself. Its three principal attributes are: attraction, facilities and accessibility.

Peculiarities of the Tourist Product

The following are some other peculiarities of the tourist product which we must understand.

- A wide range of services which the tourist requires and which constitute the tourism product in his mind cannot be provided by a single enterprise. Each of its components needs a high degree of specialisation and every enterprise produces only a part of the final product. Naturally, the need for cooperation and coordination in marketing efforts are paramount.

- Marketing of tourism is further complicated by singular dichotomy between supply and demand. Supply is inelastic as considerable fixed investment is required to expand it and highly trained manpower is needed to operate it. It cannot be adopted quickly to demand variations. The existing facilities and establishments cannot be easily modified to qualitative change.
- Tourism demand is highly unstable. Seasonal for have can affect it, Political unrest and economic instability caused by inflation and currency fluctuations can damage it.
- Trade intermediaries in tourism-travel agents, four operators, charter brokers-are powerful factors in the marketing of the tourist product. They have bargaining power in relation to the suppliers of tourist service. They can also influence the choice of a holiday destination.
- Tourism product cannot be transported to the consumer. It is the consumer who comes to the product to experience it.
- The travel agent, tour-operator or producer of the product cannot stock it or hold it in abeyance. It is a highly perishable product. An airline seat or hotel room not used today is total loss.
- Entitlement to the use of service facility in tourism product does not means that ownership passes to the user. Hotel rooms, transport seats are hired only for a specified period while the ownership remains with the proprietors is more urgent and more

Marketing of tourism product, therefore, complicated than other products.

Planning Process in Marketing

Every business organization dealing with tourism product needs a Marketing Action Plan. It can be short-term or long-term. The short-term plan will deal with immediate issues relating to cash flow required and what products will be marketed during a given period and at what price to meet the running costs and to make some profit. The long-term plan will establish goals and strategy for growth, diversification and profitability.

The Marketing Process

The first step in the marketing process is to carry out a Corporate Environment Analysis. The Corporate Environment Analysis will list the company's corporate objectives, its strengths and weaknesses. It will also look into the financial environments under which the company will have to work during a given period. The second step will be to identify the customers who will buy their products, where they live and what they want. This is called *Market Research.* Research may reveal that there is no point in advertising the beaches of India to Americans. They have enough of their own or in their neighbourhood the Caribbean Islands. Northern Europe is India's best market for beach holidays because they do not have warm water beaches. And they are also geographically closer to India and The third step is to look for the type of customers who will buy the product. Are your customers in the age group of 40-50 or do they come from the younger crowd? Are they professionals? Are they people who seek adventure or they are people looking for a cultural experience? Also who are the people who can afford your product? This is called *Market Segmentation.*

We will, therefore, focus our promotion on the market we identify through this process. The fourth step is *Formulation of the Product.* We formulate the product to suit each segment of our customers. The product must 'meet the needs of the customer. The next step is *Pricing.* The company must price the product attractively to interest the customers. It should be affordable to customers *we* seek *Distribution* come next. Where do we sell our product, in which areas and through what kind of sales network? The product should be easily accessible to enable potential customers to buy it. The next and most important part of the marketing process is to make sure that potential customers know about the product. It is called *Promotion.* It includes every aspect-mass-media, advertising, public relations, press releases, direct mail, etc., to draw the attention of customers to the product. A combination of four Ps-Product, Price, Place and Promotion is popularly called the *Marketing Mix.* The right mix for marketing purposes produces profits. Each of these elements mentioned above may be thought of as tourism marketing, but not in isolation. Together they make up marketing. It is a" cyclic process, with periodic review of product-market mix and the promotional strategy to measure their success. The strategies can be modified or changed if it is discovered that they are not effective. A marketing plan should include the following elements represented by acronym SWOT:

- *Strength: How* Hoes the product compare with other similar product
- Weaknesses: Its deficiencies in relation to competing products.
- *Opportunities:* What new markets and market segments are available for the product
- *Threats:* Who are the principal competitors to the product in the marketplace and what are they doing?

Corporate Analysis

The Corporate Analysis implies that a company decides on its goals and objectives. The goals are determined after an objective study of the current economic and market environment. The company examines its strength and weaknesses in relation to the existing competition. It must examine threats to business as well as opportunities. The goals would include achievable targets—how many tourists to attract in a given period and from which markets or market segments, etc.

Market Research

A tourist product cannot be used by everyone. Many people cannot afford it. The first step for a marketer, therefore, is to know his product well-its advantages, disadvantages, attractions and position vis-a-vis the competitive products.

He finds out all this information through research on potential users of the product. The research must provide answers to the following questions:

- What is the total size of the tourist market?
- Who are the existing customers?
- Where do they live?
- What are the present customers seeking in our product?
- What level of pricing will the customer accept?
- What are the trends in the market-past and present?
- What are the factors influencing the trend?
- Who are our potential future buyers?
- What are the strength and weakness of our product compared to the competition?

Market research depends on the types of data needed. It could be *primary or secondary data.* Primary data is available in-house or through field surveys. In-house data provides information on the performance of business, number of visitors, occupancy ratios, visitors, spending, source for business, profits, costs, etc. This information can be collected for individual businesses, groups of businesses or on regional or national level depending on the requirements.

Field Surveys

Field surveys can be done in several ways. The most frequently used method for collecting primary data through field survey is through the use of questionnaires. Questionnaires can be completed by the respondent directly or with the help of trained interviewers.

Self-completed questionnaires are often used by airlines and hotels. But, they suffer from one major disadvantage they allow no control over the sample of people filling the questionnaires and responding. Therefore, this method cannot be very useful for market research. Questionnaires are often filled by dissatisfied customers. The other method in field survey is to determine the sample in advance and use the services of trained interviewers to get the response. The questionnaires generally provide two types of data. The first demographic and socio-economic profile of the people interviewed including family composition, occupation, place of residence, their spending pattern, etc. The second type of data relates to motivation, perception, etc. The questionnaires can be designed according to the needs of an organization. In India, the questionnaire method has been more frequently used by Indian Tourism Authorities to know the visitors' profile-the plates they come from, their expenditure pattern, motivations to come to India and their perceptions, etc. It is done every four to five years.

Secondary data can be obtained from what is called Desk Research. This kind of research uses census reports, annual company reports, and surveys done by the regional and national tourist organizations and at international levels reports of IATA, ICAO, WTOJ PATA, OECD, EEC, WORLD BANK, UNESCO and other international bodies These organizations compile information on aspects of travel industry in which they are interested. Travel industry magazines are a useful sources of information. In Ask important travel industry magazines are Asia Travel Trade and TTG-Asia published from Singapore, Travel News Asia, Hong Kong, Travel Trade Report, Bangkok, Travel Trends and Trav Talk, New Delhi. Another reliable source of tourism information is an annual publication Travel Industry World Year Book-The-Big Picture, published from New York. It has been published annually for 30 years. It analyses comprehensively trends in travel industry every year in all parts of world. In USA, the US Travel Data Centre, based in Washington, product excellent reports on US tourism. The Economic Intelligence Unit, London provides some of the best reports on how tourism is shaping in different parts of the world. Of course, WTO have all kinds of reports and information on world tourism. Their publications are available for sale to non-members. For carrying out market research, it is important that the organization chosen to carry out survey is selected carefully. It should be professional, reliable and credible. The client's ability to understand the purpose and limitations of marketing research is also important.

MAIN MARKETING TOOLS

TRADE FAIRS

Travel fairs and exhibitions can be a highly-cost effective sales and marketing tool combining all the best characteristics of advertising, promotions, direct mail and selling, either through tour operators and travel agents or, in the case of public shows, directly to consumers. Benefits include direct sales, new product launches, lead generation, penetration of new markets, building and maintaining client/customer relations, market research, database building and networking. Research suggests that more than 80per cent of visitors to trade fairs are decision makers. Taking part in a trade fair without first having a clear view of why you are there is an almost certain recipe for failure.

Setting objectives is, therefore, an important starting point for any exhibition, giving direction to all aspects of your participation. Setting your objectives will make it possible to measure objectively the result of the exhibition, instead of making such a Judgement merely subjective. At the same time, objectives will help you establish budgetary requirements, motivate your staff and justify your participation next time around.

The goals you set for yourself need to be formulated as concretely as possible. They must be realistic, open to evaluation and have a time limit in order to facilitate and provide a firm base for future work. Possible objectives could include; increase in sales, meeting new clients, obtain market intelligence, launch new products, penetrate a new market, change or enhance company image, carry out market testing and study the activities of competitors.

In order to ensure that your objectives are appropriate and attainable, you need to:

- Know what you want to sell or communicate
- Know your target market
- Quantify your objectives in order to set a goal
- Ensure your targets are achievable
- Prioritize your objectives
- Communicate your objectives to your staff

Once you have defined your main goals, the next step is to give careful consideration to which sector of the travel industry you want to direct your sales and marketing efforts towards. How can you best attract your chosen targets to visit your stand? You could specifically invite companies to the fair, make pre-booked appointments or hold a reception on your stand for selected guests. By staying focused on your target market at all times, you will stand a better-than-average chance of getting your messages across and building new business. For some, having a stand of their own is the most natural way to participate, while others may find it more desirable or cost-effective to share stand space with others. Sharing with a national airline, a tourism board, a hotel or other tour operator who is not a direct competitor may enhance your presence. Since most tour operators will wish to work directly with overseas operators, it makes sense that attending wholly public fair would not be in your best interests. Your decision on where to exhibit should be made only after careful consideration of the event, the audience it is likely to attract, its timing and location and the cost, not only of exhibiting but also of attending including meals, accomm-odation and flights.

In deciding which fair(s) to participate, you should identify all the possibilities, compile as much information as possible; from organizers (attendance figures, breakdown of visitors, etc), cost implications and comments from other exhibitors. The more information you collect, the easier it will be to cut out those exhibitions that do not match your marketing objectives or your budget. Similarly, timing of the event, the size and importance of their venues and their geographical catchment area will help you reach a decision. Planning is essential to protect your investment in trade fairs, it is the key to getting the best possible return, to ensure smooth and stress free exhibiting, project a cohesive, positive and memorable message and improve your participation the next time around.

Planning for an exhibition should be thorough enough that no surprises crop up during the actual exhibition, the time when all your efforts should be directed towards sales work. One person in the business should be responsible for making all the arrangements. Most fairs will provide you with a manual which should be fully understood.

A timetable should be drawn up highlighting key tasks and deadline dates. You should draw up a budget for your participation based on the activities you plan to become involved in. The budget should also be linked to the forecasts for the benefits that you expect to achieve.

The budget could be broken down into some areas:

- Stand space
  - Space rental
  - Design and construction (for space only stands)
  - Displays
  - Furniture
  - Accessories and equipment
  - Electrical installations
  - Connections – water, telephone, fax
  - Plants and Flowers
  - Cleaning and Security Services
  - Audiovisual equipment
  - Insurance
  - Catering
  - Incidentals
- Transport of materials
  - Packing
  - Air Shipment
  - Insurance
  - Customs Fees
  - Storage
  - Handling charges
- Personnel Costs
  - Staff transportation
  - Accommodation
  - Local transportation
  - Meal allowances

  - Interpreters
  - Entertainment
- Promotional Costs
  - Telephone and Mail marketing
  - Brochures and Catalogues printing
  - Post fair distribution of materials
  - Promotional video
  - Press packs
  - Translation of material
  - Promotional give aways
  - Passes for customers
  - Advertising in official fair catalogue
  - National and international magazine advertising
  - Other advertising
  - Sponsorship of fair activities

Your stand at a travel fair should make a strong visual impact and convey at a glance who you are and what you have to offer. For most tour operators, the shell scheme option will provide the best option. It will make it easier to present your products and services, is more cost efficient and minimizes the amount of time you need to spend at the venue during buildup and break down of the exhibition. A shell scheme is a basic framework or shell erected by the organizers appointed contractor on your behalf. Take only the space you need at a fair. If you take too much, you will be left with the problem of having nothing to fill it with.

The location of your stand within the exhibition is important, though with many wellestablished fairs, you may not have much option. You have a stand of the right size, properly equipped, containing the right exhibits and staffed by knowledgeable and well-prepared personnel able to negotiate on behalf of your company. If you have the chance to choose the location for your stand, look for the busiest areas of the hall where traffic flow is likely to be high. Also, take into account the location of competitors' stands, location of service and access points (entrances, stairways, feature areas, restaurants).

The design of the stand should reflect the messages that you wish to give to your clients and potential clients. If you want to get your company better known to all visitors then an open eye-catching display is most appropriate. With graphics, they should visualize clearly what you do, have brief messages and promote benefits and not features. Ensure that the messages can be read clearly. Remember that if you choose a shell scheme you will still need to decorate it. A shell scheme will normally include a signboard, basic furniture, carpet and electrical connections. It will not do anything to promote your company. If an exhibition organizer does its job properly, it will deliver thousands of potential clients to the exhibition halls. What it will not do and cannot do is persuade those buyers to visit your stand, rather than those of your competitors. That is your job and your organization is the only one that stands to lose out if you do not do it. It is important to inform your target audience that you are exhibiting and about your profile at the show. You will also invite them to the stand and set up specific appointments with them. The key to effective promotion is to match your promotional strategy to your exhibition objectives; to coordinate your activities carefully; to explore all available avenues for promotion before, during and after the event and to heed all deadlines.

In order to promote your attendance before and during the fair, you could consider:

- Advertising in trade magazines and newspapers
- Undertaking direct mail
- Sponsoring fair events or merchandise
- Incentives and small give always
- Advertising in fair catalogue

The number of staff required to man the stand depends upon the size of your stand, the number of leads anticipated and facilities and activities on the stand. As a rule, you should allow one staff member per 4-5 square metres of floor space, this being the space required to allow two people to conduct a conversation comfortably. On person should be in charge and in attendance at the show all the time. Make sure that the staff on your stand really are friendly, approachable and well informed in the company products and services.

Staff training and briefing are essential to exhibition success; training in encouraging visitors on to the stand, how to open and close a conversation, how to qualify visitors and the impact of body language. Also make sure that your staff know what they should be selling and how. The stand should be manned at all times and should be kept tidy. The essence of sales technique if firstly to arouse interest of the prospects and discover his/her needs or problems. Then steer the conversation towards the way your products or services can solve these. Every person with whom you come into contact then receives individual attention depending on need.

The following sales techniques are important:

- Concentrate on people in your target markets
- Present briefly yourself and your product
- Chart the customer's needs and desires
- Steer the conversation towards the customer's needs and how your product/service satisfies these
- In all cases, make a note of the person's name, company, addressm etc and follow up after the fair, giving additional information and/or making your offer

The visitor information you capture at exhibitions and the way it is recorded, will have a direct effect on the speed and efficiency with which you follow up your leads. Only collecting business cards is not an effective way to compile visitor information, even if you do scribble action points on the back.

There are four steps to an effective follow-up after the fair:

1. Prioritize leads according to urgency
2. Follow up leads immediately
3. Pursue leads on an ongoing basis
4. Track leads to provide some measure of return on investment

When measuring the effectiveness of exhibition participation, there are two areas you need to look at. Firstly, the extent to which you achieved your specific objectives and secondly the extent to which the exercise proved cost effective. Look at the value of sales achieved, the number of qualified leads, the number of new contacts made, the level of awareness before and after the show, the number of promotional materials distributed, the media coverage generated, the value of market research undertaken and other benefits. The following is a suggested timetable of activities that may need to be undertaken when planning participation at a fair.

- 10-12 Months before the fair:
  - Make an initial selection of the itineraries and services that you will be selling
  - Calculate how much space you will require
  - Go over documentation from previous editions of the fair, if you were present at them
  - Draw up an initial budget
  - Get in contact with the fair organizers to let them know that you are interested in participating and request your space pre-registration
  - Examine the fair's rules and regulations
  - Fill out and submit the pre-registration and request information on promotional activities
- 8-10 Months before the fair
  - Draw up a plan and budget for the promotional activities organized prior to the fair
  - Budget for post-fair promotional activities
  - Decide on which information and sales material you will need
  - Analyse your needs for other material and where appropriate, design and develop it
  - Make allowances for trips and book tickets
  - Provide for accommodation and make reservations
- 6-8 Months before the fair
  - Design a support advertising campaign, objectives and timeframe
  - Launch the information campaign aimed at customers and trade media

  - Coordinate promotional activities with the fair organizers
  - Order promotional articles that will be handed out during the fair
  - Anticipate and organize logistics and transport tasks
  - Define the decoration, atmosphere and identity of your stand
- 4-6 Months before the fair
  - Coordinate planned activities with programmes and fair regulations
  - Stand build up, advertising material, promotional material, miscellaneous activities
  - Identify new prospective clients and send them information
  - Order fair organizational services, external services, insurance
  - Design incentives for attracting visitors to the stand
- 2-4 Months before the fair
  - Intensify marketing actions to attract visitors
  - Select and allocate functions to the personnel that will be present on the stand and decide if you need to train staff in sales, train staff in corporate image, conduct practice sessions with products and sales arguments, instruct external personnel,
  - Send information for the fair catalogue
  - Check if periodic payments have been settled with the fair organizers
- 0-2 Months before the fair
  - Check the materials that should be taken to the fair – office materials, sales material, give aways
  - Organize press activities
  - Distribute information on new products, etc to technical magazines and the fair's press office
  - Send out passes and invitations to customers
  - Collect information on the seminars and conferences that are being organized
  - Prepare a form for registering the details provided by visitors that come to your stand
- During stand build up and fair
  - Build up the stand as soon as possible
  - Checklist in hand, make sure that none of the elements, materials or services ordered for the stand are missing
  - Locate the fair organization's offices and services
  - On a daily basis, supervise stand cleaning, stocks of promotional materials
  - Exchange information with other staff on a regular basis
  - Gather competitor information, make notes and compare with equivalent aspects in your own company

- After the fair
  - Supervise stand break down and packing of material and equipment
  - Organize the transport of material, equipment and products
  - Arrange a meeting with all personnel involved in the project to analyse results
  - Launch actions for following-up leads generated at the fair

Brochures and Printed Materials

As we stated earlier, a tour operator's brochure is important because of the intangible nature of the product that is being sold. The brochure should invite people to buy the itineraries it advertises, provide the information necessary to persuade the client to purchase a holiday and create and reinforce the company's image with its clients. Most brochures are designed to an A4 format in Europe and Letter size in the US so the size of your brochure will be important according to the market you are targeting. Most brochures are printed on glossy colored paper.

The bigger the brochure, the flimsier the paper it is printed on tends to be, both to keep down production costs and to stop it becoming unmanageably heavy. Pull out price pages are normally printed on cheap colored paper. Some companies will also have slightly thicker front covers to protect the brochures in transit and on the shelves, and to create a better image. Although many operators will produce full colour brochures, it is cheaper to choose fewer colors. A full Colour brochure could include some pages that are one or two Colour (those pages used for terms and conditions, booking information, etc) to cut down costs. Colour is important. Bright colors usually signify cheaper tours. Pale and dark colors signify more expensive tours. Every brochure should contain clear, legible, comprehensive and accurate information to enable the client to exercise and informed Judgement in making his choice.

Content could include:

- A company's legal identity
- Means of travel
- Destinations or itineraries
- Dates of fixed departures (if you have them)
- Nature of accommodation and meal facilities
- Additional facilities
- Booking conditions
- Insurance details
- Price policy
- Health matters
- Arbitration
- Publication date

- Difficulty ratings
- Maps
- Pictures of attractions, accommodations or previous clients

Of course the content of your brochures may vary according to whether you are targeting the travel trade or consumers. If you are selling tours in Europe, you may like to familiarize yourself with the EC Package Travel Regulations that outlines how European tour operators must present their information and what brochures must include. The front cover of the brochure is particularly important since it is what the client will see first of all. The cover must therefore be designed to be eye-catching but must simultaneously convey certain crucial messages. It should show the company name and a logo. The choice of picture can make it clear what sort of product is on offer and also for whom the product is aimed at. The more expensive and exotic the product on offer, the less likely it is to show clients on the cover at all, preferring to concentrate on what they will see at their chosen destination.

The main part of the brochure should be clearly structured so that clients can easily identify the information they require. A contents page may be appropriate for brochures with many pages. Colored borders for pages also help in this regard. General information is usually found at the rear of the brochure. This would include guidelines for making bookings; information on what is included in the price, insurance and cancellation policies, a booking form, and health and visa requirements. If there are suitable destination marketing materials available that provide much of the destination information, then a company's promotional materials can focus more on their own particular itineraries.

The text of a brochure needs careful consideration. Firstly, there should be no grammatical or spelling mistakes. Secondly, the text should present your products in a way that will make them appealing to potential customers. For Croatian operators, the text should emphasize the the beauty of the nature and uniqueness of the culture, history, cuisine, architecture, etc. as well as the prospects for adventure, good sailing, or outdoor sports. Many brochures will also use "you", "we" and "our" to emphasize the central role of clients and their needs and how 'at home' they will feel even though they are abroad.

Photographs have the same purpose of the text, to portray the destination and products in a positive light. The photographs should complement the text and be relevant to it. Obviously the photos should be of a high quality in terms of resolution. Also, they need to be professional. It would not be appropriate for example to have pictures of clients wearing raincoats standing on a cloudy beach. There should be a good use of Colour. Many brochures will use pictures of previous clients enjoying themselves, inviting would-be buyers to imagine themselves in their place. If you use pictures of previous clients be sure that the clients are typical of those you are trying to attract

Web sites

A Well designed Web site will contain much the same information as a well conceptualized brochure. The difference here is that you have much more room for photos, and your use of Colour is limited only to the web palette of colors likely to display well on most monitors. You can also make inquiries, bookings, and other interactive functions easy for customers by using web forms, online reservations and payment, etc. Hundreds of Web sites exist with excellent features. Search (Google) company Web sites in your line of business and see which features you think are best, and try to integrate these features into your site planning.

Have a professional web developer do your site, and insist that current standards be used in the coding of your Web site. Because most search engines give sites using frames poorer rankings, for example, most new web sites are now laid out using CSS, which also makes them faster to load. Decide if you will use HTML or XHTML, make sure the site is viewable in the most popular browsers (IE, Firefox, Netscape, and Opera are just a few). Finally, make sure you do a good job of search engine optimization.

TOURISM MARKETING COMMUNICATION

The marketing mix is a traditional way to understand marketing in general. The majority of marketing practitioners consider the Mix as the toolkit of transaction marketing and archetype for operational marketing planning. While empirical evidence of the exact role and contribution of the Mix to the success of commercial organizations is very limited, several studies confirm that the 4Ps Mix is indeed the trusted conceptual platform of practitioners dealing with tactical/operational marketing issues. The marketing mix has been defined as a mixture of controllable marketing variables that the firm uses in order to pursue the sought level of sales in a targeted market. These theories have been adapted by many scholars and marketing professional, also within the tourism industry, in a number of forms. Firms marketing strategies use marketing mix variables in order to plan an operational marketing plan for their business.

The focus being on how firms can increase or improve sales, position themselves and their image in a competitive environment in which customer demands and competitors´ strategies are constantly changing. Traditional 3 marketing P´s, product, place, and promotion, can be argued to be relevant also for the analysis of multisensory marketing even though the Mix has been critized for not allowing interaction and for not capturing relationships. Multisensory marketing communication can be divided into the 5 senses. These 5 senses will be "smashed down" into separate components because this is the only way to analyze them. By doing so every sense can be analyzed towards one of the marketing p's. The marketing figure on the other hand expresses the marketing system for any organization in four constricts rings. It is an accepted way to present the marketing process.

In the inner ring is the customer involving customer orientation, customer loyalty, and consumer behaviour. In the second ring there are the traditional marketing P´s, *i.e.,* product, price, place, and promotion. The next ring represents inter-company resources such as: personal, positioning, economic resources, and relationship-based interest group resources. In the fourth ring there are determinants of tourism demand, competitors, technological development possibilities and legislation. In our research on multisensory tourism marketing communication we use the term inter medial marketing communication. We understand inter medial marketing to be interactive communication involving at least two media channels.

The easiest application for inter medial marketing is through the use of digital media. Inter medial marketing communication is thus very close to the concept of digital marketing. Urban has defined the concept of digital marketing communication as follows: "Digital marketing uses the Internet and information technology to extend and improve traditional marketing functions".Systematic idea- and development-work in media-advertising and communications technology require, just as to Viljakainen, Bäck and Lindqvist different types of knowledge in order for *e.g.,* the tourism industry to be able to develop novelties and innovations applicable on global markets. It seems that even though media is culturally bounded and a national phenomenon, new combinations of technology, media and advertisement seem to be universal.

MULTIPLE SENSES IN MARKETING COMMUNICATION

Marketing communication has been defined in new media vocabulary as company driven communication which aims directly or indirectly to influence the demand or to at least have a positive influence on demand among reference groups. With the help of marketing communication a travel company thus aims to inform and remind customers of its services and to have an impact on consumer behaviour. In addition, marketing communication aims to arouse feelings and desires for consumption, for the creation of company and product image, for sales and customer decisions. Furthermore the purpose of communication is to maintain, develop and deepen customer relations. Many people look for value fulfilment also in communication. It should thus not only be purposeful, but also enjoyable and comfortable, an aesthetical experience. For service firms, the management of the service experience is of vital importance. It does not only affect the success of the firm, but also determine customers satisfaction level, service quality perception and future behaviour *i.e.,* an intention to visit the store again.

In other words, the service experience is a result from an activity that can be defined as a process where a set of resources interact with each other and with the customers aiming at supporting the customer's processes in a value generating way. Usually the resources for service organizations are divided to two central components: backstage and frontstage. Hoffman and Turley describe backstage as to consist of those behind the scene which are invisible to the customers. Frontstage consists of those factors visible to the customers. There are many frontstage factors affecting customer's service experience. Schmitt and Lindstrom and Kotler, a customer is often attracted towards a brand based upon its sensory experience. Lindstrom and Kotler further stresses that almost our entire understanding of the world is experienced through our senses.

Our senses are our link to memory and can tap right into emotion. Smell appears to be the most persuasive sense after sight, which implies the importance for multisensory marketing. Multisensory marketing stands in this research for involving several bodily senses in marketing activities. Kahn Consulting describes it as the purposeful design and deployment of the interaction between the senses in order to stimulate a consumer's relationship with a brand; and to foster a lasting emotional connection that optimizes brand loyalty.

Multisensory marketing is in a starting phase and there is just a hand full of marketers who are using multisensory marketing in their campaigns nowadays, also in the tourism industry. It is stated by several researchers that multisensory marketing is the future of advertising and branding. Lindstrom and Kotler 2005:69, vision is the most important persuasive one with a share of 58 per cent when it comes to brand building and bonding, smell being the second most important one with a proportion of 45 per cent, hearing stands for 41 per cent, taste for 31 per cent and touch for 25 per cent.

Studies thus show that pleasant scents create pleasant states of moods. It has also been shown that we process senses differently depending on age, gender, cultural background etc. Sight is thus traditionally perceived as the most seductive sense and the most obvious one used by brands. Visual cues govern consumer behaviour. A recently published article shows that red colour enhances performance on a detail-oriented task whereas blue enhances performance on a creative task. Sound on the other hand helps us generate moods by creating feelings and emotions. Taste and smell are closely connected, although smell is 10,000 times more sensitive as it taps right into our memory. The luxurious car brand Bentley has made good use of sounds in their marketing in order for customers to perceive quality and success. Rolls Royce has successfully used scent adding to the feeling of quality. Many marketing scholars and professionals have shown some interest for the usage of multiplesenses in marketing, *e.g.,* the usage of scent in order to increase sales, to promote or evaluate products, to enhance the perception of quality, to reduce stress etc.

THE EFFECT ON ODOURS AND SCENT IN MARKETING COMMUNICATION

The physical environment or the servicescape is probably among the first of these factors customers will encounter. The reason why the servicescape is of importance is that it plays a significant role in determining the customer's satisfaction level, perceived service quality and the service experience itself. Furthermore it also affects customers' behavioural intensions. The physical environment can play a role similar to a physical good's package in that it basically communicates an image of what is included in the service.

It is apparent that different services (resorts, hotels, cruise ships, hospitals etc.) are depending on their servicescapes to communicate and create customer experiences. The physical facilities (facility exterior and interior elements) can be seen as "man-made" or constructed elements. Scent can also be adopted as a part of the different elements of physical evidence. For example, scent can be applied to facility exterior to lure customers to visit the facility interior (*e.g.*, example given of the gas stations that place fresh brewed coffee scent at the pumps to lure pay-and-go customers to stay) or simply to create a pleasant environment outside the store.

Using multiple senses in marketing is not a new thing itself, neither the use of scent for marketing and for servicescape. In cafes coffee packages have been opened in order to spread the aroma of coffee and bakers put their coffee bread on show for getting a good scent. There are approximately about 100 000 different scents in the world out of which 1000 scents are primaries and the rest of the scents are combinations. Nose as a receiver of stimuli is important. Scents are found out to strengthen communication and bonding. Features of scents are: ambience, identification and memorycap. The scents are registered in the brains faster than other senses, as the distance between the nose and the brain is short. We can identify scents with a 65 per cent accuracy whereas the visual picture is 50 per cent already after three months. There are approximately about 6-10 million cells in a human nose through which we can identify 2000-4000 different aromas.

In comparison a shepherd dog nose consists of approximately 220 million cells. Up to 75 per cent of people remember a smell even after one year. Scents can be produced naturally, for example through flowers and scent oil or artificially with the help of equipment. Odours can be interconnected with a product, to a theme, a nice shopping environment or product brand.

Scents can be used everywhere, for example in a hotel, an event or at a party. When a scent is combined with a product, the user is becoming aware of the product through its smell. The client becomes curious and at the same time the message of the product is being communicated fast and deeply into the client´s mind. The scent is asking the brain "do you want this", even though I did not come here for this purpose. A scent also differentiates the product from its competitors. Scents have been proved to increase sales. The traditional concept of servicescape has been affected by the emerge of the Internet. Web pages and communities have become a new form of servicescapes, also known as virtual servicescapes, where the customer can get in contact with any company and explore their service offerings without physically visiting it. These are the more recent forms of physical evidence, which companies may see great potential in and which they can use to communicate the service experience both before and after the service encounter, thus making the service more tangible for the customer. For example, travel agencies use their web pages as virtual servicescapes, where the customer can preview destinations and also view and take virtual tours of hotels. Often these virtual tours include a chance to see all the available rooms, how the rooms are decorated and equipped and even watch the view from the balcony live through a webcam.

The competition between companies on the market is hard and there is a lot of advertising. We encounter daily about 3000 ad-messages. Traditionally it has been evaluated that we receive visually 83 per cent of all information. Customers are being directed to buy products and services by sharing information about products, by increasing brand awareness or by guiding clients to a service purchase situation. The consumers stay for a longer time in a space in which there is a pleasant small and evaluate the products in a much more positive way. In 1965 90 per cent of the consumers 90 per cent did their daily purchase decisions prior to shopping, today 80 per cent of the consumers do their purchasing decision in the shop.

MEDIA CHANNELS

Among IAB European membership countries web-based media marketing volume in 2006 was close to 8 billion euros. Most money was spent in the United Kingdom, Germany and in France. In Finland the web-based advertising was just as to statistics 91,2 million euros and in Greece 16,3 million euros. The advertising expenditure was shared between: key word advertising 45 per cent, banner advertising 31 per cent, classified advertising 122 per cent and electronic advertising 2 per cent. IAB's corporate members believe that Internet is the ideal total media solution for difficult economic times – allowing for PR, branding and marketing in a highly targeted way, combining creativity with opportunities for customer engagement.

The proportion of web-media stood in 2006 only for about 3 per cent of total medial production just as to Viljakainen. In total marketing communications planning- and production-costs were 2, 8 billion euros in Finland during 2006 of which printed newspapers and direct advertising stood by large for the biggest proportion. All in all the share of web shopping has though been estimated to grow with 20 per cent during the next few years in Finland. There thus appears to be needs for new ways of marketing products in the web. Technology, electronic media and the internet usage is growing fast especially among young consumer groups. New types of combinations for presenting pictures together with voice and videos are emerging. Different types of media channels, internet and new publication platforms, such as the electronic books are being developed and introduced. The boundaries between massmedial targeted communication and interactive communication involving user medias have becoming blurry in the process. We are thus heading from one way communication towards various forms of interactive communication involving inter medial solutions. Multiple forms of internet and digital advertising such as billboards, skyscrapers, banners, leader boards, rectangles, floating flashes, buttons and tickets have been produced in order to attract potential consumers attention. The banners represent one of the oldest modes for internet advertising. Nowadays the term is used as a general term and more or less equivalent to internet-based marketing.

The challenge though is to make people use and click the banners, *i.e.,* new applications have been taken into use, *e.g.,* Rich media-format: Java, Flash and Shockwave-formats in interactive net advertising. The media-advertising channels and operational models have expanded during the ten last years. At the same time customer segments are being splashed down in new ways accordingly with life styles. For example e-commerce is growing annually with approximately 20 per cent. Digital channels and information technology are changing the way that companies communicate and maintain relationship with their customers. The Internet, e-mail, mobile phones, digital TV, and other evolving channels offer opportunities for frequent, costeffective, personalized, and interactive communication between the company and their customers.

VIRALMARKETING

The term was originally coined by Jeffrey Rayport, a Hardvard Business School professor. The idea being that when there is little time and a minimal budget, a virus can be a truly effective. The term "viral marketing" is commonly defined as networkenhanced word-of-mouth. As outlined by this Web Marketing Today, Dr. Ralph F. Wilson in 2005, originally published 2/1/2000, a viral campaign does six things:

- Gives away seemingly valuable products, services or content
- Provides for effortless transfer to others
- Scales easily from small to very large
- Exploits common motivations and behaviours
- Utilizes existing communication networks
- Takes advantage of others' resources

RESEARCH QUESTIONS

The main research questions in this research project are: how is the usage of multiple senses involving various media channels (*e.g.,* internet, TV, special spaces, social media) taken into consideration in tourism marketing? What kind of techniques and technologies are needed (available)? How can specific tourism companies benefit from the use of multiple senses in inter medial marketing communication in order to develop their demand/supply?

DESIGN, METHODOLOGY AND APPROACH OF THE PROJECT

The research project is designed to include work packages. The first phase is aimed at the analysis of literature and good practical cases. Research is to a significant part based on explorative literature research. The initial phase is general, beneficial for the whole tourism industry. It also includes the examination of interactions between multiple sensory modalities, such as ambient scent, background music, visual stimuli like colour and lighting.

The second phase will be made to assess the opportunities for creating and using different technologies involving smell, taste, touch, sight and sound taking into consideration the social co-experience elements and a tourism marketing communication view. Available multisensory possibilities will be evaluated and explored in existing and available virtual or real-world surroundings for specific users and situations.

The literature studies in addition to in-depth exploration of authentic cases in the tourism field will help to co-create new multisensory ways of interacting and communicating. The technological aspects will be analyzed in order to make an assessment of the current technological applications used for dispensing the multi-sensory message. Once the technological applications are combined with the use of sensory stimuli an overall picture can be given on the current profile of multi sensory marketing. The research will explore the role and opportunities of social media in connection to multisensory travel marketing. Social media offers several opportunities in relation to marketing and brand building. People value opinions and hints from their friends and contacts and this is important in spreading marketing messages and influencing decision making. When planning new ways of marketing such as multisensory marketing, it is important to create the applications so that some part of the marketing supports spreading in social media, including viral marketing. In the third phase there are made four case studies in specific tourism companies together with intermedial, digital, and viral marketing experts.

Together with tourism and intermedial partners the researchers will evaluate user experiences involving different combinations using multiple senses within tourism marketing communication. Various methods *e.g.,* service design and user based methods will be used in order to find good solutions. It includes assessment of opportunities of social media with regard to different kind of tourism services and which requirements are set on the material to be used in social media and viral marketing.

TWO CASE STUDIES OF THE EFFECTS OF USING MULTIPLE SENSES IN TOURISM MARKETING COMMUNICATION

One part of the project aims at combining different senses in authentic sales situations. The purpose of the case studies is to estimate the influence and effect that multiple marketing has on sales and the usage of products. In the first case our partner company is Helsinki Expert, an incoming travel agent. It provides a wide variety of service-bundles and products for Helsinki visitors, activities and programmes in Helsinki and elsewhere in Finland.

One of their products is an audio-guided city bus-tour in Helsinki. The travel agency was chosen as the case company for this study primarily because of their servicescape, where the research is conducted, offers an interesting and suitable environment for testing. The aim of the first case is to explore the effects of ambient scent. We are going to research, how a specific tourism company can benefit from the usage of multiple senses in a selling situation.

This study will compare two different conditions in separate time periods; one where the servicescape is constant (no additional stimuli) and the other where the servicescape is diffused with a pleasant ambient scent, moving pictures and sound congruent with the service context (design and theme) of the chosen company. Both of the time periods take one month. One of our hypotheses is that odours affect customers´ intentions to buy willingly in the scented environment. Our second case is the amusement park, Linnanmäki. We are testing the effect that the combination of scent and virus-marketing has on the amount of visitors.

TERMINATIONS

In this research project we are thus focusing on inter medial, multisensory applications applicable and beneficial within and for the tourism industry. We strongly suggest that future development of techniques and technologies for the purpose of tourism marketing communication are strongly driven by customer needs, amusement, excitement, value-added experiences, participation and interactivity. The idea of our project is to enhance the demand and to improve the availability of tourism services through new types of marketing communication involving inter medial solutions and multiple senses. We have argued that in the future the activation of sight and hearing in tourism marketing communication is not enough.

We have shown studies indicating positive correlations between the use of *e.g.,* ambient scent and consumption, the perception of wellness, quality, service experience, and bonding. There is thus some evidence on the impact of senses in order to engage emotions, feelings, bonding, the perception of quality and success. There is, however, not enough research on inter medial multisensory combinations, technological solutions and technical applications, at least not within the tourism industry. Our cases will enhance the understanding of the impact of suitable and/or possible combinations of multiple senses suitable for and within the tourism industry. The final results of this research project will give a comprehensive overview on multisensory marketing communication beneficial for service companies within the Finnish tourism industry.

Moreover, this project aims at creating marketing communication plans involving multiple senses for specific case organizations. We have already seen that the E-Commerce brought along customer empowerment, new forms of communication and interaction, global and around-the –clock operation, high degree of market transparency and difficulty in maintaining competitive advantages. We argue that the four P:s can offer a theoretical framework for the analysis of the usage of senses, involving digital and social media, co-experience, viral marketing and servicescapes even though many researches favour totally new approaches and are critical of the Mix. Internal orientation, lack of interactivity and personalisation, lack of strategic elements and lack of community building are some of the frequently mentioned weaknesses of the Mix.

TOURISM MARKETING IN DEVELOPING COUNTRIES

Tourism has become a very important and dynamic sector both in the world economy and particular in the developing countries. Its growth affects not only the activities directly linked to tourism but also other sectors. Tourism is already an important sector in some developing countries and will become so for others. Developing countries have been fast growing in tourism industry terms in the world over the last decade. Tourism is one of the most important sectors in a large number of developing countries. Increases in economic growth, disposable income and leisure time, political stability, and aggressive tourism campaigns, among others factors, have fuelled the significant growth of tourism. Developing countries have some common characteristics, such as extreme poverty and widespread conflict (including civil war and ethnic clashes), extensive political corruption, lack of political and social stability, human resource weakness (human assets index, nutrition, health, education and adult literacy), and economic vulnerability. Bangladesh is a developing country in Asia, holding high potentiality for tourism.

Bangladesh Parjatan Corporation (BPC) plays an important role for the development of tourism. For a long time, Bangladesh has been an attractive destination for tourists. But at present, its position is not significant in terms of the international tourism market. The overall objective of this research is to identify the issues and challenges in tourism marketing facing Bangladesh. The role of international tourism in generating economic benefits has long been recognised in many developing countries. The public sector may have been reluctant in the past to contribute towards tourism development, but the situation has changed and, over the years, governments' perspectives on tourism have not only evolved to include wider participation, but have also widened from the narrow focus on economic benefits to encompass environmental and societal concerns. Everything seems to suggest that developing countries look upon tourism consumption as manna from heaven that can provide a solution to all their foreign exchange difficulties. This description of tourism as 'manna from haven' has gained some support, in part because tourism is a highly visible activity.

Although tourism development results in the provision of facilities and services, there are, however, instances when these facilities are not accessible to local residents, particularly if tourism development involves the creation of tourism enclaves. In the last two decades in particular tourism has developed, especially in developing countries by their integrated tourism planning.

The specific research objectives of this study are:

- To identify development trends in Bangladesh tourism
- To evaluate the effectiveness of tourism marketing Bangladesh
- To analyse issues in tourism marketing in Bangladesh;
- To identify potential strategies that can contribute to increasing the competitiveness of Bangladesh tourism.

To conduct the research, a conceptual framework from a literature review was created and implemented using of a particular research methodology and methods.

DEFINITION, MEANING, AND CHARACTERISTICS OF DEVELOPING COUNTRIES

The terms 'the third world', 'underdeveloped countries', 'developing countries', 'poor countries', the South' and 'less-developed countries are mostly used interchangeably. However, it is not an easy task to define precisely what is meant by these terms as McQueen. Buchanan describes 'the developing country is a universe of radical scarcity. Defining and determining every dimension of men's relationship to each other... the inadequacy means of livelihood is the first and distinguishing truth of this area'. In order to give a more clear meaning of the term, it is worth quoting Todaro at some length: The 143 African, Asian and Latin American member countries of the United Nations often collectively refer to themselves as the 'Third World' or 'developing countries'.

Developing Countries, third World countries, industrialising countries, underdeveloped countries, and less developed countries are countries which, just as to the United Nations exhibit the lowest indicators of socioeconomic development, with the lowest human development ratings of all countries in the world. The World Bank classified developing countries as those having per capita income of less US$ 2200. Another concept of developing is that they have a high level of illiteracy; Afghanistan, Pakistan, Bangladesh, India, and Sudan are typical examples.

The United Nations, 120 countries are described as developing countries, and they comprise less than 20 per cent of the world's total GNP. Pearce suggests that all those nations out side of Europe, North America, Japan and

Australia have to be considered as developing countries. Most developing countries are located in Sub-Saharan Africa, Asia, Latin America, Pacific and Caribbean regions of the world. Some of these countries have fasted development rates. However, there are also countries such as India, China, Bangladesh, Nepal, and Ethiopia that are very poor.

Thus the term 'developing countries' is a very broad concept. United Nations review in 2009, and defined by the UN that developing countries as countries meeting their criteria, one of which was a three-year average estimate of gross national income per capita of less than US $950. The World Bank world economies are classified economies based on GNI per capita which is calculated using the World Bank Atlas method.

The groups are: low income, $935 or less; lower middle income, $936 - $3,705; upper middle income, $3,706 - $11,455, and high income, $11,456 or more. For example, per capita income of developing countries in year 2007-08 just as to the World Bank, International Monetary Fund and Central Intelligence Agency report as in February, 2009, such as, Pakistan $1,085; Kenya USD $680; Afghanistan, US$457; Ethiopia US$317; India, 1078; Nepal US$428; Nigeria US$401; Sri-Lanka US$2099; Vietnam US$1055; Burma US$287; Cambodia US$760; Haiti US$793, Mali US$712; Zimbabwe US$401; and Bangladesh US$690 The least developed countries are a group of countries that have been identified by the United Nations as "least developed" in terms of their low gross national income, their weak human assets and their high degree of economic vulnerability.

The term Least Developed Countries describes the world's poorest countries with following 3 criteria, such criteria are:

- Low-income criterion: based on a three-year average estimate of the gross national income per capita;
- Human resource weakness criterion: involving a composite human assets index based on indicators of:
  - Nutrition;
  - Health;
  - Education;
  - Adult literacy;
- Economic vulnerability criterion: based on indicators of the instability of agricultural production; the instability of exports of goods and services; the economic importance of non-traditional activities (share of manufacturing and modern services in GDP); merchandise export concentration; and the handicap of economic smallness.

Therefore, India, Bangladesh, and Pakistan have the common economic features of developing countries permit us to view them in a broadly similar framework. Based on common characteristics developing countries can be classified into six categories: i) low standard levels of living; ii) low incomes, inequality, poor health, and inadequate education; iii) low levels of productivity; iv) high rates of population growth and dependency burdens, substantial dependence on agricultural production and primary-products exports; v) prevalence of imperfect markets and limited information; and vi) dependence and vulnerability in international relations. Immediately after liberation, the government of Bangladesh set up the Bangladesh Parjatan Sangstha with a view to developing the tourist industry in the country. The organisation was restructured into Bangladesh Parjatan Corporation in 1973.

The corporation drew up a five-year plan within the framework of the first Five-Year Plan for economic and social development of the country to provide essential facilities and to develop natural attractions for increasing the inflow of tourists and making their stay in the country entertaining. The second, third, and fourth five-year plans and two year plans were intended to implement by the past Bangladesh governments to develop tourism sector but these plans have not been implemented properly by the government due to ministerial legacy problems.

For example, if a government has to power down before implementing a tourism development plan, the next ideal government's priority should focus on completing such partially completed projects first, but in reality, they are interested to find faults with such projects more than probing the positive aspects, and intent to formulate a new one to develop Bangladesh tourism. As a result some of the partially completed projects are let out forever. Consequently, this dreadful trend is only wasting time and money hardly developing this sector. Tourism in its modern sense is a relatively recent phenomenon, and it began in the present Bangladesh area only during the 1960s. Tourists from abroad came to see and enjoy the beaches, the scenic beauty of the landscape covered with lavish greens and the web of rivers, tribal culture, religious rituals, historical places, forests, wild life and hill resorts.

GEOGRAPHICAL CHARACTERISTICS OF BANGLADESH

Bangladesh is a developing country in South Asia, located between 20°34c to 26°38c north latitude and 88°01c to 92°42c east longitude, with an area of 147,570 square km and a population of 140 million. It is bordered on the west, north, and east by India, on the southeast by Myanmar, and the Bay of Bengal to the south. Though it is a small country, it has many diverse attractions for nature lovers as well as being rich in culture and heritage. The territorial waters of Bangladesh extend 12 nautical miles, and the exclusive economic zone of the country is 200 nautical miles. There is a large marshy jungle coastline on the Bay of Bengal popularly known as the Sundarbans - one of the largest mangrove forests in the world, the home of the Royal Bengal Tiger.

Bangladesh is located in the Ganges delta which is densely populated and it is formed by the confluence of the Ganges, Brahmaputra, and Meghna rivers and their tributaries as they flow down from the Himalayas, creating the largest riverine delta in the world. To the south is a highly irregular deltaic coastline of about 600 km, fissured by many rivers and streams flowing into the Bay of Bengal.

DEVELOPMENT AND ROLE OF TOURISM MARKETING ORGANISATION IN BANGLADESH

During the Pakistan period of rule, there was a tourism department with an office in West Pakistan. This department was assigned promotion, development and regulation of the tourism sector in Pakistan. A private sector corporation came into operation at the end of 1970. After independence, the socio-economic and political climate prevailing in the country was not encouraging for the private sector to participate in economic activities of wider magnitude.

Therefore, it became imperative for the government to come forward by promote tourism in Bangladesh. Soon after the independence of Bangladesh, the government of the newborn state realised the importance of tourism in its economic and social life. Therefore, the government decided to reorganise the tourism sector by combining both the tourism department and the private corporation into one organisation, bringing it under government responsibility for better coordination, promotion, development and marketing. Consequently, the government established the National Tourism Organisation in the name of Bangladesh Parjatan Corporation under Presidential Order No. 143, declared in November 27, 1972. BPC began in January 1973 with limited assets of the former "Pakistan Tourism Corporation" and TK.10 million sanctioned by the government. The Corporation was entrusted with the dual responsibility of developing tourism infrastructure and promoting Bangladesh as a tourist destination. Other responsibilities of the Corporation included regulation and operation of tourism activities in the country. Thus, Bangladesh Parjatan Corporation came into being as the NTO in Bangladesh.

As such, the structure of the tourism sector in Bangladesh is predominantly managed by the public sector. The public sector has played a pioneering role in the development and promotion of tourism in the country. Government involvement in the tourism sector is channelled through BPC, which is under the Ministry of Civil Aviation and Tourism. As a semiautonomous organisation it enjoys wide power and authority, including the right to acquire and dispose of property; construct and run hotels, restaurants and other tourists facilities; operate duty free shop, transportation and car rental; establish training institutes; and invest its funds as it deems proper. Due to neglect by successive governments, BPC totally failed to achieve the objectives for which it was created. Had there been no private sector tour operators in the country things would have been even more precarious. They have kept the hope of tourism alive, almost without government support. Private sector involvement in tourism in Bangladesh is still not adequate however, and the Bangladesh government has taken remedial measures to encouraging the private sector to play a positive role in the development and diversification of tourist facilities to promote domestic and international tourism in the country.

A large proportion of investments have been made in hotel businesses and tour operations. Private sector investors now are as showing a keen interest to participate in the tourism sector. Tour operators have a significant role to play in tourism business. Over 40 private tour operators have already been engaged in tourism marketing in Bangladesh. Some of them conduct only domestic tours while others offer both domestic and outbound tours. Thirty two such private tour operators are members of an association named "Tours Operator Association of Bangladesh", formed to carry out their activities more efficiently, to lobby the BPC and the government for the realisation of justified rights and to promote the country's tourism together. Travel agencies in both the destination and the tourist generating countries also play important roles in the promotion and development of tourism in a country. There are 235 travel agencies in Bangladesh; most of them are members of the Association of Travel Agents of Bangladesh. These travel agencies are licensed by the Registration Authority under the Ministry of Civil Aviation and Tourism and controlled by the same authority under the Travel Agencies Registration and control ordinance of 1977, which says that the travel agencies are involve themselves in travel arrangements only.

BANGLADESH TOURISM MARKETING PRODUCTS AND TOURIST ATTRACTIONS

The world thinks of Bangladesh as poor, flood-ravaged, and more of a disaster zone than a travel destination. In some respects, the world is right but hiding behind these images is a country with a rich history, a strange beauty, and some interesting attractions but it is not, however, a destination for everyone. Bangladesh is a country with rich traditions, natural beauty, beaches, forests, lakes, hills, wild lives, archaeological attractions, monuments, handicrafts, sanctuaries, religious festivals, cultural heritage, tribal culture and architecture, incredible greenery, mighty rivers and attractive river cruises, sunny beaches, colourful tribal life and attractive cultural functions that offer great tourist attractions.

Tourism involves travelling for pleasure, enjoy and education. It is also a business of attracting tourists and providing for their accommodation and entertainment. In many countries, tourism is an industry for earning revenue and foreign exchange. The many businesses that grow concurrently with the development of tourism include airlines, shipping, hotels and restaurants, finance companies, tour operators, travel agents, car rental firms, caterers and retail establishments and together, they contribute significantly to the overall development of a country's economy and to its cultural diversification and adaptation. The Moorish traveller Ibn Batuta who visited Bengal in the fourteenth century described Bengal as the wealthiest and cheapest land of the world and stated that it was known as 'a hell full of bounties' In the seventeenth century French traveller Francois Bernie observed and stated "Egypt has been represented in every age as the finest and most fruitful country in the world, and even our modern writers deny that there is any other land of peculiarly favoured by nature; but the knowledge I have acquired of Bengal during two visits paid to that kingdom inclines me to believe that pre-eminence ascribed to Egypt is rather due to Bengal".

Bangladesh has the world's longest 120 km unbroken sea beach sloping here down to the blue water of the Bay of Bengal in Cox's Bazar, Parki beach, and Kuakata. Such a long sea beach covering miles of golden sands, soaring cliffs, surfing waves, all of these make Cox's Bazar the tourist capital of Bangladesh. The tourists can enjoy the charming beauty of the sunset behind the waves of the sea. Its appeal makes Cox's Bazar one of the most attractive tourist spots in the world. In addition to that, there are other beaches like Inani beach in Ukhia, Cox's Bazar, St. Martin Island, and Patengha beach which are also attractive to foreign as well as local tourists. In Bangladesh, there are some attractive hilly regions which also are considered beautiful tourism spots and attract a large number of tourists. These hilly regions show significant differences from the rest of the country because the indigenous inhabitants belong to different ethnic minorities who have a distinctive lifestyle from the majority of the population.

TOURIST ARRIVALS IN BANGLADESH

The number of tourist arrivals in Bangladesh has increased to 397,410 in 2007 from 113,242 in 1991 which shows an average annual growth rate of 9 per cent. The tourist arrivals increased in 2003 by 18 per cent and 16 per cent in 2007 over the preceding year. In general, the statistics show a very good and positive trend. This rate can be considered very high for those countries that have already matured in the market, but for a new market entry, like Bangladesh, the growth rate is not very impressive.

BANGLADESH TOURISM MARKETING STRATEGY

The most important challenge for destination marketing therefore is to bring all individual partners together to cooperate rather than compete and to pool resources towards developing an integrated marketing mix and delivery system. Bangladesh, as a vacation destination, has many facets. It is endowed with almost all the natural potentials that attract tourist. These include: Cox's Bazaar, the longest unbroken clean and sandy beach in the world; Sundarbans, the home of the majestic Royal Bengal tigers, Dhaka, the capital known as the city of mosques and muslin; Rangamati, the heart of the panoramic lake district; Sylhet, land of fascinating hills and tea gardens; Chittagong, the largest port city of the country and known as the city of shrines; Mainamati, Mahasthangarh and Paharpur, archaeological treasures of Hindu and Buddhist rule in the country from 300 BC to 1200 AD.

Riverine beauty, colourful tribal culture and simple village life are the main factors for attracting visitors. These kind of things are need to be explored by the tourism marketing promotion and need to formulate tourism marketing strategic plan either by the Bangladesh government organisation or the private sectors.

Therefore, the objectives of the tourism marketing strategy in Bangladesh are now outlined:

- To consolidate Bangladesh's position as a tourist destination in the established generating markets at regional and international levels by utilizing different marketing tools such as web sites;
- To target new and potential markets by identifying and monitoring changing designs and needs for various market types such as China, Japan, East European and South America, and South Asian countries;
- To enhance Bangladesh's competitive position in the intercontinental destination market by mobilizing effective promotional measures supported by attractive proposals and appealing tourism products. The Bangladesh government promotes Sundarban and Cox's Bazar, St. Martin Island and the Fort William, and House of Ahasan Monzil, Sonargaon as preferred tourism destination areas. However, the Bangladeshi government decided to; diversify Bangladeshi's tourism products: to meet the demands of the general public; to increase its tourist's market share in a competitive region; to strive to realise the country's potential in terms of, MICE, sport and adventure; to promote Bangladeshi's scenic beauty, diverse wildlife, eco-tourism and diversity of cultures and heritage; promote it in terms of its unique selling points as an all season destination; and
- To pay special attention to tourist arrivals from Europe, South Asia, USA, Gulf Cooperation Council Countries, East Asia and the Pacific Rim, Australia and New Zealand and others. BTO opened new regional offices in these countries to support and enhance the value of Bangladesh as a tourism destination.

METHODOLOGY PHILOSOPHICAL PERSPECTIVES

All research is based on underlying assumptions about what forms 'valid' research and which research methods are suitable. In order to conduct and/or evaluate qualitative research, it is important to know what these assumptions are. The most relevant philosophical assumptions are those which relate to the underlying epistemology of the research. Epistemology refers to assumptions about knowledge and how it can be obtained. Orlikowski and Baroudi, following Chua, suggest three categories of research philosophy, positivist, interpretive and critical. In social research these differences are not always precise. Qualitative research can be positivist, interpretive, or critical. However, these three approaches are philosophically different.

There is considerable disagreement as to whether these research "models" or underlying epistemologies are necessarily opposed or can be accommodated within one study. The research paradigm been selected for this study is an interpretivist paradigm; and therefore, the following ontological and epistemological positions are adopted: Ontological position: subjective; and epistemological position: Interpretive paradigm.

In order to achieve the research objectives, this research is divided into two parts, one is exploratory research, and the other causal research in marketing in tourism. As little is known about marketing in tourism in Bangladesh, an exploratory study is appropriate to accomplish the objectives. Exploratory research is conducted when not much is known about the situation at hand or when little information is available on how similar problems or research issues have been solved in the past. Exploratory research, therefore, is useful for generating new ideas, factors or hypothesis, as well as developing techniques for measuring and locating future data. This exploratory research will also adopt a qualitative approach, because this approach is useful to uncover what lies behind the phenomenon about which little is known, which is compatible with the rationale for exploratory studies. Exploratory research is used principally to gain a deeper understanding of something.

However, considering the objectives of this research is to generate variables related to tourism marketing to be used in the research, a qualitative approach is more appropriate as an initial study than a quantitative one. Churchill, exploratory studies are; literature search, survey, analysis of the case, and focus group. This research will conduct an analysis of a case study. To summarize, exploratory research will provide an opportunity to formulate and develop hypotheses for a more precise investigation in the secondary stage of the research with regard to the competitiveness of tourism marketing.

The exploratory research will be incorporated in building detailed and relevant questionnaires for the secondary stage of research. After identifying the first objective, this research will move on to the remaining objectives. These relate to the identification of different variables and relationships among the variables and this research will be a case-effect relationship or hypotheses testing study, which normally adopts a quantitative approach. Sekaran, studies that engage in hypothesis testing usually explain the nature of certain relationships or identify establish differences among the variables or the independence of two or more factors in a situation. All three are relevant to these research objectives. Multivariate data analysis will be used for the causal study in this research because various dependent and independent variable are involved with regard to effectiveness measures of tourism marketing as a promotional tool in Bangladesh. Causal Research explores the effect of one thing on another and more specifically, the effect of one variable on another. The research is used to measure what impact a specific change will have on existing norms and allows market researchers to predict hypothetical scenarios upon which an agency can base its business plan.

Causal research is a way of seeing how actions taken now will affect a business in the future. Hypothesis testing will be one of the parts of this research and for this reason a descriptive approach will also be partly employed to present not only the characteristics of respondent groups, but also their general perception about the effectiveness and competitiveness of tourism marketing in Bangladesh The research incorporates a triangulation technique. Triangulation can be used when data are obtained from a number of sources and individuals using a variety of methods with a particular emphasis on the function of confirmation and completeness. With regards to the triangulation, this research will be used two different methods, one is analysis of case study that will be exploratory research and the other is multivariate analysis which will be causal research. Both will be combined to accomplish research objectives.

Different data sources, including government reports, photos, articles, newspaper articles, meetings minutes and interview's will be collected and analysed. However, there are diverse debates on triangulation with regard to its usefulness and effectiveness. Triangulation is expected to reduce the risk that research conclusions can reflect the systematic biases or limitations of specific methods and allows researchers to gain a better assessment of the validity and generality of their explanations. Triangulation is also suggested as a powerful solution to the problem of relying too much on any single data source. However, triangulation is also criticised for having constraints and drawbacks that may affect the effectiveness of the strategy. In general, mixed research methods are considered as one of the three paradigms in which quantitative and qualitative techniques or other paradigm characteristics are confined in one overall study. The two major types of mixed research are distinguished as mixed method and mixed model research. Mixed model research is that in which the researcher mixes both qualitative and quantitative research approaches within a stage of the study or across two stages of the research process. As such, a researcher might conduct a survey and use a questionnaire that is composed of multiple closed-ended or quantitative type items as well as several open-ended or qualitative type items. A researcher might also collect qualitative data but then quantify this. When different approaches are used to focus on the same phenomenon and they provide the same result, they have validation which means they have superior evidence as the result. Other important reasons for doing mixed research are to complement one set of results with another, to expand a set of results, or to discover something that would have been missed if only a qualitative or a quantitative approach had been used.

DATA COLLECTION AND ANALYSIS

The data collection technique chosen for this research is in-depth face-to-face interviews. The interview is an appropriate technique by which to gather information and data from a questionnaire. The main advantage of an interview is that the researcher can provide clarification to questions if needed during the interview session. This can lead to an increase in the quality, accuracy, and the amount of data obtained. The interviews were conducted in Bengali as well as English, depending on the needs of the person being interviewed.

DATA COLLECTION

This study utilized a self-administered survey method. Once the final measurement scales and the survey questionnaire had been developed, the survey package, including a cover letter and survey questionnaire, was distributed to the selected tourism stakeholders in Dhaka, Bangladesh. As well, a departing foreign tourist survey was conducted at the Zia International Airport, Bangladesh using a survey questionnaire.

STUDY POPULATION AND SAMPLING DESIGN

The population can be defined as the entire group under study as specified by the objectives of the research. The objectives of this study are to investigate tourism stakeholders' perceptions and attitudes towards tourism promotional effectiveness and its development, and the population of this study are tourism stakeholders and departing foreign tourists. Specifically, the stakeholder target population includes members or groups that are government officials, tourism authorities, local tourism agencies, tourism related operators, and tourism planning and development companies in the capital city of Dhaka, Bangladesh.

The sample of tourism stakeholders for this study was collected by a judgement sampling method from the identified sampling frame. The major source of the sampling frame was the Tour Operators Association of Bangladesh homepage, which was used by the researcher to produce a list of possible respondents their addresses, and other details.

This information source contains over 150 tourism stakeholders. A second source, the internet homepage of the Bangladesh Parjatan Corporation provided directories and resources about tourism stakeholders. It provided foreign and local/regional visitor information, destination marketing organizations, and local and state tourism attractions and sites. Once tourism stakeholders were identified, a set of criteria was applied, and it was determined whether or not individuals would be included in the sampling frame for this study. Different categories of population were selected based on the research objectives and specific criteria. These population are:

- Secretary of the MoCAT
- Chairman of the BPC;
- Owners of the private tour operators;
- Foreign tourists visiting country;
- Director of Marketing and Sales, Biman Bangladesh Airlines; and
- Owners of the Travel Agencies.

These are the major role players in the marketing activities of the tourism marketing industry in Bangladesh.

TOURISM ECONOMICS

Most of the tourism activity also involves economic costs, including the direct costs incurred by tourism businesses, government costs for infrastructure to better serve tourists, as well as congestion and related costs borne by individuals in the community. Community decisions over tourism often involve debates between industry proponents touting tourism's economic impacts (benefits) and detractors emphasizing tourism's costs.

Sound decisions rest on a balanced and objective assessment of both benefits and costs and an understanding of who benefits from tourism and who pays for it. Businesses and public organizations are increasingly interested in the economic impacts of tourism at national, state, and local levels. One regularly hears claims that tourism supports X jobs in an area or that a festival or special event generated Y million dollars in sales or income in a community. "Multiplier effects" are often cited to capture secondary effects of tourism spending and show the wide range of sectors in a community that may benefit from tourism. Tourism's economic benefits are touted by the industry for a variety of reasons. Claims of tourism's economic significance give the industry greater respect among the business community, public officials, and the public in general. This often translates into decisions or public policies that are favourable to tourism.

Community support is important for tourism, as it is an activity that affects the entire community. Tourism businesses depend extensively on each other as well as on other businesses, government and residents of the local community. Economic benefits and costs of tourism reach virtually everyone in the region in one way or another. Economic impact analyses provide tangible estimates of these economic interdependencies and a better understanding of the role and importance of tourism in a region's economy.

Tourism's economic impacts are therefore an important consideration in state, regional and community planning and economic development. Economic impacts are also important factors in marketing and management decisions. Communities therefore need to understand the relative importance of tourism to their region, including tourism's contribution to economic activity in the area. A variety of methods, ranging from pure guesswork to complex mathematical models, are used to estimate tourism's economic impacts. Studies vary extensively in quality and accuracy, as well as which aspects of tourism are included. Technical reports often are filled with economic terms and methods that non-economists do not understand. On the other hand, media coverage of these studies tend to oversimplify and frequently misinterpret the results, leaving decision makers and the general public with a sometimes distorted and incomplete understanding of tourism's economic effects.

How can the average person understand these studies sufficiently to separate good studies from bad ones and make informed choices? The purpose of this bulletin is to present a systematic introduction to economic impact concepts and methods. The presentation is written for tourism industry analysts and public officials, who would like to better understand, evaluate, or possibly conduct an economic impact assessment. The bulletin is organized around ten basic questions that either are asked or should be asked about the economic impacts of tourism.

ECONOMIC ISIMPACT ANALYSIS

A variety of economic analyses are carried out to support tourism decisions. As these different kinds of economic analysis are frequently confused, let's begin by positioning economic impact studies within the broader set of economic problems and techniques relevant to tourism. These same techniques may be applied to any policy or action, but we will define them here in the context of tourism. Each type of analysis is identified by the basic question(s) it answers and the types of methods and models that are appropriate. Benefit cost analysis and economic impact analysis are frequently confused as both discuss economic "benefits".

There are two clear distinctions between the two techniques. B/C analysis addresses the benefits from economic efficiency while economic impact analysis focuses on the regional distribution of economic activity. The income received from tourism by a destination region is largely off-set by corresponding losses in the origin regions, yielding only modest contributions to net social welfare and efficiency. B/C analysis includes market and non-market values (consumer surplus), while economic impact analysis is restricted to actual flows of money from market transactions.

While each type of economic analysis is somewhat distinct, a given problem often calls for several different kinds of economic analysis. An economic impact study will frequently involve a demand analysis to project levels of tourism activity. In other cases demand is treated as exogenous and the analysis simply estimates impacts if a given number of visitors are attracted to the area. A comprehensive impact assessment will also examine fiscal impacts, as well as social and environmental impacts. Be aware that an economic impact analysis, by itself, provides a rather narrow and often one-sided perspective on the impacts of tourism. Studies of the economic impacts of tourism tend to emphasize the positive benefits of tourism. On the other hand environmental, social, cultural and fiscal impact studies tend to focus more on negative impacts of tourism. This is in spite of the fact that there are negative economic impacts of tourism (*e.g.,* seasonality and lower wage jobs) and in many cases positive environmental and social impacts (*e.g.,* protection of natural and cultural resources in the area and education of both tourists and local residents). An economic impact assessment (EIA) traces changes in economic activity resulting from some action.

An EIA will identify which economic sectors benefit from tourism and estimate resulting changes in income and employment in the region. Economic impact assessment procedures do not assess economic efficiency and also do not generally produce estimates of the fiscal costs of an action. For many problems economic impact analysis will be part of a broader analysis. Environmental, social, and fiscal impacts are often equally important concerns in a balanced assessment of impacts. An economic impact analysis will assess the contribution of tourism activity to a region's economy. The basic questions an economic impact study usually addresses are:

- How many jobs in the area does tourism support?
- How much tax revenue is generated from tourism?
- How much do tourists spend in the area?
- What portion of sales by local businesses is due to tourism?
- How much income does tourism generate for households and businesses in the area?

An economic impact analysis also reveals the interrelationships among economic sectors and provides estimates of the changes that take place in an economy due to some existing or proposed action. The most common applications of economic impact analysis to tourism are:

1. To evaluate the economic impacts of changes in the supply of recreation and tourism opportunities. Supply changes may involve a change in quantity, such as the opening of new facilities, closing of existing ones, or expansions and contraction in capacity. Supply changes may also involve changes in quality, including changes in (a) the quality of the environment, (b) the local infrastructure and public services to support tourism, or (c) the nature of the tourism products and services that are provided in an area.
2. To evaluate the economic impacts of changes in tourism demand. Population changes, changes in the competitive position of the region, marketing activity or changing consumer tastes and preferences can alter levels of tourism activity, spending, and associated economic

activity. An economic impact study can estimate the magnitude and nature of these impacts.

3. To evaluate the effects of policies and actions which affect tourism activity either directly or indirectly. Tourism depends on many factors at both origins and destinations that are frequently outside the direct control of the tourism industry itself. Economic impact studies provide information to help decision makers better understand the consequences of various actions on the tourism industry as well as on other sectors of the economy. For example, increased air pollution standards have been opposed in some regions due to the predicted economic consequences of the closing of plants that cannot meet the new standards. Tourism interests counter these arguments with estimates of the potential gains in income and jobs in tourism industries that depend on good air quality and visibility.
4. To understand the economic structure and interdependencies of different sectors of the economy. Economic studies help us better understand the size and structure of the tourism industry in a given region and its linkages to other sectors of the economy. Such understandings are helpful in identifying potential partners for the tourism industry as well as in targeting industries as part of regional economic development strategies. Issues such as economic growth, stability, and seasonality may be addressed as part of these studies.
5. To argue for favourable treatment in allocation of resources or local tax, zoning or other policy decisions. By showing that tourism has significant economic impacts, tourism interests can often convince decision-makers to allocate more resources for tourism or to establish policies that encourage tourism. Tax abatements and other incentives frequently given to manufacturing firms have also been granted to hotels, marinas and other tourism businesses based on demonstrated economic impacts in the local area.
6. To compare the economic impacts of alternative resource allocation, policy, management or development proposals. Economic impact analyses are commonly used to assess the relative merits of distinct alternatives. The economic contribution of expanded tourism offerings may be compared for example with alternatives such as resource extraction activities (mining, timber harvesting) or manufacturing. Impacts of alternative tourism development proposals may also be evaluated, *e.g.,* tourism strategies that emphasize outdoor recreation, camping development, a convention facility, or a factory outlet mall.

Tourism has a variety of economic impacts. Tourists contribute to sales, profits, jobs, tax revenues, and income in an area. The most direct effects occur within the primary tourism sectors —lodging, restaurants, transportation, amusements, and retail trade. Through secondary effects, tourism affects most sectors of the economy. An economic impact analysis of tourism activity normally focuses on changes in sales, income, and employment in a region resulting from tourism activity. A simple tourism impact scenario illustrates. Let's say a region attracts an additional 100 tourists, each spending $100 per day. That's $10,000 in new spending per day in the area. If sustained over a 100 day season, the region would accumulate a million dollars in new sales. The million dollars in spending would be distributed to lodging, restaurant, amusement and retail trade sectors in proportion to how the visitor spends the $100. Perhaps 30per cent of the million dollars would leak out of the region immediately to cover the costs of goods purchased by tourists that are not made in the local area (only the retail margins for such items should normally be included as direct sales effects). The remaining $700,000 in direct sales might yield $350,000 in income within tourism industries and support 20 direct tourism jobs. Tourism industries are labour and income intensive, translating a high proportion of sales into income and corresponding jobs.

The tourism industry, in turn, buys goods and services from other businesses in the area, and pays out most of the $350,000 in income as wages and salaries to its employees. This creates secondary economic effects in the region. The study might use a sales multiplier of 2.0 to indicate that each dollar of direct sales generates another dollar in secondary sales in this region. Through multiplier effects, the $700,000 in direct sales produces $1.4 million in total sales. These secondary sales create additional income and employment, resulting in a total impact on the region of $1.4 million in sales, $650,000 in income and 35 jobs.

While hypothetical, the numbers used here are fairly typical of what one might find in a tourism economic impact study. A more complete study might identify which sectors receive the direct and secondary effects and possibly identify differences in spending and impacts of distinct subgroups of tourists (market segments). One can also estimate the tax effects of this spending by applying local tax rates to the appropriate changes in sales or income. Instead of focusing on visitor spending, one could also estimate impacts of construction or government activity associated with tourism. There are several other categories of economic impacts that are not typically covered in economic impact assessments, at least not directly. For example:

Changes in prices — tourism can sometimes inflate the cost of housing and retail prices in the area, frequently on a seasonal basis.

Changes in the quality and quantity of goods and services — tourism may lead to a wider array of goods and services available in an area (of either higher or lower quality than without tourism).

Changes in property and other taxes — taxes to cover the cost of local services may be higher or lower in the presence of tourism activity. In some cases, taxes collected directly or indirectly from tourists may yield reduced local taxes for schools, roads, etc. In other cases, locals may be taxed more heavily to cover the added infrastructure and service costs. The impacts of tourism on local government costs and revenues are addressed more fully in a fiscal impact analysis.

Economic dimensions of "social" and "environmental" impacts — There are also economic consequences of most social and environmental impacts that are not usually addressed in an economic impact analysis. These can be positive or negative. For example, traffic congestion will increase costs of moving around for both households and businesses. Improved amenities that attract tourists may also encourage retirees or other kinds of businesses to locate in the area.

Induced Effects

A standard economic impact analysis traces flows of money from tourism spending, first to businesses and government agencies where tourists spend their money and then to:

Other businesses — supplying goods and services to tourist businesses,

Households — earning income by working in tourism or supporting industries, and

Government — through various taxes and charges on tourists, businesses and households

Formally, regional economists distinguish direct, indirect, and induced economic effects. Indirect and induced effects are sometimes collectively called secondary effects. The total economic impact of tourism is the sum of direct, indirect, and induced effects within a region. Any of these impacts may be measured as gross output or sales, income, employment, or value added. Direct effects are production changes associated with the immediate effects of changes in tourism expenditures.

For example, an increase in the number of tourists staying overnight in hotels would directly yield increased sales in the hotel sector. The additional hotel sales and associated changes in hotel payments for wages and salaries, taxes, and supplies and services are direct effects of the tourist spending.

Indirect effects are the production changes resulting from various rounds of re-spending of the hotel industry's receipts in other backward-linked industries (*i.e.,* industries supplying products and services to hotels). Changes in sales, jobs, and income in the linen supply industry, for example, represent indirect effects of changes in hotel sales. Businesses supplying products and services to the linen supply industry represent another round of indirect effects, eventually linking hotels to varying degrees to many other economic sectors in the region. Induced effects are the changes in economic activity resulting from household spending of income earned directly or indirectly as a result of tourism spending. For example, hotel and linen supply employees supported directly or indirectly by tourism, spend their income in the local region for housing, food, transportation, and the usual array of household product and service needs. The sales, income, and jobs that result from household spending of added wage, salary, or proprietor's income are induced effects.

By means of indirect and induced effects, changes in tourist spending can impact virtually every sector of the economy in one way or another. The magnitude of secondary effects depends on the propensity of businesses and households in the region to purchase goods and services from local suppliers. Induced effects are particularly noticed when a large employer in a region closes a plant. Not only are supporting industries (indirect effects) hurt, but the entire local economy suffers due to the reduction in household income within the region. Retail stores close and leakages of money from the region increase as consumers go outside the region for more and more goods and services.

Similar effects in the opposite direction are observed when there is a significant increase in jobs and household income. Final demand is the term used by economists for sales to the final consumers of goods and services. In almost all cases, the final consumers of tourism goods and services are households. Government spending is also considered as final demand. The same methods for estimating impacts of visitor spending can be applied to estimate the economic impacts of government spending, for example, to operate and maintain a park or visitor center.

Regional Models

An input-output model (I-O model) is a mathematical model that describes the flows of money between sectors within a region's economy. Flows are predicted by knowing what each industry must buy from every other industry to produce a dollar's worth of output. Using each industry's production function, I-O models also determine the proportions of sales that go to wage and salary income, proprietor's income, and taxes. Multipliers can be estimated from input-output models based on the estimated re-circulation of spending within the region. Exports and imports are determined based upon estimates of the propensity of households and firms within the region to purchase goods and services from local sources (often called RPC's or regional purchase coefficients). The more a region is self-sufficient and purchases goods and services from within the region, the higher the multipliers for the region.

Input-output models make a number of assumptions. The basic ones are that:

- All firms in a given industry employ the same production technology (usually assumed to be the national average for that industry), and produce identical products.
- There are no economies or diseconomies of scale in production or factor substitution. I-O models are essentially linear — double the level of tourism activity/production and you double all of the inputs, the number of jobs, etc.

- The model doesn't explicitly keep track of time, but analysts generally report the impact estimates as if they represent activity within a single year.
- One must assume that the various model parameters are accurate and represent the current year.

I-O models are firmly grounded in the national system of accounts, which relies on a standard industrial classification system (SIC codes) and various federal government economic censuses, in which individual firms report sales, wage and salary payments and employment. I-O models will generally be at least a few years out-of-date, although this isn't usually a major problem unless the region's economy has changed significantly. An I-O model represents the region's economy at a particular point in time. Tourist spending estimates are generally price adjusted to the year of the model.

Multiplier computations for induced effects generally assume that jobs created by additional spending are new jobs, involving new households in the area. Induced effects are computed assuming linear changes in household spending with changes in income. Estimates of induced effects may be inflated due to the violation of these assumptions. Induced effects tend to account for the vast majority of the secondary effects of tourism, and therefore should be used with caution.

CONCLUSION

The value of the promotion channel depends on its capacity to reach consumers and satisfy their interests and needs. In the tourism sector, the means of promotion constitute an active and open way of getting information for tourists. Most of the consumer and tourist behaviour models incorporated the search of external information as an important component. Advice given by relatives and friends, tourist guides, tourist offices and brochures are among the most used and appreciated sources of tourist information. However, Gitelson and Crompton concluded that information sources do not stimulate purchase of destination and that brochures are only a part of the destination marketing.

The criterion most commonly used in order to determine whether one type of information source is more important than others was the fact that a great percentage of consumers may have access to it. In this sense, upon review of a large body of literature on destination image and information search, it is clear that destination image is an important aspect of tourism development due to its impact on both supply and demand side aspects of marketing. In this case, it has proved that the use of information sources as promotion tools has a strong influence on the formation of tourist destination images. Furthermore, this work has also revealed that the image generated by tourist brochures is firmly related to actual destination image. This research shows that the inclusion of image and tourist information in one model not only serves to highlight the importance of image, but also provides a better explanation for destination choice. Brochures and guides have proved to be the most valued information sources. In addition, tourists tend to prefer impersonal information sources. Nevertheless, personal experience probably appears to be the most important information source. This means that all contacts between the tourist and the destination, companies and travel agents at a personal and direct level, have a decisive influence on the perception and image of a given tourist destination.

Tourists long for satisfactory travelling experiences, and tourist businesses and public institutions should consider this fact and be aware of experience marketing strategies. Tourists use external information sources as a first step when planning their holiday travel. As a result, it is essential for entrepreneurs and tourism promoters to know exactly what kind of information should be included in tourist brochures and guides, in order to encourage the process of decision-making. At the same time, it is also important to analyse the effect of information on tourist behaviour and image. The process of destination image formation implies two fundamental issues. On the one hand, it suggests that individuals may have made up a specific destination image even before visiting and using promotional information sources.

The measurement of this basic image is an essential factor in the design of experience marketing strategies, so that destination promotion strategies may be modified to efficiently respond to the strengths and weaknesses, accuracies and inaccuracies of destination image. On the other hand, it is necessary to differentiate the image perceived by consumers who have already visited the destination from the image formed by those who have not; due to the fact that image alters upon travel to destination. This study indicates the influence of image variables on the respondents' perceptions, especially quality of accommodation and different customs and culture.

With regard to this question, the results indicate a relationship between overall destination attractiveness and the image induced by brochures. The results also indicate the influence of functional attributes on consumers' perceptions. The conceptual implications of this research pertain to the multidimensional aspects of the destination image.

10

Tourist Motivation and Statistics

According to Moutinho (1987:16), motivation is 'a state of need, a condition that exerts a push on the individual towards certain types of action that are seen as likely to bring satisfaction'. In this respect Cooper *et al.* (1993:20) rightly acknowledge that 'demand for tourists at the individual level can be treated as a consumption process which is influenced by a number of factors. These may be a combination of needs and desires, availability of time and money, or images, perceptions and attitudes'.

Not surprisingly, this is an incredibly complex area of research and it is impossible within a chapter such as this to overview the area in depth. Nevertheless, P. Pearce's (1993) influential work in this field outlined a 'blueprint for tourist motivation', arguing that in an attempt to theorise tourist motivation one must consider the following issues:

- The conceptual place of tourism motivation;
- Its task in the specialism of tourism;
- Its ownership and users;
- Its ease of communication;
- Pragmatic measurement concerns;
- Adopting a dynamic approach;
- The development of multi-motive perspectives;
- Resolving and clarifying intrinsic and extrinsic motivation approaches.

To date no all-embracing theory of tourist motivation has been developed which has been adapted and legitimised by researchers in other contexts. This is largely due to the multidisciplinary nature of the research issues identified above and the problem of simplifying complex psychological factors and behaviour into a set of constructs and ultimately a universally acceptable theory that can be tested and proved in various tourism contexts. As a result, Cooper *et al.* (1993:20) prefer to view the individual as a central component of tourism demand to understand what motivates the tourist to travel. Their research rightly acknowledges that:

No two individuals are alike, and differences in attitudes, perceptions and motivation have an important influence on travel decisions [where] attitudes depend on an individual's perception of the world. Perceptions are mental impressions of ... a place or travel company and are determined by many factors which include childhood, family and work experiences. However, attitudes and perceptions in themselves do not explain why people want to travel. The inner urges which initiate travel demand are called travel motivators.

If one views the tourist as a consumer, then tourism demand is formulated through a consumer decision-making process, and therefore one can discern four elements which initiate demand:

- *Energisers of demand*: Factors that promote an individual to decide on a holiday;
- *Filterers of demand*: Which means that even though motivation may prevail, constraints on demand may exist in economic, sociological or psychological terms;
- *Affecters*: Which are factors that may heighten or suppress the energisers that promote consumer interest or choice in tourism;
- *Roles*: Where the family member involved in the purchase of holiday products and the arbiter of group decision-making on choice of destination, product, and the where, when and how of consumption.

These factors underpin the tourist's process of travel decision-making although it does not explain why people choose to travel.

TOURIST MOTIVATIONS AND MARKET SEGMENTATION

Each destination offers a variety of products and services to attract tourists. From the destinations' point of view, it is very important to know why tourists choose this destination and how the tourists feel about the place they visited. Analysis of tourist motivation attempts to extend the theoretical and empirical evidence on the causal relationship among the push and pull motivations, satisfaction, and destination loyalty. Motivation has been referred to as psychological/biological/social needs and wants, including internal and external forces.

Uysal and Hagan, these forces describe how individuals are pushed by motivation variables into making travel decisions and how they are pulled or attracted by destination attributes. "Push" factors are defined as origin-related and refer the intangible, intrinsic desires of the individual traveller, such as desire to escape, rest and relaxation, adventure, health and prestige. "Pull" factors are defined mainly related to the attractiveness of a given destination and tangible characteristics such as beaches, accommodation and recreation facilities and cultural and historical resources. Quite a number of literatures have studied tourist motivation from biological, psychological, sociological and anthropological aspects. Tourism motivation is a multi-motive dimensional. Tourists often have more than one motive for choosing a certain destination, for example, people can choose one destination with a motive of relaxation in a pleasant safe place combined with visiting a local historical heritage. Motivation is also a dynamic and flexible variable. The design of a motivation list 'must be flexible enough to incorporate individual changes across the life-span and consider the effects of broad cultural force on tourist motivation'.

For example, a person may change his travel preferences as he moves through the family life cycle from a single-career person to a more family-oriented person, his motives for choosing destinations may be changed accordingly. The travel market is often divided into four types of markets: personal business travel, government or corporate business travel, visiting friends and family, and leisure travel. Each type of market can be sub-divided further into segments. Market segmentation is based on the profiles of target groups and measuring the attractiveness of the market. Destinations select one or a few segments as their target markets and develop the products and marketing strategies accordingly.

Effective market segmentation must exhibit the following characteristics:

- *Measurability*: The degree to which the size and purchasing power of the segments can be measured. Certain segmentation variables are difficult to measure;
- *Accessibility*: The degree to which the segment can be effectively reached and served;
- *Substantiality*: The degree to which the segments are large and/or profitable enough;
- *Action ability*: The degree to which effective programmes can be designed for attracting and serving the segments.

There are a number of objects dealing with tourism motivation, tourist perception and market positioning. Positioning involves identifying potential visitors' perception of the strong attributes of a destination, comparing them with their perceptions of the attributes of competitive destinations, and selecting those which differentiate a destination from its competitors. These features are then emphasized and form the cornerstone of marketing strategy.

Calantone point out that multinational tourism research requires researchers to investigate the problem of multinational origin, multinational destination, and multi-attribute criteria. Tourism planners should have a sound understanding of tourist perceptions and how they may differ across countries. Chen and Uysal use a new approach that could be applied to market positioning studies from a regional perspective. Different criteria are applied in this research.

- First, a regional perspective can identify a destination as an urban or a rural/peripheral area.
- Second, types of accommodation distinguish the same 'desires' and 'needs' of tourists, therefore, it can identify the market segments.

- Third, tourism markets show the potential directions for marketing, the same origins might have the same personal behaviours.
- Fourth, after the above three criteria, the markets can be further segmented by tourist motivation and activities in order to understand what kind of products, services and experiences tourists really desire, then the market planners can have a deep understanding of tourists needs, so that they can make appropriate marketing strategies for the segments.

Kozak gives an analysis of tourist motivations by comparing British and German tourists who have visited Mallorca and Turkey. The analysis uses cross-tabulation, factor analysis and a series of independent t-tests to evaluate quantitative data. The findings show that personal motivation and destination attributes should be used for destination positioning studies.

Efforts to understand the factors motivating tourists to visit a particular destination and how likely it is to be different from those of others visiting other destinations could help destination planners to set marketing strategies. It will also help the destination to build a self image for marketing and differentiating its own products and services from those of competing destinations.

DATA AND TOURISM PROFILE

The data for this study are based on a large survey that Danish Tourism Organization undertook in 2004. Visit Denmark conducted a survey of approximately 7,600 leisure tourists in all regions of Denmark, which covered both domestic and foreign tourists, and five different accommodation types, *i.e.,* all types except yachting. The questionnaire was designed with the purposes of both economic analysis and tourism marketing analysis. Apart from the tourist profile, such as age, gender, household types, income level, party sizes and length of stay, tourist motivation and activities that tourists made at the destination and their satisfaction are also included in the questionnaire. Bornholm and Copenhagen are chosen amongst 14 destinations for further investigation in this study.

From the sample analysis, it is seen that the tourist characteristics within these two types of segments are significant different from each other. Families with children tend to come to Bornholm, as shown that the party size with more than 3-4 persons accounted for 44per cent at Bornholm, while tourists in Copenhagen are relatively younger, single or couples without children. 39per cent of tourists stayed one week and 37per cent stayed for more than one week at Bornholm. Only 7per cent of tourists at Bornholm stayed for 1-3 nights, while in Copenhagen 64per cent of tourists stayed for 1-3 nights. From Statistics Denmark's tourism information it is seen that 91per cent of all tourist nights in Copenhagen are spent at hotels, while the nature-beach tourists stay at summer cottages and camping sites. The spending patterns of these two segments show that tourism spend more in big cities than rural/peripheral destination; hotel guests spend more than those staying at camping sites and holiday cottages. In the Danish survey 22 motives are included in a list of things that may affect tourists to choose the destinations.

These motives are grouped into seven factors by a rotated component matrix analysis:

- Nature (beach, forest, clean environment, safe place to stay and few tourists);
- Local ways of life (people in general, enjoying local food, shopping and other motives);
- attractions (children friendly, attraction/amusement, possibility of activities);
- Value for money (good/cheap transport, price level/inexpensive, possibility for spa, health and fitness)
- Physical activities (golfing, bicycle, fishing, sailing);
- cultural and museum (museum/cultural, historical heritage, special events, theatre, musical festival;
- Visit family and friends and possibility of playing golf.

STATISTICAL RESULTS AND EXPLANATION

A variety of analytical tools are applied in the analysis, including correlation and multivariate statistical techniques such as a factor analysis and multiple regression analysis. The point of departure is to check the differences in tourist motivation between the different types of destination, different types of accommodation and different tourism markets. Statistic tests show that tourist motivations have no direct relation with their satisfaction; it is found that activities that tourists made at destinations have influence on the tourist satisfaction. The activities like long walks or hikes and relaxation contribute positively to satisfaction. Those tourists who were less active in participating in activities are less satisfied than those who are very active participants.

DIFFERENCE IN MOTIVATION BY DESTINATIONS

An analysis of variance shows that motives for visiting Denmark are significantly different depending on destination. The tests are carried out for each of 22 different motives; it can identify tourism motivation for choosing different destinations, *i.e.,* different county regions in Denmark. Tourist motive for nature shows the greatest difference between the various destinations.

The motive for good/cheap transport is the least difference between 16 destinations in Denmark, which is followed by motive of possibility for yachting. The differences in motivation by destination Copenhagen, Bornholm, rest of Denmark, and Denmark as whole. It is seen that most tourists choose to visit

Bornholm because of nature, clean country and safety place, however, tourists also come with motivation of attraction, possibility of activities, children friends, possibility for bicycling and cultural, historical heritage.

Copenhagen attracts tourists by attractions and amusement many museums, cultural and historical heritage, many shopping possibilities and many restaurants. The main motives for tourists choosing Denmark as destination are nature, clean country, and safety place; also people in general, children friendly, attractions and amusement and possibility for activities. All these factors are scored by more than 40per cent of tourists.

DIFFERENCE IN MOTIVATION BY TYPES OF ACCOMMODATION

A second analysis of variance shows that motives for visiting Denmark are also significantly different depending on type of accommodation. The tests are conducted again for each of the 22 different motives. Tourists' motive for nature shows the greatest difference between the various accommodations. The tourists come to enjoy the nature, they are more likely to choose summer cottages, camping sites and holiday centres. Tourists with motives for cultural, historical and special events, are more likely to stay at hotels and youth hostels. Sport-active tourists more likely choose camping sites; and tourists focusing more on value for money more likely choose to stay in holiday centres.

DIFFERENCE IN MOTIVATION BY TOURISM MARKETS

A third analysis of variance shows that motives for visiting Denmark are also significantly different depending on market. The difference in motivation by tourist markets. A high proportion of tourists from all nationalities think nature, clean country and safety are important influencing factors for the destination choice. However, there are significant differences between nationalities with respect to the proportion of tourists who think these attributes are important. It is shown that German tourists are more likely motivated by possibilities of angling and bicycling than other tourists; Swedish/Norwegian tourists are more likely motivated by short distance to destination, inexpensive and attraction and amusement. In the analysis of variance with destination as the dependent variable, the average F-value for the 22 motives was 25.

For type of accommodation, the average F-value was 80, and for market it was also very large, namely 72. Therefore when segmenting the market for potential holiday visitors to Denmark, both market and types of accommodation are relevant criteria.

TOURIST SATISFACTION BY PARTICIPATION IN ACTIVITIES AT DESTINATIONS

Tourists are more satisfied with their holidays at Bornholm than those who visit Copenhagen or the rest of Denmark in term of overall satisfaction.

For Denmark as a destination as a whole overall satisfaction among leisure tourists was 4.48 on a scale from 1 to 5, with a 95per cent confidence interval ranging from a low of 4.47 and a high of 4.50.

Average satisfaction for tourists who visit Bornholm is 4.63, for those who visit Copenhagen it is 4.39. Average scores in satisfaction at Bornholm for all types of accommodation are higher than those corresponding types of accommodation in Copenhagen and the rest of Denmark. Tourist satisfaction by their participation in activities at destinations. The level of participation in each activity is scaled from 1 – 5, representing from no participation, a lower level to a higher level of participation. NO represents non-participation in the category of activities. LOW represents for answers 2-4 and HIGH shows a higher level of participation in activity.

The weighted average scores for satisfaction on a scale from 1 to 5 for these three types of tourists, namely 'non-participation', 'lower level of participation' and 'higher level of participation'. For nearly all activities, tourists at Bornholm are more satisfied than the tourists who visited Copenhagen and the rest of Denmark. Tourists at Bornholm are more satisfied with 'long walks or hikes', 'visiting attractions', 'swimming', 'cultural events', 'relax' and 'sunbathe' with relative higher percentage of respondents.. Tourists in Copenhagen are relatively more satisfied with 'shopping', 'cultural events', 'meeting new friends' and 'eating at restaurants' with also higher percentage of respondents, etc. In most cases at all regions the tourists with a higher level of participation are more satisfied than those with lower level of participation in activities.

MARKETING STRATEGIES FOR CITY-BREAKER AND NATURE-BEACHES TOURISM

Tourism markets are characterized by multinational origin, multinational or multi-regional destinations and multiple motives. Segmentation criteria should consider the points concerning measurability, accessibilities, substantiality of market segments. Destination planners should be aware of its comparative and competitive advantage in relation to other destinations. Comparative advantage involves the resources available to a destination, while competitive advantage relates to a destination's ability to use these resources.

Demographical trends in the main tourism markets and the changes in tourist motives should also be considered, as individual choice and tourism satisfaction do have influence on the destination development. Demographical trends in most western countries show growing shares of senior people and decreasing shares of young people in the population. This has been observed from the destinations in Denmark that tourist arrivals have decreased from the German families with small children and young people. The purpose of analyzing the target markets and motivations for destination choice is to understand the needs and desire of tourists better. Destinations can use the analysis to make appropriate strategies for tourism products and marketing mix. The object uses two typical destinations as case studies to show the difference both in destination attributes and tourism motives for visiting the destination. The marketing strategies discussed here are focused also on these two types of destination. It should be noticed that some destinations have both features, such as one destination could be a rural-coastal area that is also close to a large city; or a destination has both cultural heritage, and at the same time it has an attractive natural environment.

It really depends on how large the destination area is defined. Another notice is that the authors do not suggest that each destination should only make their own marketing efforts; instead it is suggested to have a cooperative strategy between the different regions, coordinated by a national or regional tourism organization. Each accommodation would need to find the right balance between marketing through destination marketing organizations and accommodation brand marketing. Many hotels in Denmark and in Europe in general are unbranded, and therefore the booking platform may to some extent take on the role of a brand.

MARKETING STRATEGY FOR CITY-BREAKER TOURISM

City-breakers have a diversified background related to age, nationality, family types and income. They stay on average 4-5 days, but they stay at genuine hotels and spend much more than the nature-beach tourists, who generally stay at lower cost forms of accommodation. City-breakers are also relatively more interested in activities and culture attraction. It is suggested that marketing strategies for city destinations should concentrate on the attractions, activities development and event arrangement. Tourists from far away countries typically fly to the destination and are attracted by seeing the city and experience the activities happening in the city, however they are also interested in people in general, to experience every day life in the cities, including shopping.

For the repeat or domestic visitors, they are attracted to the city by the variety of activities, such as new shows in the theatres and opera houses or music festivals, new exhibitions, sport arrangements. It is suggested that destinations like large cities continuously focus on the needs of relatively widely covered tourists, such as events tourism and cultural tourism. Destination planners should follow the new trends in the tourism development, such as more and more tourists prefer prolonged weekend holidays to the large cities to be relaxed or enjoy some cultural experience.

City marketing planners can accordingly make some effective activities to attract this type of tourists. City destinations have possibilities to explore new markets, such as Eastern European countries, Asian and South American countries.

Following the rapid economic development in recent years in some developing countries, residents in these countries can afford to have long-haul travel 16 experience. The large cities are often the first choice when they are going abroad. Therefore city destinations should make appropriate products and marketing strategies for the target markets. A large city like Copenhagen should market itself with the unique attractions and diversified services in the city. The attractions, such as Tivoli and new Opera House, can be flagships for marketing.

The survey shows that 53per cent of those visiting Copenhagen sited the attractions/amusements as an important motive for coming. Besides the wide selection and variety of restaurants and shopping opportunities, good and cheap transport facilities to and at the destination are favourable attributes for Copenhagen to attract tourists.

MARKETING STRATEGY FOR NATURE-BEACHES TOURISM

Nature-beach tourists are more family-types with more emphasis on relaxation. The average length of stay for this kind of tourists is around 8-9 days. They enjoy beach or forest, few tourists at destination, clean environment, children friendly and possibilities of different activities, such as golfing, bicycling, fishing and most likely swimming. The destination at rural and peripheral areas should have the quality of providing good, clean environment to attract tourists coming again.

Certain facilities, such as possibilities for tourists to play golf, bicycling, fishing, should be available at destinations. Provincial destinations can also arrange children friendly activities, like mini-Tivoli and other small-scale amusement parks to attract tourists with children. At the same time destinations are facing the challenge of decreasing share of tourists with children, it is worthwhile starting to investigate the senior tourist markets to attract more retired people to visit the nature-beach destinations. The wonderful island of Bornholm should emphasize its unique nature, sited by a whopping 93per cent of visitors, including its rocky cliffs on the north coast and its white sandy beaches on the south coast. Also in the area of cycling possibilities the island is far ahead of the rest of the country.

Also the island has a strong cultural and historical heritage, which is mentioned by 44per cent of visitors, which is a higher percentage even than those visiting the capital of Denmark. Bornholm is the only place in Denmark with round churches, and there are five of them, and also there is an ancient castle ruin. The rest of Denmark, as most of them have attributes of nature and rural or coastal features, could also use nature or unspoiled environment to attract tourists. Nature, for one: 80per cent site Nature as an important reason for visiting other provinces. Also the facts that these other provinces are child friendly and the price level is relatively low. Angling is quite popular at mainland provinces of Denmark, sited by 15per cent. But actually, the Baltic Sea along the coasts of Bornholm has got tremendous amounts and sizes of salmon, and one weekend in the spring there is a huge trolling competition, an event which should perhaps be emphasized even more by Destination Bornholm. Analyzing tourist satisfaction shows that more active tourists are more satisfied with destinations.

The results reflect the fact that tourists desire for experiences at destination. Destination marketing planners should investigate the possibilities of arranging more tourism activities. The regional cooperation needs to be further coordinated and more marketing efforts and investment is required. For the national marketing organization of Denmark it would be better to emphasize the variety of accommodation offers rather than the different regions, since motives vary more between different types of accommodation than between different regions. However, there is also great variation in motives between regions.

HIERARCHY MODEL AND TOURIST MOTIVATION

Within the social psychology of tourism there is a growing literature which has built upon Maslow's work (discussed earlier in relation to recreation) to identify specific motivations beyond the concept of needing 'to get away from it all' pioneered by Grinstein (1955), while push factors motivating individuals to seek a holiday exist, and pull factors (*e.g.,* promotion by tourist resorts and tour operators) encourage as attractors.

Ryan's (1991:25-9) analysis of tourist travel motivators (excluding business travel) identifies the following reasons commonly cited to explain why people travel to tourist destinations for holidays, which include:

- A desire to escape from a mundane environment;
- The pursuit of relaxation and recuperation functions;
- An opportunity for play;
- The strengthening of family bonds;
- Prestige, since different destinations can enable one to gain social enhancement among peers;
- Social interaction;
- Educational opportunities;
- Wish fulfilment;
- Shopping.

From this list, it is evident that while all leisure involves a temporary escape of some kind, 'tourism is unique in that it involves real physical escape reflected in travelling to one or more destination regions where the leisure experience transpires ... [thus] a holiday trip allows changes that are multi-dimensional: place, pace, faces, lifestyle, behaviour, attitude. It allows a person temporary withdrawal from many of the environments affecting day to day existence'

(Leiper (1984) cited in D.G. Pearce (1995:19). Within most studies of tourist motivations these factors emerge in one form or another, while researchers such as Crompton (1979) emphasise that socio-psychological motives can be located along a continuum, Iso-Ahola (1980) theorised tourist motivation in terms of an escape element complemented by a search component, where the tourist is seeking something.

However, Dann's (1981) conceptualisation is probably one of the most useful attempts to simplify the principal elements of tourist motivation into:

- Travel as a response to what is lacking yet desired;
- Destination pull in response to motivational push;
- Motivation as fancy;
- Motivation as classified purpose;
- Motivation typologies;
- Motivation and tourist experiences;
- Motivation as definition and meaning.

This was simplified a stage further by McIntosh and Goeldner (1990) into:

- Physical motivators;
- Cultural motivators;
- Interpersonal motivators;
- Status and prestige motivators.

On the basis of motivation and using the type of experiences tourists seek, Cohen (1972) distinguished between four types of travellers:

- The organised mass tourist, on a package holiday, who is highly organised. Their contact with the host community in a destination is minimal.
- The individual mass tourist, who uses similar facilities to the organised mass tourist but also desires to visit other sights not covered on organised tours in the destination.
- The explorers, who arrange their travel independently and who wish to experience the social and cultural lifestyle of the destination.
- The drifter, who does not seek any contact with other tourists or their accommodation, preferring to live with the host community.

Clearly, such a classification is fraught with problems, since it does not take into account the increasing diversity of holidays undertaken and inconsistencies in tourist behaviour. Other researchers suggest that one way of overcoming this difficulty is to consider the different destinations tourists choose to visit, and then establish a sliding scale similar to Cohen's (1972) typology, but which does not have such an absolute classification.

In contrast, Plog (1974) devised a classification of the US population into psychographic types, with travellers distributed along a continuum from psychocentrism to allocentrism. The psychocentrics are the anxious, inhibited and less adventurous travellers while at the other extreme the allocentrics are adventurous, outgoing, seeking new experiences due to their inquisitive personalities and interest in travel and adventure.

D.G. Pearce (1995) highlights the spatial implications of such conceptualisations, that each tourist type will seek different destinations which will change through time. However, criticisms by P. Pearce (1993) indicate that Plog's model is difficult to use because it fails to distinguish between extrinsic and intrinsic motivations without incorporating a dynamic element to encompass the changing nature of individual tourists. P. Pearce discounts such models, suggesting that individuals have a 'career' in their travel behaviour where people 'start at different levels, they are likely to change levels during their life-cycle and they can be prevented from moving by money, health and other people. They may also retire from their travel career or not take holidays at all and therefore not be part of the system'.

These are:

- A concern with biological needs;
- Aafety and security needs;
- Relationship development and extension needs;
- Special interest and self-development needs;
- Fulfilment or self-actualisation needs.

Cooper *et al.* (1993:23) argue that 'the literature on tourism motivation is still in an immature phase of development, it has been shown that motivation is an essential concept behind the different patterns of tourism demand'. From the existing literature on tourist motivation, the problems of determining tourist motivation may be summarised as follows:

- Tourism is not one specific product, it is a combination of products and experiences which meet a diverse range of needs.
- Tourists are not always conscious of their deep psychological needs and ideas. Even when they do know what they are, they may not reveal them.
- Tourism motives may be multiple and contradictory (push and pull factors).
- Motives may change over time and be inextricably linked together (*e.g.,* perception, learning, personality and culture are often separated out but they are all bound up together) and dynamic conceptualisations such as P. Pearce's (1993) leisure ladder are crucial to advancing knowledge and understanding in this area.

Having examined some of the issues associated with what motivates tourists to travel, attention now turns to the process of measurement and recording tourist demand using statistical measures.

TOURISM STATISTICS

Ritchie argued that 'an important part of the maturing process for any science is the development or adaptation of consistent and well-tested measurement techniques and methodologies which are well-suited to the types of problems encountered in practice'. In this context, the measurement of tourists, tourism activity and the effects on the economy and society in different environments is crucial to the development of tourism as an established area of study within the confines of social science.

Burkart and Medlik (1981) provide a useful insight into the development of measurements of tourism phenomena by governments during the 1960s and their subsequent development through to the late 1970s. While it is readily acknowledged by most tourism researchers that statistics are a necessary feature to provide data to enable researchers, managers, planners, decision-makers and public and private sector bodies to gauge the significance and impact of tourism on destination areas, Burkart and Medlik (1981:74) identify four principal reasons for statistical measurement in tourism:

- To evaluate the magnitude and significance of tourism to a destination area or region;
- To quantify the contribution to the economy or society, especially the effect on the balance of payments;
- To assist in the planning and development of tourism infrastructure and the effect of different volumes of tourists with specific needs;
- To assist in the evaluation and implementation of marketing and promotion activities where the tourism marketer requires information on the actual and potential markets and their characteristics.

Consequently, tourism statistics are essential to the measurement of the volume, scale, impact and value of tourism at different geographical scales from the global to the country level down to the individual destination. Yet an information gap exists between the types of statistics provided by organisations for and the needs of users. The compilation of tourism statistics provided by organisations associated with the measurement of tourism has established methods and processes to collect, collate and analyse tourism statistics (World Tourism Organisation (WTO) 1996), yet these have been understood by only a small number of researchers and practitioners. Thus this section attempts to demystify the apparent sophistication and complexity associated with the presentation of statistical indicators of tourism and their value to spatial analysis, since geographers have a strong quantified methods tradition, which is reflected in the use and reliance upon such indicators to understand spatial variations and patterns of tourism activity.

All too often, undergraduate and many postgraduate texts assume a prior knowledge of tourism statistics and they are only dealt with in a limited way by most tourism texts, and where such issues are raised they are usually discussed in over-technical texts aimed at a limited audience (*e.g.,* Frechtling 1996). A commonly misunderstood feature which is associated with tourism statistics is that they are a complete and authoritative source of information (*i.e.,* they answer all the questions posed by the researcher). Other associated problems are that statistics are recent and relate to the previous year or season, implying that there is no time lag in their generation, analysis, presentation and dissemination to interested parties. In fact, most tourism statistics are 'typically measurements of arrivals, trips, tourist nights and expenditure, and these often appear in total or split into categories such as business or leisure travel'. Furthermore, the majority of published tourism statistics are derived from sample surveys, with the results being weighted or statistically manipulated to derive a measure which is supposedly representative of the real-world situation. In reality, this often means that tourism statistics are subject to significant errors depending on the size of the sample. The statistical measurement of tourists is far from straightforward, and Latham (1989) identifies a number of distinctive and peculiar problems associated with the tourist population:

- Tourists are a transient and highly mobile population, making statistical sampling procedures difficult when trying to ensure statistical accuracy and rigour in methodological terms.
- Interviewing mobile populations such as tourists is often undertaken in a strange environment, typically at ports or points of departure or arrival where there is background noise which may influence responses.
- Other variables, such as the weather, may affect the responses.

Even where sampling and survey-related problems can be minimised, one has to treat tourism statistics with a degree of caution because of additional methodological issues that can affect the results. For example, tourism research typically comprises:

- Pre-travel studies of tourists' intended travel habits and likely choice of destination (intentional studies);
- Studies of tourists in transit to provide information on their actual behaviour and plans for the remainder of their holiday or journey (actual and intended studies);
- Studies of tourists at the destination or at specific tourist attractions and sites, to provide information on their actual behaviour, levels of satisfaction, impacts and future intentions (actual and intended studies);
- Post-travel studies of tourists on their return journey from their destination or on-site experience or once they have returned to their place of residence (post-travel measures).

In an ideal world, where resource constraints are not a limiting factor on the generation of statistics, each of the aforementioned approaches should be used to provide a broad spectrum of research information on tourism and tourist behaviour. In reality, organisations and government agencies select a form of research which meets their own particular needs. In practice, most tourism statistics are generated with practical uses in mind and they may usually, though not exclusively, be categorised as follows:

- Measurement of tourist volume, enumerating arrivals, departures and the number of visits and stays;
- Expenditure-based surveys which quantify the value of tourist spending at the destination and during the journey;
- The characteristics and features of tourists to construct a profile of the different markets and segments visiting a destination.

However, before any tourism statistics can be derived, it is important to deal with the complex and thorny issue of defining the population - the tourist. Therefore, how does one define and differentiate between the terms *tourism* and *tourist*?

The terms *travel* and *tourism* are often interchanged within the published literature on tourism, though they are normally meant to encompass 'the field of research on human and business activities associated with one or more aspects of the temporary movement of persons away from their immediate home communities and daily work environments for business, pleasure and personal reasons'. These two terms tend to be used in differing contexts to mean similar things, although there is a tendency for the United States to continue to use the term 'travel' when in fact they mean tourism. Despite this inherent problem which may be little more than an exercise in semantics, it is widely acknowledged that the two terms are used in isolation or in unison to 'describe' three concepts:

- The movement of people;
- A sector of the economy or an industry;
- A broad system of interacting relationships of people (including their need to travel outside their communities and services that attempt to respond to these needs by supplying products).

From this initial starting point, one can begin to explore some of the complex issues in arriving at a working definition of the terms *tourism* and *tourist*. In a historical context, Burkart and Medlik (1981:41) identify the historical development of the term *tourism*, noting the distinction between the endeavours of researchers to differentiate between the concept and technical definitions of tourism. The concept of tourism refers to the 'broad notional framework, which identifies the essential characteristics, and which distinguishes tourism from the similar, often related, but different phenomena'.

In contrast, technical definitions have evolved through time as researchers modify and develop appropriate measures for statistical, legislative and operational reasons implying that there may be various technical definitions to meet particular purposes. However, the concept of tourism, and its identification for research purposes, is an important consideration in this instance for tourism statistics so that users are familiar with the context of their derivation. While most tourism books, articles and monographs now assume either a standard definition or interpretation of the concept of tourism, which is usually influenced by the social scientists' perspective (*i.e.,* a geographical, economic, political, sociological approach or other disciplines), Burkart and Medlik's (1981) approach to the concept of tourism continues to offer a valid assessment of the situation where five main characteristics are associated with the concept.

- Tourism arises from the movement of people to, and their stay in, various destinations.
- There are two elements in all tourism: the journey to the destination and the stay including activities at the destination.
- The journey and the stay take place outside the normal place of residence and work, so that tourism gives rise to activities which are distinct from those of the resident and working populations of the places, through which tourists travel and in which they stay.
- The movement to tourist destinations is of a temporary, short-term character, with the intention of returning home within a few days, weeks or months.
- Destinations are visited for purposes other than taking up permanent residence or employment remunerated from within the places visited (Burkart and Medlik 1981:42).

Furthermore, Burkart and Medlik's (1981) definition of tourism as a concept is invaluable because it rightly recognises that much tourism is a leisure activity which involves a discretionary use of time and money, and recreation is often the main purpose for participation in tourism. But this is no reason for restricting the total concept in this way and the essential characteristics of tourism can best be interpreted to embrace a wider concept. All tourism includes some travel but not all travel is tourism, while the temporary and short-term nature of most tourist trips distinguishes it from migration. Therefore, from the broad interpretation of tourism, it is possible to consider the technical definitions of tourism.

TECHNICAL DEFINITIONS OF TOURISM

Technical definitions of tourism are commonly used by organisations seeking to define the population to be measured, and there are three principal features which normally have to be defined:

- Purpose of travel (*e.g.* the type of traveller, be it business travel, holiday-makers, visits to friends and relatives or for other reasons).
- The time dimension involved in the tourism visit, which requires a minimum and a maximum period of time spent away from the home area and the time spent at the destination. In most cases, this would involve a minimum stay of more than 24 hours away from home and less than a year as a maximum.

- Those situations where tourists may or may not be included as tourists, such as cruise passengers, those tourists in transit at a particular point of embarkation/departure and excursionists who stay less than 24 hours at a destination (*e.g.,* the European duty-free cross-channel day-trip market).

Among the most recent attempts to recommend appropriate definitions of tourism was the World Tourism Organisation (hereafter WTO) International Conference of Travel and Tourism in Ottawa in 1991 which reviewed, expanded and developed technical definitions, where tourism comprises 'the activities of a person travelling outside his or her usual environment for less than a specified period of time and whose main purpose of travel is other than exercise of an activity remunerated from the place visited', where 'usual environment' is intended to exclude trips within the areas of usual residence and also frequent and regular trips between the domicile and the workplace and other community trips of a routine character, where 'less than a specified period of time' is intended to exclude long-term migration, and 'exercise of an activity remunerated from the place visited' is intended to exclude only migration for temporary work. The following definitions were developed by the WTO:

- International tourism: consists of inbound tourism.
- Visits to a country by non-residents and outbound tourism residents of a country visiting another country.
- Internal tourism: residents of a country visiting their own country.
- Domestic tourism: internal tourism plus inbound tourism (the tourism market of accommodation facilities and attractions within a country).
- National tourism: internal tourism plus outbound tourism (the resident tourism market for travel agents and airlines) (WTO, cited in Chadwick 1994:66).

In order to improve statistical collection and improve understanding of tourism, the United Nations (UN) (1994) and the WTO (1991a) also recommended differentiating between visitors, tourists and excursionists (day trippers). The WTO (1991a) recommended that an international tourist be defined as: 'a visitor who travels to a country other than that in which he/she has his/her usual residence for at least one night but not more than one year, and whose main purpose of visit is other than the exercise of an activity remunerated from within the country visited'; and that an international excursionist (*e.g.,* cruise ship visitors) be defined as 'a visitor residing in a country who travels the same day to a country other than which he/she has his/her usual environment for less than 24 hours without spending the night in the country visited and whose main purpose of visit is other than the exercise of an activity remunerated from within the country visited'.

Similar definitions were also developed for domestic tourists, with domestic tourists having a time limit of 'not more than six months' (WTO 1991a; UN

1994). Interestingly, the inclusion of a same-day travel, 'excursionist' category in UN/WTO technical definitions of tourism makes the division between recreation and tourism even more arbitrary, and there is increasing international agreement that 'tourism' refers to all activities of visitors, including both overnight and same-day visitors (UN 1994:5). Given improvements in transport technology, same-day travel is becoming increasingly important to some countries, with the UN (1994:9) observing, 'day visits are important to consumers and to many providers, especially tourist attractions, transport operators and caterers'. Chadwick (1994) moves the definition of tourists a stage further by offering a typology of travellers (tourists) which highlights the distinction between tourists (travellers) and non-travellers (non-tourists) which is summarised.

It is also useful because it illustrates where technical problems may occur in deciding which groups to include in tourism and which to exclude. From this classification of travellers, the distinction between international and domestic tourism needs to be made. Domestic tourism normally refers to tourists who travel from their normal domicile to other areas within a country. In contrast, international tourism normally involves a tourist leaving their country of origin to cross into another country which involves documentation, administrative formalities and movement to a foreign environment.

DOMESTIC TOURISM STATISTICS

D.G. Pearce (1995a) acknowledges that the scale and volume of domestic tourism worldwide exceeds that of international tourism, though it is often viewed as the poorer partner in the compilation of statistics. For example, most domestic tourism statistics tend to underestimate the scale and volume of flows since certain aspects of domestic tourist movements are sometimes ignored in official sources. The 'visits to friends and relatives, the use of forms of accommodation other than hotels (for example, second homes, camp and caravan sites) and travel by large segments of a population from towns to the countryside are not for the most part included'. This is supported by the WTO, who argue that 'there are relatively few countries that collect domestic travel and tourism statistics. Moreover some countries rely exclusively on the traditional hotel sector, thereby leaving out of account the many travellers staying in supplementary accommodation establishments or with friends and relatives'. Therefore, the collection of domestic tourism statistics requires the use of different data sources aside from the more traditional sources such as hotel records which identify the origin and duration of a visitor's stay.

To assist in the identification of who to include as a domestic tourist, the WTO (1983) suggests the following working definition: 'any person, regardless of nationality, resident in a country and who travels to a place in the same country for not more than one year and whose main purpose of visit is other than following an occupation remunerated from within the place visited.' Such a definition includes domestic tourists where an overnight stay is involved and domestic excursionists who visit an area for less than 24 hours and do not stay overnight. In fact, Latham (1989:66) points to the variety of definitions which exist aside from those formulated by WTO and the following issues complicate matters further:

- *Purpose of visit*: All countries using this concept define a domestic tourist as one who travels for a purpose other than to perform a remunerated activity.
- *The length of trip and/or distance travelled*: Certain definitions state that travellers should, for example, be involved in an overnight stay and/or travel a prescribed minimum distance.
- *Type of accommodation*: For practical reasons, some countries restrict the concept of domestic tourism to cover only those persons using commercial accommodation facilities (after Latham 1989:66).

Problems in applying WTO definitions may also reflect an individual country's reasons for generating such statistics, which may not necessarily be to contribute to a better understanding of statistics *per se*. For example, WTO (1981) identified four uses of domestic tourism statistics:

- To calculate the contribution of tourism to the country's economy, whereby estimates of tourism's value to the Gross Domestic Product is estimated due to the complexity of identifying the scope of tourism's contribution.
- To assist in the marketing and promotion of tourism, where government-sponsored tourism organisations seek to encourage its population to take domestic holidays rather than to travel overseas for a discussion of this activity among Pacific Rim countries).
- To aid the regional development policies of governments which harness tourism as a tool for area development where domestic tourists in congested environments are encouraged to travel to less developed areas and to improve the quality of tourism in different environments.
- To achieve social objectives, where socially oriented tourism policies may be developed for the underprivileged which requires a detailed understanding of the holiday-taking habits of a country's nationals.

Regional and local tourist organisations also make use of such data to develop and market destinations and different businesses within the tourism sector. But how is domestic tourism measured? Burkart and Medlik (1981) argue that two principal features need to be measured: first, the volume, value and characteristics of tourism among the population of the country; second, the same data relating to individual destinations within the country.

The WTO (1981, cited in Latham 1989) considers the minimum data requirements for the collection of domestic tourism statistics in terms of arrivals and tourist nights in accommodation classified by:

- Month;
- Type of grade of accommodation establishment;
- Location of the accommodation establishment and overall expenditure on domestic tourism.

Latham (1989) argues that it is possible to generate additional data from such variables including length of stay, occupancy rate and average expenditure. Many countries also collate supplementary information beyond the minimum standards identified by WTO, where the socioeconomic characteristics of tourists are identified, together with their use of tourist transport and purpose of visit, though the cost of such data collection does mean that the statistical basis of domestic tourism in many less developed countries remains poor.

The methods used to generate domestic tourism statistics are normally based on the estimates of volume, value and scale derived from sample surveys due to the cost of undertaking large-scale surveys of tourist activities.

The immediate problem facing the user of such material is the type of errors and degree of accuracy which can be attached to such data. For example, Latham (1989) identifies the following sample surveys which are now used to supplement data derived from hotel records:

- *Household surveys*, where the residents of a country are interviewed in their own home to ascertain information of tourist trips for the purpose of pleasure. A useful example of a pan-European study is the EC Omnibus study. Even so, little progress has been made internationally to collate common data on household surveys since the OECD's attempt in 1967 to outline the types of data which national travel surveys should collect.
- *Destination surveys*, where high levels of tourist activity occur in a region or resort. Such studies frequently compile statistics on accommodation usage, sample surveys of visitors and may be linked to existing knowledge derived from household surveys.
- *En route surveys*, where tourists are surveyed en route to examine the characteristics and features of tourists. Although it is a convenient way to interview a captive audience depending upon the mode of transport used, the results may not necessarily be as representative without a complete knowledge of the transport flows for the mode of tourist transport being surveyed.

The problem of incomplete questionnaires or non-response may occur where such surveys require a respondent to post the form back to the surveyor.

INTERNATIONAL TOURISM STATISTICS

The two principal organisations which collate data on international tourism are the World Tourism Organisation (WTO) and the Organisation for Economic Cooperation and Development (OECD). In addition, international regional tourism organisations such as the Pacific Asia Travel Association and the ASEAN Tourism Working Group also collect international tourism statistics. Page (1994b) reviews the major publications of the first two organisations in relation to international tourism, noting the detailed contents of each.

In the case of the WTO, the main source is the *Yearbook of Tourism Statistics*, which contains a summary of the most salient tourism statistics for almost 150 countries and territories. In the case of the OECD, their *Tourism Policy and International Tourism* (referred to as the 'Blue Book') is less comprehensive, covering only 25 countries, but it does contain most of the main generating and receiving areas. While the main thrust of the publication is government policy and the obstacles to international tourism, it does expand on certain areas not covered in the WTO publication.

In contrast to domestic tourism, statistics on international tourism are normally collected to assess the impact of tourism on a country's balance of payments, though as Withyman (1985:69) argued: Outward visitors seem to attract less attention from the pollsters and the enumerators. Of course, one country's outward visitor is another country's (perhaps several countries) inward visitor, and a much more welcome sort of visitor, too, being both a source of revenue and an emblem of the destination country's appeal in the international market. This has meant that governments have tended to be generally more keen to measure inward than outward tourism, or at any rate, having done so, to publish the results.

This statement indicates that governments are more concerned with the direct effect of tourism on their balance of payments. Yet such statistics are also utilised by marketing arms of national tourism organisations to base their decisions on who to target in international campaigns. The wider tourism industry also makes use of such data as part of their strategic planning and for more immediate purposes where niche markets exist. Even so, Shackleford (1980) argued that the collection of tourism statistics should be a responsibility of the state to meet international standards for data collection (WTO 1996). However, it is increasingly the case that only when the economic benefits of data collection can be justified will national governments continues to compile tourism statistics.

Where resource constraints exist, the collection and compilation of tourism statistics may be impeded. This also raises important methodological issues related to what exactly is being measured. As Withyman (1985:61) argued: 'In the jungle of international travel and tourism statistics, it behoves the explorer to step warily; on all sides there is luxuriant growth. Not all data sources are what they appear to be - after close scrutiny some show themselves to be inconsistent and often unsuitable for the industry researcher and planner.' The key point Withyman (1985) recognises is the lack of comparability in tourism data in relation to what is measured (*e.g.*, is it visitor days or visitor nights?)

and the procedures and methodology used to measure international tourism. Frechtling (1976) concluded that the approaches taken by national and international agencies associated with international tourism statistics were converging towards common definitions of trip, travel and traveller.

Yet the principal difficulty which continues to be associated with this is whether business travel should be considered as a discrete activity in relation to tourism. Chadwick (1994:75) notes that 'the consensus of North American opinion seems to be that, despite certain arguments to the contrary ... business travel should be considered part of travel and tourism'. While BarOn (1984) examines the standard definitions and terminology of international tourism as used by the UN and WTO, research by Ngoh (1985) is useful in that it considers the practical problems posed by such definitions when attempting to measure international tourism and find solutions to the difficulties. Latham (1989) suggests that the main types of international tourism statistics collated relate to:

- Volume of tourists;
- Expenditure by tourists;
- The profile of the tourist and their trip characteristics.

As is true of domestic tourism, estimates form the basis for most statistics on international tourism since the method of data collection does not generate exact data. For example, volume statistics are often generated from counts of tourists at entry/exit points (*i.e.,* gateways such as airports and ports) or at accommodation. But such data relate to numbers of trips rather than individual tourists since one tourist may make more than one trip a year and each trip is counted separately. In the case of expenditure statistics, tourist expenditure normally refers to tourist spending within a country and excludes payments to tourist-transport operators.

Yet deriving such statistics is often an indirect measure based on foreign currency estimates derived from bank records, from data provided by tourism service providers or more commonly from social surveys undertaken directly with tourists. Research by White and Walker (1982) and Baretje (1982) directly questions the validity and accuracy of such methods of data collection, examining the main causes of bias and error in such studies. According to Edwards (1991:68-9), 'expenditure and receipts data apart, tourist statistics are usually collected in one of the five following ways':

- Counts of all individuals entering or leaving the country at all recognised frontier crossings, often using arrival/departure cards where high-volume arrivals/departures are the norm. Where particularly large volumes of tourist traffic exist, a 10 per cent sampling framework is normally used (*i.e.,* every tenth arrival/ departure card). Countries such as New Zealand actually match the arrival/departure cards, or a sample, to examine the length of stay.

- Interviews carried out at frontiers with a sample of arriving and/or departing passengers to obtain a more detailed profile of visitors and their activities within the country. This will often require a careful sample design to gain a sufficiently large enough sample with the detail required from visitors on a wide range of tourism data including places visited, expenditure, accommodation usage and related items.
- Selecting a sample of arrivals and providing them with a self-completion questionnaire to be handed in or posted. This method is used in Canada but it fails to incorporate those visitors travelling via the United States by road.
- Sample surveys of the entire population of a country including travellers and non-travellers, though the cost of obtaining a representative sample is often prohibitive.
- Accommodation arrivals and nights spent are recorded by hoteliers and owners of the accommodation types covered. The difficulty with this type of data collection is that accommodation

As a government-sponsored survey which began in 1961, the International Passenger Survey now covers all ports of entry/exit to the UK. It is based on a stratified random sample of tourists arriving and departing from the UK by air and sea. According to Latham (1989:64), IPS' four principal aims are:

- To collect data for the travel account (which acts to compare expenditure by overseas visitors to the UK with expenditure overseas by visitors from the UK) of the balance of payments;
- To provide detailed information on foreign visitors to the UK, and on outgoing visitors travelling overseas.
- To provide data on international migration.
- To provide information on routes used by passengers as an aid to aviation and shipping authorities. owners have no incentive to record accurate details, particularly where the tax regime is based on the turnover of bed-nights.

The final area of data collection is profile statistics, which examine the characteristics and travel habits of visitors. For example, the UK's International Passenger Survey (IPS) is one survey that incorporates volume, expenditure and profile data on international tourism.

Bibliography

A M Bagulia.: *Encyclopaedia of Travel Agency Management (3 Vols-Set)*, Anmol Publication, Delhi, 2006.

A.P. Rastogi.: *Air Travel Ticketing and Fare Construction*, Aman Publication, Delhi, 2007.

A.P. Rastogi.: *Travel Agency Operations*, Aman Publications, Delhi, 2007.

Ajit Baral, Bela Malik, Pant, Jagannath Adhikari, Purna Basnet and Usha Titikshu.: *By the Way : Travels Through Nepal's Conflict*, Martin Chautari, 2008.

Awnsham and John Churchill.: *A Collection of Voyages and Travels: Volume-II*, AES Publishers, New Delhi, 2002.

B S Badan and Harish Bhatt.: *Financial Management of Travel and Tourism*, Commonwealth Publication, New Delhi, 2007.

Banwari Lal Raheja.: *Food Management in Hotel, Travel and Tourism*, Arise Publication, Delhi, 2006.

Bayard Taylor.: *Central Asia : Travels in Cashmere, Little Tibet, and Central Asia*, Cosmo Publication, Delhi, 2005.

C.H. Payne.: *Jahangir and the Jesuits With an Account of the Travels of Benedict Goes and the Mission to Pegu*, Munshiram Manoharlal, Delhi, 1997.

Debi Singh Tewatia.: *A Journey Less Travelled*, Universal Law Publication, Delhi, 2011.

Dinesh Kaushik.: *Financial Management of Travel and Tourism*, Vishvabharti Publication, Delhi, 2006.

Fisher, Michael.: *Beyond the Three Seas: Travellers' Tales from Mughal India*, Random House India, 2008.

Gulshan Soni.: *Consumer Protection in Hospitality Travel and Tourism*, Aman Publication, Delhi, 2011.

H A Newell.: *Agra and Fatehpur Sikri : A Traveller's History*, Spring Books, 2004.

Jagmohan Negi.: *Air Travel : Ticketing and Fare Construction (With Examination Questions)*, Kanishka Publication, Delhi, 2004.

Kunal Sinha.: *An Ordinary Traveller*, Bluejay Books, Delhi, 2002.

L K Singh.: *Management of Travel Agency*, Isha Books, Delhi, 2008.

L K Singh.: *Marketing in Service Industry-Airline, Travel Tours and Hotel*, Isha Books, Delhi, 2008.

Lalita Sharma.: *An Introduction to Ecotourism*, Centrum Press, Delhi, 2003.

M C Metti.: *Customer Service and Hotel Management*, Anmol Publication, Delhi, 2008.

Michael H. Fisher.: *Counterflows to Colonialism : Indian Travellers and Settlers in Britain 1600-1857*, Permanent Black, 2004.

Mohit Sen.: *A Traveller and the Road : The Journey of an Indian Communist*, Rupa and Co, Delhi, 2003.

Monobina Gupta.: *Left Politics in Bengal : Time Travels Among Bhadralok Marxists*, Orient Blackswan, Delhi, 2010.

Niral Mehta.: *Encyclopaedia of Travel and Tourism*, Anmol Publication, Delhi, 2006.

P.C. Sinha.: *Encyclopaedia of Travel, Tourism and Ecotourism (10 Vols-Set)*, Anmol Publication, Delhi, 2005.

Parvez Dewan.: *Amazing Ladakh : Travel Trekking Religion Culture Wildlife*, Manas Publications, Delhi, 2012.

Rowe.: *Career Award Travel and Tourism: Standard Level*, Cambridge University Press, 2003.

Samanth Subramanian.: *Following Fish: Travels around the Indian Coast*, Penguin Publication, Delhi, 2010.

Sarika Bajpai.: *Marketing Perspective for Travel and Tourism*, Shri Sai Printographers, Delhi, 2007.

T. Filippi Ippolito De Desideri/Filippo.: *An Account of Tibet - The Travels of Ippolito Desideri of Pistoia S.J., 1712-1727*, AES, 1995.

W. Baker Samuel.: *Eight Years in Ceylon: Travels in the Island about the Year 1850 with Notes on Cultivation, Sport, History and Future Prospects*, AES Publication, Chennai, 1994.

Index